CONTENTS
paris

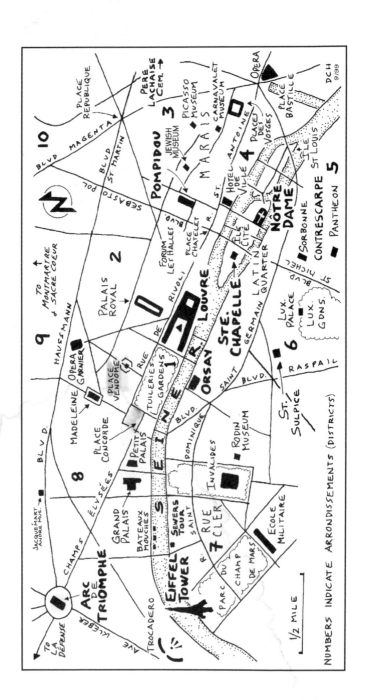

NUMBERS INDICATE ARRONDISSEMENTS (DISTRICTS)

INTRODUCTION

paris

Paris—the City of Lights—has been a beacon of culture for centuries. As a world capital of art, fashion, food, literature, and ideas, it stands as a symbol of all the fine things that human civilization can offer. Come prepared to celebrate, rather than judge, the cultural differences, to capture the romance and *joie de vivre* that Paris exudes.

Paris offers sweeping boulevards, chatty crêpe stands, chic boutiques, and world-class art galleries. Sip decaf with deconstructionists in a sidewalk café, then step into an Impressionist painting in a tree-lined park. Climb Notre-Dame and rub shoulders with the gargoyles. Cruise the Seine, zip up the Eiffel Tower, and saunter down the Champs-Elysées. Master the Louvre and Orsay museums. Save some after-dark energy for one of the world's most romantic cities.

This Information Is Accurate and Up-to-Date

This book is updated every year. Most publishers of guidebooks that cover a city from top to bottom can afford an update only every two or three years. Since this book is selective, covering only the places we think make the top week or two in and around Paris, we can update it each summer (we even do a winter check-up). Even with an annual update, however, things change. But if you're traveling with the current edition of this book, we guarantee you're using the most up-to-date information available (for the latest, check www.ricksteves.com/update). This book will help you have an inexpensive, hassle-free trip. Use this year's edition. Saving a few bucks by traveling on old information is not smart. If you're packing an old book, you'll learn the seriousness of your mistake . . . in Paris. Your trip costs at least $10 per waking hour. Your time is valuable. This guidebook saves lots of time.

Welcome to Our Paris City Guide

This book is organized in the following way:

Paris Orientation includes tourist information, public-transportation basics, and easy-to-read maps. The "Planning Your Time" section offers a suggested schedule with thoughts on how to best use your limited time.

Sights provides a succinct overview of Paris' most important sights. They're arranged by neighborhood and include ratings: ▲▲▲—Don't miss; ▲▲—Try hard to see; ▲—Worthwhile if you can make it; no rating—Worth knowing about.

The **Walks** cover five of Paris' most enjoyable neighborhoods: Historic Paris (Notre-Dame and Sainte-Chapelle), Champs-Elysées, Marais, rue Cler (near the Eiffel Tower), and Montmartre.

The **Self-Guided Museum Tours** take you through Paris' most interesting museums: Louvre, Orsay, Rodin, Marmottan, L'Orangerie, Cluny, Carnavalet, Pompidou Center, and Les Invalides military museums, including Napoleon's Tomb.

Daytrips covers nearby sights, including the great châteaux of Versailles (includes self-guided tour), Vaux-le-Vicomte, Fontainebleau, and Chantilly; Chartres' majestic cathedral (includes self-guided tour); the Impressionist retreats of Monet's Giverny and van Gogh's Auvers-sur-Oise; and, *finalement*, Disneyland Paris. Accommodations are listed for Versailles, Fontainebleau, Chartres, Giverny, and Auvers-sur-Oise.

Sleeping in Paris is a guide to our favorite hotels, from budget deals to cushy splurges in three cozy neighborhoods, with orientation tips geared to make you feel at home.

Eating in Paris offers good-value restaurants ranging from inexpensive eateries to romantic bistros, arranged by neighborhood, with a special section on "Grand Cafés."

Paris with Children includes our top 10 recommendations to keep your kids (and you) happy in Paris.

Shopping in Paris helps you shop painlessly and enjoyably, without letting it overwhelm your vacation or ruin your budget. Here, you can read up on Paris' great department stores, neighborhood boutiques, flea markets, and outdoor food markets.

Paris at Night is a guide to entertainment and evening fun, with music, bus tours, and river cruises, plus information on how to easily translate *Pariscope* magazine, the weekly entertainment guide.

Transportation Connections covers connections by train and plane, with detailed information on Paris' two airports and six train stations, laying the groundwork for your smooth arrival and departure.

The **appendix** includes a Paris history, a climate chart,

telephone tips, French survival phrases, and a handy almanac of resources.

Throughout the book, when you see a ✪ in a listing, it means that the sight is covered in much more depth in one of our walks or self-guided tours—a page number will tell you just where to look to find more information.

Browse through this book and choose your favorite sights. Then have a *fantastique* trip! You'll become your own guide with our self-guided walks and museum tours. Traveling like a temporary local, you'll get the absolute most out of every mile, minute, and dollar. You won't waste time on mediocre sights because, unlike other guidebooks, this one covers only the best. Since lousy, expensive hotels are a major financial pitfall, we've worked hard to assemble the best accommodations values. And, as you explore the city we know and love, we're happy you'll be meeting some of our favorite Parisians.

Trip Costs

Five components make up your trip costs: airfare, surface transportation, room and board, sightseeing/entertainment, and shopping/miscellany.

Airfare: Don't try to sort through the mess. Find and use a good travel agent. A basic round-trip U.S.–Paris flight costs $700 to $1,100, depending on where you fly from and when (even cheaper in winter).

Surface Transportation: For a typical one-week visit, allow about $50 for Métro tickets and a couple of daytrips. Add an additional $70 if you opt for taxi rides to and from the airport (or save money by taking a shuttle, airport bus, or the RER).

Room and Board: You can thrive in Paris on $80 a day per person for room and board. An $80-a-day budget allows $5 for breakfast, $10 for lunch, $20 for dinner, and $45 for lodging (based on 2 people splitting the cost of an $90 double room). That's doable. Students and tightwads do it on $40 ($20 per bed, $15–20 for meals and snacks). But budget sleeping and eating require using the skills and information covered in this book (and in much greater depth in *Rick Steves' Europe Through the Back Door*).

Sightseeing and Entertainment: Get the Paris Museum and Monument Pass, which covers most sights in Paris (for more information, see Sights chapter, page 32). You'll pay about $25 for a three-day pass and $35 for a five-day pass. (While you can buy the pass through some U.S. travel agents, it's easy and cheaper to buy in Paris). Without a museum pass, figure $5 to $7 per major sight (e.g., Rodin-$5, Louvre-$6.50), $4 for minor ones (climbing church towers), and $25 for bus tours and splurge experiences (concerts in Sainte-Chapelle). An overall average of $15 a day works for most. Don't skimp here. After all, this category directly powers most of the experiences all the other expenses are designed to make possible.

Shopping and Miscellany: Figure $3 per ice-cream cone, coffee, or soft drink. Shopping can vary in cost from nearly nothing to a small fortune. Good budget travelers find that this category has little to do with assembling a trip full of lifelong and wonderful memories.

Exchange Rate
We've priced things throughout this book in the euro currency. France, along with 11 other member countries of the European Union, has adopted the euro currency.

> 1 euro (€) = about 90 cents, and €1.10 = about $1.

One euro is broken down into 100 cents. You'll find coins ranging from 1 cent to 2 euros, and bills from 5 euros to 500 euros. To convert prices in euros into dollars, take 10 percent off the price in euros: €25 = $22.50, and €140 = $126. For information on the euro, see the European Central Bank's Web site: www.euro.ecb.int.

Prices, Times, and Discounts
The prices in this book, as well as the hours and telephone numbers, are accurate as of mid-2001. Europe is always changing, and we know you'll understand that this, like any other guidebook, starts to yellow even before it's printed—especially this transition year of 2002, with the materialization of the euro currency. Because it's possible that the French might adjust prices a bit in 2002, depending on current exchange rates, the prices in this book are approximate.

In Europe—and in this book—you'll use the 24-hour clock. After 12 noon, keep going—13:00, 14:00, and so on. For anything over 12, subtract 12 and add p.m. (14:00 is 2:00 p.m.).

While discounts for sights and transportation are listed for only the most important sights in this book, students with International Student Identification Cards, teachers with proper identification, and youths under 18 often get big discounts—but only if they ask.

When to Go
Late spring and fall have the best weather and the biggest crowds. Summers are generally hot and dry; if you wilt in the heat, look for the rare room with air-conditioning. It's fairly easy to find rooms

in summer, and while many French businesses close in August, you'll hardly notice. Paris makes a great winter getaway. Airfares are cheap, the cafés are cozy, and the city feels lively but not touristy. The only problem—weather—is fixed by dressing correctly. Expect cold and rain, but no snow.

Red Tape, Business Hours, and Parking

You need a passport but no visa or shots to travel in France.

Most shops are open Monday through Saturday (10:00–19:00) and closed Sunday, though many small markets, *boulangeries* (bakeries), and the like are open Sunday mornings until noon. On Mondays, some businesses are closed until 14:00, and possibly all day. Saturdays are like weekdays (but most banks are closed).

If you have a car, street parking is free after 19:00, on weekends, and in August. Otherwise ask your hotelier for suggestions (figure about €15–25 per day in a parking garage).

Banking

Bring your ATM, credit, or debit card, along with traveler's checks in dollars as a backup.

The best and easiest way to get cash in euros is to use the omnipresent French bank machines (always open, lower fees, quick processing); you'll need a four-digit PIN (numbers only, no letters) with your Visa or MasterCard. Some ATM bankcards will work at some banks, though Visa and MasterCard are more reliable. Before you go, verify with your bank that your card will work. Bring two different cards or two copies of the same card; demagnetization can be a problem. "Cash machine" in French is *distributeur automatique des billets*, or D.A.B. (day-ah-bay).

Regular banks have the best rates for cashing traveler's checks. For a large exchange, it pays to compare rates and fees. The Bank of France (Banque de France) usually offers the best rates, and branches are generally open 09:30 to 12:30 for change (you'll find a Banque de France near the Louvre at 31 rue Croix des Petits Champs, Métro: Palais Royal; and on place de la Bastille where rue St. Antoine meets the place, Métro: Bastille). Standard banking hours vary, though most are open Tuesday through Friday from 09:00 to 16:30. Some branches are open Saturday morning, and many are closed on Monday.

Post offices, train stations, and tourist offices usually change money if you can't get to a bank. Post offices (which take cash or American Express checks) give a good rate, have longer hours, and charge no fee. Banks at train stations, tourist offices, and airports offer mediocre rates.

Just like at home, credit (or debit) cards work easily at larger hotels, restaurants, and shops. Smaller businesses prefer payment in local currency. Smart travelers function with hard local cash and a major credit card.

If using traveler's checks, don't be petty about changing money. The greatest avoidable money-changing expense is having to waste time every few days returning to a bank. Change 10 days' or two weeks' worth of money, get big bills, stuff them in your money belt, and travel!

The Language Barrier and that French Attitude

You've no doubt heard that Parisians are "mean and cold and refuse to speak English." This is an out-of-date preconception left over from the de Gaulle days. Parisians are as friendly as any other people and no more disagreeable than New Yorkers. Like many big cities, Paris is a massive melting pot of international cultures (your evening hotel receptionist is just as likely to speak French with an accent as not). And, without any doubt, Parisians speak more English than Americans speak French. Be reasonable in your expectations: Waiters are paid to be efficient, not chatty. And Parisian postal clerks are every bit as speedy, cheery, and multi-lingual as ours are back home.

The biggest mistake most Americans make when traveling in France is trying to do too much with limited time. Hurried, impatient travelers who miss the subtle pleasures of people-watching from a sun-dappled café and taking walks in the countryside often misinterpret French attitudes. By slowing your pace and making an effort to understand French culture, you're much more likely to have a richer experience. Parisians take great pride in their customs, cling-ing to their belief in cultural superiority despite the fact that they're no longer a world superpower. Let's face it—it's tough to keep on smiling when you've been crushed by a Big Mac, Mickey-Moused by Disney, and drowned in instant coffee. Your hosts are cold only if you decide to see them that way. Polite and formal, the French respect the fine points of culture and tradition. In France, strolling down the street with a big grin on your face (and saying hello to people you don't know) is a sign of senility, not friendliness (seri-ously). Parisians think that Americans, while friendly, are hesitant to pursue more serious friendships. Recognize sincerity and look for kindness. Give them the benefit of the doubt.

Communication difficulties in France are exaggerated. To hurdle the language barrier, bring a small English/French dictio-nary, a phrase book (look for ours), a menu reader, and a good supply of patience. In transactions, a small notepad and pen mini-mize misunderstandings about prices; have vendors write the price down. If you learn only five phrases, learn and use these:

bonjour (good day), *pardon* (pardon me), *s'il vous plaît* (please), *merci* (thank you), and *au revoir* (goodbye). The French place great importance on politeness. Begin every encounter with "*Bonjour, madame/monsieur*" and end every encounter with "*Au revoir, madame/monsieur.*"

The French are language perfectionists—they take their language (and other languages) seriously. Often they speak more English than they let on. This isn't a tourist-baiting tactic but is timidity on their part to speak another language less than fluently. Start any conversation with "*Bonjour, madame/monsieur. Parlez-vous anglais?*" and hope they speak more English than you speak French.

Travel Smart

Reread this book as you travel. Buy a phone card and use it for reservations and confirmations. Enjoy the friendliness of the local people and don't let one rude person ruin your day. Ask questions. Most locals are eager to point you in their idea of the right direction. Wear your money belt. Those who expect to travel smart, do.

Plan ahead for banking, laundry, post-office chores, and picnics. Mix intense and relaxed periods. Every trip (and every traveler) needs at least a few slack days. Pace yourself. Assume you will return.

As you read through this book, plan your itinerary. Note the days when sights are closed. Sundays have pros and cons, as they do for travelers in the United States (special events and weekly markets, limited hours, shops and banks closed, limited public transportation, no rush hours). Saturdays are virtually weekdays. Popular places are even more popular on weekends and inundated on three-day weekends. In 2002, be ready for unusually big crowds during these holiday periods: Easter week (March 29–April 6), Labor Day weekend (May 1–5), VE Day and Ascension weekend (May 8–12), Pentecost weekend (May 17–20, religious holiday on May 19), Bastille Day (July 14), Assumption (Aug 15), All Saints' Day weekend (Oct 30–Nov 1, religious holiday on Nov 1), Armistice Day (Nov 11), and the winter holidays (late Dec–early Jan). Many sights close on the actual holiday (check with a tourist office).

French Tourist Offices in the United States

France's national tourist offices in the United States are a wealth of information. Before your trip, request any specific information you may want (such as city maps and schedules of upcoming festivals).

French Government Tourist Offices: For questions and brochures (on regions, barging, the wine country, and so on), call 410/286-8310. Ask for the Discovery Guide. Materials delivered in 4 to 6 weeks are free; there's a $4 shipping fee for information delivered in 5 to 10 days.

Their Web site is www.franceguide.com and their offices are in...

New York: 444 Madison Ave., 16th floor, New York, NY 10022, fax 212/838-7855, e-mail: info@francetourism.com.

Illinois: 676 N. Michigan Ave. #3360, Chicago, IL 60611-2819, fax 312/337-6339, e-mail: fgto@mcs.net.

California: 9454 Wilshire Blvd. #715, Beverly Hills, CA 90212, fax 310/276-2835, e-mail: fgto@gte.net.

For the latest on Paris, visit www.pariscope.fr (in French).

Recommended Guidebooks

For most travelers, this book is all you need. But if you'd like more information, you may want to buy an additional guidebook. The Michelin Green Guide, which is somewhat scholarly, and the more readable *Paris Access* guide are both well-researched. Of the multitude of other guidebooks on France and Paris, many are high on facts and low on opinion, guts, or personality. To better understand the French, read *French or Foe* (by Polly Platt) and *Fragile Glory* (by Richard Bernstein). *The Course of French History* (by Pierre Goubert) provides a reasonably succinct and good summary of French history. If you'll be traveling elsewhere in France, consider *Rick Steves' France, Belgium & the Netherlands 2002*.

Rick Steves' Books and Videos

Rick Steves' Europe Through the Back Door 2002 gives you budget travel tips on minimizing jet lag, packing light, planning your itinerary, traveling by car or train, finding budget beds without reservations, changing money, avoiding rip-offs, outsmarting thieves, hurdling the language barrier, staying healthy, taking great photographs, using your bidet, and lots more. The book also includes chapters on 35 of Rick's favorite "Back Doors."

Rick Steves' Country Guides are a series of eight guidebooks covering the Best of Europe; France, Belgium, and the Netherlands (co-written with Steve Smith); Great Britain; Ireland; Italy; Spain and Portugal; Scandinavia; and Germany, Austria, and Switzerland. They're updated annually and come out in December and January.

My **City Guides**, updated annually, include this book and *Rick Steves' London* and *Rome* (available in January), and—new for 2002—Venice and Florence (available in March). With the sleek Eurostar train, London is just three hours from Paris. Consider combining the two cities (and books) for a great visit.

Rick Steves' Europe 101: History and Art for the Traveler (with Gene Openshaw, 2000) gives you the story of Europe's people, history, and art. Written for smart people who were sleeping in their history and art classes before they knew they were going to Europe, *101* really helps Europe's sights come alive.

Rick Steves' Mona Winks (with Gene Openshaw, 2001) gives you fun, easy-to-follow, self-guided tours of Europe's top 25 museums and cultural sites. All of the *Mona Winks* chapters on Paris are included in this Paris guidebook. But if you'd like similar coverage for the great museums in London, Amsterdam, Venice, Florence, and Rome, *Mona*'s for you.

My *Rick Steves' French Phrase Book* (1999) is a fun, practical tool for independent budget travelers. This handy book has everything you'll need, including a menu decoder, conversational starters for connecting with locals, and an easy-to-follow telephone template for making hotel reservations.

My latest television series, *Rick Steves' Europe*, features a new half-hour show on Paris. Of a combined total of 68 episodes (from my new series and the original series, *Travels in Europe with Rick Steves*), two shows cover Paris and seven half-hour shows cover other parts of France. These air on public television throughout the United States. They are also available in information-packed home videos, along with my 90-minute slideshow lecture on France, Belgium, and the Netherlands (call us at 425/771-8303 for our free newsletter/catalog).

Rick Steves' Postcards from Europe, my autobiographical book, packs 25 years of travel anecdotes and insights into the ultimate 3,000-mile European adventure. Through my guidebooks, I share my favorite European discoveries with you. *Postcards* introduces you to my favorite European friends.

All of my books are published by Avalon Travel Publishing (www.travelmatters.com).

Maps

The maps in this book, drawn by Dave Hoerlein, are concise and simple. Dave, who is well-traveled in Paris, designed these maps to help you orient quickly and get to where you want to go painlessly. Once in Paris, simply pick up the free Paris map at your hotel and you're ready to travel.

Tours of Paris and France by Rick Steves and Steve Smith

Travel agents will tell you about all the normal tours of Paris and France, but they won't tell you about ours. At Europe Through the Back Door, we organize and lead one-week tours of Paris and longer tours covering the highlights of France. The Paris tours, limited to 20 people, take place off-season (Feb–April and Oct–Dec) when crowds and airfares are manageable. For a longer tour, choose from "Paris and the Heart of France" (14 days), "Provence and the South of France" (15 days), and the "Best of Village France" (18 days). These depart each year from April through October, are limited to 24 people per group, and have big, roomy buses and two great guides. For details, call us at 425/771-8303 or check www.ricksteves.com.

Transportation

Transportation concerns within Paris are limited to the subway, buses, and taxis, all covered extensively in the Orientation chapter. If you have a car, stow it. You don't want to drive in Paris. For all the specifics on transportation throughout France by train or car, see *Rick Steves' France, Belgium & the Netherlands 2002*.

Telephones, Mail, and E-mail

An efficient card-operated system has virtually replaced coin-operated public phones throughout Europe. Insert the card in the phone and dial away.

Buy a **phone card** (*une télécarte*) from any post office or train station or from most newsstands and tobacco shops (*tabac*). France has two denominations of phone cards: *une petite* costs about €7; *une grande* about €15. When you use the *télécarte* (simply take the phone off the hook, insert the card, and wait for a dial tone) the price of the call (local or international) is automatically deducted.

France's latest phone card (Kertel, pron: *care-tel)* is not inserted into the phone but allows you to dial from the comfort of your hotel (or anywhere) and charge the call to the card for lower rates than with a *télécarte* (€8 and €15 cards available). It's simple to use, instructions are provided in English, and the card is sold wherever *télécartes* are sold. And while per-minute rates are cheaper with Kertel than a *télécarte*, it's slower to use (more numbers to dial), so local calls are quicker with a *télécarte* from a phone booth.

USA Direct Services: Despite the expense, some travelers prefer to use American calling cards (AT&T, MCI, and Sprint numbers listed in appendix). Calling-card calls were a fine deal until direct-dial rates were cut in half. Now it's cheaper to make your international calls using a European phone card (whether French or Kertel). Definitely avoid using your American calling card for calls between European countries; it's far cheaper to call direct.

Dialing Direct: France has a dial-direct 10-digit telephone system. There are no area codes. To call to or from anywhere in France, including Paris, you dial the 10 numbers directly. All Paris numbers start with 01.

To call France from another country, start with the international access code (00 if you're calling from a European country;

011 from the United States and Canada), dial France's country code (33), and then drop the initial zero of the 10-digit local number and dial the remaining nine digits. For example, the phone number of a good hotel in Paris is 01 47 05 49 15. To call it from home, dial 011-33-1 47 05 49 15.

To dial out of France, start your call with its international code (00), then dial the country code of the country you're calling. To call our office in the United States, dial 00 (France's international access code), 1 (U.S. country code), then 425/771-8303 (our area code plus local number).

For a list of international access codes and country codes, see the appendix. European time is six/nine hours ahead of the East/West Coasts of the United States.

Mail: The hours of French post offices (called PTT for Postal, Telegraph, and Telephone) vary, though most are open weekdays from 08:00 to 19:00 and Saturday morning from 08:00 to 12:00. Stamps and phone cards are also sold at *tabac* (tobacco) shops. It costs about €0.70 to mail a postcard to the United States.

To arrange for mail delivery, reserve a few hotels along your route in advance and give their addresses to friends. Or you can use American Express Company's mail services (available to anyone who has at least one American Express traveler's check). Allow 10 days for a letter to arrive. Phoning is so easy that we've dispensed with mail stops altogether.

E-mail: E-mail is catching on among hoteliers; we've added e-mail addresses for hotels whenever available. As for Internet access, ask at your hotel for the nearest Internet (an-ter-net) café.

Sleeping

A comfortable hotel in Paris costs less than a comparable hotel in London or in most major U.S. cities. It's a great hotel city. Still, you should reserve in advance to secure the best hotel for you. We like places that are clean, small, central, traditional, friendly, and a good value. Most places we list have at least four of these six virtues.

Paris Hotels

In this book, the price for a double room will normally range from $40 (very simple, toilet and shower down the hall) to $190 (maximum plumbing and more), with most clustering around $80–$90. A triple and a double are often the same room, with a small double bed and a sliver single, so a third person sleeps very cheaply. Most hotels have a few singles, triples, and quads. While groups sleep cheap, traveling alone can be expensive—a single room usually costs about the same as a double. Hotels cannot legally allow more in the room than what's shown on their price list.

Receptionists are often reluctant to mention the cheaper rooms. Study the room price list posted at the desk. Understand it. You'll save about $15 on the average if you get a room with a "shower down the hall" rather than in your room; ask for a room without a shower (*sans douche*) rather than with a shower (*avec douche*). A room with a bathtub (*salle de bain*) costs $5 to $10 more than a room with a shower. A double bed (*grand lit*) is $5 to $10 cheaper than twins (*deux petits lits*). Hotels are inclined to give you a room with a tub (which the French prefer). If you prefer a double bed and a shower, you'll need to ask for it, and you'll save up to $20 (compared to the cost of a twin-bedded room with a tub). If you'll take twins *or* a double, ask for a room for two (*chambre pour deux;* shambruh pur duh) to avoid being needlessly turned away.

The French have a simple hotel rating system (zero through four stars) depending on amenities. One and two-star hotels are the best budget values, though some three-star hotels (and even a few 4-star hotels) can justify the extra cost. Unclassified hotels (no stars) can be bargains or depressing dumps. Look before you leap and lay before you pay (upon departure). Hotels in France must charge a daily tax (*taxe du séjour*) that is normally added to the bill. It varies from €0.50 to €1 per day per person depending on the number of stars the hotel has. While some hotels include it in the price list, most add it to your bill.

You'll almost always have the option of breakfast at your hotel, which is pleasant and convenient, but, at €6 to €9, it can be much more than the price of breakfast at the corner café. While hotels hope you'll spring for their breakfast, this is optional unless otherwise noted.

Rooms are safe. Still, keep cameras and money out of sight. Towels aren't routinely replaced every day; drip-dry and conserve. If that French Lincoln-log pillow isn't your idea of comfort, American-style pillows (and extra blankets) are usually in the closet or available on request. To get a pillow, ask for "*Un oreiller, s'il vous plaît*" (un oar-ray-yay, see-voo-play). If you're planning to visit Paris in the summer, the extra expense of an air-conditioned room can be money well spent. (When using the air-conditioner, remember 20 degrees Celsius = 68 degrees Fahrenheit).

Making Reservations

Reserve ahead for Paris, the sooner the better. May, June, September, and October are busiest. If you're not sure how long you'll stay, guess long. You can always cancel the last days once there (48 hours advance notice is generally required), but it's very hard to add days at the last minute. We've taken great pains to list telephone numbers with long-distance instructions (see "Telephones,

Sleep Code

To give maximum information in a minimum of space, we
use these codes to describe accommodations listed in this
book. Prices listed are per room, not per person.

- **S** = Single room (or price for one person in a double).
- **D** = Double or Twin. French double beds can be very small.
- **T** = Triple (generally a double bed with a single).
- **Q** = Quad (usually two double beds).
- **b** = Private bathroom with toilet and shower or tub.
- **s** = Private shower or tub only. (The toilet is down the hall.)
- **CC** = Accepts credit cards (Visa and MasterCard, rarely American Express).
- **no CC** = Does not accept credit cards; pay in local cash.
- ***** = French hotel rating system, ranging from zero to four stars.

According to this code, a couple staying at a "Db-€90,
CC" hotel would pay a total of 90 euros (or about $81) for a
double room with a private bathroom. The hotel accepts
credit cards or cash in payment.

Mail, and E-mail" above, and the appendix). Use the telephone and
convenient telephone cards. Most hotels listed are accustomed to
English-only speakers. A hotel receptionist will trust you and hold
a room until 16:00 without a deposit, though some will ask for a
credit-card number. Honor (or cancel by phone) your reservations.
Long distance is cheap and easy from public phone booths. Don't
let these people down—we promised you'd call and cancel if for
some reason you won't show up. Don't needlessly confirm rooms
through the tourist office; it'll take a commission.

To reserve from home, call, fax, e-mail, or write the hotel.
E-mail is preferred when possible. Phone and fax costs are reasonable, and simple English is usually fine. To fax, use the fax form in
the appendix (online at www.ricksteves.com/reservation). If you're
writing, add the zip code and confirm the need and method for a
deposit. A two-night stay in August would be "two nights, 16/8/02
to 18/8/02"—Europeans write the date day/month/year, and
European hotel jargon uses your day of departure.

If you send a reservation request and receive a response with
rates stating that rooms are available, this is not a confirmation.
You must confirm that the rates are fine and that indeed you want

the room. One night's deposit is generally required. A credit card will usually be accepted as a deposit, though you may need to send a signed traveler's check or a bank draft in the local currency. If you give your credit-card number for the deposit, the hotel may bill one night's stay to your card (most let you know this in advance). Don't give your credit-card number as a deposit unless you're absolutely sure you want to stay there on the dates you requested and are clear that they have a room available. If you don't show up, you'll be billed for one night, and if you cancel in advance, you may not receive your entire deposit back. Reconfirm your reservations a few days in advance for safety.

Hostels

Parisian hostels charge about $20 per bed. Some require a hostel membership; the best don't. Get a hostel card before you go if you need one. Travelers of any age are welcome if they don't mind dorm-style accommodations and meeting other travelers. Travelers without a hostel card can generally spend the night for a small extra "one-night membership" fee at those places requiring membership. Cheap meals are sometimes available, and kitchen facilities are usually provided for do-it-yourselfers.

Apartments

It's easy, though not necessarily cheaper, to rent a furnished apartment in Paris. Consider this option if you're either traveling with a family or staying two weeks or longer. For listings, see the end of the Sleeping chapter (on page 265).

Eating in Paris

Parisians eat long and well. Relaxed lunches, three-hour dinners, and endless hours sitting in outdoor cafés are the norm. They have a legislated 35-hour workweek and a self-imposed 36-hour eat-week. Parisians spend much of their five annual weeks of paid vacation at *la table*. Local cafés, cuisine, and wines become a highlight of any Parisian adventure—sightseeing for your palate. Even if the rest of you is sleeping in a cheap hotel, let your taste buds travel first-class in Paris. (They can go coach in England.) You can eat well without going broke, but choose carefully—you're just as likely to blow a small fortune on a mediocre meal as you are to dine wonderfully for $20.

Breakfast

Petit déjeuner (puh-tee day-zhu-nay) is typically *café au lait* (coffee with hot milk), hot chocolate, or tea; a roll with butter and marmalade; and a croissant. Don't expect much variety for breakfast, but the bread is fresh and the coffee is good. While available at your hotel (€6–9), breakfasts are cheaper at the corner café. It's entirely acceptable to buy a croissant or roll at a nearby bakery and eat it with your cup of coffee (no refills) at a café. Some hotels offer a *petit-déjeuner buffet*—consisting of cereal, yogurt, cheese, fruit, and bread—generally worth the higher cost. If the morning urge for an egg gets the best of you, drop into a café and order *une omelette* or *oeufs sur le plat* (fried eggs). You could also buy or bring plastic bowls and spoons from home, buy a box of French cereal and a small box of milk, and eat in your room before heading out for coffee. We carry fruit and a package of La Vache Qui Rit (Laughing Cow) cheese to supplement the morning jelly.

Picnics

Great for lunch or dinner, French picnics can be first-class affairs and adventures in high cuisine. Be daring. Try the smelly cheeses, ugly pâtés, sissy quiches, and minuscule (usually drinkable) yogurts. Local shopkeepers are accustomed to selling small quantities of produce. Try the tasty salads to go and ask for *une fourchette en plastique* (a plastic fork).

Gather supplies early for a picnic lunch; you'll probably visit several small stores to assemble a complete meal, and many close at noon. Look for a *boulangerie* (bakery), a *crémerie* (cheeses), a *charcuterie* (deli items, meats, and pâtés), an *épicerie* or *alimentation* (small grocery with veggies, drinks, and so on), and a *pâtisserie* (delicious pastries). For fine picnic shopping, check out our street market recommendations in the Shopping in Paris chapter.

Local *supermarchés* offer less color and cost, more efficiency, and adequate quality. Department stores often have supermarkets in the basement. For a quick meal-to-go, look for food stands and bakeries selling take-out sandwiches and drinks. For an affordable sit-down meal, try a *crêperie* or café. See "Café Culture," below.

Café Culture

French cafés (or *brasseries*) provide reasonable light meals and a refuge from museum and church overload. Feel free to order only a bowl of soup or a salad for lunch or dinner at a café. They are carefully positioned viewpoints from which to watch the river of local life flow by. It's easier for the novice to sit and feel comfortable in a café when you know the system.

Check the price list first. Prices, which must be posted prominently, vary wildly between cafés. Cafés charge different prices for the same drink depending upon where you want to be seated. Prices are posted: *comptoir* (counter/bar) or the more expensive *salle* (seated).

Your waiter probably won't overwhelm you with friendliness.

Notice how hard they work. They almost never stop. Cozying up to clients (French or foreign) is probably the last thing on their minds.

The standard menu items (generally served day and night) are the Croque Monsieur (grilled cheese sandwich) and Croque Madame (Monsieur with a fried egg on top). The *salade composée* (com-po-zay) is a hearty chef's salad. Sandwiches are least expensive but plain unless you buy them at the *boulangerie* (bakery). To get more than a piece of ham *(jambon)* on a baguette, order a sandwich *jambon-crudité* (crew-dee-tay), which means garnished with lettuce, tomatoes, cucumbers, and so on. Omelets come lonely on a plate with a basket of bread. The *plat du jour* (daily special) is your fast, hearty hot plate for €9 to €12. At most cafés (though never at a restaurant), feel free to order only appetizers—which many find lighter, more fun, and more interesting than entrées. Regardless of what you order, bread is free; to get more, just hold up your bread basket and ask, "*Encore, s'il vous plaît.*"

Coffee: To order coffee, here is the lingo.

- *un express* (uh nex-press) = shot of espresso
- *une noisette* (oon nwah-zette) = shot of espresso with a shot of milk
- *café au lait* (kah-fay oh lay) = coffee with lots of milk; also called *un grand crème* (uh grahn krem = big) or *un petit crème* (uh puh-tee krem = average)
- *un café allongé* (uh kah-fay al-own-zhay) = cup of coffee, closest to American style
- *un décaffiné* (uh day-kah-fee-nay) = decaf, and can modify any of the above drinks

By law, the waiter must give you a glass of tap water with your coffee if you request it; ask for "*un verre d'eau*" (uh vayre dough).

Wine and Beer: House wine at the bar is cheap (about €2 per glass, cheapest by the *pichet*, or pitcher), and the local beer is cheaper on tap (*une pression*) than in the bottle (*bouteille*).

Tipping: While prices include service, tip, and tax, it's polite to round up for a drink or meal well-served (e.g., if your bill is €19, leave €20); this bonus tip generally isn't more than 5 percent of the bill.

Restaurants

Choose restaurants filled with locals, not places with big neon signs boasting, "We Speak English." Consider your hotelier's opinion. If a restaurant doesn't post its menu (*la carte*) outside, move along.

If you want the menu, ask for *la carte* (and order à la carte like the locals do); if you ask for the *menu* (muh-noo), you'll get a fixed-price meal. *Menus*, which offer three or four courses, are generally a good value: You get your choice of soup, appetizer, or salad; your choice of three or four main courses with vegetables; plus a cheese course and/or a choice of desserts. Service is included, but wine or drinks are generally extra. Restaurants that offer a *menu* for lunch often charge about €6 more for the same *menu* at dinner.

If you'd rather dine à la carte, ask the waiter for help deciphering the French. Go with his or her recommendations and anything *de la maison* (of the house). Galloping gourmets should bring a menu translator; the Marling Menu Master is excellent. The wines are often listed in a separate *carte des vins*.

In France, an entrée is the first course and *le plat* is the main course. *Le plat* or *le plat du jour* (plate of the day) is the main course with vegetables (usually €9–12). If all you want is a salad, find a café instead. Soft drinks and beer cost €1.50 to €3, and a bottle or carafe of house wine costs €10 to €15. To get a waiter's attention, simply say, "*S'il vous plaît*" (see-voo-play)—please.

Drinks

In stores, unrefrigerated soft drinks and beer are one-half the price of cold drinks. Milk and boxed fruit juice are the cheapest drinks. Avoid buying drinks-to-go at streetside stands; you'll find them far cheaper in a shop. Try to keep a water bottle with you. Water quenches your thirst better and cheaper than anything you'll find in a store or café. We drink tap water in Paris.

Parisians are willing to pay for bottled water with their meal (*eau minérale*; oh mee-nay-rahl) because they prefer the taste over tap water. If you prefer a free pitcher of tap water, ask for *une carafe d'eau* (oon kah-rahf doh). Otherwise, you may unwittingly buy bottled water.

To save money when ordering beer, ask for a beer on tap (*une pression*; oon pres-yon) or a draft beer (un *demi*; uh duh-mee), which are cheaper than bottled. France's best beer is Alsatian; try Krônenburg or the heavier Pelfort. *Une panaché* (pan-a-shay) is a refreshing French shandy (7-Up and beer).

To get inexpensive wine at a restaurant, order table wine in a pitcher (*un pichet*; pee-shay) rather than bottled. If all you want is a glass of wine, ask for *un verre de vin* (uh vehr duh van).

You could drink away your children's inheritance if you're not careful. The most famous wines are the most expensive, while lesser-known taste-alikes remain a bargain. If you like brandy, try a *marc* (regional brandy, e.g., *marc de Bourgogne*) or Armagnac, cognac's cheaper twin brother. Pastis, a popular apéritif, is a sweet anise or licorice drink that comes on the rocks with a glass of water (cut it to taste with lots of water).

For a fun, bright, nonalcoholic drink, order *un diabolo menthe* (dee-ablo mont, 7-Up with mint syrup). Kids love the local lemon-ade (*citron pressé*; see-trone preh-say) and the flavored syrups mixed with bottled water (*sirops à l'eau*; see-roe allo). The ice cubes melted after the last Yankee tour group left.

Stranger in a Strange Land

We travel all the way to Europe to enjoy differences—to become temporary locals. You'll experience frustrations. Certain truths that we find "God-given" or "self-evident," like friendly waiters, ice in drinks, bottomless cups of coffee, hot showers, body odor smelling bad, and bigger being better, are suddenly not so true. One of the benefits of travel is the eye-opening realization that there are logical, civil, and even better alternatives. Paris is an understand-ably proud city. To enjoy its people, you need to celebrate the differences. A willingness to go local ensures that you'll enjoy a full dose of Parisian hospitality.

Back Door Manners

While updating our guidebooks, we hear over and over again that our readers are considerate and fun to have as guests. Thank you for traveling as temporary locals who are sensitive to the culture. It's fun to follow you in our travels.

Send Us a Postcard, Drop Us a Line

If you enjoy a successful trip with the help of this book and would like to share your discoveries, please fill out and send the survey at the end of this book to Europe Through the Back Door, Box 2009, Edmonds, WA 98020. We personally read and value all feedback. Thanks in advance—it helps a lot.

For our latest travel information, tap into our Web site: www.ricksteves.com. To check for any updates to this book, visit www.ricksteves.com/update. Our e-mail address is rick @ricksteves.com. Anyone is welcome to request a free issue of our Back Door quarterly newsletter (call 425/771-8303 or order it online at www.ricksteves.com).

Judging from all the positive feedback and happy postcards we receive from travelers who have used this book, it's safe to assume you'll enjoy a great, affordable vacation—with the finesse of an independent, experienced traveler.

From this point, "we" (your coauthors) will shed our respec-tive egos and become "I."

Thanks, and *bon voyage*!

BACK DOOR TRAVEL PHILOSOPHY
As Taught in *Rick Steves' Europe Through the Back Door*

Travel is intensified living—maximum thrills per minute and one of the last great sources of legal adventure. Travel is freedom. It's recess, and we need it.

Experiencing the real Europe requires catching it by surprise, going casual... "Through the Back Door."

Affording travel is a matter of priorities. (Make do with the old car.) You can travel—simply, safely, and comfortably—anywhere in Europe for $80 a day plus transportation costs. In many ways, spending more money only builds a thicker wall between you and what you came to see. Europe is a cultural carnival, and, time after time, you'll find that its best acts are free and the best seats are the cheap ones.

A tight budget forces you to travel close to the ground, meeting and communicating with the people, not relying on service with a purchased smile. Never sacrifice sleep, nutrition, safety, or cleanliness in the name of budget. Simply enjoy the local-style alternatives to expensive hotels and restaurants.

Extroverts have more fun. If your trip is low on magic moments, kick yourself and make things happen. If you don't enjoy a place, maybe you don't know enough about it. Seek the truth. Recognize tourist traps. Give a culture the benefit of your open mind. See things as different but not better or worse. Any culture has much to share.

Of course, travel, like the world, is a series of hills and valleys. Be fanatically positive and militantly optimistic. If something's not to your liking, change your liking. Travel is addictive. It can make you a happier American, as well as a citizen of the world. Our Earth is home to six billion equally important people. It's humbling to travel and find that people don't envy Americans. They like us, but, with all due respect, they wouldn't trade passports.

Globe-trotting destroys ethnocentricity. It helps you understand and appreciate different cultures. Travel changes people. It broadens perspectives and teaches new ways to measure quality of life. Many travelers toss aside their hometown blinders. Their prized souvenirs are the strands of different cultures they decide to knit into their own character. The world is a cultural yarn shop. And Back Door Travelers are weaving the ultimate tapestry. Come on, join in!

paris

ORIENTATION

Many people fall in love with Paris. Some see the essentials and flee, overwhelmed by the huge city. With the proper approach and a good orientation, you'll fall head over heels for Europe's capital city.

This orientation to the City of Lights will illuminate your trip. The day plans—for visits of one to seven days—will help you prioritize the many sights. You'll tap into Paris' information sources for current events. Most important, you'll learn to navigate Paris by Métro, bus, taxi, or foot. For most travelers, the key to the city is a Métro ticket.

Arrival in Paris

For a comprehensive rundown on Paris' six train stations and two airports, see "Transportation Connections" on page 295.

Planning Your Time

Paris in One, Two, or Three Busy Days

Sights are listed in descending order of importance. If you have only one day, just do Day 1 (below); for two days, add Day 2. If you want to fit in Versailles on a three-day visit, try the afternoon of the second (easier) or third day.

Day 1

Morning: Follow Historic Paris Walk, featuring Ile de la Cité, Notre-Dame, Latin Quarter, and Sainte-Chapelle (consider lunch at nearby Samaritaine view café).

Afternoon: Tour the Louvre.

Evening: Cruise Seine River or take illuminated Paris by Night bus tour.

Day 2
Morning: Follow Champs-Elysées Walk from Arc de Triomphe down the grand Champs-Elysées boulevard to Tuileries Gardens (consider lunch at a café in the Tuileries Gardens).
Midday: Cross the pedestrian bridge from the Tuileries Gardens, then tour the Orsay Museum.
Afternoon: Tour the Rodin Museum or Napoleon's Tomb, or visit Versailles (take RER direct from Orsay).
Evening: Enjoy Trocadero scene and twilight ride up the Eiffel Tower.

Day 3
Morning: Follow Marais Walk.
Afternoon: Stay in the Marais and tour your choice of the Carnavalet Museum, Pompidou Center, or Jewish Art and History Museum. (Or visit Versailles.)
Evening: Take Montmartre Walk, featuring Sacré-Coeur.

Paris in Five to Seven Days without Going In-Seine
Day 1
Morning: Follow Historic Paris Walk, featuring Ile de la Cité, Notre-Dame, Latin Quarter, Cluny Museum, and Sainte-Chapelle.
Afternoon: Enjoy the Luxembourg Gardens and relax in a nearby café (see "Les Grands Cafés de Paris" in the Eating chapter), or tour the nearby Pompidou Center.
Evening: Cruise Seine River or take illuminated Paris by Night bus tour.

Day 2
Morning: Tour the Louvre (arrive 15 min befire opening). Lunch at Café Le Nemours.
Afternoon: Follow Champs-Elysées Walk from Arc de Triomphe down the grand Champs-Elysées boulevard to Tuileries Gardens. (Reversing the morning and afternoon also works well because the Champs-Elysées Walk leaves you near the Louvre, though most have more energy for museums in the morning.)
Evening: Take Montmartre Walk, featuring Sacré-Coeur.

Day 3
Morning: Tour Orsay Museum (arrive 15 min before opening).
Midday: Tour Rodin Museum (picnic or café lunch in gardens).
Afternoon: Visit Napoleon's Tomb, then take the Rue Cler Walk and relax at the Café du Marché.
Evening: Enjoy dinner on the Ile St. Louis.

Daily Reminder

Monday: These sights are closed today—Orsay, Rodin, Marmottan, Montmartre, Carnavalet, Catacombs, Giverny, and Versailles; the Louvre is more crowded because of this, but the Richelieu wing stays open until 21:45. Some small stores don't open until 14:00. Street markets such as rue Cler and rue Mouffetard are dead today. Some restaurants and banks are closed. It's discount night at most cinemas.

Tuesday: Many museums are closed today, including the Louvre, Picasso, Cluny, and Pompidou Center, as well as the châteaux of Chantilly and Fontainebleau. The Eiffel Tower, Orsay, and Versailles are particularly busy today.

Wednesday: All sights are open (Louvre until 21:45). The weekly *Pariscope* magazine comes out today. School is out, so many kids' sights are busy. Some cinemas offer discounts.

Thursday: All sights are open (except the Sewer Tour). The Orsay is open until 21:45. Department stores are open late.

Friday: All sights are open (except the Sewer Tour). Afternoon trains and roads leaving Paris are crowded; TGV (*train à grande vitesse*; tay-zhay-vay) reservation fees are higher.

Saturday: All sights are open (except the Jewish Art and History Museum). The fountains run at Versailles (July–Sept) and Vaux-le-Vicomte hosts candlelight visits (May–Oct); otherwise avoid weekend crowds at area châteaux. Department stores are busy. The Jewish Quarter is quiet.

Sunday: Some museums are two-thirds price all day and/or free the first Sunday of the month, thus more crowded (e.g., Louvre, Orsay, Rodin, Cluny, Pompidou, and Picasso). The fountains run at Versailles (early April–early Oct). Most of Paris' stores are closed on Sunday, but shoppers will find relief in the lively Marais neighborhood—the Jewish Quarter— and in Bercy Village, where many stores are open. Look for organ concerts at St. Sulpice and possibly other churches. The American Church sometimes offers a free evening concert at 18:00 (Sept–May only). Most recommended restaurants in the rue Cler neighborhood are closed for dinner.

Day 4

Morning: Catch the RER and arrive early (09:00) at Versailles. Tour palace interior.

Midday: Have lunch on Versailles' market square.

Afternoon: Take the shortcut from the market square to

Versailles' gardens, and visit Le Hameau and Trianon Palaces. Return to Paris with some time for shopping.
Evening: Attend a concert at Sainte-Chapelle.

Day 5
Morning: Follow Marais Walk and tour the Carnavalet Museum. Lunch at Nectarine on place des Vosges or have a falafel on rue des Rosiers.
Afternoon: Tour the Pompidou Center and/or the Jewish Art and History Museum.
Evening: Enjoy Trocadero scene and twilight ride up the Eiffel Tower.

Days 6 and 7
Choose from:
Shopping and cafés
Montmartre and Sacré-Coeur (by day)
Picasso, Cluny, Marmottan, or Jacquemart-Andre Museums, or Garnier Opéra
Daytrip to Chartres
Daytrip to Vaux-le-Vicomte and Fontainebleau
Daytrip to Disneyland Paris
Evening: Night bus or boat tour (whichever you have yet to do)

Paris: A Verbal Map
Paris is split in half by the Seine River, divided into 20 *arrondissements* (proud and independent governmental jurisdictions), and circled by a ring-road freeway (the *périphérique*). You'll find Paris easier to navigate if you know which side of the river you're on, which *arrondissement* you're in, and which subway (Métro) stop you're closest to. If you're north of the river (the top half of any city map), you're on the Right Bank (*rive droite*). If you're south of it, you're on the Left Bank (*rive gauche*). Most of your sightseeing will take place within five blocks of the river.

Arrondissements are numbered, starting at Notre-Dame (ground zero) and moving in a clockwise spiral out to the ring road. The last two digits in a Parisian zip code are

PARIS ARRONDISSEMENTS

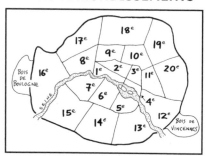

the *arrondissement* number. The notation for the Métro stop is "Mo." In Parisian jargon, Napoleon's tomb is on *la rive gauche* (the Left Bank) in the *7ème* (7th *arrondissement*), zip code 75007, Mo: Invalides. Paris Métro stops are used as a standard aid in giving directions, even for those not using the Métro. As you're tracking down addresses, these definitions will help: *place* (square), *rue* (road), and *pont* (bridge).

Tourist Information

Avoid the Paris tourist offices (abbreviated TI in this book) because of their long lines, short information, and €0.75 charge for maps. This book, the *Pariscope* magazine (described below), and one of the freebie maps available at any hotel are all you need. The main TI is at 127 avenue des **Champs-Elysées** (daily 09:00–20:00, tel. 08 36 68 31 12—phone tree, or 01 49 52 53 10), but the other TIs are less crowded: at **Gare de Lyon** (daily 08:00–20:00, tel. 01 43 43 33 24, answered by live English-speaker), at the **Eiffel Tower** (May–Sept daily 11:00–18:42, yes, 18:42, closed off-season, tel. 01 45 51 22 15), and at the **Louvre** (Wed–Mon 10:00–19:00, closed Tue). Both **airports** have handy TIs (called ADP) with long hours and short lines (see the Transportation Connections chapter).

Paris' TIs have an official Web site (www.paris-touristoffice .com) offering practical information on hotels, special events, museums, children's activities, fashion, nightlife, and more. Two other Web sites that are entertaining and at times useful are www .bonjourparis.com (which claims to offer a virtual trip to Paris with interactive French lessons; tips on wine and food; and news on the latest Parisian trends) and the similar www.paris-anglo.com (with informative stories on visiting Paris, plus a directory of over 2,500 English-friendly businesses).

For a complete schedule of museum hours and English-language museum tours, pick up the free *Musées, Monuments Historiques, et Expositions* booklet from any museum.

Pariscope: The *Pariscope* weekly magazine (or one of its clones, €0.50 at any newsstand) lists museum hours, art exhibits, concerts, music festivals, plays, movies, and nightclubs. Smart tour guides and sightseers rely on this for all the latest (www.pariscope.fr, in French). See "Tour of *Pariscope*" on page 290.

Maps: While Paris is littered with free maps, they don't show all the streets. You may want the huge Michelin #10 map of Paris. For an extended stay, I prefer the pocket-size, street-indexed *Paris Pratique* (€6) with an easy-to-use Métro map.

Bookstores: There are many English-language bookstores in Paris where you can pick up guidebooks (for nearly double their American prices). A few of the best: Shakespeare & Company (daily 12:00–24:00, some used travel books, 37 rue de la Boucherie, across the river from Notre-Dame, tel. 01 43 26 96 50), W. H. Smith (248 rue de Rivoli, Mo: Concorde, tel. 01 44 77 88 99), and Brentanos (37 avenue de L'Opéra, Mo: Opéra, tel. 01 42 61 52 50).

American Church: The American Church is a nerve center for the American émigré community. It distributes a free, handy, and insightful monthly English-language newspaper called the *Paris Voice* (with useful reviews of concerts, plays, and current events; available at about 200 locations in Paris, www.parisvoice .com) and an advertisement paper called *France—U.S.A. Contacts* (full of useful information for those seeking work or long-term housing). The church faces the river between the Eiffel Tower and Orsay Museum (reception open Mon–Sat 09:30–22:30, Sun 09:00–19:30, 65 quai d'Orsay, Mo: Invalides, tel. 01 40 62 05 00).

Helpful Hints

Theft Alert: Use your money belt and never carry a wallet in your back pocket or a purse over your shoulder. Thieves thrive in tourist areas and the Métro (at stations and in subway cars).

Paris Museum Pass: This worthwhile pass, covering most sights in Paris, is available at major Métro stations, TIs, and museums. For detailed information, see page 32.

Museum Strategy: Arriving 20 minutes before major museums open is line-time well spent. Remember, most museums require you to check daypacks and coats, and important museums have metal detectors that will slow your entry. If you're still ahead of the pack when you enter, consider hustling to the most popular works first.

Toilets: Carry small change for pay toilets, or walk into any sidewalk café like you own the place and find the toilet in the back. The toilets in museums are free and generally the best you'll find, and if you have a museum pass, you can drop into almost any museum for the clean toilets. Modern, super-sanitary, street-booth toilets provide both relief and a memory (coins required, don't leave small children inside unattended). Keep some toilet paper or tissues with you, as some toilets are poorly supplied.

Getting around Paris

By Métro: Europe's best subway is divided into two systems— the Métro (for puddle-jumping everywhere in Paris) and the RER (which connects suburban destinations with a few stops in central Paris). You'll be using the Métro for almost all your trips (runs daily from 05:30 until 00:30). Occasionally, you'll find the RER more convenient as it makes fewer stops (like an express bus).

In Paris, you're never more than a 10-minute walk from a Métro station. One ticket takes you anywhere in the system with unlimited transfers. Save 40 percent by buying a *carnet* (car-nay) of 10 tickets for €9 at any Métro station (a single ticket is €1.30, kids 4–10 pay €4.75 for a carnet). Métro tickets work on city buses, though one ticket cannot be used as a transfer between subway and bus.

The new, overpriced, single or multi-day *Paris Visite* Métro pass gives you free run of all Métro, RER, and bus routes in central Paris (and discounts at minor sights). You're better off buying carnets of 10 tickets (see above) and getting three days' use out of one carnet (most travelers use 3–4 tickets/day). But if you want to know more about the *Paris Visite* pass: It covers three progressively larger zones (zones 1–3, 1–5, and 1–8; sold at any Métro station, no photo required). Zones 1 through 3 include central Paris and virtually all tourist needs (1 day-€8.50 for adults or €4.50 for kids under 12; 2 days-€13.75/€7; 3 days-€18.30/€9; and 5 days-€27/€13.75; no 4-day option). Zones 4 through 8 add suburban destinations, such as Versailles, Disneyland Paris, and the airports, for which you're better off buying individual tickets. The pass begins when you validate it (on bus or at Métro turnstile) and lasts for the consecutive number of days purchased. Note that tourists can no longer can buy the cheaper *Carte Orange* week- or month-long passes; these are now available only for residents of Paris.

To get to your destination, determine the closest "Mo" stop and which line or lines will get you there. The lines have numbers, but they're best known by their direction or end-of-the-line stop. (For example, the La Défense/Château de Vincennes line runs between La Défense in the west and Vincennes in the east.)

Once in the Métro station, you'll see blue-and-white signs directing you to the train going in your direction (e.g., "direction: La Défense"). Insert your ticket in the automatic turnstile, pass through, and reclaim and keep your ticket until you exit the system. Fare inspectors regularly check for cheaters and accept absolutely no excuses from anyone. I repeat, keep that ticket until you leave the Métro system.

Transfers are free and can be made wherever lines cross. When you transfer, look for the orange *correspondance* (connections) signs when you exit your first train, then follow the proper direction sign.

Before you *sortie* (exit), check the helpful *plan du quartier* (map of the neighborhood) to get your bearings, locate your destination, and decide which *sortie* you want. At stops with several *sorties*, you can save lots of walking by choosing the best exit.

Thieves spend their days in the Métro. Be on guard. For example, if your pocket is picked as you pass through a turnstile, you end up stuck on the wrong side while the thief strolls away. Any jostle or commotion (especially when boarding or leaving trains) is likely the sign of a thief or team of thieves in action.

Key Words for the Métro and RER

- *direction* (dee-rek-see-ohn): direction
- *ligne* (leen-yuh): line
- *correspondance* (kor-res-pohn-dahns): transfer
- *sortie* (sor-tee): exit
- *carnet* (kar-nay): cheap set of 10 tickets
- *Pardon, madame/monsieur* (par-dohn, mah-dahm/mes-yur): Excuse me, lady/bud.
- *Je descend* (juh day-sahn): I'm getting off.
- *Donnez-moi mon porte-monnaie!*: Give me back my wallet!

Etiquette

- When waiting at the platform, get out of the way of those exiting their train. Board only once everyone is off.
- Avoid using the hinged seats when the car is jammed; they take up valuable standing space.
- In a crowded train, try not to block the exit. If you're blocking the door when the train stops, step out of the car and to the side, let others off, then get back on.
- Talk softly in the cars. Listen to how quietly Parisians can communicate and follow their lead.
- On escalators, stand on the right, pass on the left.

Paris has a huge homeless population and over 11 percent unemployment; expect a warm Métro welcome by panhandlers, musicians, and those selling magazines produced by the homeless community.

By RER: The RER (Réseau Express Régionale; air-ay-air) is the suburban train system serving destinations such as Versailles, Disneyland Paris, and the airports. These routes are indicated by thick lines on your subway map and identified by letters A, B, C, and so on. The RER works like the Métro but can be speedier (if it serves your destination directly) because it makes only a few stops within the city. One Métro ticket is all you need for RER rides within central Paris. You can transfer between the Métro and RER systems with the same ticket. Unlike the Métro, you need to insert your ticket in a turnstile to exit the RER system, and also unlike the Métro, signage can vary between RER stations, meaning you have to pay attention and verify that you're heading the right direction (RER lines often split at the end of the line leading to different signed *Destinations*—study your map and you'll do fine*)*. To travel outside the city (to Versailles or the airport, for example), you'll need to buy a separate, more expensive ticket at the station window before boarding; make sure your stop is served by checking the signs over the train platform (not all trains serve all stops).

By City Bus: The trickier bus system is worth figuring out. Métro tickets are good on both bus and Métro, though you can't use the same ticket to transfer between the two systems. One ticket gets you anywhere in central Paris, but if you leave the city center (shown as zone 1 on the diagram on board the bus), you must validate a second ticket. While the Métro shuts down about 00:30, some buses continue much later. Schedules are posted at bus stops. Handy bus-system maps *(plan des autobus)* are available in any Métro station and are provided in your *Paris Pratique* map book if you invest (€6).

Big system maps, posted at each bus and Métro stop, display the routes. Individual route diagrams show the exact routes of the lines serving that stop. Major stops are painted on the side of each bus. Enter through the front doors. Punch your Métro ticket in the machine behind the driver, or pay the higher cash fare. Get off the bus using the rear door. Even if you're not certain you've figured it out, do some joyriding (outside of rush hour). Lines #24, #63, and #69 are Paris' most scenic routes and make a great introduction to the city. Bus #69 is particularly handy, running between the Eiffel Tower, rue Cler (recommended hotels), Orsay, Louvre, Marais (recommended hotels), and the Père Lachaise Cemetery. The handiest bus routes are listed for each hotel area recommended (see the Sleeping chapter, page 249).

By Taxi: Parisian taxis are almost reasonable. A 10-minute ride costs about €8 *sans baggage* (versus €1 to get anywhere in town on the Métro). You can try waving one down (a glowing white light on the roof means it's free), but it's easier to ask your hotel to call for you or ask for the nearest taxi stand *(Où est une station de taxi?*; oo ay oon stah-see-ohn duh taxi). Taxi stands are indicated by a circled "T" on many city maps, including Michelin's #10 Paris. A typical taxi takes up to three people (maybe 4 if you're polite and pay €2 extra); groups can use a *grand taxi*, which must be booked in advance (ask your hotel to call). If a taxi is summoned by phone, the meter starts as soon as the call is received. Higher rates are charged at night from 19:00 to 7:00, all day Sunday, and to either airport. There's a €1 charge for each piece of baggage. To tip, round up to the next euro (minimum €0.50). Taxis are tough to find on Friday and Saturday nights, especially after the Métro closes (around 00:30). If you need to catch a train or flight early in the morning, consider booking a taxi the night before.

By Foot: Be careful! Parisian drivers are notorious for ignoring pedestrians. Never assume you have the right of way, even in a crosswalk. When crossing a street, keep your pace constant and don't stop suddenly. By law, drivers must miss pedestrians by one meter/three feet (1.5 meters/5 feet in the countryside). Drivers carefully calculate your speed and won't hit you, providing you don't alter your route or pace. Watch out for a lesser hazard: *merde*. Parisian dogs decorate the city's sidewalks with 16 tons of droppings a day. People get injured by slipping in it.

Organized Tours of Paris

Bus Tours: Paris Vision offers handy bus tours of Paris, day and night (advertised in hotel lobbies); their "Illuminated Paris" tour is much more interesting and is explained on page 292.

Far better daytime bus tours are the hop-on hop-off double-decker buses that connect Paris' main sights while providing running commentary (ideal in good weather when you can sit on top; see also Bâteau-Bus under Boat Tours below). Two companies provide hop-on hop-off bus service: **L'Open Tours** and **Les Cars Rouges** (pick up their brochures showing routes and stops from any TI or on their buses). The yellow buses of L'Open Tours provide more extensive coverage, with three different routes rolling by most of the important sights in Paris (the Paris Grand Tour offers the best introduction). Tickets are good for any route. Buy your tickets from the driver (€23/1-day ticket, €25/2-day ticket, kids 4–11 pay €11.50 for 1 or 2 days). Two or three buses depart hourly from about 10:00 to 18:00; expect to wait 10 to 20 minutes at each stop. You can hop off at any stop, then catch a later bus following the same circuit. You'll see these bright-yellow topless double-decker buses all over town—pick one up at the first important sight you visit, or start your tour at the Eiffel Tower stop (the first street on non-river side of the tower, tel. 01 42 66 56 56). **Les Cars Rouges'** bright red buses offer largely the same service with fewer stops on a single, Grand Tour Route for less money (2-day tickets, €21-adult, €10-kids 4–12, tel. 01 53 95 39 53).

Boat Tours: Several companies offer one-hour boat cruises on the Seine (by far, best at night). The huge, mass-production **Bâteaux-Mouches** boats depart every 20 to 30 minutes from pont de l'Alma's right bank, the centrally located pont Neuf, and right in front of the Eiffel Tower, and are convenient to rue Cler hotels (€7, €4 for ages 4–12 and over 65, daily 10:00–22:30, useless taped explanations in 6 languages and tour groups by the dozens, tel. 01 42 25 96 10). The smaller and more intimate **Vedettes de pont Neuf** depart only once an hour from the center of pont Neuf (twice an hour after dark), but they come with a live guide giving explanations in French and English and are convenient to Marais and Contrescarpe hotels (€8.50, €4 for ages 4–12 and over 65, tel. 01 46 33 98 38). From early April to early November, **Bâteau-Bus** operates boats on the Seine, connecting seven key stops about every 25 minutes: Eiffel Tower, Champs-Elysées, Orsay/place de la Concorde, Louvre, Notre-Dame, Hôtel de Ville, and St. Germain-des-Près. Pick up a schedule at any stop (or TI) and use them as a scenic alternative to the Métro. Tickets are available for one day (€10, €5.50 under 12), and two days (€12, €6 under 12); boats run from 10:00 to 19:00, and until 21:00 June through September. **Paris Canal** departs twice daily for three-hour, one-way cruises between the Orsay and Parc de la Vilette. You'll cruise up the Seine then along a quiet canal through non-touristy Paris, accompanied by English explanations (€15, €8.50 for kids 4–11, €11.50 for ages 12–25, tel. 01 42 40 96 97); the one-way trips depart at 09:30 from quai Anatole France (near the Orsay), and from Parc de la Vilette (at Folie des Visites du Parc) at 14:30.

Walking Tours: Paris Walking Tours offers a variety of excellent two-hour walks nearly daily for €10 (tel. 01 48 09 21 40 for recorded schedule in English, fax 01 42 43 75 51, www.pariswalkingtours.com). They focus on the Marais, Luxembourg Gardens, Garnier Opéra, Montmartre, and Hemingway's Paris. Ask about their family-friendly tours. Call ahead a day or two to learn their schedule and starting point. No reservations are required. These are thoughtfully prepared, humorous, and relaxing walking tours led by British or American guides. Don't hesitate to stand close to the guide to hear. For Lost Generation fans, **Paris Literary Promenades** takes you through areas once popular with literary giants from Joyce to Beckett to Hemingway (€9, late May–mid-Oct, daily except Wed at 14:30 and 19:00, 2 hrs, tours depart from place de l'Odeon, tel. 01 48 07 80 72 or cellular 06 03 27 73 52). You can also hire a Parisian as your personal guide. Arnaud Servignat (tel. 06 72 77 94 50, fax 01 42 57 00 38, e-mail: arnotour@noos.fr) and Marianne Siegler (tel. 01 42 52 32 51) are licensed local guides who freelance for individuals and families ($150/4 hrs, $250/day).

Bike Tours: Mike's Bullfrog Bike Tours—like a frat party on wheels—attracts a college crowd for its boisterous three-to four-hour rolls through Paris (€20, May–Nov daily at 11:00, also at 15:30 June–July, no CC, in English, no bikes or reservations needed, meet at south pillar of Eiffel Tower, cellular 06 09 98 08 60, www.mikesbiketours.com).

Excursion Tours: Many companies offer minivan and big bus tours to regional sights, including all of the daytrips described in this book. **Paris Walking Tours** are the best, with informative and fun afternoon visits to the Impressionist artist retreats of Giverny and Auvers-sur-Oise (€47–56, includes admissions, tel. 01 48 09 21 40 for recording in English, fax 01 42 43 75 51, www.pariswalkingtours.com). **Paris Vision** offers mass-produced,

full-size bus and minivan tours to several popular regional destinations, including the Loire Valley, Champagne region, D-Day
beaches, and Mont St. Michel. Their minivan tours are more
expensive but more personal, in English, and offer pick-up at
your hotel (€130–200/person). Their full-size bus tours are multi-
lingual and cost about half the price of a minivan tour—worth
it for some simply for the ease of transportation to the sights (full-
size buses depart from 214 rue de Rivoli, Mo: Tuileries, tel. 01 42
60 30 01, fax 01 42 86 95 36, www.parisvision.com).

paris

SIGHTS

These sights are arranged by neighborhood for handy sightseeing. When you see a ⭐ in a listing, it means the sight is covered in much more depth in one of our walks or self-guided tours.

Paris Museum Pass: All of the sights listed in this chapter are covered by a Paris museum pass, except for the Eiffel Tower, Montparnasse Tower, Marmottan Museum, Garnier Opéra, Notre-Dame treasury, Jacquemart-André Museum, Jewish Art and History Museum, Grande Arche at La Défense, Jeu de Paume Exhibition Hall, Catacombs, Paris Story film, and the ladies of Pigalle. Outside Paris, the pass covers the châteaux of Versailles, Chantilly, and Fontainebleau.

In Paris, there are two classes of sightseers: Those with a museum pass and those who stand in line. Serious sightseers save time and money by getting this pass. Sold at museums, main Métro stations (including Ecole Militaire and Bastille stations), and TIs (even at the airports), the pass pays for itself in two admissions and gets you into most sights with no lining up (1 day-€13, 3 consecutive days-€26, 5 consecutive days-€39, no youth or senior discount). Try to avoid buying the pass at a major museum (such as the Louvre) where supply can be spotty and lines long.

The pass isn't worth buying for children, as most museums are free for those under 18. The free museum and monuments directory that comes with your pass lists the latest hours, phone numbers, and specifics on what kids pay. The cutoff age for free entry varies from 5 to 18. Most major art museums let young people under 18 in for free, but anyone over age five has to pay to tour the sewers—go figure.

The pass is not activated until the first time you use it (you enter the date on the pass).

Included sights (and admission prices without the pass)

you're likely to visit: Louvre (€7), Orsay (€7), Sainte-Chapelle (€5.50), Arc de Triomphe (€6), L'Orangerie (about €6), Les Invalides Museums/Napoleon's Tomb (€6), Carnavalet Museum (€5.50), Conciergerie (€5.50), Victor Hugo's House (€3), Panthéon (€5.50), Sewer Tour (€4), Cluny Museum (€6), Pompidou Center (€5), Notre-Dame towers (€5.50) and crypt (€3), Picasso Museum (€5), and the Rodin Museum (€4). Outside Paris, the pass covers the Palace of Versailles (€7) and its Trianons (€5); Château of Fontainebleau (€5.50); and Château of Chantilly (€6).

Tally it up—and remember, an advantage of the pass is that you skip to the front of lines, saving hours of waiting, especially in summer (though everyone must pass through the slow-moving metal-detector lines, and some places can't accommodate a bypass lane, such as Notre-Dame's tower). With the pass you'll pop painlessly into sights that you're walking by (even for a few minutes) that might otherwise not be worth the expense (e.g., Notre-Dame crypt, Conciergerie, Victor Hugo's House, and the Panthéon).

Museum Tips: The Louvre and many other museums are closed on Tuesday. The Orsay, Rodin, Marmottan, Carnavalet, and Versailles are closed Monday. Most museums offer reduced prices on Sunday. Many sights stop admitting people 30 to 60 minutes before they close, and many begin closing rooms 45 minutes before the actual closing time. For the fewest crowds, visit very early, at lunch, or very late. Most museums have slightly shorter hours October through March. French holidays can really mess up your sightseeing plans (Jan 1, May 1, May 8, July 14, Nov 1, Nov 11, and Dec 25). The best Impressionist art museums are the Orsay, L'Orangerie (scheduled to re-open in 2002), and Marmottan (see our self-guided tours of these).

Paris Museums near the Tuileries Gardens

The Tuileries Gardens were once the private property of kings and queens. Paris' grandest public park links these museums: Louvre, L'Orangerie (due to re-open in 2002), Jeu de Paume, and the Orsay.

▲▲▲**Louvre**—This is Europe's oldest, biggest, greatest, and second-most-crowded museum (after the Vatican). It's packed with Greek and Roman masterpieces, medieval jewels, Michelangelo statues, and paintings by the greatest artists from the Renaissance to the Romantics (mid-1800s).

Cost: €7, €5 after 15:00 and on Sun, free on first Sun of month and for those under 18, covered by museum pass.

Hours: Wed through Mon 09:00 to 18:00, closed Tue, all wings open Wed until 21:45, Richelieu Wing (only) until 21:45 on Mon. Closed Jan 1, Easter, May 1, Nov 1, and Dec 25.

—— MUSEUMS NEAR TUILERIES GARDENS ——

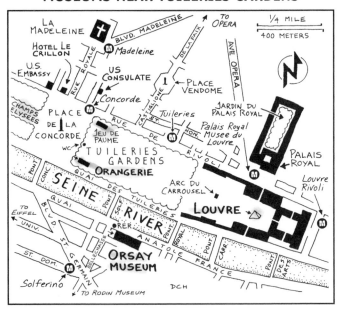

Tel. 01 40 20 51 51 or 01 40 20 53 17 for recorded information, www.louvre.fr.

Location: At Palais Royal/Musée du Louvre Métro stop. The old Louvre Métro stop, called Louvre Rivoli, no longer goes to the Louvre. ✪ See Louvre Tour on page 91.

▲**L'Orangerie**—After a two-year renovation, this museum is due to re-open sometime in 2002. To find out exactly when, ask at a Paris TI or another museum (e.g., Louvre or Orsay). This small, quiet, and often overlooked museum houses Monet's water lilies and a scattering of other great Impressionist works (about €6, price and hours not set, covered by museum pass, located in Tuileries Garden near place de la Concorde, Mo: Concorde).

Jeu de Paume—This one-time home to the Impressionist art collection now located in the Orsay hosts rotating exhibits of top contemporary artists (€6, not covered by museum pass, Tue 12:00–21:30, Wed–Fri 12:00–19:00, Sat–Sun 10:00–19:00, closed Mon, on place de la Concorde, just inside Tuileries Garden on rue de Rivoli side, Mo: Concorde).

▲▲▲**Orsay Museum**—This is Paris' 19th-century art museum (actually, art from 1848–1914), and it includes Europe's greatest collection of Impressionist works.

Cost: €7, €5 after 16:15, on Sun, and for ages 18–25, free for youth under 18 and for anyone first Sunday of month, covered by museum pass. English-language tours usually run daily except Sun at 11:30, cost €5.50, take 90 minutes, and are also available on audioguide (€5). Tel. 01 40 49 48 48.

Hours: June 20–Sept 20 Tue–Sun 09:00–18:00, Sept 21–June 19 Tue–Sat 10:00–18:00, Sun 09:00–18:00, Thu until 21:45 all year, closed Mon. Last entrance is 45 minutes before closing.

Location: Above the RER-C stop called Musée d'Orsay; the nearest Métro stop is Solferino, three blocks south of the Orsay. From the Louvre, it's a 15-minute walk downstream to the Orsay. ✪ See Orsay Tour on page 112.

Historic Core of Paris: Notre-Dame, Sainte-Chapelle, and More

✪ All of these sights are covered in detail in the Historic Paris Walk (plus map) on page 47. Only the essentials are listed here.

▲▲**Notre-Dame Cathedral**—The 700-year-old cathedral is packed with history and tourists (free, daily 08:00–18:45; treasury-€2.50, not covered by museum pass, daily 09:30–17:30; ask about the free English tours, normally Wed and Thu at 12:00 and Sat at 14:30; Mo: Cité, Hôtel de Ville, or St. Michel; clean €0.50 toilets in front of church near Charlemagne's statue). ✪ See page 47.

You can climb the north **tower** (€5.50, daily April–Sept 09:00–18:00, Oct–March 10:00–17:30, covered by museum pass), or descend to the **crypt**. The Paris Archaeological Crypt is a worthwhile 15-minute stop with your museum pass (€3, Tue–Sun 10:00–17:30, closed Mon, enter 100 meters in front of church). You'll see Roman ruins, trace the street plan of the medieval village, and see diagrams of how early Paris grew and grew, all thoughtfully explained in English.

▲▲**Deportation Memorial (Mémorial de la Déportation)**—This memorial to the 200,000 French victims of the Nazi concentration camps draws you into their experience (free, April–Sept daily 10:00–12:00, 14:00–19:00, Oct–March daily 10:00–12:00, 14:00–17:00, east tip of the island Ile de la Cité, behind Notre-Dame and near Ile St. Louis, Mo: Cité). ✪ See page 53.

Ile St. Louis—This residential island behind Notre-Dame is known for its restaurants (see Eating chapter), great Bertillon ice cream (31 rue St. Louis en l'Ile), and shops (along rue St. Louis en l'Ile). ✪ See page 54.

Cité "Métropolitain" Stop and Flower Market—On place Louis Lepine, between Notre-Dame and Sainte-Chapelle, you'll find an early-19th-century subway entrance and a flower market (that chirps with a bird market on Sun).

▲▲▲**Sainte-Chapelle**—This triumph of Gothic church architecture is a cathedral of glass like no other (€5.50, €8 combo-ticket covers Conciergerie, both covered by museum pass, daily April–Sept 09:30–18:30, Oct–March 10:00–17:00, Mo: Cité, tel. 01 48 01 91 35 for concert information). ✪ See page 58.

▲**Conciergerie**—Marie Antoinette was imprisoned here, as were 2,600 others on the way to the guillotine (€5.50, €8 combo-ticket covers Sainte-Chapelle, both covered by museum pass, daily April-Sept 09:30–18:30, Oct–March 10:00–17:00, good English descriptions). ✪ See page 62.

▲**Samaritaine Department Store Viewpoint**—For a great, free viewpoint, take the elevator to the ninth floor and walk to the eleventh-floor rooftop panorama (daily 09:30–19:00, reasonably priced café on 10th-floor terrace, supermarket in basement, Mo: Pont Neuf, tel. 01 40 41 20 20). ✪ See page 287.

Southwest Paris: Eiffel Tower Neighborhood

▲▲▲**Eiffel Tower**—It's crowded and expensive but worth the trouble. Go early (by 08:45) or late in the day (after 18:00, after 20:00 in summer) to avoid most crowds; weekends are worst. Pilier Nord (the north pillar) has the biggest elevator and, therefore, the fastest-moving line. A TI/ticket booth is between the Pilier Nord and Est (east pillar). The stairs (yes, you can walk up partway) are next to the Jules Verne restaurant entry. A sign in the jammed elevator tells you to beware of pickpockets.

The tower is 300 meters (1,000 feet) tall; in hot weather it's 15 centimeters (6 inches) taller. It covers 2.5 acres and requires 50 tons of paint. Its 7,000 tons of metal are spread out so well at the base that it's no heavier per square inch than a linebacker on tiptoes. Visitors to Paris may find *Mona Lisa* to be less than expected, but the Eiffel Tower rarely disappoints, even in an era of skyscrapers.

Built a hundred years after the French Revolution (and in the midst of an Industrial one), the tower served no function but to impress. Bridge-builder Gustave Eiffel won the contest for the 1889 Centennial World's Fair by beating out such rival proposals as a giant guillotine. To a generation hooked on technology, the tower was the marvel of the age, a symbol of progress and of man's ingenuity. To others it was a cloned-sheep monstrosity. The writer Maupassant routinely ate lunch in the tower just so he wouldn't have to look at it.

Delicate and graceful when seen from afar, it's massive—even a bit scary—from close up. You don't appreciate the size until you walk toward it; like a mountain, it seems so close but takes forever to reach. There are three observation platforms, at 60, 120, and

──── SOUTHWEST PARIS: ────
EIFFEL TOWER NEIGHBORHOOD

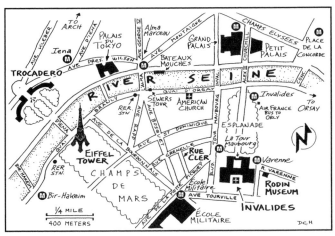

270 meters (200, 400, and 900 feet); the higher you go, the more
you pay. Each requires a separate elevator (and a line), so plan on
at least 90 minutes if you want to go to the top and back. For most,
the view from the second level is plenty. As you ascend through the
metal beams, imagine being a worker, perched high above nothing,
riveting this giant erector set together. On top, all of Paris lies
before you, with a panorama guide. On a good day you can see
for 65 kilometers (40 miles).

The first level has exhibits, a post office (daily 10:00–19:00,
cancellation stamp will read Eiffel Tower), snack bar, WCs, and
souvenirs. Read the informative signs (in English) describing the
major monuments, see the entertaining free movie on the history
of the Tower, and don't miss a century of fireworks, including the
entire millennium blast, on video. Then consider a drink or a sandwich overlooking all of Paris at the snack café (outdoor tables in
summer) or at the city's best view bar/restaurant, **Altitude 95**
(€15 lunches, €34–46 dinners, dinner seatings at 19:00 and 21:00,
reserve well ahead for a view table; before you ascend to dine, drop
by the booth between the north/*nord* and east/*est* pillars to pick
up a pass that enables you to skip the line; tel. 01 45 55 20 04,
fax 01 47 05 94 40).

The second level has the best views (walk up the stairway
to get above the netting), a small cafeteria, WCs, and an Internet
gimmick to have your photo at the Eiffel Tower sent into cyber-
space (La Gallerie des Visiteurs).

Cost and Hours: It costs €4 to go to the first level, €7 to the second, and €10 to go all the way for the 270-meter view (900 feet; not covered by museum pass). On a budget? You can climb the stairs to the second level for only €3 (daily March–Sept 09:00–24:00, Oct–Feb 09:30–23:00, shorter lines at night, Mo: Trocadero, RER: Champ de Mars, tel. 01 44 11 23 23).

The best place to view the tower is from Trocadero Square to the north (a 10-min walk across the river, and a happening scene at night); for a kid's angle on the tower and Trocadero, see the Paris with Children chapter (page 281). Consider arriving at the Trocadero Métro stop for the view, then walking toward the tower. Another great viewpoint is the long, grassy field, le Champ de Mars, to the south (after about 20:00, the *gendarmes* look the other way as Parisians stretch out or picnic on the grass). However impressive it may be by day, it's an awesome thing to see at twilight, when the tower becomes engorged with light and virile Paris lies back and lets night be on top.

▲**Paris Sewer Tour (Egouts)**—This quick and easy visit takes you along a few hundred meters of underground water tunnel. Its interesting displays and English descriptions explain the evolution of the world's longest sewer system. (If you lined up Paris' sewers, they would reach beyond Istanbul.) Don't miss the slide show, the fine WCs just beyond the gift shop, and the occasional tours in English (€4, covered by museum pass, Sat–Wed 11:00–17:00, closed Thu–Fri, where pont de l'Alma greets the Left Bank, Mo: Alma Marceau, RER Pont de l'Alma, tel. 01 47 05 10 29).

▲▲**Napoleon's Tomb and Les Invalides Army Museum**—The emperor lies majestically dead inside several coffins under a grand dome—a goose-bumping pilgrimage for historians. Napoleon is surrounded by Europe's greatest military museum in the Hôtel des Invalides, providing fascinating coverage of Napoleon, World War I, and World War II. The dome glitters with 26 pounds of gold (€6, ages 12–17 and students-€5, under 12 free, covered by museum pass, daily April–Sept 09:00–17:45, Napoleon's Tomb open June 15–Sept 15 until 18:45, Oct–March 10:00–16:45, Mo: La Tour Maubourg or Varennes, tel. 01 44 42 37 72). ✪ See Napoleon's Tomb & Les Invalides Tour on page 188.

▲▲**Rodin Museum**—This user-friendly museum is filled with passionate works by the greatest sculptor since Michelangelo. See *The Kiss*, *The Thinker*, *The Gates of Hell*, and many more (€4, €2.75 on Sun and for students, free for youth under 18 and for anyone first Sun of month, covered by museum pass; €0.75 for gardens only, which may be Paris' best deal, as many works are well-displayed in the beautiful gardens; Tue–Sun 09:30–17:45, closed Mon and at 17:00 off-season; near Napoleon's Tomb, 77 rue de

Varennes, Mo: Varennes, tel. 01 44 18 61 10). ✪ See Rodin Museum Tour on page 169.

▲▲**Marmottan**—In this private, intimate, less-visited museum, you'll find more than 100 paintings by Claude Monet (€6, not covered by museum pass, Tue–Sun 10:00–17:30, closed Mon, 2 rue Louis Boilly, Mo: La Muette, follow museum signs 6 blocks through a delightful kid-filled park to museum, tel. 01 44 96 50 33). Combine this fine museum with a stroll down one of Paris' most pleasant shopping streets, the rue de Passy (from La Muette Métro stop). ✪ See Marmottan Tour on page 177.

Southeast Paris: Latin Quarter

✪ The Historic Paris Walk, on page 47, dips into the Latin Quarter.

▲**Latin Quarter**—This Left Bank neighborhood, just opposite Notre-Dame, was the center of Roman Paris. But the Latin Quarter's touristy fame relates to its intriguing artsy, bohemian character. This was perhaps Europe's leading university district in the Middle Ages, when Latin was the language of higher education. The neighborhood's main boulevards (St. Michel and St. Germain) are lined with cafés—once the haunts of great poets and philosophers, now the hangout of tired tourists. While still youthful and artsy, the area has become a tourist ghetto filled with cheap North African eateries.

▲▲**Cluny Museum (Musée National du Moyen Age)**—This treasure trove of medieval art fills the old Roman baths, offering close-up looks at stained glass, Notre-Dame carvings, fine goldsmithing and jewelry, and rooms of tapestries (€6, €4 on Sun, covered by museum pass, Wed–Mon 09:15–17:45, closed Tue, near the corner of boulevards St. Michel and St. Germain, Mo: Cluny, tel. 01 53 73 78 00). ✪ See Cluny Museum Tour on page 203.

St. Germain-des-Près—A church was first built on this site in A.D. 452. The church you see today was constructed in 1163 and is all that's left of a once sprawling and powerful monastery. The colorful interior reminds us that Gothic churches originally were painted in bright colors. The area around the church hops at night with venerable cafés, fire-eaters, mimes, and scads of artists (Mo: St. Germain-des-Près).

▲**St. Sulpice Organ Concert**—For pipe-organ enthusiasts, this is a delight. The Grand-Orgue at St. Sulpice has a rich history, with a line of 12 world-class organists (including Widor and Dupre) going back 300 years. Widor started the tradition of opening the loft to visitors after the 10:30 service on Sundays. Daniel Roth continues to welcome guests in three languages while playing five keyboards at once. The 10:30 Sunday Mass is followed by a high-powered

──── SOUTHEAST PARIS: LATIN QUARTER ────

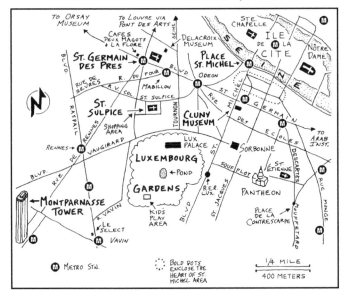

25-minute recital at 11:40. Then, just after noon, the small, unmarked door is opened (left of entry as you face the rear). Visitors scamper like 16th notes up spiral stairs, past the 18th-century Stairmasters that were used to fill the billows, into a world of 7,000 pipes, where they can watch the master performing the next Mass. You'll generally have 30 minutes to kill (there's a plush lounge) before the organ plays; visitors can leave at any time. If late or rushed, show up around 12:30 and wait at the little door. As someone leaves, you can slip in (Mo: St. Sulpice or Mabillon). The nearby St. Germain market is open Sundays and a delight.

▲▲**Luxembourg Gardens**—Paris' most beautiful, interesting, and enjoyable garden/park/recreational area is a great place to watch Parisians at rest and play. (See Paris with Children, page 281.) These private gardens are property of the French Senate (housed in the château) and have special rules governing their use (e.g., where cards can be played, where dogs can be walked, where joggers can run, when and where music can be played). The brilliant flower plantings are completely changed three times a year, and the boxed trees are brought out of the *orangerie* in May. Challenge the card and chess players to a game (near the tennis courts), or find a free chair near the main pond and take a breather. Notice any pigeons? The story goes that a poor

Ernest Hemingway used to hand-hunt (read: strangle) them here. Paris Walking Tours offers a good tour of the park (see "Organized Tours," page 29). The grand neoclassical-domed Panthéon, now a mausoleum housing the tombs of several great Frenchmen, is a block away and is only worth entering if you have a museum pass. The historic cafés of Montparnasse are a few blocks from the southwest-corner exit of the park (rue Vavin, see "Les Grands Cafés de Paris," page 278). The park is open until dusk (Mo: Odéon, RER: Luxembourg). If you enjoy the Luxembourg Gardens and want to see more, visit the more elegant Parc Monceau (Mo: Monceau) and the colorful Jardin des Plantes (Mo: Jussieu or Gare d'Austerlitz, RER: Luxembourg).

Montparnasse Tower—This 59-floor superscraper is cheaper and easier to get to the top of than the Eiffel Tower, and has the added bonus of offering one of Paris' best views—since the Eiffel Tower is in it and the Montparnasse Tower isn't. Buy the photo guide to the city, then go to the rooftop and orient yourself (€8, not covered by museum pass, daily in summer 09:30–23:30, off-season 10:00–22:00, disappointing after dark, entrance on rue l'Arrivé, Mo: Montparnasse). The tower is an efficient stop when combined with a daytrip to Chartres, which begins at the Montparnasse train station.

▲**Catacombs**—These underground tunnels contain the anonymous bones of six million permanent Parisians. In 1785, the Revolutionary government of Paris decided to make its congested city more spacious and sanitary by emptying the city cemeteries (which traditionally surrounded churches) into an official ossuary. The perfect locale was the many kilometers of underground tunnels from limestone quarries, which were, at that time, just outside the city. For decades, priests led ceremonial processions of black-veiled, bone-laden carts into the quarries, where the bones were stacked into piles 1.5 meters (5 feet) high and as much as 24 meters (80 feet) deep behind neat walls of skull-studded tibia. Each transfer was completed with the placement of a plaque indicating the church and district where that stack of bones originated and the date they arrived.

From the entry of the catacombs, a spiral staircase leads 18 meters (60 feet) down. Then you begin a 1.5-kilometer-long (1 mile) subterranean walk. After several blocks of empty passageways, you ignore a sign announcing: "Halt, this is the empire of the dead." Along the way, plaques encourage visitors to reflect upon their destiny: "Happy is he who is forever faced with the hour of his death and prepares himself for the end every day." You emerge far from where you entered, with white limestone-covered toes, telling anyone in the know you've been underground gawking at bones. Note to wannabe Hamlets: An attendant checks your bag at the exit for stolen souvenirs (€5, not covered by museum pass, 1 place Denfert-Rochereau, Mo: Denfert-Rochereau, Tue–Fri 14:00–16:00, Sat–Sun 09:00–11:00, 14:00–16:00, closed Mon, tel. 01 43 22 47 63).

Northwest Paris: Champs-Elysées, Arc de Triomphe, and Beyond

⭐ Take the Champs-Elysées Walk (page 66) for a pleasant downhill stroll connecting the sights from the enduring Arc de Triomphe to the historic place de la Concorde.

▲▲**Champs-Elysées**—This famous boulevard is Paris' backbone, with the greatest concentration of traffic. From the Arc de Triomphe down the Champs-Elysées, all of France seems to converge on place de la Concorde, the city's largest square. While the boulevard has become a bit Americanized, a walk here is a must. Take the Métro to the Arc de Triomphe (Mo: Etoile) and saunter down the Champs-Elysées (Métro stops every few blocks: Etoile, George V, FDR). ⭐ See page 66.

▲▲▲**Arc de Triomphe**—Napoleon had the magnificent Arc de Triomphe commissioned to commemorate his victory at the battle of Austerlitz. Climb to the top for a mesmerizing view of the traffic that swirls around the arch (€6, covered by museum pass, June–Sept daily 09:30–23:00, Oct–May daily 09:30–22:00, Mo: Etoile, use underpass to reach arch, tel. 01 43 80 31 31). ⭐ See page 66.

▲**Le Palais Garnier (a.k.a. "The Old Opera")**—This grand palace of the belle époque was built for Napoleon III and finished in 1875 (after completing this project, the architect—Garnier—went south to do the casino in Monte Carlo). From the grand Avenue de l'Opéra, once lined with Paris' most fashionable haunts, the newly-restored facade seems to say "all power to the wealthy." While huge, the actual theater seats only 2,000. The real show was before and after, when the elite of Paris—out to see and be seen—strutted their elegant stuff in the extravagant lobbies. Think of the grand marble stairway as a theater itself. As you wander the halls and gawk at the decor, imagine the place filled with the beautiful people of the day. The massive foundations straddle an underground lake (creating the mysterious world of the Phantom of the Opera). Tourists can peek from two boxes into the actual red velvet theater to see Marc Chagall's colorful ceiling (1964) playfully dancing around the eight-ton chandelier. Note the box seats next to the stage—the most expensive in the house, with an obstructed view of the stage but just right if you're there only to be seen. The elitism of this place prompted Mitterand to have a people's opera house built in the 1980s (symbolically on place

de la Bastille, where the French Revolution started in 1789).
This left the Garnier Opéra home only to a ballet and occasional
concerts. While the library-museum is of interest to opera buffs,
anyone will enjoy the second-floor grand foyer and Salon du
Glacier, iced with decor typical of 1900 (€5, not covered by
museum pass, daily 10:00–17:00 except when in use for performance, English tours summers only, normally at 14:00, call to
confirm; enter through the front off place de l'Opéra, Mo:
Opéra, tel. 01 40 01 22 53). American Express and the Paris
Story film are on the left side of the Opéra and the venerable
Galeries Lafayette department store is just behind.

Paris Story Film—This entertaining film gives a good and
painless overview of Paris's turbulent and brilliant past, covering
2,000 years in 45 fast-moving minutes. The theater's wide-screen
projection and cushy chairs provide an ideal break from bad
weather and sore feet and make it fun with kids (€8, kids 6–18-€5,
families with 2 kids and 2 parents-€21, not covered by museum
pass, shows are on the hour from 09:00–18:00 daily, next to
Opéra at 11 rue Scribe, Mo: Opéra, tel. 01 42 66 62 06).

▲▲Musée Jacquemart-André—This thoroughly enjoyable
museum showcases the lavish home of a wealthy, art-loving 19th-
century Parisian couple. After wandering the grand boulevards,
you now get inside for an intimate look at the lifestyles of the
Parisian rich and fabulous. Edouard André and his wife Nélie
Jacquemart—who had no children—spent their lives and fortunes
designing, building, and then decorating a sumptuous mansion.
What makes this visit so rewarding is the fine audioguide tour
(in English, free with admission). And to make it even more memo-
rable, the place is strewn with paintings by Rembrandt, Botticelli,
Uccello, Mantegna, Bellini, Boucher, Fragonard—enough to make
a painting gallery famous. Plan on spending an hour with the audioguide (€8, not covered by museum pass, daily 10:00–18:00, elegant
café, 158 blvd. Haussmann, Mo: Miromesnil, tel. 01 42 89 04 91).

▲Grande Arche de La Défense—On the outskirts of Paris, the
centerpiece of Paris' ambitious skyscraper complex (La Défense)
is the Grande Arche. Built to celebrate the 200th anniversary of
the 1789 French Revolution, the place is big—38 floors on more
than 200 acres. It holds offices for 30,000 people. Notre-Dame
Cathedral could fit under its arch. The La Défense complex is an
interesting study in 1960s land-use planning. More than 100,000
workers commute here daily, directing lots of business and devel-
opment away from downtown and allowing central Paris to retain
its more elegant feel. This makes sense to most Parisians, regardless of whatever else they feel about this controversial complex.
You'll enjoy city views from the Arche elevator (€7, under 18-€5,

not covered by museum pass, daily 10:00–19:00, includes a film on its construction and art exhibits, RER or Mo: La Défense, follow signs to Grande Arche or get off 1 stop earlier at Esplanade de la Défense and walk through the interesting business complex, tel. 01 49 07 27 57).

Northeast Paris: Marais Neighborhood and More

✪ To connect the sights with a fun, fact-filled stroll leading from place de la Bastille to the Pompidou Center, take the Marais Walk on page 73.

▲▲**Pompidou Center**—Europe's greatest collection of far-out modern art is housed in the Musée National d'Art Moderne, on the top floor of this colorful, exoskeletal building. Once ahead of its time, this 20th-century art (remember that century?) has been waiting for the world to catch up with it. After so many Madonnas and Children, a piano smashed to bits and glued to the wall is refreshing. Ride the escalator for a great city view from the café terrace on top, and don't miss the free exhibits on the ground floor (€5, covered by museum pass, audioguide-€4, Wed–Mon 11:00–21:00, closed Tue; to use escalator you need a ticket for the museum or a museum pass, good mezzanine-level café is cheaper than cafés outside, Mo: Rambuteau, tel. 01 44 78 12 33).

The Pompidou Center and its square are lively, with lots of people, street theater, and activity inside and out—a perpetual street fair. Kids of any age enjoy the fun, colorful fountain (called *Homage to Stravinsky*) next to the Pompidou Center. ✪ See Pompidou Center Tour on page 139.

▲▲**Museum of Art and History of Judaism (Hôtel d'Aignan)**—This remarkable museum, located in a beautifully restored Marais mansion, tells the story of Judaism throughout Europe, from the Roman destruction of Jerusalem to the theft of famous artworks during World War II. Helpful audioguides and many English explanations make this an enjoyable history lesson (red numbers on small signs indicate the number you should press on your audioguide). Move along at your own speed. The museum illustrates the cultural unity maintained by this continually dispersed population. You'll learn about the history of Jewish traditions from Bar Mitzvahs to menorahs, and see exquisite traditional costumes and objects around which daily life revolved. Don't miss the explanation of "the Dreyfus affair," a major event in early 1900 French politics. You'll also see photographs of and paintings by famous Jewish artists, including Chagall, Modigliani, and Soutine. The small section devoted to the deportation of Jews from Paris is moving (€6, ages 18–25-€4, under 18 free, not covered by museum pass, Mon–Fri 11:00–18:00, Sun 10:00–18:00, closed

Sat, 71 rue du Temple, Mo. Rambuteau or Hôtel de Ville, tel. 01 53 01 86 53).

▲**Picasso Museum (Hôtel Salé)**—This is the world's largest collection of Pablo Picasso's paintings, sculptures, sketches, and ceramics, and includes his personal collection of Impressionist art. It's well-explained in English and worth ▲▲▲ if you're a fan (€5, covered by museum pass, Wed–Mon 09:30–18:00, closed Tue, 5 rue Thorigny, Mo: St. Paul or Chemin Vert, tel. 01 42 71 25 21).

▲▲**Carnavalet Museum**—The tumultuous history of Paris is well-displayed in this converted Marais mansion. Explanations are in French only, but many displays are fairly self-explanatory. You'll see paintings of Parisian scenes, French Revolution para-phernalia, old Parisian store signs, a small guillotine, a model of 16th-century Ile de la Cité (notice the bridge houses), and rooms full of 15th-century Parisian furniture (€5.50, covered by museum pass, Tue–Sun 10:00–17:40, closed Mon, 23 rue de Sévigné, Mo: St. Paul, tel. 01 42 72 21 13). ✪ See Carnavalet Museum Tour on page 153.

Victor Hugo's House—France's literary giant lived in this house on place des Vosges from 1832 to 1848. Inside are posters adver-tising theater productions of his works, paintings of some of his most famous character creations, and a few furnished rooms (€3, covered by museum pass, Tue–Sun 10:00–17:40, closed Mon, 6 place des Vosges, tel. 01 42 72 10 16).

▲**Promenade Plantée Park**—This three-kilometer long (2 mile) narrow garden walk on a viaduct was once used for train tracks and is now a joy. It runs from place de la Bastille (Mo: Bastille) along Avenue Daumesnil to Saint-Mandé (Mo: Michel Bizot). Part of the park is elevated. At times, you'll walk along the street until you pick up the next segment. From place de la Bastille, take avenue Daumesnil (past Opéra building) to the intersection with avenue Ledru Rollin; walk up the stairs and through the gate (free, opens Mon–Fri at 08:00, Sat–Sun at 09:00, closes at sunset). The shops below the viaduct's arches make for entertain-ing window-shopping.

▲**Père Lachaise Cemetery**—Littered with the tombstones of many of the city's most illustrious dead, this is your best one-stop look at the fascinating, romantic world of "permanent Parisians." More like a small city, the place is confusing, but maps will direct you to the graves of Chopin, Molière, Edith Piaf, Oscar Wilde, Gertrude Stein, Heloïse, and Abelard. In section 92, a series of statues memorializing World War II makes the French war experience a bit more real (helpful €1.50 maps at flower store near entry, across street from Métro stop, closes at dusk, Mo: Père Lachaise or bus #69).

North Paris: Montmartre

✪ Connect the sights with the Montmartre Walk on page 84.

▲▲**Sacré-Coeur and Montmartre**—This Byzantine-looking church, while only 130 years old, is impressive (daily until 23:00). One block from the church, the place du Tertre was the haunt of Toulouse-Lautrec and the original bohemians. Today it's mobbed with tourists and unoriginal bohemians, but it's still fun (go early in the morning to beat the crowds). Take the Métro to the Anvers stop (1 Métro ticket buys your way up the funicular and avoids the stairs) or the closer but less scenic Abbesses stop. A taxi to the top of the hill saves time and sweat.

Pigalle—Paris' red-light district, the infamous "Pig Alley," is at the foot of Butte Montmartre. *Ooh la la*. It's more shocking than dangerous. Walk from place Pigalle to place Blanche, teasing desperate barkers and fast-talking temptresses. In bars, a €150 bottle of cheap champagne comes with a friend. Stick to the bigger streets, hang on to your wallet, and exercise good judgment. Cancan can cost a fortune, as can con artists in topless bars. After dark, countless tour buses line the streets, reminding us that tour guides make big bucks by bringing their groups to touristy night-clubs like the famous Moulin Rouge (Mo: Pigalle or Abbesses).

Disappointments de Paris

Here are a few negatives to help you manage your limited time:

La Madeleine is a big, stark, neoclassical church with a postcard facade and a postbox interior. The famous aristocratic deli behind the church, Fauchon, is elegant, but so are many others handier to your hotel.

Paris' **Panthéon** (nothing like Rome's) is another stark neoclassical edifice, filled with mortal remains of great Frenchmen who mean little to the average American tourist.

The **Bastille** is Paris' most famous nonsight. The square is there, but confused tourists look everywhere and can't find the famous prison of Revolution fame. The building's gone and the square is good only as a jumping-off point for the Marais Walk (see page 73) or Promenade Plantée Park (see page 45).

Finally, the **Latin Quarter** is a frail shadow of its character-istic self. It's more Tunisian, Greek, and Woolworth's than old-time Paris. The café life that turned on Hemingway and endeared boul' Miche and boulevard St. Germain to so many poets is also trampled by modern commercialism.

HISTORIC
PARIS
WALK

From Notre-Dame to Sainte-Chapelle

paris

Paris has been the capital of Europe for centuries. We'll start where it did, on the Ile de la Cité, with forays into both the Left and Right Banks, on a walk that laces together the story of Paris: Roman, medieval, the Revolution, café society, the literary scene of the '20s, and the modern world. Allow four hours to do this five-kilometer (3-mile) walk justice.

Orientation

Many sights that charge admission are covered by the Paris museum pass, which for many is a great time and money saver.
Notre-Dame: Free, daily 08:00–18:45; treasury-€2.50 (not covered by museum pass), daily 09:30–17:30; Sunday Mass at 08:00, 08:45, 10:00, 11:30, 12:30, and 18:30. Leaflet with church schedule at booth inside entrance. Free English tours, normally Wed and Thu at 12:00 and Sat at 14:30. The tower climb takes 400 steps and €5.50— worth it for the gargoyle's-eye view of the cathedral, Seine, and city (daily April–Sept 09:00–18:00, Oct–March 10:00–17:30, covered by museum pass, no bypass line for passholders, long lines at peak times).
Paris Archaeological Crypt: €3, covered by museum pass, under 27 and over 60 free, €5 combo-ticket with Carnavalet Museum; Tue–Sun 10:00–17:30, closed Mon, entry 100 meters (325 feet) in front of the cathedral.
Deportation Memorial: Free, April–Sept daily 10:00–12:00, 14:00–19:00, Oct–March daily 10:00–12:00, 14:00–17:00.
Sainte-Chapelle and Conciergerie: €5.50 each, €8 together, daily April–Sept 09:30–18:30, Oct–March 10:00–17:00, Mo: Cité.

NOTRE-DAME

• *Start at the Notre-Dame Cathedral on the island in the River Seine, the physical and historic bull's-eye of your Paris map (closest Métro stops*

HISTORIC PARIS WALK

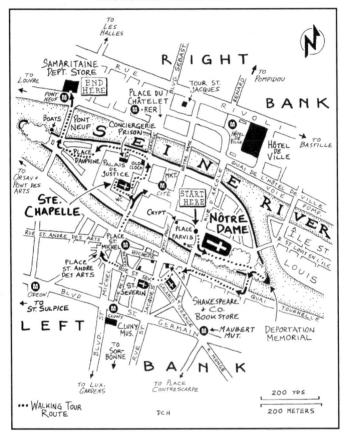

are Cité, Hôtel de Ville, and St. Michel, each requiring a short walk). On the square in front of the cathedral, stand far enough back to take in the whole facade. Look at the circular window in the center.

For centuries, the main figure in the Christian "pantheon" has been Mary, the mother of Jesus. Common people petition her in times of trouble to gain comfort and to ask her to convince God to be compassionate with them. The church is dedicated to "Our Lady" (Notre-Dame), and there she is, cradling God, right in the heart of the facade, surrounded by the halo of the rose window. Though the church is massive and imposing, it has always stood for the grace and compassion of Mary, the "mother of God."

Imagine the faith of the people who built this. They broke

ground in 1163 with the hope
that someday their great-great-
great-great-great-great grand-
children might attend the dedication Mass two centuries later.
Look up the 60-meter (200-foot)
bell towers and imagine a tiny
medieval community mustering
the money and energy to build
this. Master masons supervised,
but the people did much of the
grunt work themselves for free—
hauling the huge stones from
distant quarries, digging a

9-meter-deep (30-foot) trench to lay the foundations, and treading
like rats on a wheel designed to lift the stones up, one by one. This
kind of backbreaking, arduous manual labor created the real hunch-
backs of Notre-Dame.

• *"Walk this way" toward the cathedral, and view it from the bronze
plaque on the ground marked...*

Point Zero

You're standing at the very center of France, from which all
distances are measured. The "Cité" started here in the third century B.C. In 52 B.C., the Romans booted out the Parisii tribe and
built their government palace at the end of the square behind you
and the Temple of Jupiter where the cathedral sits. Two thousand
years of dirt and debris have raised the city's altitude. The archaeological crypt nearby offers a fascinating look at the remains
of the earlier city and church below today's street level.

Still facing the church, you see on your right a grand equestrian statue of Charlemagne ("Charles the Great"), whose reign
marked the birth of modern Europe. Crowned in A.D. 800, he
briefly united much of Europe during the Dark Ages. (Maybe
even greater than Charles are nearby pay toilets—the cleanest
you'll find in downtown Paris.)

Before renovation 150 years ago, this square was much smaller,
a characteristic medieval shambles facing a rundown church,
surrounded by winding streets and countless buildings (look at the
outlines marked in the pavement of the square, showing the medieval
street plan). The huge church bell towers rose above this tangle
of smaller buildings, inspiring Victor Hugo's story of a deaf, bell-
ringing hunchback who could look down on all Paris.

• *Now turn your attention to the church facade. Look at the left doorway
and, to the left of the door, find the statue with his head in his hands.*

NOTRE-DAME FACADE

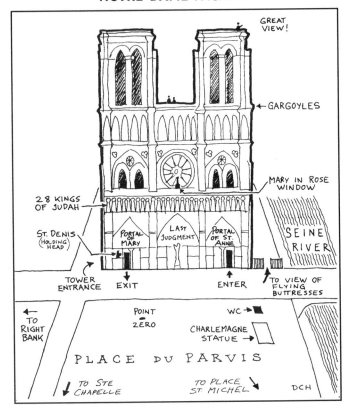

GREAT VIEW!

← GARGOYLES

MARY IN ROSE WINDOW

28 KINGS OF JUDAH

ST. DENIS (HOLDING HEAD)

PORTAL OF MARY

LAST JUDGMENT

PORTAL OF ST. ANNE

SEINE RIVER

TOWER ENTRANCE   EXIT   ENTER   TO VIEW OF FLYING BUTTRESSES

← TO RIGHT BANK

POINT ZERO

WC →

CHARLEMAGNE STATUE →

PLACE DU PARVIS

↓ TO STE CHAPELLE

TO PLACE ST. MICHEL ↘

DCH

Notre-Dame Facade

When Christianity began making converts in Roman Paris, the Bishop of Paris was beheaded. But these early Christians were hard to keep down. St. Denis got up, tucked his head under his arm, headed north, paused at a fountain to wash it off, and continued until he found just the right place to meet his maker. The Parisians were convinced of this miracle, Christianity gained ground, and a church soon replaced the pagan temple.

By the way, Christians think Montmartre (the one hill overlooking Paris) is named for

this martyr (pagans think it was named after a Roman temple of Mars—Mount of Mars—which once stood here). Denis eventually died on the edge of town where the church of St. Denis was built (famous in history books as the first Gothic church, but not much to see today).

• *Now look above the central doorway, where you'll find scenes from the Last Judgment.*

Central Portal

It's the end of the world, and Christ sits on the throne of judgment (just under the arches, holding his hands up). Below him, an angel and a demon weigh souls in the balance. The good people stand to the left, looking up to heaven. The naughty ones to the right are chained up and led off to...a six-hour tour of the Louvre on a hot day. Notice the crazy sculpted demons to the right, at the base of the arch.

• *Above the arches is a row of 28 statues, known as...*

The Kings of Judah

In the days of the French Revolution (1789–1793), these Biblical kings were mistaken for the hated French kings, and Notre-Dame represented the oppressive Catholic hierarchy. The citizens stormed the church, crying, "Off with their heads!" Plop, they lopped off the crowned heads of these kings with glee, creating a row of St. Denises that wasn't repaired for decades.

But the story doesn't end there. A schoolteacher who lived nearby collected the heads and buried them in his backyard for safekeeping. There they slept until 1977, when they were accidentally unearthed. Today you can stare into the eyes of the original kings in the Cluny Museum, a few blocks away (see page 203).

• *Enter the church and find a spot to view the long, high central aisle.*

Notre-Dame Interior

Remove your metaphorical hat and become a simple bareheaded peasant, entering the dim medieval light of the church. Take a minute to let your pupils dilate, to take in the subtle, mysterious light show God beams through the stained-glass windows. Follow the slender columns up to the praying-hands arches of the ceiling and contemplate the heavens. Let's say it's dedication day for this great stone wonder. The priest intones the words of the Mass that echo through the hall: "*Terribilis est locus iste*"—"This place is *terribilis*," meaning awe-inspiring or even terrifying. It's a huge, dark, earthly cavern lit with an unearthly light.

This is Gothic. Taller and filled with light, this was a major improvement over the earlier Romanesque style. Gothic architects needed only a few structural columns, topped by pointed arches that crisscross the columns to support the weight of the roof. This let them build higher than ever, freeing up the walls for windows. The church is designed in the shape of a cross, with the altar where the cross beams intersect.

• *Walk up to the main altar.*

The Altar

This marks the spot where Mass is said and the bread and wine of communion are prepared and distributed. In olden days, there were no chairs. The church can hold up to 10,000 faithful. Join the statue of Joan of Arc (*Jeanne d'Arc*, in the right transept) in gazing up to the rose-shaped window, the only one of the three with its original medieval glass.

This was the holy spot for Romans, Christians . . . and even atheists. When the Revolutionaries stormed the church, they gutted it and turned it into a "Temple for the Cult of Reason." A woman dressed up like the Statue of Liberty held court at the altar as a symbol of the divinity of Man. France today, while nominally Catholic, remains aloof from Vatican dogmatism. Instead of traditional wooden confessional booths, notice the open, glass-walled room where modern sinners seek counseling as much as forgiveness.

Just past the altar are the walls of the choir, where more intimate services can be held in this spacious building. The aisles are lined with chapels, each dedicated to a particular saint. The faithful can pause at their favorite, light a candle as an offering, and meditate in the cool light of the stained glass. (The nearby treasury, containing lavish robes and golden relic-holders, probably isn't worth the entry fee.)

• *Amble around the ambulatory, spill back outside, and make a U-turn left. Walk to the back end of the church along the side that faces the river.*

Notre-Dame Side View

Along the side of the church, you'll notice the flying buttresses. These 15-meter (50-foot) stone "beams" that stick out of the church were the key to the complex architecture of Gothic. The pointed arches we saw inside caused the weight of

the roof to push outward rather than downward. The "flying" buttresses support the roof by pushing back inward. Gothic architects were masters at playing architectural forces against each other to build loftier and loftier churches.

Picture Quasimodo running around along the railed balcony at the base of the roof among the gargoyles. These grotesque beasts sticking out from pillars and buttresses represent souls caught between heaven and earth. They also function as rain spouts when there are no evil spirits to battle.

The neo-Gothic 90-meter (300-foot) spire is a product of the 1860 reconstruction of the dilapidated old church. Around its base are apostles and evangelists (the green men) as well as Viollet-le-Duc, the architect in charge of the work. Notice how the apostles look outward, blessing the city, while the architect (at top) looks up the spire, marveling at his fine work.

• *Behind Notre-Dame, squeeze through the tourist buses, cross the street, and enter the iron gate into the park at the tip of the island.*

Deportation Memorial (Mémorial de la Déportation)

This memorial to the 200,000 French victims of the Nazi concentration camps draws you into their experience. As you descend the steps, the city around you disappears. Surrounded by walls, you have become a prisoner. Your only freedom is your view of the sky and the tiny glimpse of the river below.

Enter the dark, single-file chamber up ahead. Inside, the circular plaque in the floor reads, "They descended into the mouth of the earth and they did not return."

The hallway stretching in front of you is lined with 200,000 lighted crystals, one for each French citizen that died. Flickering at the far end is the eternal flame of hope. The tomb of the unknown deportee lies at your feet. Above, the inscription reads, "Dedicated to the living memory

of the 200,000 French deportees sleeping in the night and the fog, exterminated in the Nazi concentration camps." Above the exit as you leave is the message you'll find at all Nazi sights: "Forgive, but never forget."

Ile St. Louis

Back on street level, look across the river to the Ile St. Louis. If the Ile de la Cité is a tug laden with the history of Paris, it's towing this classy little residential dinghy laden only with boutiques, characteristic restaurants, and famous sorbet shops. This island wasn't developed until much later (18th century). What was a swampy mess is now harmonious Parisian architecture.

• *From the tip of the Ile de la Cité, cross the bridge to the Left Bank and turn right. Walk along the river, toward the front end of Notre-Dame. Stairs detour down to the riverbank if you need a place to picnic. This side view of the church from across the river is one of Europe's great sights.*

LEFT BANK (RIVE GAUCHE)

The Left Bank of the Seine—"left" if you were floating downstream—still has many of the twisting lanes and narrow buildings of medieval times. The Right Bank is more modern and business-oriented, with wide boulevards and stressed Parisians in suits. Here along the riverbank, the "big business" is books, displayed in the green metal stalls on the parapet. These literary entrepreneurs pride themselves on their easy-going business style. With flexible hours and literally no overhead, they run their businesses as they have since medieval times.

• *When you reach the bridge (pont au Double) that crosses over in front of Notre-Dame, veer to the left across the street to a small park (square Viviani). Go through the park to the small rough-stone church of St. Julien-le-Pauvre. You'll pass Paris' oldest inhabitant, a false acacia tree ("Robinier") that may once have shaded the Sun King.*

Medieval Paris (1000–1400)

This church dates from the 12th century, and the area around it keeps the same feel. A half-timbered house stands to the right of the entrance. Many buildings in medieval times were built like this, with a wooden frame filled in with a plaster of mud, straw, and dung. Back then, the humble "half-timbered" structure would have been hidden by a veneer of upscale stucco.

Looking along nearby rue Galande, you'll see a few old houses built every which way. In medieval days, people were piled on top of each other, building at all angles, as they scrambled for this prime real estate near the main commercial artery of the day—the Seine. The smell of fish competed with the smell of neighbors in this knot of humanity.

These narrow streets would have been dirt (or mud). Originally, the streets sloped from here down into the mucky Seine, until modern quays cleaned that up. Many Latin Quarter lanes were named for their businesses or crafts. The rue de la Boucherie

(or "Butcher Street," just around the corner, in the direction of the river) was where butchers slaughtered livestock. The blood and guts drained into the Seine and out of town.
• *At #37 rue de la Boucherie is...*

Shakespeare & Company Bookstore

In addition to hosting butchers and fish-mongers, the Left Bank has been home to scholars, philosophers, and poets since medieval times. This funky bookstore— a reincarnation of the original shop from the 1920s—has picked up the literary torch. In the '20s it was famous as a meeting place of Paris' literary expatriate elite. Ernest Hemingway, who is said to have strangled and cooked pigeons in the park, borrowed books from here to survive. Fitzgerald, Joyce, and Pound also got their English fix here.

Today the bookstore does its best to carry on that literary tradition. Struggling writers are given free accommodations upstairs in tiny, book-lined rooms with views of Notre-Dame. Downstairs, travelers enjoy the best selection of used English books in Paris. Pick up *Paris Voice*, a newspaper published for today's American expatriates, and say hi to George.

• *Return to St. Julien-le-Pauvre, follow it to rue Galande, then turn right (west) on rue Galande, which immediately intersects the busy rue St. Jacques (also called rue du Petit Pont). Way back in Roman times, the rue St. Jacques was the straight, wide, paved road that brought chariots racing in and out of the city. (Roman-iacs can see remains from the 3rd-century baths, along with a fine medieval collection, at the Cluny Museum, 2 blocks to the left; see tour on page 203.) Cross rue St. Jacques and walk straight, pausing at the small Gothic church of St. Severin, then continue straight, into the Latin Quarter.*

St. Severin

Don't ask me why, but it took a century longer to build this church than Notre-Dame. This is flamboyant, or "flame-like," Gothic, and you can see the short, prickly spires meant to make this building flicker in the eyes of the faithful. The church gives us a close-up look at gargoyles. This weird, winged species of flying mammal, now extinct, used to swoop down on unwary peasants, occasionally carrying off small children in their beaks. Today they're most impressive in thunderstorms, when they vomit rain.

The Latin Quarter

While it may look more like the Tunisian Quarter today, this area is the Latin Quarter, named for the language you'd have heard on these streets if you walked them in the Middle Ages. The university, one of the leading educational institutions of medieval Europe, was (and still is) nearby.

A thousand years ago, the "crude" or vernacular local languages were sophisticated enough to communicate basic human needs, but if you wanted to get philosophical, the language of choice was Latin. The educated elite of Dark Ages Europe was a class that transcended nations and borders. From Sicily to Sweden, they spoke and corresponded in Latin. The most Latin thing about this area now is the beat you may hear coming from some of the subterranean jazz clubs.

Along rue St. Severin, you can still see the shadow of the medieval sewer system. (The street slopes into a central channel of bricks.) In the days before plumbing and toilets, when people still went to the river or neighborhood wells for their water, flushing meant throwing it out the window. Certain times of day were flushing times. Maids on the fourth floor would holler *"Garde de l'eau!"* ("Look out for the water!") and heave it into the streets, where it would eventually wash down into the Seine.

• *At #22 rue St. Severin, you'll find the skinniest house in Paris, two windows wide. Continue along rue St. Severin to . . .*

Boulevard St. Michel

Busy boulevard St. Michel (or "boul' Miche") is famous as the main artery for bohemian Paris, culminating a block away (to the left), where it intersects boulevard St. Germain. Although nowadays you're more likely to find pantyhose at 30 percent off, there are still many cafés, boutiques, and bohemian haunts nearby.

The Sorbonne—the University of Paris' humanities department—is also close, if you want to make a detour. (Turn left on boulevard St. Michel and walk two blocks. The entrance is at #47 rue des Ecoles, or just gaze at the dome from the place de La Sorbonne courtyard.) Founded as a theology school around the radical Peter Abelard, it became the alma mater for Thomas Aquinas, Loyola, Erasmus, and John Calvin. Children of kings and nobles were sent here to become priests, though many returned as heretics, having studied radical new secular ideas as well. Paris still is a world center for new intellectual trends.

• *Cross boulevard St. Michel. Just ahead is a tree-filled square lined with cafés and restaurants.*

Place Saint Andre des Arts

In Paris, most serious thinking goes on in cafés. (For more information, see "Les Grands Cafés de Paris," page 278.) For centuries, these have been social watering holes, where you can buy a warm place to sit and stimulating conversation for the price of a cup of coffee. Every great French writer— from Voltaire and Rousseau to Sartre and Derrida—had a favorite haunt.

Paris honors its writers. If you visit the Panthéon (a few blocks down boulevard St. Michel and to the left), you will find French writers and scientists buried in a setting usually reserved for warriors and politicians.

• *Adjoining this square on the river side is the triangular place St. Michel, with a Métro stop and a statue of St. Michael killing a devil.*

Place St. Michel

You're standing at the traditional core of the Left Bank's artsy, liberal, hippie, bohemian district of poets, philosophers, and winos. You'll find international eateries, far-out bookshops, street singers, pale girls in black berets, jazz clubs, and— these days—tourists. Small cinemas show avant-garde films, almost always in the *version originale* (v.o.). For colorful wandering and café sitting, afternoons and evenings are best. In the morning, it feels sleepy. The Latin Quarter stays up late and sleeps in.

In less commercial times, place St. Michel was a gathering point for the city's malcontents and misfits. Here, in 1871, the citizens took the streets from the government troops, set up barricades "Les Miz"-style, and established the Paris Commune. In World War II, the locals rose up against their Nazi oppressors (read the plaques by the St. Michel fountain).

And in the spring of 1968, a time of social upheaval all over the world, young students battled riot batons and tear gas, took over the square, and declared it an independent state. Factory workers followed their call to arms and went on strike, toppling the de Gaulle government and forcing change. Eventually,the students were pacified, the university was reformed, and the Latin Quarter's original cobblestones were replaced with pavement, so future scholars could never again use the streets as weapons.

• *From place St. Michel, look across the river and find the spire of Sainte-Chapelle church, with its weathervane angel. Cross the river on pont St. Michel and continue along boulevard du Palais.*

On your left, you'll see the doorway to Sainte-Chapelle. But first, carry on another 30 meters (100 feet) and turn right at a wide pedestrian street, the rue de Lutece.

Cité "Metropolitain" Stop

Of the 141 original early-20th-century subway entrances, this is one of 17 survivors now preserved as a national art treasure. (New York's Museum of Modern Art even exhibits one.) The curvy, plantlike ironwork is a textbook example of Art Nouveau, the style that rebelled against the erector-set squareness of the Industrial Age.

The flower market on place Louis Lepine is a pleasant detour. On Sundays, this square chirps with a busy bird market. And across the way is the Prefecture de Police, where Inspector Clouseau of Pink Panther fame used to work, and where the local resistance fighters took the first building from the Nazis in August of 1944, leading to the allied liberation of Paris a week later.

• *Pause here to admire the view. Sainte-Chapelle is a pearl in an ugly architectural oyster, part of a complex of buildings that includes the Palace of Justice (to the right of Sainte-Chapelle, behind the iron and bronze gates).*

Return to the entrance of Sainte-Chapelle. You'll need to pass through a metal detector to get into Sainte-Chapelle. Walk through the security scanner. Toilets are ahead on the left. The line into the church may be long. (Museum passholders can go directly in.) Enter the humble ground floor (and check the concert schedule if interested).

SAINTE-CHAPELLE

Sainte-Chapelle, the triumph of Gothic church architecture, is a cathedral of glass like no other. It was built in 1248 for St. Louis IX

(France's only canonized king) to house the supposed Crown of Thorns. Its architectural harmony is due to the fact that it was completed under the direction of one architect and in only five years—unheard of in Gothic times. Recall that Notre-Dame took over 200 years.

The exterior is ugly. But those fat buttresses are all the support needed to hold up the roof, opening up the walls for stained glass. The design clearly shows an Old Regime approach to worship. The basement was for staff and more common folks. Royal Christians

SAINTE-CHAPELLE

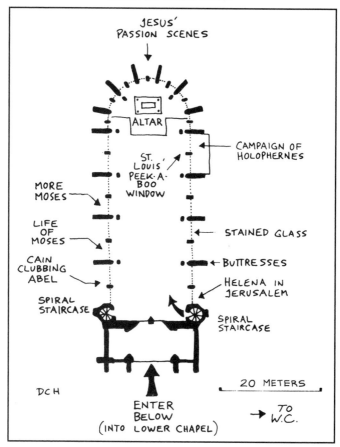

JESUS' PASSION SCENES

ALTAR

CAMPAIGN OF HOLOPHERNES

ST. LOUIS' PEEK·A· BOO WINDOW

MORE MOSES

LIFE OF MOSES

STAINED GLASS

CAIN CLUBBING ABEL

BUTTRESSES

HELENA IN JERUSALEM

SPIRAL STAIRCASE

SPIRAL STAIRCASE

20 METERS

DCH

ENTER BELOW (INTO LOWER CHAPEL)

TO W.C.

worshiped upstairs. The paint job, a 19th-century restoration, helps you imagine how grand this small, painted, jeweled chapel was. (Imagine Notre-Dame painted like this....)

• *Climb the spiral staircase to the Haute Chapelle. Leave the rough stone of the earth and become enlightened.*

The Stained Glass

Fiat lux. "Let there be light." From the first page of the Bible, it's clear, light is important. Light shining through stained glass was a symbol of God's grace shining down to earth, and Gothic architects used their new technology to turn dark stone buildings into lanterns of light. For me, the glory of Gothic shines brighter here than in any other church.

There are 15 separate panels of stained glass, with more than 1,100 different scenes, mostly from the Bible. In medieval times, scenes like these helped teach Bible stories to the illiterate. These cover the entire Christian history of the world, from the Creation in Genesis (first window on the left), to the

coming of Christ (over the altar), to the end of the world (the round "rose"-shaped window at the rear of the church). Each individual scene is interesting, and the whole effect is overwhelming.

Let's look at a single scene. Head toward the altar to the fourth big window on the right. Look at the bottom circle, second from the left. It's a battle scene (the campaign of Holophernes) showing three soldiers with swords slaughtering three men. The background is blue. The men have different colored clothes—red, blue, green, mauve, and white. Notice some of the details. You can see the folds in the robes, the hair, facial features... and look at the victim in the center—his head is splotched with blood!

Craftsmen made glass (which is, essentially, melted sand), coloring it by mixing in metals like cobalt (blue) or copper (green). Then they'd assemble pieces of different colored glass to make, say, the soldier in blue with a green shield (upper right). The pieces were held together by lead. Details like the folds in the robes (see the victim in white, lower left) came by either scratching on the glass or by baking in imperfections. It was a painstaking process

It takes 13 tourists to build a Gothic church: six columns, six buttresses, and one steeple.

of finding just the right colors, fitting them together to make a scene... and then multiplying by 1,100. (Note: The sun lights up different windows at different times of day. Overcast days give the most even light. On bright sunny days, some sections are glorious while others look like a sheet of lead.)

Other scenes worth a look:

1) Cain clubbing Abel (first window on the left, second row of circles, far right—Cain is in red).

2) The life of Moses (second window, the bottom row of diamond panels). First panel shows baby Moses in a basket, placed by his sister in the squiggly brown river. Next, he's found by the pharaoh's daughter. Then, he grows up. And finally, he's a man, a prince of Egypt on his royal throne.

3) In the next window (third on left), you'll see various scenes of Moses. He's often given "horns" because of a medieval mistranslation of the Biblical description of his "aura" of holiness.

4) Over the altar are scenes from Jesus' arrest and crucifixion. Stand at the stairs in front and look over the altar and through the canopy to find Jesus being whipped (left), Jesus in purple being crowned with thorns (right), Jesus in yellow carrying his cross (a little above), and, finally, Jesus on the cross being speared by a soldier (above, left).

5) Helena, the mother of Constantine—the first Christian Roman emperor—travels to Jerusalem to find relics of Jesus' Crucifixion (first window to the right, lowest level).

If you can't read much into the individual windows, you're not alone. For some tutoring, a little book with color photos is on sale downstairs with the postcards.

The altar was raised up high (notice the staircase for the priest) to better display the relic around which this chapel was built—the Crown of Thorns. This was the crown put on Jesus when the Romans were torturing and humiliating him before his execution. King Louis was convinced he'd found the real McCoy and paid three times as much money for it as was spent on this entire chapel. Today the supposed Crown of Thorns is kept in the Notre-Dame Treasury and shown only on Good Friday.

Notice the little private viewing window in the wall to the right of the altar. Louis was both saintly and shy. He liked to be able to go to church without dealing with the rigors of public royal life. Here he could worship still dressed in his jammies.

Lay your camera on the ground and shoot the ceiling. Those pure and simple ribs growing out of the slender columns are the essence of Gothic structure.

Palais de Justice

As you walk around the church exterior, look down and notice how much Paris has risen in the 800 years since Sainte-Chapelle was built. You're in a huge complex of buildings that has housed the local government since ancient Roman times. It was the site of the original Gothic palace of the early kings of France. The only surviving medieval parts are Sainte-Chapelle and the Conciergerie prison.

Most of the site is now covered by the giant Palais de Justice, home of France's supreme court, built in 1776. *"Liberté, Egalité, Fraternité"* over the doors is a reminder that this was also the headquarters of the Revolutionary government. Here they doled out justice, condemning many to torture in the Conciergerie downstairs or to have their heads removed by "Monsieur de Paris"—the guillotine.

Paris' Palais de Justice in 1650, with Sainte-Chapelle, the Conciergerie, and Pont Neuf (then 30 years old) in the background.

• *Now pass through the big iron gate to the noisy boulevard du Palais and turn left (toward the Right Bank).*

On the corner is the site of the city's oldest public clock (1334). While the present clock is Baroque, it still manages to keep accurate time.

Turn left onto quai d'Horloge and walk along the river. The round medieval tower just ahead marks the entrance to the Conciergerie. Even if you don't pay to see the Conciergerie, you can visit the courtyard and lobby. Step past the serious-looking guard into the courtyard.

Conciergerie

The Conciergerie, a former prison and place of torture, is a gloomy place. Kings used it to torture and execute failed assas-

sins. The leaders of the Revolution put it to similar good use. The tower next to the entrance, called "the babbler," was named for the painful sounds that leaked from it.

Look at the stark printing above the doorways. This was a no-nonsense revolutionary time. Everything, including lettering, was subjected to the test of reason. No frills or we chop 'em off.

Marie-Antoinette was imprisoned here. During a busy eight-month period in the Revolution, she was one of 2,600 prisoners kept here on their way to the guillotine.

The interior (requires ticket, free with museum pass), with its huge vaulted and pillared rooms, echoes with history but is pretty barren. You can see Marie-Antoinette's cell, with a collection of Marie-Antoinette mementos. In another room, a thought-provoking list of those made "a foot shorter at the top" by the guillotine includes ex-King Louis XVI, Charlotte Corday (who murdered Marat in his bathtub), and the chief Revolutionary who got a taste of his own medicine—Maximilien Robespierre.

• *Back outside, wink at the flak-vested guard, turn left, and continue your walk along the river. Across the river, you can see the rooftop observatory of the Samaritaine department store, where we'll end this walk. At the first corner, veer left into a sleepy triangular square called "place Dauphine."*

Place Dauphine

It's amazing to find such coziness in the heart of Paris. This city of two million is still a city of neighborhoods, a collection of villages. The French Supreme Court building looms behind like a giant marble gavel. Enjoy the village-Paris feeling in the park. You may see lawyers on their lunch break playing *boules*.

• *Walk through the park to the statue of Henry IV, who in 1607 inaugurated the Pont Neuf. (If you need a romantic hideaway in the midst of this mega-city, take the steps down into the park on the tip of the island and dangle your legs over the prow of this concrete island.) From the statue, turn right onto the old bridge. Walk to the little nook halfway across.*

Pont Neuf

The Pont Neuf, or "new bridge," is now Paris' oldest. Its 12 arches span the widest part of the river. The fine view includes the park on the tip of the island (note Seine boats), the Orsay, and the Louvre. These turrets were originally for vendors and street entertainers. In the days of Henry, who originated the promise of "a chicken in every pot," this would have been a lively scene.

• *The first building you'll hit on the Right Bank is the venerable old department store, Samaritaine. Go through the door, veer left, and catch the elevator to the ninth floor. Climb two sets of stairs to the panorama level. (Don't confuse the terrace level with the higher, better panorama. Light meals are served on the terrace. Public WCs on fifth and ninth floors.)*

THE REST OF PARIS

From the circular little crow's nest of the building, ponder the greatest skyline in Europe. Retrace the walk you just made, starting with Notre-Dame and Sainte-Chapelle. Then spin counterclockwise (or run down the stairs to hop on the Métro) and check out the rest of Paris:

The **Pompidou Center**, the wild and colorful rectangular tangle of blue and white pipes and tubes, is filled with art that makes this building's exterior look tame. See tour on page 139.

Sacré-Coeur is a neo-Romanesque church topping Montmartre. This is an atmospheric quarter after dark, its streets filled with strolling tourists avoiding strolling artists. ✪ See Montmartre Walk, page 84.

The **Louvre** is the largest building in Paris, the largest palace in Europe, and the largest museum in the Western world. ✪ See Louvre Tour, page 91.

Stretching away from the Louvre, the **Tuileries Gardens**, place de la Concorde, and the Champs-Elysées lead to the Arc de Triomphe. The gardens are Paris' "Central Park," filled with families at play, cellists in the shade, carousels, pony rides, and the ghost of Maurice Chevalier.

The gardens overlook the grand **place de la Concorde**, marked by an ancient obelisk, where all of France seems to converge. It was "guillotine central" during the Revolution and continues to be a place of much festivity.

Europe's grandest boulevard, the **Champs-Elysées**, runs uphill from place de la Concorde about 1.5 kilometers (1 mile) to the Arc de Triomphe. While pretty globalized, and with rich-and-single aristocrats more rare than ever, it's still the place you're most likely to see Sylvester Stallone. ✪ See Champs-Elysées Walk, page 66.

Napoleon began constructing the magnificent **Arc de Triomphe** in 1806 to commemorate his victory at the battle of Austerlitz. It was finished in 1836, just in time for the emperor's funeral parade. Today it commemorates heroes of past wars. There's no triumphal arch bigger (50 meters/165 feet high, 40 meters/130 feet wide). And, with 12 converging boulevards, there's no traffic circle more thrilling, either on foot or behind the wheel. See page 66.

Paris, the capital of Europe, is built on an appropriately monumental plan, with an axis that stretches from the Louvre, up the Champs-Elysées, past the Arc de Triomphe, all the way to the modern Grande Arche among the skyscrapers at **La Défense**. (Find the faint shadow of this arch, just above the Arc de Triomphe.)

The **Orsay Museum**, the train-station-turned-art-museum, is just beyond the Louvre on the Left Bank. See tour on page 112.

The body of Napoleon lies under the gilded dome. The giant building is **Les Invalides**, designed to house his wounded troops.

Today it houses a fine military museum. See page 188. The **Rodin Museum** is nearby. See page 169.

The **Eiffel Tower** is a thousand-foot exclamation point built as a temporary engineering stunt to celebrate the 100th anniversary of the French Revolution. Paris decided to let it be an exception to a downtown building code that allows the skyline to be broken only by a few prestigious domes and spires. See page 36.

The 52-story **Montparnasse Tower**, a city in itself (5,000 workers, 210 meters/700 feet high) reminds us that, while tourists look for hints of Louis and Napoleon, work-a-day Paris looks to the future.

CHAMPS-ELYSÉES WALK

Leaving Paris without strolling the Champs-Elysées is like walking out of a great restaurant before dessert. This is Paris at its most Parisian: monumental sidewalks, stylish shops, grand cafés, and glimmering showrooms. This walk covers about five kilometers (3 miles) and takes three hours if done completely. The Arc de Triomphe (open daily until 23:00 in summer) and Champs-Elysées are best at night. Métro stops are located every three blocks on the Champs-Elysées (zhahn-zay-lee-zay).

Start by taking the Métro to the Arc de Triomphe. At the Métro stop Charles de Gaulle Etoile, follow *sortie* Champs-Elysées/ Avenue Friedland to "access Arc de Triomphe" signs. Exit at the top of the Champs-Elysées and face the Arc de Triomphe. The TI and underground WCs are on the other (left) side of Champs-Elysées, and an underground walkway leading to the arch should be in front of you on the right side of the Champs-Elysées. Get to that arch (worthwhile even if you don't climb it; there's no charge to wander around the base).

Ascend the **Arc de Triomphe** via the 230 steps or the elevator if you're disabled—sorry, no discount for walkers (€6, covered by museum pass, daily June–Sept 09:30–23:00, Oct–May 09:30–22:00, skip the line if you have a pass or don't want to go to the top of the arch, Mo: Etoile, tel. 01 43 80 31 31).

A small museum near the top explains its history; the exhibits are in French, but there's a good video in English. Begun in 1806, the arch was intended to honor Napoleon's soldiers, who, in spite of being vastly outnumbered by the Austrians, scored a remarkable victory at the battle of Austerlitz. Napoleon died prior to its completion. But it was finished in time for his funeral procession to pass underneath, carrying his remains from exile in St. Helena to Paris. The Arc de Triomphe is dedicated to the glory of all French armies.

CHAMPS-ELYSÉES WALK

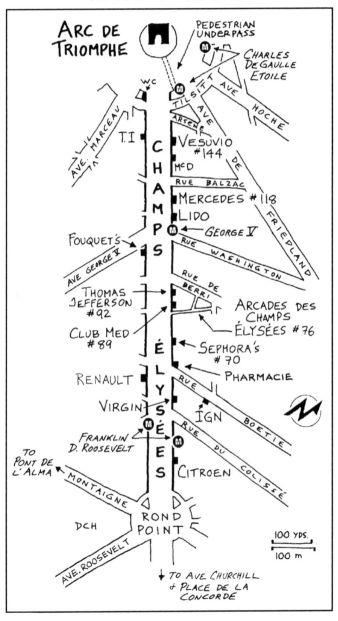

From the rooftop viewpoint, get your bearings with the circular orientation tables. Opposite the Champs-Elysées, the avenue Grande Armée leads to the skyscraper ghetto of the La Défense suburb. Notice what a contrast the skyscrapers make to the uniform height of buildings closer to the arch. French President Mitterand had the huge, white **Grande Arche de La Défense** built as a centerpiece of this mini-Manhattan (see page 43). It's part of the huge axis capped by the arch you're standing on and the Louvre. The wide boulevard lined with grass and trees a little to your left is avenue Foch (named after a WWI hero) and is the best address to have in Paris (the Shah of Iran and Aristotle Onassis had homes here). The Bois de Boulogne Park is the big green carpet at the end of avenue Foch. While the arch was under construction, the land below you was a rural forest, looking much like the Bois de Boulogne.

Walk to the Champs-Elysées side and scan the cityscape of downtown Paris. Notice the symmetry. The beauty of Paris— basically a flat basin with a river running through it—is man-made. The key to this beauty is the relationship between the width of its grand boulevards and the uniformity in the height and design of the buildings. To the right, the rude **Montparnasse Tower** looks lonely out there, standing like the box the Eiffel Tower came in. It served as a wake-up call in the early 1970s to preserve the building height restriction and strengthen urban design standards.

The 12 boulevards that radiate from the Arc de Triomphe were part of Baron Haussmann's master plan for Paris: The creation of a series of major boulevards, intersecting at diagonals with monuments (such as the Arc de Triomphe) as centerpieces of those intersections. His plan did not anticipate the automobile—obvious when you watch the traffic scene below. Gaze down at what appears to be a chaotic traffic mess. Motorcycles are fair game. Pedestrians are used as target practice. But watch how smoothly it really functions. Cars entering the circle have the right of way; those in the circle must yield. Still, there are plenty of accidents, often caused by tourists who don't understand the rules of the game. Tired of related disputes, insurance companies split the fault and damages of any Arc de Triomphe accident 50–50.

Look straight down the **Champs-Elysées**. The first street was built at the lower end in the early 1600s by Queen Marie de Medici, a short extension of her Tuileries Gardens. It soon became the place to cruise in your carriage. (It still is today—traffic can be jammed up even at midnight.) One hundred years later, it was extended uphill to where you are now.

Like its Roman ancestors, this arch has served as a parade gateway for triumphal armies (French or foe) and important ceremonies. From 1941 to 1944, a large swastika flew from here as Nazis goose-stepped down the Champs-Elysées. Allied troops marched triumphantly under this arch in August 1944.

Descend the arch and stand on the bronze plaque at the foot of the **Tomb of the Unknown Soldier** (from World War I). Daily at 18:30, the flame is rekindled and new flowers set in place. On the columns you'll see lists of battle victories and officers (with a line under the names of those who died in battle).

Still facing the Tomb of the Unknown Soldier, walk to the front of the arch's massive column to your left and see its most famous sculpture. *The Departure of the Volunteers*, or *La Marseillaise*, was a rousing effort to rally the troops by what looks like an ugly reincarnation of Joan of Arc. On the right side of this column, a scene a little over halfway up the arch shows Napoleon's confident pose as he oversees his victory at Austerlitz.

Walk out to the traffic circle and look down the Champs-Elysées. Plan your walking attack from here. The Louvre is the building at the very end of the avenue through the Tuileries Gardens. Our walk turns right off the Champs-Elysées about halfway there. Notice how the left sidewalk is more popular with pedestrians. While the left side is most interesting, cross over at least once for the exhilarating view from the center of the avenue's 10 lanes. The **tourist information office** is immediately on the right at #127. Le Drugstore (next door) has a small grocery store in the back.

Cross back under the tunnel to the top of the Champs-Elysées. The *nouveau* Champs-Elysées is a revitalized avenue with new street benches, lamps, broader sidewalks, and an army of green-suited workers with small machines designed to keep Paris' most famous avenue spic-and-span.

Start your descent. The first tiny street you cross, rue de Tilsitt, is part of a shadow ring road—an option for drivers who'd like to avoid the chaos of the arch, complete with stoplights. Be careful of speedy cars on these cross streets as you descend.

On the first block down, stop by Café Vesuvio (#144, reasonable prices) to enjoy fine views of the arch with its rooftop bristling with tourists. The Big Macs for sale a few doors down are just as popular among the French as they are at home.

At the Peugeot (#136) or the flashy Mercedes showrooms (#118), you can pick up your new sedan and a leather jacket and purse to match. Test drives are a problem.

Next to the Mercedes showroom is the famous **Lido**, Paris' largest cabaret—check out the photos, video, and prices. These sensational shows pull out every stop for floor customers. Movie-going on the Champs-Elysées is also popular. Check to see if there are films you recognize, then look for the showings (*séances*); if there is a "v.o." (*version originale*) next to the time, the film will be in its original language.

Now cross the boulevard where the elegant avenue George V (home to several 4-star hotels and the Crazy Horse Saloon) spills into the Champs-Elysées. **Fouquet's café-restaurant**, under the orange awning, serves the most expensive shot of espresso I found in Paris, but the setting is tops. Since the early 1900s, Fouquet's has been a favorite of French actors and actresses. The welcome mat of golden plaques honors winners of France's Oscar-like film awards, the Césars (see "Les Grands Cafés de Paris," page 278).

Cross back to the lively side. At #92, a wall plaque marks the place Thomas Jefferson lived while minister to France (1785–89). A plaque just below marks the spot where Robert Birlinger died fighting the Germans during the liberation of Paris in August 1944.

Nearby are several **arcades**. My favorite is the Arcade des Champs-Elysées, at #76. This refuge of the belle époque seems out of place today. Wander in.

Just down *les Champs*, glide down Sephora's ramp at #74 into a vast hall of cosmetics and **perfumes** (Mon–Sat 10:00–24:00, closed Sun). The young woman at the wheel of scents will explain how it works. Tell her your fantasy, and she'll point you toward it. Grab a black basket and dive into a lifetime of fragrant samples. The music, composed just for Sephora, made me crave cosmetics. Halfway down on your left in red flashing numbers are the current prices of perfumes (*cours des parfums*) in cities throughout the world. Notice that Paris is hardly the cheapest.

The English **pharmacy** is open until midnight at the corner on rue Boetie, and map-lovers can detour one block down this street to the *Espace IGN* (Institut Géographique National), France's version of the National Geographic Society (Mon–Fri 09:30–19:00, Sat 11:00–12:30, 14:00–18:30, closed Sun).

Virgin Megastore sells a world of **music** one block farther down the Champs-Elysées. The Disney, Gap, and Quicksilver stores are reminders of global economics—the French seem to love these stores as much as Americans do. And near the bottom of the Champs-Elysées, Renault and Citroën showrooms glare across the avenue, each offering late-night cafés (Renault, opposite Sephora, also has a cool concept-car exhibit, worth crossing the Champs for).

At the Rondpoint, the shopping ends and the park begins. This leafy circle is always colorful, lined with flowers or seasonal decorations (thousands of pumpkins at Halloween, hundreds of trees at Christmas).

Now it's decision time. You have three options: 1) You can continue straight (by Métro or foot) to reach place de la Concorde and the Tuileries Gardens; 2) A hard right turn here takes you to the river and pont de l'Alma, down Paris' most exclusive shopping street, the avenue Montaigne, where you need an appointment to buy a dress; 3) You can finish the walk with me.

If you're still with me, walk a block past Rondpoint, then turn right on avenue Churchill and walk between the glass- and steel-domed **Grand and Petit Palais** exhibition halls, built for the 1900 World's Fair. Today, these examples of the "can do" spirit of the early 20th century host a variety of exhibits (details at TIs or in *Pariscope*). Impressive temporary exhibits fill the huge Grand Palais (drop in to see what's on; €8, not covered by museum pass), while the Petit Palais (left side) houses a permanent collection of 19th-century paintings by Delacroix, Cézanne, Monet, and others (€8.50, covered by museum pass).

Cross the river on **pont Alexandre**, eyeing the golden dome of Les Invalides. Les Invalides was built by Louis XIV as a veteran's hospital for his battle-weary troops (see Napoleon's Tomb Tour on page 188); in the Esplanade des Invalides, possibly the largest slice of accessible grass in Paris, soccer balls and Frisbees fill the air.

This exquisite bridge, spiked with golden statues and iron work lamps, was built to celebrate a turn-of-the-20th-century treaty between France and Russia. Like the two palaces we just passed, it's a fine example of belle époque exuberance. Notice the elegant street lamps on the railing. The barges under the bridge are some of more than 2,000 houseboats on the Seine.

At the end of the bridge, turn left and follow the Seine past the Air France bus terminal and Ministry of Foreign Affairs (#37) to the Greek temple–like **Assemblée Nationale** (at the next bridge). France's 600 members of parliament convene here. If the gates are open, climb to the top of the steps for a fantastic view over the place de la Concorde.

From here, **pont de la Concorde** leads to place de la Concorde. The bridge, built of stones from the Bastille prison (which was demolished by the Revolution in 1789), symbolizes that, with good government, *concorde* (harmony) can come from chaos. Walk to the far (right) side of the bridge and begin crossing it. Stand near the center of the bridge and gaze upriver. If you use a clock as a compass, the L'Orangerie hides behind the trees at 10:00 and the tall building with the skinny chimneys (at 11:00) is the architectural caboose of the sprawling Louvre Palace. The park between is the Tuileries Gardens. The thin spire of Sainte-Chapelle is dead center at 12:00, with the twin towers of Notre-Dame to its right. The Orsay Museum is closer on the right and connected with the Tuileries Gardens via a fine new pedestrian bridge (the next bridge upriver).

Leaving the bridge, you'll cross a freeway underpass similar to the one at pont de L'Alma, three bridges downstream, where Princess Diana lost her life in the tragic 1997 car accident.

Continue to the **place de la Concorde**, the 21-acre square with the obelisk. Walk to the island in the center from the cross-walk on the far side of the square (be careful out there). During the Revolution, this was the place de la Revolution. Over 1,300 heads lost their bodies here during the Reign of Terror. The guillotine sat here. A bronze plaque in the ground in front of the obelisk memorializes the place where Louis XVI and Marie-Antoinette, among many others, were made a foot shorter on top. Three worked the guillotine: One managed the blade, one held the blood bucket, and one caught the head, raising it high to the roaring crowd.

Look for **Le Crillon**, Paris' most exclusive hotel, to the left of the twin buildings that guard the entrance to rue Royale (which leads to the Greek-style Basilique de la Madeleine). Eleven years before the king lost his head on this square, Louis XVI met with Benjamin Franklin in this hotel to sign a treaty recognizing the United States as an independent country. (The American embassy is located next door.) For an affordable splurge, consider high tea at Le Crillon; see "Les Grands Cafés de Paris," page 278.

The 2,300-year-old **obelisk of Luxor** now forms the center-piece of place de la Concorde. It was carted here from Egypt in 1829, a gift to the French king. The gold pictures on the obelisk tell the story of its incredible journey.

The obelisk also forms a center point along a line locals call the "royal perspective." From this straight line (Louvre—Obelisk—Arc de Triomphe—Grand Arche de la Défense) you can hang a lot of history. The Louvre symbolizes the old regime (divine-right rule by kings and queens). The obelisk and place de la Concorde symbolize the people's revolution (cutting off the king's head). The Arc de Triomphe calls to mind the triumph of nationalism (victori-ous armies carrying national flags under the arch). And the huge modern arch in the distance, surrounded by the headquarters of multinational corporations, heralds a future where business entities are more powerful than nations.

The beautiful **Tuileries Gardens** lead through the iron gates to the Louvre (with a public WC just inside on the right). Pull up a chair next to the pond or find one of the cafés in the gardens.

MARAIS
WALK

paris

This walk takes you through one of Paris' most characteristic quarters, the Marais, and finishes in the artsy Beaubourg neighborhood. When in Paris, you naturally want to see the big sights, but to experience the city you need to visit a vital neighborhood—like the Marais.

The **Marais** neighborhood contains more pre-Revolutionary lanes and buildings than anywhere else in town, and is more atmospheric than touristy. It's medieval Paris. This is how much of the city looked until the mid-1800s, when Napoleon III had Baron Haussmann blast out the narrow streets to construct broad boulevards (wide enough for the guns and ranks of the army, too wide for revolutionary barricades), creating modern Paris.

This walk is about five kilometers (3 miles) long. Allow two hours, and add another hour for each of these museums you might visit en route: Carnavalet, Picasso, Jewish History, and the Pompidou Center. Paris Walks offers in-depth guided tours of this area; see "Organized Tours," page 29.

Start by riding the Métro to the Bastille stop. Exit the Métro, following signs to rue St. Antoine (not the signs to rue du Faubourg St. Antoine). Ascend onto a noisy square dominated by the bronze Colonne de Juillet (July Column).

1. Place de la Bastille: There are more revolutionary images in the Métro station murals than on the square. Victims of the revolutions of 1830 and 1848 are buried in a vault 55 meters (180 feet) below this gilded statue of liberty. The actual Bastille, a royal fortress-then-prison that once symbolized old-regime tyranny and now symbolizes the Parisian emancipation, is long gone. While only a brick outline of the fortress' round turrets survives (under the traffic where rue St. Antoine hits the square), the story of the Bastille is indelibly etched into the city's psyche.

MARAIS WALK

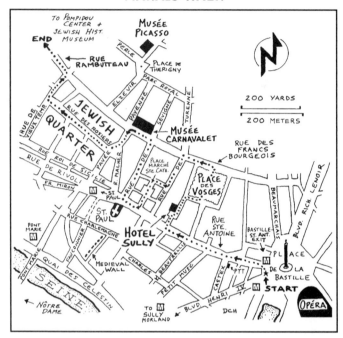

For centuries, the Bastille was used to defend the city (mostly from its own people). On July 14, 1789, the people of Paris stormed the prison, releasing its seven prisoners and hoping to find arms. They demolished the brick fortress and decorated their pikes with the heads of a few bigwigs. By shedding blood, the leaders of the gang made sure it would be tough to turn back the tides of revolution. Ever since, the French have celebrated July 14 as their independence day—Bastille Day.

The flashy, glassy-gray, and controversial **Opéra-Bastille** dominates (some say overwhelms) the square. In a symbolic

attempt to bring high culture to the masses, former French President François Mitterand chose this square for the opera that would replace Paris' earlier "palace of the rich," the Garnier-designed opera house (see page 42). Designed by the Canadian architect Carlos Ott, this grand

Bastille Day in France

Bastille Day—July 14th, the symbolic kickoff date of the
French Revolution—was made the French national holiday
in 1880. Traditionally, Parisians party at place de la Bastille
starting at 20:00 on July 13th (but the best parties are on the
numerous smaller squares where firefighter units sponsor
dances). Then, near midnight, there's a fireworks display at
the Eiffel Tower. And at 10:00 on the morning of the 14th, a
grand military parade fills the Champs-Elysées.

Parisian project was opened with fanfare by Mitterrand on the
200th Bastille Day, July 14, 1989. How much high culture the
masses have actually enjoyed here is a subject of debate. (For
opera ticket information, see page 292.)
• *Turn your back to the square to look down rue St. Antoine. In
1350, there was a gate to the city here, Porte St. Antoine, defended
by a "bastille"—a drawbridge between two towers.*

*Passing the Banque de France on your right (opposite a fine
map of the area), head down rue St. Antoine about four blocks into
the Marais. Leave rue Saint Antoine at #62 and walk through
two elegant courtyards of* **Hôtel de Sully** *(open until 19:00, fine
bookstore inside).*

2. Hôtel de Sully: Originally a swamp (*marais*) during the
reign of Henry IV, this area became the hometown of the French
aristocracy. In the 17th century, big shots built their private
mansions (*hôtels*), like this one, close to Henry's place des Vosges.
Typically, they would have a carriage-friendly courtyard separat-
ing the mansion from the noisy and very public street. The
peaceful backyard often came with an orangerie or greenhouse
for homegrown fruits and veggies through the winter (as you'll
see here). *Hôtels* that survived the revolution now house museums, libraries, and national institutions. The aristocrats may be
gone, but the Marais—which, until the 1970s, was a dumpy
bohemian quarter—is today a thriving, trendy, real community
and a joy to explore.
• *Continue through Hôtel de Sully to the places des Vosges; the small
door on the far right corner of the second courtyard pops you out into
one of Paris' finest squares—a romantic place for dinner; see page 272.
(If the Hôtel's entrance is closed, backtrack to rue de Biraque to reach
place des Vosges.)*

3. Place des Vosges: Study the architecture: Nine pavilions

per side. Note some of the brickwork is real, some is fake. Walk to
the center, where Louis XIII sits on a horse, surrounded by locals
enjoying their community park. Children frolic in the sandbox,
lovers warm benches, and pigeons guard their fountains while trees
shade this retreat from the glare of the big city. Henry IV built this

centerpiece of the Marais in
1605. As hoped, it turned the
Marais into Paris' most exclusive neighborhood. As the
nobility flocked to Versailles
in a later age, this too was
a magnet for the rich and
powerful of France. With
the Revolution, the aristocratic elegance of this quarter
became working-class, filled with gritty shops, artisans, immigrants, and Jews. **Victor Hugo** lived at #6, and you can visit his
house (€3, covered by museum pass, Tue–Sun 10:00–17:40,
closed Mon, marked by the French flag in the corner closest to
the Bastille; see page 45).
• *Walk behind Louis' horse, turning left in the arcade, and exit the
place des Vosges. Turn left immediately on rue de Turenne, make a
right on rue de Jarente, then pop into the adorable place du Marché
Ste. Catherine on the left (several good restaurants, see page 272).
Exit the square on rue Caron, angle right across rue St. Antoine, and
enter St. Paul Church.*

4. St. Paul Church: St. Paul Church is a Jesuit church, inspired

by the original Gesu church in Rome. France's royalty and aristocracy worshiped here in the 17th century to make a pro-Catholic
statement as the Church battled (and burned) the protesting Huguenots. Walking out the back side of the church (behind the altar)
you come to a long asphalt playground bounded by the best surviving piece of Paris' first protective wall, built in the 12th century
(complete with 2 towers), which defined and protected Paris in
the Middle Ages.
• *Retrace your steps to rue St. Antoine, with a possible diversion into the
Village Saint Paul (a collection of interesting antique shops facing the old
wall, open Thu–Mon 11:00–19:00). Cross rue St. Antoine at the St. Paul
Church and walk up rue de Sévigné. In three blocks, you'll come to the
Carnavalet Museum, which focuses on the history of Paris and is housed
inside another Marais mansion (€5.50, covered by museum pass, Tue–
Sun 10:00–17:40, closed Mon, 23 rue de Sévigné). ★ See Carnavalet
Tour on page 153. Turn left onto rue des Francs Bourgeois (peeking*

through the Carnavalet's gate on the right) and turn left at the post office onto rue Parée. The Picasso Museum, described on page 45, is up one block to the right (€5, covered by museum pass, Wed–Mon 09:30–18:00, closed Tue, 5 rue Thorigny). From rue Parée, turn right onto rue des Rosiers (named for the roses which once lined the city wall), which runs straight for three blocks through Paris' Jewish Quarter, lively every day except Saturday.

5. Paris' Jewish Quarter: Considered the largest in Western

Europe, Paris' Jewish quarter grew in three waves. First, with Jews escaping 19th-century East European pogroms (surprise attacks on villages). Next, with Jews fleeing Nazi Germany (before 75 percent of the Jewish population was taken to concentration camps). And, most recently, with Algerian exiles (both Jewish and Muslim—living together peacefully here in Paris). Rue des Rosiers, the main drag, is lined with colorful shops and kosher eateries. Rue des Ecouffes (named for a bird of prey) is a derogatory reminder of the moneychangers' shops that once lined this lane. Check out Jo Goldenberg's delicatessen/restaurant (first corner on left, #7 rue des Rosiers) which serves typical—but not kosher—East European Jewish cuisine. A plaque on the wall and the planters (to keep potential car bombs at a distance) remind locals of the 1982 terrorist bombing here, which left six people dead. You'll be tempted by kosher pizza and plenty of €4 falafel-to-go joints (*emporter* = to go). The best falafels (sit-down or to go) are at #34. The Sacha Finkelsztajn Yiddish bakery (#27) is also good.

• *Rue des Rosiers dead-ends into rue du Vieille du Temple (where the Jewish Quarter's main drag meets Paris' gay district—generally to the left and along nearby Avenue Ste. Croix de la Bretonnerie). Turn right. Frank Bourgeois is waiting at the corner postcard/print shop. Turn left on rue des Francs Bourgeois, which leads past the national archives (peek inside the courtyard) and turns into rue Rambuteau, then continue for several blocks on rue Rambuteau. As you approach the Pompidou Center, you'll pass within a few doors of the Jewish Art and History Museum—to the right on rue du Temple (€6, ages 18–25-€4, under 18 free, not covered by museum pass, Mon–Fri 11:00–18:00, Sun 10:00–18:00, closed Sat, 71 rue du Temple, see page 44). The pipes and glass of the Pompidou Center mark your exit from the Marais and reintroduce you to the 21st century. Pass that huge building on your left to join the fray in front of the center.*

6. Pompidou Center: Survey this popular spot from the

top of the sloping square. Tubular escalators lead up to a great view and the modern art museum (€5, covered by museum pass, Wed–Mon 11:00–21:00, closed Tue). ✪ See Pompidou Center

Tour on page 139. The Pompidou Center follows with gusto the 20th-century architectural axiom, "form follows function." To get a more spacious and functional interior, the guts of this exoskeletal building are draped on the outside and color coded: vibrant red for people lifts, cool blue for air-conditioning, eco-green for plumbing, don't-touch-it yellow for electrical stuff, and white for bones (compare the Pompidou Center to another exoskeletal building, Notre-Dame). Enjoy

the adjacent **Homage to Stravinsky** fountains. Jean Tingley designed these as a tribute to the composer: Every fountain represents one of his hard-to-hum scores. For low-stress meals, try **Le Mélodine**, a self-service cafeteria at the Rambuteau Métro stop, or the fun **Dame Tartine**, which overlooks the *Homage to Stravinsky* fountains and serves a young clientele good, inexpensive meals.

• *With your back to the Pompidou Center's escalators, walk the cobbled pedestrian mall, crossing the busy boulevard Sebastopol to the ivy-covered pavilions of* **Les Halles**. *Paris' down-and-dirty central produce market of 800 years was replaced by a glitzy but soulless shopping center in the late 1970s. The mall's most endearing layer is its grassy rooftop park. The Gothic St. Eustache church overlooking this contemporary scene has a famous 8,000-pipe organ. For a more soulful (rue Cler–like) shopping experience, find your way behind St. Eustache church and cross rue Etienne Marcel onto the delightfully traffic-free rue Montorgueil.*

RUE CLER
WALK

The Art of Parisian Living

paris

Paris is changing fast, but a stroll down this street puts you into a thriving, traditional Parisian neighborhood.

Shopping for groceries is an integral part of daily life here. Parisians shop almost daily for three good reasons: Refrigerators are small (expensive electricity, tiny kitchens), produce must be fresh, and it's an important social event. Shopping is a chance to hear about the butcher's vacation plans, see photos of the florist's new grandchild, relax over *un café*, and kiss the cheeks of friends (twice for regular acquaintances, three times for friends you haven't seen in a while).

Rue Cler—traffic-free since 1984—offers plenty of space for tiny stores and their shoppers to spill into the street. It's an ideal environment for this ritual to survive and for you to explore. The street is lined with all the necessary shops—wine, cheese, chocolate, bread—as well as a bank and a post office. And the shops of this community are run by people who've found their niche: boys who grew up on quiche, girls who know a good wine.

If you wish to learn the fine art of living Parisian-style, rue Cler provides an excellent classroom. And if you wish to assemble the ultimate French picnic, there's no better place. This is the only walking tour in this guidebook you should start hungry.

Do this walk when the market is open and lively (Tue–Sat 08:30–13:00 or 17:00–19:00, Sun 08:30–12:00, dead on Mon). Remember that these shops are busy serving regular customers, be careful not to get in the way, and please be sensitive to their needs.

1. Boulangerie: Start your walk where the pedestrian section of rue Cler does, at rue de Grenelle (Mo: Ecole Militaire). The corner bakery is typical of a newer breed of bakeries, with space in the corner for coffee drinkers and fast-fooders. The almond croissants here are famous among locals.

RUE CLER WALK

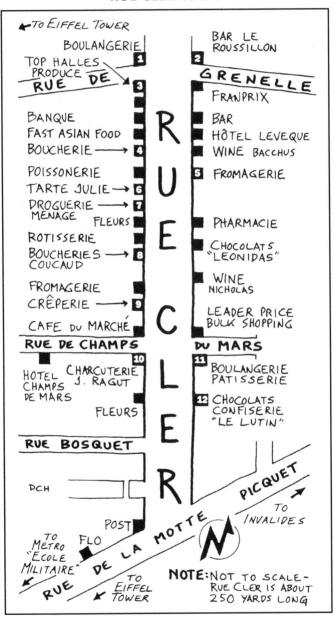

←TO EIFFEL TOWER

BOULANGERIE **1**

TOP HALLES PRODUCE
RUE DE **3**

BANQUE
FAST ASIAN FOOD
BOUCHERIE ⟶ **4**

POISSONERIE
TARTE JULIE ⟶ **6**
DROGUERIE ⟶ **7**
MENAGE
FLEURS

ROTISSERIE
BOUCHERIES ⟶ **8**
COUCAUD

FROMAGERIE
CRÊPERIE ⟶ **9**

CAFE DU MARCHÉ

RUE DE CHAMPS

10
HOTEL CHARCUTERIE
CHAMPS J. RAGUT
DE MARS
FLEURS

RUE BOSQUET

DCH

POST
FLO
TO
METRO
"ECOLE
MILITAIRE"
RUE
TO
EIFFEL
TOWER

BAR LE ROUSSILLON **2**

GRENELLE
FRANPRIX

BAR
HÔTEL LEVEQUE
WINE BACCHUS

5 FROMAGERIE

PHARMACIE
CHOCOLATS "LEONIDAS"

WINE NICHOLAS

LEADER PRICE
BULK SHOPPING

DU MARS

11 BOULANGERIE
PATISSERIE

12 CHOCOLATS
CONFISERIE
"LE LUTIN"

PICQUET
TO
INVALIDES

DE LA MOTTE

NOTE: NOT TO SCALE—
RUE CLER IS ABOUT
250 YARDS LONG

R U E   C L E R

2. Café Roussillon:
This café across the street is typical. Drinks at the always-active bar (*comptoir*) are about half the price of drinks at the tables. The "*tickets restaurant*" and "*cheque déjeuner*" decals on the door advertise that this café accepts lunch checks. In France, an employee lunch subsidy program is an expected perk. Employers issue checks (worth about €5 or $4) for the number of days an employee works in a month. Few workers bring sack lunches. A good lunch is sacred.

3. Top Halles Produce:

Fresh produce is trucked in each morning from the huge Rungis market near Orly Airport. Rungis' location, outside of town, is handy for small farmers bringing in their goods. Notice the lack of bags (paper or plastic?). Most locals bring their own.

Parisians shop with their noses. Try it. Insist on quality. Smell the cheap Spanish strawberries. Then smell the French Gariguette. Find the herbs. Is today's delivery in? *Ooh la la*, look at the price of those melons. What's the country of origin? It must be posted. If they're out of season, they come from Guadeloupe. Many people buy only French products.

The Franprix across the street is a small Safeway-type store. Opposite Hôtel Leveque is Asie Traiteur. Fast Asian food to go is popular in Paris. These shops—about as common as bakeries now—are making an impact on Parisian eating habits.

4. Boucherie:
Next to Asie Traiteur is the Triperie/Boucherie butcher shop. Look for things you may want to avoid in restaurants: *rognons* (kidneys), *foie* (liver), *coeur de boeuf* (heart of beef). Next door is fish, brought in daily from ports on the English Channel, just 160 kilometers (100 miles) away. Anything wiggling? Across the street is a wine shop. Next to that, smell the...

5. Fromagerie:
A long, narrow, canopied cheese table brings the *fromagerie* into the street. Wedges, cylinders, balls, and miniature hockey pucks all powdered white, gray, and burnt marshmallow—it's a festival of mold. Much of the street cart is devoted only to the goat cheeses. *Ooh la la* means you're impressed. If you like cheese, show greater excitement with more *la*s. *Ooh la la la la*. My local friend held the stinkiest glob close to her nose, took an orgasmic breath, and exhaled, "Yes, it smells like zee feet of angels." Try it.

Step inside and browse through some of the 400 different

types of French cheese. In the
back room are *les meules*, the
big, 170-pound wheels of cheese
(250 gallons of milk go into each
wheel). The "hard" cheeses are
cut from these. Don't eat the skin
of these big ones... they roll them
on the floor. But the skin on
the smaller cheeses—the Brie, the

Camembert—is part of the taste. "It completes the package."

At dinner tonight, you can take the cheese course just before
or as the dessert. On a good cheese plate you have a hard cheese
(like Emmenthaler), a flowery cheese (maybe Brie or Camembert),
a blue, and a goat.

6. Tarte Julie: Perhaps the most tempting storefront on rue Cler is Tarte Julie's.
The front windows are filled with various
pies. The shop's classy old storefront is a
work of art that survives from the previous
occupant. The inset stones and glass advertise horse meat: *Boucherie Chevaline*. The
decorated front, from the '30s and signed
by the artist, would fit in a museum. But it
belongs right here. And everyone knows this
is a place for a fine tart, not horse meat.

7. Droguerie Ménage and More: This French drugstore
sells everything but drugs. It's the classic kitchen/hardware store
where you buy corkscrews, brooms, knives, and so on.

Wander on past the flower shop, pharmacy (in France, the
first diagnosis and prescription are made by the pharmacist—if it's
out of his league, he'll recommend a doctor), rotisserie (quarter of
a roasted chicken with a salad and a drink to go?), and another wine
shop. In France, when invited to dinner, you'll find it's bad style to
bring a bottle of wine. The host cooks with a particular wine in
mind. Bring flowers or chocolates instead.

8. Boucherie: At Boucheries Coucaud, sort through pigeons,
quail, and rabbit. Hoist a duck and check the feet; they should be
rough and calloused—an indication that they weren't stuck in an
industrial kennel but ran wild on a farm. While Americans prefer beef,
pork, and chicken, the French eat more rabbit, lamb, duck, and horse.

9. Crêperie and More: Almost next door, you'll find the smallest

business on rue Cler, the Crêperie. Savory crêpes come with ingredients we'd put in an omelet (cheese, ham, mushrooms, and so on). They're called *galettes*, and the pancake is made from buckwheat flour. Dessert crêpes are made of wheat flour and come with everything you might enjoy on your ice-cream sundae. The Café du Marché, on the corner, is the best place to sit and enjoy the rue Cler action. For a reasonable meal, grab a chair and the waiter will prop the chalky menu listing the *plat du jour* (blue plate special) on an empty chair. The shiny, sterile Leader Price grocery store (across the street) is a French Costco selling bulk items. Because storage space is so limited in most Parisian apartments, bulk purchases are unlikely to become a big deal here.

10. Charcuterie J. Ragut: Across the street, a *charcuterie* sells mouthwatering deli food to go (try their homemade potato chips). Because kitchens are so small, these gourmet delis are handy, allowing hosts to concentrate on the main course and buy beautifully prepared side dishes to complete a fine dinner. Notice the system: Pay the cashier and return with the receipt to pick up your food.

11. Boulangerie: Locals debate the merits of rue Cler's rival *boulangeries*. It's said that a baker cannot be both good at bread and good at pastry: When you do good bread, you have no time to do good pastry. The baker at the rue Grenelle bakery (stop #1) specializes in pastry. The bread suffers. Here, the baker does good bread. He has a man who does the tasty little pastries for him.

12. Le Lutin Gourmand Chocolats Confiseries:

Serious Corinne recently took over the shop from a woman who kept this neighborhood in fine chocolates for 30 years. The wholesalers want you to take the new products, but she keeps the old traditional candies, too. "The old ladies, they want the same sweets they had 80 years ago."

Corinne dips and decorates her chocolates in the back, where the merchants used to live. As was the tradition in rue Cler shops, the merchants lived and produced in the back and sold in the front. Please don't enter her tiny store unless you plan to buy.

Rue Cler ends at the post office. The Ecole Militaire Métro stop is just around the corner. If you bought a rue Cler picnic, you'll find benches and gardens nearby. From the post office, avenue la Motte Picquet leads to two fine parks: Turn left for Les Invalides or right for the Eiffel Tower. *Bon appétit!*

paris

MONTMARTRE
WALK

While tourists usually make the almost obligatory trek to the top of Paris' Montmartre, eat an overpriced crêpe, and marvel at the view, most miss out on the neighborhood's fascinating charm and history, both uncovered by this short walk. To avoid the crowds, arrive in the morning by 09:30. If crowds don't get you down, come for the sunset and stay for dinner. I've included several restaurants on this tour. This walk is best done under clear skies—the views can be sensational. There are four sights you can enter on this tour: the Basilica of Sacré-Coeur (daily until 23:00), the church of St. Pierre, the Dalí Museum (daily 10:00–18:00), and the Montmartre Museum (Tue–Sun 11:00–18:00, closed Mon).

You'll walk about three kilometers (2 miles) up and down on this 90-minute, 12-stop tour. To avoid the climb, either take the funicular (described below) or catch a taxi (about €11 from the Eiffel Tower or Bastille to Sacré-Coeur) and begin the tour at the church on top.

To reach Sacré-Coeur by Métro, get off at Anvers. When you exit the Métro, look up the only real hill in Paris. The peeling and neglected Elysées Montmartre theater across the street is the oldest cancan dance hall in Paris, and it sets the stage for this area in transition (it's a rowdy rock-and-roll dance hall today). People have always moved to this area for cheap rent. It still feels neglected, though some urban gentrification is underway as young professionals restore neglected apartments and hotels renovate for a more upscale clientele.

Walk two blocks up rue de Steinkerque (the street to the right of Elysées Montmartre), through waves of tourists and past cheap clothing and souvenir shops (inexpensive postcards) to the grassy parkway below the white Sacré-Coeur church. The dips in the landscapes are from old gypsum quarries. Hike toward the church or ride the funicular (costs 1 Métro ticket, to the left, past the merry-go-round). The best view is just below the last flight of stairs.

1. Sacré-Coeur Church and View: From Paris' highest point (130 meters/430 feet), the City of Lights fans out at your feet. The big triangular roof on your left is the Gare du Nord train station; the golden dome out there on the right is Les Invalides. The colorful Pompidou Center is straight ahead, and the domed Panthéon lies just beyond to the right, on Paris' only other (and far smaller) butte. The Montparnasse Tower is farther off to the right, and the skyscrapers beyond define the southern limit of central Paris. Now walk up to the church.

The Sacré-Coeur ("Sacred Heart") **church**, with its onion domes and bleached-bone pallor, looks ancient but was built only a century ago by Parisians chastened by German invaders. Otto von Bismark's Prussian army laid siege to Paris for more than four months in 1870. Things got so bad for residents that urban hunting for dinner (to cook up cats and dogs) became accepted behavior. The church was erected as a "praise the Lord anyway" gesture after France's humiliation by Germany.

The five-dome, Romano-Byzantine basilica took 40 years to build. The church is dedicated to the "sacred heart" of Jesus, which enables Him to understand human needs and feelings. The contrast between the brilliant white exterior and the sooty interior is jarring. Explore the impressive mosaics, especially of Christ with his sacred heart, above the altar. Walk clockwise around the ambulatory behind the altar. Notice the colorful mosaic stations of the cross as you walk behind the altar on your right. Between stations VII and VIII, rub St. Peter's bronze foot and look up to the ceiling.

For an unobstructed panoramic view of Paris, climb 80 meters (260 feet) up the tight and claustrophobic spiral stairs to the top of the **dome** (€2, daily June–Sept 09:00–19:00, Oct–May 10:00–18:00, access is outside church and downstairs to the right, especially worthwhile if you have kids with excess energy). Skip the crypt (€2); it's just a big empty basement.

• *Leaving the church, turn right and follow the tree-lined street with the view to your left. At rue St. Eleuthere, turn right and walk uphill to the Church of St. Pierre (at top on right).*

2. Church of St. Pierre: Originally a headquarters for nuns, the church is one of Paris' oldest—some say Dante prayed here. Older still are the four gray columns inside that may have stood in a temple of Mercury and Mars in Roman times (2 flank the entrance and 2 are behind the altar.) The name "Montmartre" comes from the Roman "Mount of Mars," though later generations,

──MONTMARTRE WALK──

```
300 YARDS
300 METERS
IIII = STAIRS
```

❶ SACRE COEUR
❷ ST. PIERRE
❸ PLACE DU TERTRE
❹ DALI MUSEUM
❺ MONTMARTRE MUSEUM
❻ VINEYARD
❼ LAPIN AGILE
❽ BATEAU LAVOIR
❾ MOULIN DE LA GALETTE
❿ VAN GOGH'S HOUSE
⓫ MOULIN ROUGE
⓬ PIG ALLEY
⓭ RENOIR'S HOUSE
⓮ TOULOUSE-LAUTREC'S HOUSE

thinking of their beheaded patron St. Denis, preferred a less pagan version, "Mount of Martyrs."

In front of the church, the Café and Cabaret La Bohème remind visitors that the community was a haunt of the bohemian crowd in the 19th and early 20th centuries. The artist-filled place du Tertre awaits.

3. Bohemian Montmartre—Place du Tertre: In 1800,
a wall separated Paris from this village on the hill. You had to pay a toll to get in. Montmartre was a mining community (the local gypsum was the original plaster of Paris) where the wine flowed cheap and easy. Life here was a working-class festival of cafés, bistros, and dance halls. Painters came here for the ruddy charm, the light, and the low rents. In 1860, Montmartre was annexed into the growing city of Paris. The "bohemian" ambience

survived and attracted sophisticated Parisians ready to get down and dirty in the belle époque of cancan.

Lined with cafés and filled with artists, hucksters, and tourists, the scene mixes charm and kitsch in ever-changing proportions. The place du Tertre artists, who at times outnumber the tourists, are the great-great-grandkids of the Renoirs, van Goghs, and Picassos who once roamed here—poor, carefree, seeking inspiration, and occasionally cursing a world too selfish to bankroll their dreams.

The Syndicat d'Initiative across the square is a tourist office (daily 10:00–19:00). Find it, then turn left and walk along the square.

4. Dalí Museum: Escape from place du Tertre via the downhill corner. At the Patachou restaurant (great views from its backyard tables, €27 dinner *menu*), turn right into the tiny place du Calvaire for a great view.

Past the café Chez Plumeau is the quiet Salvador Dalí Museum. The museum—a beautifully lit, black gallery with the right music—offers a walk through statues, etchings, and paintings by Dalí. Don't miss the printed interview on the exit stairs (€6, not covered by museum pass, daily 10:00–18:00, well-described in English, 11 rue Poulbot).

From the museum, follow rue Poulbot as it curves to the rue Norvins, the spine and main tourist drag of the community (you'll pass the Butte en Vigne restaurant at #5 rue Poulbot—inexpensive and decent plats du jour and *menus*). Turn left down rue Norvins and walk 20 steps to the crossroads with rue des Saules. The venerable *boulangerie* on the left (dating from 1900) is one of the last surviving bits of the old-time community. From here, we'll side-trip three blocks down the backside of the *mont*, then return to carry on past the *boulangerie*.

From the boulangerie, walk to the Auberge de la Bonne Franquette on rue des Saules (allow €14 for lunch, €24 for dinner, classic Montmartre ambience and good French onion soup). At its doorway, notice the dome of Sacré-Coeur rising above the rooftops. Painters such as Maurice Utrillo (1883–1955) captured views like this, making the neighborhood famous. Utrillo, the son of a free-spirited single mom, grew up in Montmartre's streets. He fought, broke street lamps, and haunted the cafés and bars, buying drinks with masterpieces. A very free spirit, he's said to have exposed himself to strangers on the street, yelling, "I paint with this!"

5. Montmartre Museum: Follow rue des Saules downhill into the less-touristed backside of Montmartre. A right up rue Cortet (just before Maison Rose restaurant) leads up an exclusive street with vine-covered homes to the Montmartre Museum, at

#12. Utrillo once lived here with his mom. (Composer Erik Satie lived at #16.) The museum fills eight rooms in this creaky 17th-century manor house with paintings, posters, old photos, music, and memorabilia re-creating the traditional cancan and cabaret Montmartre scene (€4, not covered by museum pass, Tue–Sun 11:00–18:00, closed Mon, reasonably well-described in English).
• *Return to the rue des Saules and walk downhill past the Maison Rose restaurant one block to Paris' last remaining vineyard.*

6. Clos Montmartre Vineyard: What originally drew

artists to Montmartre was its country charm. With vineyards, wheat fields, windmills, animals, and a village tempo of life, it was the perfect escape from grimy Paris. Today's vineyard is off-limits to tourists except during the annual grape-harvest fest (first Sat in Oct), when a thousand costumed locals bring back the boisterous old days and the vineyard's annual production of 300 liters is auctioned off to support local charities.
• *Continue downhill to the foot of the vineyard.*

7. Lapin Agile Cabaret: The faded poster above the door

gives the place its name. A rabbit (*lapin*) makes an agile leap out of the pot while balancing the bottle of wine which now—rather than be cooked in—he can drink. This was the village's hot spot. Picasso and other artists and writers would gather for "performances" that ranged from serious poetry, dirty limericks, sing-alongs, and parodies of the famous to anarchist manifestos. Once, to play a practical joke on the avant-garde art community, patrons tied a paintbrush to the tail of the owner's donkey and entered the "abstract painting" that resulted in the Salon. Called "Sunset over the Adriatic," it won critical acclaim and sold for a nice price.

You now have two options. Most will want to walk back up the rue des Saules to the bakery at the top of the hill, where we'll continue our walk. If you have a reserve of energy, 15 extra minutes, and want to see more of Montmartre (including Renoir's home), walk up the rue des Saules and turn right at la Maison Rose. Follow rue de l'Abbreuvoir onto the small walkway at the curve, and you'll pass Renoir's home, at #6. Walk down the steps at the walkway's end, then stroll up through the small park (notice the formal *boules* court overseen by a fascinated St. Denis). Turn left at the top of the park onto rue Junot, which turns into rue Norvins. The bakery is at the top of rue Norvins.
• *Once reunited at the bakery, we all go downhill (along place Jean Baptiste Clement), hugging the buildings on our left—don't curve right on rue Lepic. Turn right on rue Ravignan and follow it to the "TIM Hôtel." Next door, at 13 place Emile-Goudeau, is Bâteau-Lavoir.*

8. Bâteau-Lavoir, Picasso's Studio: A humble window display marks the place where modern art was born. Here, in a lowly artists' abode (destroyed by fire in 1970), as many as 10 artists lived and worked. The fading photos in the window show Picasso and the studio where he and his friends Georges Braque and Juan Gris revolutionized art. Sharing paints, ideas, and girl-friends, they created art, such as Picasso's *Demoiselles d'Avignon*, that shocked the world. Modigliani and the poet Apollinaire also lived here. Later (when he was one of France's richest men), Picasso wrote, "I know one day we'll return to Bâteau-Lavoir. It was there that we were really happy—where they thought of us as painters, not strange animals."

• *Backtrack uphill to the corner (where you'll see the only surviving bit of the burned studio—complete with artist-pleasing skylights), turn left on rue d'Orchampt, squirt out the end, and (at rue Lepic and rue d'Orchampt) come face-to-face with a wooden windmill. (If you're hungry, detour to Le Montagnard restaurant, uphill 1 block at 102 rue Lepic, offering cozy, country-elegant dining at fair prices.)*

9. Moulin de la Galette:

Only two windmills (*moulins*) remain on a hill that was once dotted with them. Originally, they pressed grapes and crushed stones. When the gypsum mines closed and vineyards sprouted apartments, this windmill turned into a popular outdoor dance hall. Renoir's *Bal du Moulin de La Galette* (at the Orsay) shows it in its heyday—a sunny Sunday afternoon in the leafy gardens, with ordinary folk dancing, eating, and laughing. Some call it the quintessential Impressionist painting.

• *Rue Lepic winds down the hill. The green-latticed building to your right was part of the Moulin de la Galette. Continue past the main entry of Moulin de la Galette down rue Lepic to the rue Durantin. At this intersection, look down rue Tourlaque one block to the building with the tall, brick-framed art studio windows and heavy Mansart roof. Toulouse-Lautrec lived here. Continue down rue Lepic and, at # 54, find ...*

10. Van Gogh's House: In the two short years (1886–1888) he stayed here with his brother, Vincent van Gogh transformed from a gloomy Dutch painter of brown and gray peasant scenes into an inspired visionary with wild ideas and Impressionist colors.

• *Follow the rue Lepic downhill as it makes a hard right at #36 and continue to place Blanche; check out the horse butcher at #30 as you descend.*

Notice the happy horses on the price stickers. This leg of the rue Lepic is little changed from when Vincent lived here. Enjoy that notion for the delightful last stretch of rue Lepic before it hits the big street and a big change. On busy place Blanche is the . . .

11. Moulin Rouge: *Ooh*
la la! The new Eiffel Tower at
the 1889 World's Fair was
nothing compared to the sight
of pretty cancan girls spreading their legs at the newly
opened "Red Windmill."
The nightclub seemed to
sum up the belle époque—
the age of elegance, opulence, sophistication, and worldliness. On
most nights, you'd see a small man in a sleek black coat, checked
pants, a green scarf, and a bowler hat peering through his pince-
nez glasses at the dancers and making sketches of them—Henri
de Toulouse-Lautrec. Perhaps he'd order an absinthe, the dense
green liqueur that was the toxic muse for so many great (and forgotten) artists. Toulouse-Lautrec's sketches of dancer Jane Avril
and comic La Goulue hang in the Orsay. Walk in and mull over
the photos, show options, and prices.

12. Pig Alley: The stretch of boulevard de Clichy from place
Blanche eastward (toward Sacré-Coeur) to place Pigalle is the den
mother of all iniquities. Plaster of Paris from the gypsum found
on this mount was loaded sloppily at place Blanche . . . the white
place. Today sex shops, peep shows, live sex shows, and hotdog
stands line the busy boulevard de Clichy. Dildos abound.

Although raunchy now, the area has always been the place
where bistros had tax-free status, wine was cheap, and prostitutes
roamed free. WWII GIs nicknamed Pigalle "Pig Alley."

End your tour at the place Blanche Métro stop (if you want
to skip the raunchiness) or hike through Pigalle, escaping home
from the fine Art Nouveau Métro stop, Pigalle.

LOUVRE TOUR

Paris walks you through history in three world-class museums—the Louvre (ancient world to 1850), the Orsay (1850–1914, including Impressionism), and the Pompidou (20th century to today). Start your art-yssey at the Louvre. The Louvre's collection—more than 30,000 works of art—is a full inventory of Western civilization. To cover the entire collection in one visit is in-Seine. We'll enjoy just three of the Louvre's specialties—Greek sculpture, Italian painting, and French painting.

Orientation

Cost: €7, €5 after 15:00 and on Sun, free on first Sun of month and for those under 18, covered by museum pass. Tickets good all day; reentry allowed.

Hours: Wed–Mon 09:00–18:00, closed Tue. All wings open Wed until 21:45. On Mon, only the Richelieu wing is open until 21:45. Galleries start closing 30 minutes early. Closed Jan 1, Easter, May 1, Nov 1, and Dec 25. Crowds are worst on Sun, Mon, Wed, and mornings. Save money by visiting after 15:00.

Getting There: The Métro stop Palais Royal/Musée du Louvre is closer to the entrance than the stop called Louvre Rivoli.

There is no grander entry than through the pyramid, but metal detectors create a long line at times. There are several ways to avoid the line. Museum-pass holders can use the group entrance in the pedestrian passageway between the pyramid and rue de Rivoli (facing the pyramid with your back to the Tuileries Gardens, go to your left, which is north; under the arches you'll find the entrance and escalator down). Otherwise, you can enter the Louvre underground from the Carrousel shopping mall, which is connected to the museum. Enter the mall at 99 rue de Rivoli (the door with the red awning) or directly from the Métro stop Palais Royal/

——— THE LOUVRE—A BIRD'S-EYE VIEW ———

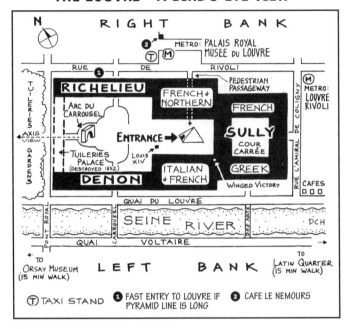

Musée du Louvre (exit following signs to "Musée du Louvre").
The taxi stand is across rue de Rivoli next to the Métro station.
Information: Pick up the free *Louvre Handbook* in English at the
information desk under the pyramid as you enter. Tel. 01 40 20
51 51, recorded info tel. 01 40 20 53 17, www.louvre.fr.
Checkrooms: The coat check—which can have a torturously
slow line (drop in the morning, pick up in the afternoon)—does
not take bags. The bag check (which doesn't take coats that are
not stuffed into bags) is separate from the coat check and generally has almost no line.
Photography: Photography without a flash is allowed.
Cuisine Art: The underground shopping mall has a dizzying assortment of good-value eateries (up the escalator near the inverted
pyramid). There's also a post office, handy TI, SNCF train office,
glittering boutiques, and the Palais-Royal Métro entrance. Stairs
at the far end take you right into the Tuileries Gardens, a perfect
antidote to the stuffy, crowded rooms of the Louvre. For a fine
light lunch, cross rue de Rivoli to the venerable Café Le Nemours
(adjacent to the Comédie Française, see the Eating chapter).
Length of Our Tour: Two hours.

Louvre Tours: The 90-minute English-language tours leave six times daily except Sun (€5.50, tour tel. 01 40 20 52 09). Clever €5 digital audioguides (after ticket booths, at top of stairs) give you a directory of about 130 masterpieces, allowing you to dial a rather dull commentary on included works as you stumble upon them. I recommend the free, self-guided tour described below. **Starring:** *Venus de Milo, Winged Victory, Mona Lisa*, Raphael, Michelangelo, and the French painters.

Surviving the Louvre

Pick up the map at the information desk under the pyramid as you enter. The Louvre, the largest museum in the Western world, fills three wings in this immense U-shaped palace. The north wing (Richelieu) houses French, Dutch, and Northern art. The east wing (Sully) houses the extensive French painting collection.

For this tour, we'll concentrate on the Louvre's south wing (Denon), which houses the superstars: ancient Greek sculpture, Italian Renaissance painting, and French neoclassical and Romantic painting.

Expect changes. The Louvre is in flux for several years as they shuffle the deck. If you can't find a particular painting, ask a guard where it is. Point to the photo in your book and ask, *"Où est?"* (oo ay).

THE TOUR BEGINS—
GREEK STATUES (600 B.C.–A.D. 1)

Every generation defines beauty differently. For Golden Age Greeks, beauty was balance, combining opposites in just the right propor-tions. They thought that the human body— especially the female form—embodied the order they saw in the universe. In the Louvre, we'll see a series of "Venuses" throughout history. Their different poses and gestures tell us about the people that made them. We'll see how the idea of beauty (as balance) began in ancient Greece, how it evolved into Hellenism (tipping the balance from stability to movement), and then how it resurfaced in the Renaissance, 2,000 years later.

• *From inside the big glass pyramid, you'll see signs to the three wings. Head for the Denon wing.*

—— PRE-CLASSICAL GREECE ——

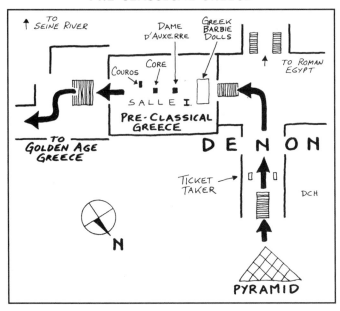

Escalate up one floor. After showing your ticket, take the first left you can, climbing a set of stairs to the brick-ceilinged Salle (Room) 1: "La Grèce préclassique." Enter prehistory.

Pre-Classical Greece

These statues are noble but crude. The Greek Barbie dolls (3000 B.C.) are older than the pyramids, as old as writing itself. These pre-rational voodoo dolls whittle women down to their life-giving traits. Farther along, a woman (*Dame d'Auxerre*) pledges allegiance to stability. Another (*Core*) is essentially a

column with breasts. A young naked man (*Couros*) seems to have a gun to his back—his hands at his sides, facing front, with sketchy muscles and a mask-like face. "Don't move."

The early Greeks, who admired such statues, found stability more attractive than movement. Like their legendary hero, Odysseus, the Greek people had spent generations wandering, war-weary, and longing for the comforts of a secure home.

The noble strength and sturdiness of these works looked beautiful.

• *Exit Salle 1 at the far end and climb the stairs one flight. At the top, veer 10-o'clock left, where you'll soon see* Venus de Milo *rising above a sea of heads. As you approach her, you'll pass the ornate Antiquités Romaines Hall (we'll return here later). Next, turn right into Salle 7 (Salle du Parthenon), where you'll find two carved panels from the Parthenon on the wall.*

Golden Age Greece

The great Greek cultural explosion that changed the course of history happened in a 50-year stretch (around 450 B.C.) in Athens, a Greek town smaller than Muncie, Indiana. The Greeks dominated the ancient world through brain, not brawn, and the art shows their love of rationality and order.

In a sense, we're all Greek. Democracy, mathematics, theater, philosophy, literature, and science were practically invented in ancient Greece. Most of the art that we'll see in the Louvre either came from Greece or was inspired by it.

Parthenon Frieze (Fragment de la Frise des Panathénées), c. 440 B.C.

These stone fragments once decorated the exterior of the greatest Athenian temple, the Parthenon. The right panel shows a half-man/half-horse creature sexually harassing a woman. It tells the story of  how these rude centaurs crashed a party of humans. But the Greeks fought back and threw the brutes out, just as Athens (metaphorically) conquered its barbarian neighbors and became civilized.

The other relief shows the sacred procession of young girls who marched up the hill every four years with an embroidered veil for the 12-meter-high (40 feet) statue of Athena, the goddess of wisdom. The maidens, carved in only a few centimeters of stone, are amazingly realistic—more so than anything we saw in the pre-Classical period. They glide along horizontally (their belts and shoulders all in a line), while the folds of their dresses drape down vertically. The man in the center is relaxed and realistic. Notice the veins in his arm.

GREEK STATUES

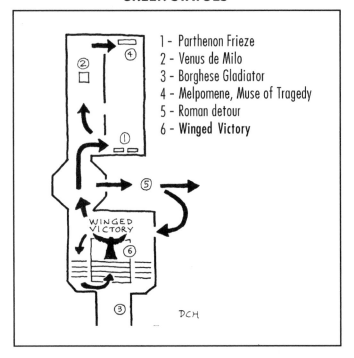

1 - Parthenon Frieze
2 - Venus de Milo
3 - Borghese Gladiator
4 - Melpomene, Muse of Tragedy
5 - Roman detour
6 - Winged Victory

Greeks of the Golden Age valued the golden mean—that is, balance. The ideal person was well-rounded—an athlete and a bookworm, a lover and a philosopher, a realtor who plays the piano, a warrior and a poet. In art, the balance between timeless stability and fleeting movement made beauty. The maidens' pleated dresses make them look as stable as fluted columns, but their arms and legs step out naturally—the human form is emerging from the stone.

• *Now seek the Goddess of Love. You'll find her floating above a sea of worshiping tourists. It's been said that, among the warlike Greeks, this was the first statue to unilaterally disarm.*

Venus de Milo (*Aphrodite*), c. 100 B.C.

The *Venus de Milo* (or Goddess of Love, from the Greek island of Milos) created a sensation when it was discovered in 1820. Europe was already in the grip of a classical fad, and this statue seemed to sum up all that ancient Greece stood for. The Greeks pictured their gods in human form, telling us they had an optimistic view of the human race.

Most "Greek" statues are actually later Roman copies. This is a rare Greek original. This "epitome of the Golden Age" was actually sculpted three centuries later, though in the style of the earlier.

Venus de Milo is a harmonious balance of opposites. *Venus* is stable, resting her weight on one leg (called *contrapposto*, or "counterpose"), yet her other leg is slightly raised, ready to take a step. This slight movement sets her whole body in motion, though she remains perfectly still.

Split *Venus* down the middle (left and right) and see how the two halves balance each other. As she lifts her left leg, her right shoulder droops down. And as her knee points one way, her head turns the other. The twisting pose gives an S-curve to her body (especially noticeable from the back view) that the Greeks and succeeding generations found beautiful.

Other opposites balance as well, like the rough-cut texture of her dress (size 14) that sets off the smooth skin of her upper half. She's actually made from two different pieces of stone plugged together at the hips (the seam is visible). The face is realistic and anatomically accurate, but it's also idealized, a goddess, too generic and too perfect. This isn't any particular woman but Everywoman—all the idealized features that the Greeks found beautiful.

What were her missing arms doing? Some say her right arm held her dress while her left arm was raised. Others say she was hugging a man statue or leaning on a column. I say she was picking her navel.

• *This statue is interesting and different from every angle. Remember the view from the back—we'll see it again later. Orbit* Venus. *Make your reentry to Earth as you wander among Greek statues. Try to find even one that's not* contrapposto. *Retracing your steps, find the "Antiquités Romaines" hall and take a loop...*

Roman Detour

The Romans were great conquerors but bad artists. Fortunately for us, they had a huge appetite for Greek statues and made countless copies. They took the Greek style and wrote it in capital letters—like the huge statue of Melpomene, holding the frowning mask of tragic plays.

One area the Romans excelled

in was realistic portrait busts, especially of their emperors, who were worshiped as gods on earth. Stroll among the Caesars and try to see the man behind the public persona—Augustus, the first emperor, and his wily wife, Livia; Nero ("Neron"), who burned part of his own city; Hadrian, who popularized the beard; crazy Caligula; the stoic Marcus Aurelius; Claudius of "I" fame; and the many faces of the ubiquitous Emperor Inconnu.

The Roman rooms also contain sarcophagi and an impressive mosaic floor. Weary? Relax with the statues in the Etruscan Lounge.

• *This Roman detour deposits you at the base of stairs leading up to the dramatic* Victory of Samothrace. *We'll be there momentarily, but first—to continue the evolution of Greek art from Golden Age balance to the more exuberant Hellenistic Age, find the ...*

Borghese Gladiator (Guerrier Combattant, Dit Gladiateur Borghese)

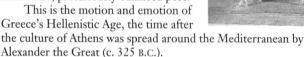

We see a fighting gladiator at the peak of action. He blocks a blow with the shield that used to be attached to his left arm, while his right hand, weighted with an early version of brass knuckles, prepares to deliver the counterpunch. His striding motion makes a diagonal line from his left foot up his leg, along the body and out the extended arm. It's a dramatic, precariously balanced pose.

This is the motion and emotion of Greece's Hellenistic Age, the time after the culture of Athens was spread around the Mediterranean by Alexander the Great (c. 325 B.C.).

The earlier Golden Age Greeks might have considered this statue ugly. His rippling, knotted muscles are a far cry from the more restrained Parthenon sculptures and the soft-focus beauty of *Venus*. And the statue's off-balance pose leaves you hanging, like an unfinished melody. But Hellenistic Greeks loved these cliff-hanging scenes of real-life humans struggling to make their mark. The artist himself made his mark, signing the work proudly on the tree trunk: "Agasias of Ephesus, son of Dositheos, did this."

• *Now ascend the staircase, to the ...*

Winged Victory of Samothrace (Victoire de Samothrace)

This woman with wings, poised on the prow of a ship, once stood on a hilltop to commemorate a great naval victory. Her clothes are windblown and sea-sprayed, clinging to her body like the winner of a wet T-shirt contest. (Notice the detail in the folds of her dress around the navel, curving down to her hips.) Originally, her right arm was stretched high, celebrating the victory like a Super Bowl champion, waving a "we're-number-one" finger.

This is the *Venus de Milo* gone Hellenistic—a balance of opposites that produces excitement, not grace. As *Victory* strides forward,

the wind blows her and her wings back. Her feet are firmly on the ground, but her wings (and missing arms) stretch upward. She is a pillar of vertical strength while the clothes curve and whip around her. These opposing forces create a feeling of great energy, making her the lightest two-ton piece of rock in captivity.

In the glass case nearby is *Victory*'s open right hand, discovered in 1950, a century after the statue itself was unearthed. Also in the case is *Victory*'s finger. When the French discovered this was in Turkey, they negotiated with the Turkish government for rights

to it. Considering all the other ancient treasures the French had looted from Turkey in the past, the Turks thought it only appropriate to give France the finger.

• *Enter the octagonal room to the left as you face the* Winged Victory, *with Icarus bungee-jumping from the ceiling. Bench yourself under a window and look out toward the pyramid.*

FRENCH HISTORY
The Louvre as a Palace

The Louvre, a former palace, was built in stages over several centuries. On your right (the east wing) was the original medieval fortress. Next, another palace, the Tuileries, was built 500 meters to the west—in the open area past the pyramid and past the triumphal arch. Succeeding kings tried to connect these two palaces, each one adding another section onto the long, skinny north and south wings. Finally, in 1852, after three centuries of building, the two palaces were connected, creating a rectangular Louvre. Soon after that, the Tuileries Palace burned down during a riot, leaving the U-shaped Louvre we see today.

The glass pyramid was designed by the American architect I. M. Pei. Many Parisians hated the pyramid, like they used to hate another new and controversial structure 100 years ago—the Eiffel Tower.

The doorway leads to the Apollo Gallery, or Galerie d'Apollon (although the gallery is closed for renovation for several years, the

jewels are on display in the Sully
wing). The plaque above the
doorway explains that France's
Revolutionary National Assembly
(the same people who brought
you the guillotine) founded this
museum in 1793. What could be
more logical? You behead the

king, inherit his palace and art collection, open the doors to the
masses, and, Voilà! You've got Europe's first public museum. Major
supporters of the museum are listed on the walls—notice all the
Rothschilds.

• *The Italian collection ("Peintures Italiennes") is on the other side of the*
Winged Victory. *Cross in front of the* Victory *to the other side and
pause at the two fresco paintings on the wall to the left.*

ITALIAN RENAISSANCE

A thousand years after Rome fell,
plunging Europe into the Dark
Ages, the Greek ideal of beauty
was "reborn" in 15th-century
Italy. This was the Renaissance,
the cultural revival of ancient art.

In these two frescoes by
the Italian Renaissance artist
Botticelli, we see echoes of
ancient Greece. The maidens, with their poses, clear sculptural
lines, and idealized beauty, are virtual *Venus de Milo*s with clothes.
The Renaissance was a time of great optimism, exploration, and
liberation, and here we see it in its fresh-faced springtime.

The key to Renaissance painting was realism, and for the
Italians "realism" was spelled "3-D." Painters were inspired by
the realism and balanced beauty of Greek sculpture.

• *The Italian collection—including* Mona Lisa—*is scattered throughout
the next few rooms (Salles 3 & 4), in the long Grand Gallery, and in
adjoining rooms. To see the paintings in chronological order may require
a little extra shoe leather. When in doubt, show the photo to a guard
and ask,* "Où est, s'il vous plaît?" *(It rhymes.)*

Medieval and Early Italian
Renaissance (1200–1500)

Painting a 3-D world on a 2-D surface is tough, and after a millennium of Dark Ages, artists were rusty. Living in a religious age, they
painted mostly altarpieces full of saints, angels, Madonnas-and-
bambinos, and crucifixes floating in an ethereal gold-leaf heaven.

Gradually, though, they brought these otherworldly scenes
down to earth.

Cimabue—*The Madonna of the Angels*

During the Age of Faith (1200s), most
every church in Europe had a painting like
this one. Mary was a cult figure—bigger
than even the 20th-century Madonna—
adored and prayed to by the faithful for
bringing baby Jesus into the world.

And most every painting followed
the same "Byzantine" style: Somber iconic
faces, stiff poses, elegant folds in the robes,
and generic angels, all laid flat on a gold
background like cardboard cutouts.
Violating 3-D space, the angels at the
"back" of Mary's throne are the same size as those holding the front.

Still, Cimabue (c. 1240–1302; chee-MAH-bway) is considered
the first painter to experiment with Renaissance techniques. He uses
the throne to give some sense of foreground and background, and
puts shading ("modeling") around the edge of figures to make them
look rounded. The work has Renaissance symmetry, three angels on
each side, with the top ones bending in to frame the Virgin.

Cimabue was the first "name" artist in a world of anonymous
craftsmen. His proud personality (Cimabue is a nickname meaning
"bullheaded") was legendary. And the legend grew when, one day, he
came across a shepherd boy sketching his sheep. Cimabue took young
Giotto in, and raised him to shatter the icons of the medieval style.

Giotto—*St. Francis of Assisi Receiving the Stigmata (and Francis Preaching to the Birds)*

Francis of Assisi (1181–1226), a wandering
Italian monk of renowned goodness,
breathed the spirit of the Renaissance into
medieval Europe. His humble love of man
and nature inspired artists to portray real
human beings with real emotions living in
a physical world of beauty.

Here, Francis kneels on a rocky Italian
hillside, pondering the pain of Christ's tor-
ture-execution. Suddenly he looks up, star-
tled, to see Christ himself, with six wings,
hovering above. Christ shoots lasers from
his wounds to burn marks on the hands,
feet, and side of the empathetic monk.

Like a good filmmaker, the artist Giotto (1266–1337; JOT-toh) doesn't just *tell* us what happened in the past, he *shows* us in present tense, freezing the scene at the most dramatic moment. Though the perspective is crude—Francis' hut is smaller than he is, and Christ is somehow shooting at Francis while facing us—Giotto gives a glimpse of the 3-D world of the coming Renaissance.

In the predella (the panel of paintings below the altarpiece), birds gather at Francis' feet to hear him talk about God. Giotto catches the late arrivals in mid-flight, an astonishing technical feat for an artist more than a century before the Renaissance. The simple gesture of Francis' companion speaks volumes about his amazement. Breaking the stiff, iconic mold for saints, Francis bends forward at the waist to talk to his fellow creatures, while the tree bends down symmetrically to catch a few words from the beloved hippie of Assisi.

Painters such as Giotto, Fra Angelico, and Uccello broke Renaissance ground by learning to paint realistic, 3-D humans. They placed them in a painted scene with a definite foreground, background, and middle ground to create the illusion of depth. Composition was simple but symmetrically balanced in the Greek style. Art was a visual sermon, appreciated for its moral message, not its beauty.

• *The long Grand Gallery displays Italian Renaissance painting, some masterpieces, some not. Mona Lisa is at the far end. (Note that in 2003, Mona will have her own room, likely within the Salle des Etats, midway down the Grand Gallery to your right.)*

The Grand Gallery

The Grand Gallery was built in the late 1500s to connect the old palace with the Tuileries Palace. From the doorway, look to the far end—where *Mona* is waiting—and consider this challenge: I hold the world's record for the Grand Gallery Heel-Toe-Fun-Walk-Tourist-Slalom, going end to end in one minute 58 seconds, two injured. Time yourself. Along the way, notice some of the . . .

THE GRAND GALLERY

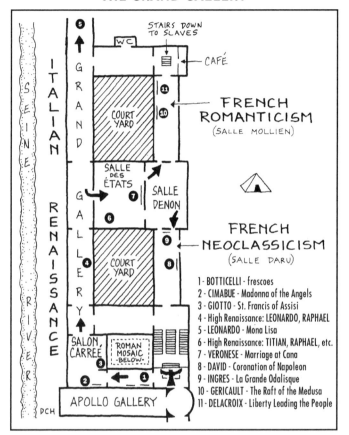

1 - BOTTICELLI - frescoes
2 - CIMABUE - Madonna of the Angels
3 - GIOTTO - St. Francis of Assisi
4 - High Renaissance: LEONARDO, RAPHAEL
5 - LEONARDO - Mona Lisa
6 - High Renaissance: TITIAN, RAPHAEL, etc.
7 - VERONESE - Marriage at Cana
8 - DAVID - Coronation of Napoleon
9 - INGRES - La Grande Odalisque
10 - GERICAULT - The Raft of the Medusa
11 - DELACROIX - Liberty Leading the People

Features of Italian Renaissance Painting

1. **Religious:** Lots of Madonnas, children, martyrs, and saints.
2. **Symmetrical:** The Madonnas are flanked by saints, two to the left, two to the right, and so on.
3. **Realistic:** Real-life human features are especially obvious in the occasional portrait.
4. **Three-Dimensional:** Every scene gets a spacious setting with a distant horizon.
5. **Classical:** You'll see some Greek gods and classical nudes, but even Christian saints pose like Greek statues, and Mary is a "Venus" whose face and gestures embody all that was good in the Christian world.

Mantegna—*St. Sebastian*

This isn't the patron saint of acupuncture. St. Sebastian was a Christian martyr, although here he looks more like a classical Greek statue. Notice the *contrapposto* stance (all of his weight resting on one leg) and the Greek ruins scattered around him. His executioners look like ignorant medieval brutes bewildered by this enlightened Renaissance man. Italian artists were beginning to learn how to create human realism and earthly beauty on the canvas. Let the Renaissance begin.

Italian High Renaissance (1500–1600)

The two masters of Renaissance grace and balance were Raphael and Leonardo da Vinci.

Leonardo was the consummate Renaissance man. Musician, sculptor, engineer, scientist, and sometimes painter, he combined knowledge from all areas to create beauty. If he were alive today, he'd create a Unified Field theory in physics—and set it to music.
• *Look for the following masterpieces by Leonardo and Raphael in the Grand Gallery.*

Leonardo da Vinci—*Virgin, Child, and St. Anne* (*La Vierge, l'Enfant Jésus, et Sainte Anne*)

Three generations—grandmother, mother, and child—are arranged

in a pyramid form with Anne's face as the peak and the lamb as the lower right corner. Within this balanced structure, Leonardo sets the figures in motion. Anne's legs are pointed to our left. (Is Anne *Mona*? Hmm.) Her daughter Mary, sitting on her lap, reaches to the right. Jesus looks at her playfully while turning away. The lamb pulls away from him. But even with all the twisting and turning, this is still a placid scene. It's as orderly as the geometrically perfect universe created by the Renaissance god.

There's a psychological kidney punch in this happy painting. Jesus, the picture of childish joy, is innocently playing with a lamb—the symbol of his inevitable sacrificial death.

The Louvre has the greatest collection of Leonardos in the

world—all five of them. Look for the neighboring *Madonna of the Rocks* and his androgynous *John the Baptist*.

Raphael—*La Belle Jardinière*

Raphael (roff-eye-ELL) perfected the style Leonardo pioneered. This Madonna, Child, and John the Baptist is also a balanced pyramid with hazy grace and beauty. Mary is a mountain of maternal tenderness (the title translates as "The Beautiful Kindergarten Teacher"), eyeing her son with a knowing look. Jesus looks up innocently, standing *contrapposto* like a chubby Greek statue.

With Raphael, the Greek ideal of beauty reborn in the Renaissance reached its peak. His work spawned so many imitators who cranked out sickly sweet, generic Madonnas that we often take him for granted. Don't. This is the real thing.

• *The* Mona Lisa *is at the end of the Grand Gallery (until 2003, when she'll likely move into the Salle des Etats, midway down the Grand Gallery)—regardless, follow the signs and crowds.*

Leonardo da Vinci—*Mona Lisa*

Leonardo was already an old man when François I invited him to France. Determined to pack light, he took only a few paintings with him. One was a portrait of a Lisa del Giocondo, the wife of a wealthy Florentine merchant. When Leonardo arrived, François immediately

fell in love with the painting, making it the centerpiece of the small collection of Italian masterpieces that would, in three centuries, become the Louvre museum. He called it *La Gioconda*. We know it as a contraction of the Italian for "my lady Lisa"—*Mona Lisa*.

Advance warning: *Mona* may disappoint you. She's smaller than you'd expect, darker, engulfed in a huge room, and hidden behind a glaring pane of glass. So, you ask, "Why all the hubbub?" Let's take a closer look. Like any lover, you've got to take her for what she is, not what you'd like her to be.

The famous smile attracts you first. Leonardo used a hazy technique called *sfumato*, blurring the edges of *Mona*'s mysterious smile. Try as you might, you can never quite see the corners of her mouth. Is she happy? Sad? Tender? Or is it a cynical supermodel's smirk? Every viewer reads it differently, projecting his own mood onto *Lisa*'s enigmatic face. *Mona* is a Rorschach inkblot...so how are you feeling?

Now look past the smile and the eyes that really do follow you (most eyes in portraits do) to some of the subtle Renaissance elements that make this work work. The body is surprisingly massive and statuelike, a perfectly balanced pyramid turned at an angle so that we can see its mass. Her arm is resting lightly on the chair's armrest almost on the level of the frame itself, like she's sitting in a window looking out at us. The folds of her sleeves and her gently folded hands are remarkably realistic and relaxed. The typical Leonardo landscape shows distance by getting hazier and hazier.

The overall mood is one of balance and serenity, but there's also an element of mystery. Her smile and long-distance beauty are subtle and elusive, tempting but always just out of reach, like strands of a street singer's melody drifting through the Métro tunnel. *Mona* doesn't knock your socks off, but she winks at the patient viewer.
• *Backtrack through the Grand Gallery and take a left into the Salle des Etats...*

Titian—*Pastoral Symphony* (*Le Concert Champêtre*)

Venus enters the Renaissance in this colorful work by Titian the Venetian (they rhyme). The nymph turning toward the well at left is like a Titian reconstruction of the *Venus de Milo*, but what a difference! The Greek Venus was cold and virginal, but these babes are hot, voluptuous, sensual. The two couples are "making music," if you catch my drift.

The three figures on the grass form a pyramid, giving the scene a balanced, classical beauty, but this appeals more to the senses than to the mind. The golden glow of the skin, the ample flesh, and the hazy outlines became the standard of female nudes for centuries. French painters, especially, learned from Titian's rich colors and sensual beauty.
• *The huge canvas at the far end of the Salle des Etats is...*

Veronese—*Marriage at Cana*

Stand 10 steps away from this enormous canvas to where it just fills your field of vision, and suddenly... you're in a party! Pull

up a glass of wine. This
is the Renaissance love
of beautiful things gone
hog-wild. Venetian
artists like Veronese
painted the good life of
rich, happy-go-lucky
Venetian merchants.

In a spacious set-
ting of Renaissance
architecture, we see
colorful lords and ladies decked out in their fanciest duds, feasting
on a great spread of food and drink while the musicians fuel the
fires of good fun. Servants prepare and serve the food, jesters play,
and animals roam. In the upper left, a dog and his master look on.
A sturdy linebacker in yellow pours wine out of a jug, while nearby a ferocious cat battles a lion. The man in white samples some
wine and thinks, "Hmm, not bad." The wedding couple at the
far left is almost forgotten.

Believe it or not, this is a religious work showing the wedding
celebration where Jesus turned water into wine. And there's Jesus
in the dead center of 130 frolicking figures, wondering if maybe
wine coolers might not have been a better choice. With true
Renaissance optimism, Venetians pictured Christ as a party animal,
someone who loved the created world as much as they did.

Now, let's hear it for the band! On bass—the bad cat with
the funny hat—Titian the Venetian! And joining him on viola—
Crazy Veronese!

• *Exit behind the* Marriage at Cana *into the Salle Denon. The dramatic
Romantic room is to your left, and the grand neoclassical room is to your
right. They feature the most exciting French canvases in the Louvre.
In the neoclassical room, kneel before the largest canvas in the Louvre.*

FRENCH PAINTING—
NEOCLASSICAL (1780–1850)

J. L. David—*The Coronation of Napoleon*

France's last kings lived in a fantasy world, far out of touch with
the hard lives of their subjects. Then the people revolted, and this
decadent world was decapitated—along with the head of state,
Louis XVI. Then, after a decade of floundering under an ineffi-
cient revolutionary government, France was united by a charismatic, brilliant, temperamental upstart general who kept his feet
on the ground, his eyes on the horizon, and his hand in his coat—
Napoleon Bonaparte.

Napoleon quickly conquered most of Europe and insisted on being made emperor (not merely king) of this "New Rome." He staged an elaborate coronation ceremony in Paris. The painter David (dah-veed) recorded it for posterity.

We see Napoleon holding aloft the crown—the one we saw in the Apollo Gallery. He has just made his wife, Josephine, the empress, and she kneels at his feet. Seated behind Napoleon is the pope, who journeyed from Rome to place the imperial crown on his

 head. But Napoleon felt that no one was worthy of the task. At the last moment, he shrugged the pope aside, grabbed the crown, held it up for all to see . . . and crowned himself. The pope looks p.o.'d.

The radiant woman in the gallery in the background center wasn't actually there. Napoleon's mother couldn't make it to see her boy become the most powerful man in Europe, but he had her painted in anyway. (There's a key on the frame telling who's who in the picture.)

The traditional place of French coronations was the ultra-Gothic Notre-Dame cathedral. But Napoleon wanted a setting that would reflect the glories of Greece and the grandeur of Rome. So interior decorators erected stage sets of Greek columns and Roman arches to give the cathedral the architectural political correctness you see in this painting. (The *Pietà* statue on the right edge of the painting is still in Notre-Dame today.)

David was the new republic's official painter and propagandist, in charge of costumes, flags, and so on for all public ceremonies and spectacles. (Find his self-portrait with curly gray hair in the *Coronation*, way up in the second balcony, directly above Napoleon's crown.) His "neoclassical" style influenced French fashion. Take a look at his *Madame Juliet Récamier* portrait on the opposite wall, showing a modern Parisian woman in ancient garb and Pompeii hairstyle reclining on a Roman couch. Nearby paintings, such as *The Death of Socrates* and the *Oath of the Horatii (Le Serment des Horaces)*, are fine examples of neoclassicism, with Greek subjects, patriotic sentiment, and a clean, simple style.

Ingres—*La Grande Odalisque*
Take *Venus de Milo*, turn her around, lay her down, and stick a hash pipe next to her and you have the *Grande Odalisque*. OK,

maybe you'd have to add a vertebra or two.

Using clean, polished, sculptural lines, Ingres (ang-gruh, with a soft "gruh") exaggerates the S-curve of a standing Greek nude. As in the *Venus de Milo*, rough folds of cloth set off her smooth skin. The face, too, has a touch of *Venus*' idealized features (or like Raphael's kindergarten teacher), taking nature and improving on it. Contrast the cool colors of this statuelike nude with Titian's golden girls. Ingres preserves *Venus*' backside for posterior—I mean, posterity.
• *Cross back through the Salle Denon and into a room gushing with . . .*

ROMANTICISM (1800–1850)

Géricault—*The Raft of the Medusa* (*Le Radeau de la Méduse*)

Not every artist was content to copy the simple, unemotional style of the Golden Age Greeks. Like the ancient Hellenists, they wanted to express motion and emotion. In the artistic war between hearts and minds, the heart style was known as Romanticism. It was the complete flip side of neoclassicism, though they both, flourished in the early 1800s.

What better setting for an emotional work than a shipwreck? This painting was based on the actual sinking of the ship *Medusa* off the coast of Africa. The survivors barely did, floating in open seas on a raft, suffering hardship and hunger, even resorting to cannibalism—all the exotic elements for a painter determined to shock the public and arouse its emotions.

That painter was young Géricault (zher-ee-ko). He'd honed his craft sketching dead bodies in the morgue and the twisted faces of lunatics in asylums. Here he paints a tangle of bodies and lunatics sprawled over each other. The scene writhes with agitated, ominous motion—the ripple of muscles, churning clouds, and choppy seas. On the right is a deathly green corpse sprawled overboard. In the face of the man at left cradling a dead body, we see the despair of spending weeks stranded in the middle of nowhere.

But wait. There's a stir in the crowd. Someone has spotted something. The bodies rise up in a pyramid of hope culminating in a waving flag. They wave frantically, trying to catch the attention of the tiny ship on the horizon, their last desperate hope...which did finally save them. Géricault uses rippling movement and powerful colors to catch us up in the excitement. If art controls your heartbeat, this is a masterpiece.

Delacroix—*Liberty Leading the People* (*La Liberté Guidant le Peuple*)

France is the symbol of modern democracy. The French weren't the first to adopt it (Americans were), nor are they the best working example of it, but they've had to work harder to achieve it than any other country. No sooner would they throw one king or dictator out than they'd get another. They're now working on their fifth republic.

In this painting, the year is 1830. The Parisians have taken to the streets once again to fight royalist oppressors. There's a hard-bitten proletarian with a sword (far left), an intellectual with a top hat and a sawed-off shotgun, and even a little boy brandishing pistols.

Leading them on through the smoke and over the dead and dying is the figure of Liberty, a strong woman waving the French flag. Does this symbol of victory look familiar? It's the *Winged Victory*, wingless and topless.

To stir our emotions, Delacroix (del-ah-kwah) uses only three major colors—the red, white, and blue of the French flag.

This symbol of freedom is a fitting tribute to the Louvre, the first museum ever opened to the common rabble of humanity. The good things in life don't belong only to a small wealthy part of society, but to everyone. The motto of France is "Liberté, Egalité, Fraternité"—liberty, equality, and the brotherhood of all.

• *Exit the room at the far end (past the café) and go downstairs, where you'll bump into the bum of a large, twisting male nude looking like he's just waking up after a thousand-year nap.*

Michelangelo Buonarotti—*Slaves*, c. 1513

These two statues by earth's greatest sculptor are a fitting end to this museum—works that bridge the ancient and modern worlds. Michelangelo, like his fellow Renaissance artists, learned from the Greeks. The perfect anatomy, twisting poses, and idealized faces look like they could have been done 2,000 years earlier.

The so-called *Dying Slave* (also called the Sleeping Slave, who looks like he should be stretched out on a sofa) twists listlessly against his T-shirt-like bonds, revealing his smooth skin. Compare the polished detail of the rippling, bulging left arm with the sketchy details of the face and neck. With Michelangelo, the body does the talking. This is probably the most sensual nude ever done by the master of the male body.

The *Rebellious Slave* fights against his bondage. His shoulders turn one way while his head and leg turn the other, straining to get free. He even seems to be trying to free himself from the rock he's made of. Michelangelo said that his purpose was to carve away the marble to reveal the figures God put inside. This *Slave* shows the agony of that process and the ecstasy of the result.

• Finished? I am. *Où est la sortie?*

ORSAY
TOUR

paris

The Musée d'Orsay (mew-zay dor-say) houses French art of the 1800s (specifically, art from 1848–1914), picking up where the Louvre leaves off. For us, that means Impressionism, the art of sun-dappled fields, bright colors, and crowded Parisian cafés. The Orsay houses the best general collection of Manet, Monet, Renoir, Degas, van Gogh, Cézanne, and Gauguin anywhere. If you like Impressionism, visit this museum. If you don't like Impressionism, visit this museum. I personally find it a more enjoyable and rewarding place than the Louvre. Sure, ya gotta see *Mona* and *Venus de Milo*, but after you get your gottas out of the way, enjoy the Orsay.

Orientation

In the summer of 2002, the main entry to the Orsay will re-open after renovation. Until then, visitors are admitted through a temporary entry facing the river. Because of this renovation, some paintings described in this tour (generally only those on the ground floor) may be moved to a new location. If you can't find a particular painting, ask a room guard.

Cost: €7; €5 after 16:15, on Sun, and for ages 18 to 25; free for youth under 18 and for anyone first Sun of month; covered by museum pass. Tickets are good all day. Museum-pass holders can enter to the left of the main entrance (during the renovation, they can walk to the front of the line and show their passes).

Hours: June 20–Sept 20 Tue–Sun 09:00–18:00, Sept 21–June 19 Tue–Sat 10:00–18:00, Sun 09:00–18:00, Thu until 21:45 all year, closed Mon. Last entrance is 45 minutes before closing. Galleries start closing 30 minutes early. Note: The Orsay is crowded on Tue, when the Louvre is closed.

Getting There: Above the RER-C stop called Musée d'Orsay.

The nearest Métro stop is Solferino, three blocks south of the Orsay. Bus #69 from the Marais and rue Cler neighborhoods stops at the museum on the river side (Quai Anatole France). From the Louvre, it's a lovely 15-minute walk through the Tuileries and across the river on the pedestrian bridge to the Orsay. Taxis wait in front of the museum on Quai Anatole France.

Information: The booth near the entrance gives free floor plans in English (tel. 01 40 49 48 48).

Photography: Photography without a flash is allowed.

Cuisine Art: The elegant second-floor restaurant has a pricey but fine buffet and salad bar. A simple fourth-floor café is sandwiched between the Impressionists.

Length of Our Tour: Two hours.

Orsay Tours: English-language tours usually run daily (except Sun) at 11:30. The 90-minute tours cost €5.50 and are available on audioguide (€5). Tours focusing on the Impressionists are offered Tuesdays at 14:30 and Thursdays at 18:30 (in English, €5.50). I recommend the free, self-guided tour described below.

Starring: Manet, Monet, Renoir, Degas, van Gogh, Cézanne, and Gauguin.

❋ *Gare d'Orsay: The Old Train Station*

• *Pick up a free English map upon entering, buy your ticket, and check your bag. Belly up to the stone balustrade overlooking the main floor and orient yourself.*

Trains used to run right under our feet down the center of the gallery. This former train station, or *gare*, barely escaped the wrecking ball in the 1970s when the French realized it'd be a great place to house their enormous collections of 19th-century art scattered throughout the city.

The main floor has early 19th-century art (as usual, Conservative on the right, Realism on the left). Upstairs (not visible from here) is the core of the collection—the Impressionist rooms. Finally, we'll end the tour with "the other Orsay" on the mezzanine level. Clear as Seine water? *Bon.*

THE ORSAY'S 19TH "CENTURY" (1848–1914)

Einstein and Geronimo. Abraham Lincoln and Karl Marx. The train, the bicycle, the horse and buggy, the automobile, and the balloon. Freud and Dickens. Darwin's *Origin of Species* and the

──── ORSAY GROUND FLOOR—OVERVIEW ────

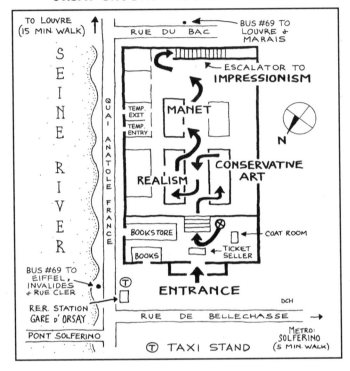

Church's Immaculate Conception. Louis Pasteur and Billy the Kid. V. I. Lenin and Ty Cobb.

The 19th century was a mix of old and new side by side. Europe was entering the modern Industrial Age, with cities, factories, rapid transit, instant communication, and global networks. At the same time, it clung to the past with traditional, rural—almost medieval—attitudes and morals.

According to the Orsay, the "19th century" began in 1848 with the socialist and democratic revolutions (Marx's *Communist Manifesto*). It ended in 1914 with the pull of an assassin's trigger, igniting World War I and ushering in the modern world.

The museum shows art that is also both old and new, conservative and revolutionary. We'll start with the Conservatives and early rebels on the ground floor, then head upstairs to see how a few visionary young artists bucked the system and revolutionized the art world, paving the way for the 20th century.

• *Walk down the steps to the main floor, a gallery filled with statues.*

Conservative Art

No, this isn't ancient Greece. These statues are from the same century as the Theory of Relativity. It's the Conservative art of the French schools that was so popular throughout the 19th century. It was popular because it's beautiful. The balanced poses, the perfect anatomy and sweet faces, the curving lines, the gleaming white stone—all this is very beautiful. (I'll be bad-mouthing it later, but for now appreciate the exquisite craftsmanship of this "perfect" art.)
• *Take your first right into the small Room 1, marked "Ingres." Look for a nude woman with a pitcher of water.*

Ingres—*The Source* (*La Source*)

Let's start where the Louvre left off. Ingres (ang-gruh, with a soft "gruh"), whelp cap the Louvre collection, championed a neoclassical style. *The Source* is virtually a Greek statue on canvas. Like *Venus de Milo*, she's a balance of opposite motions—her hips tilt one way, her breasts the other; one arm goes up, the other down; the fluid curve of her body is matched by the water falling from the pitcher.

Ingres worked on this over the course of 35 years and considered it his "image of perfection." Famous in its day, *The Source* influenced many artists whose classical statues and paintings are in the Orsay gallery.

In this and the next few rooms, you'll see more of these visions of idealized beauty—nude women in languid poses, Greek myths, and so on. The "Romantics," like Delacroix, added bright colors, movement, and emotion to the classical coolness of Ingres.
• *Walk uphill (quickly, this is background stuff) to the last room, with a pastel blue-green painting.*

Cabanel—*Birth of Venus* (*Naissance de Venus*)

This goddess is a perfect fantasy, an orgasm of beauty. The Love Queen stretches back seductively, recently birthed from the ephemeral foam of the wave. This is art of a pre-Freudian society, when sex was dirty and mysterious and had to be exalted into a more pure and divine form. The sex drive was channeled into an acute sense of beauty. French folk would literally swoon in ecstasy before these works of art.

Get a feel for the ideal beauty and refined emotion of these Greek-style works. You'll find a statue with a pose similar to Venus' back out in the gallery. Go ahead, swoon. If it feels good, enjoy it.

• *Now, take a mental cold shower, grab a bench in the main gallery of statues, and read on.*

Academy and Salon

Who liked this stuff? The art world was dominated by two conservative institutions: The Academy (the state art school) and the Salon, where works were exhibited to the buying public.

Now let's literally cross over to the "wrong side of the tracks," to the art of the early rebels.

• *Head back toward the entrance and turn right into Room 4, marked "Daumier" (opposite the Ingres room).*

REALISM—EARLY REBELS

Daumier—36 Caricature Busts (Ventre Legislatif)

This is a liberal's look at the stuffy bourgeois establishment that controlled the Academy and the Salon. In these 36 bustlets, Daumier, trained as a political cartoonist, exaggerates each

subject's most distinct characteristic to capture with vicious precision the pomposity and self-righteousness of these self-appointed arbiters of taste. The labels next to the busts give the name of the person being caricatured, his title or job (most were members of the French parliament), and an insulting nickname (like "gross, fat, and satisfied" and Monsieur "Platehead"). Give a few nicknames yourself. Can you find Reagan, Clinton, Yeltsin, Thatcher, and Gingrich?

These people hated what you're about to see. Their prudish faces tightened as their fantasy world was shattered by the Realists.

• *Go uphill four steps and through a few Romantic and pastoral rooms to the final room, #6.*

Millet—*The Gleaners* (*Les Glaneuses*)

Millet (mee-yay) shows us three gleaners, the poor women who pick up the meager leavings after a field has already been harvested by the wealthy. Millet grew up on a humble farm. He didn't attend the Academy and hated the uppity Paris art scene. Instead of idealized

── CONSERVATIVE ART & EARLY REALISM ──

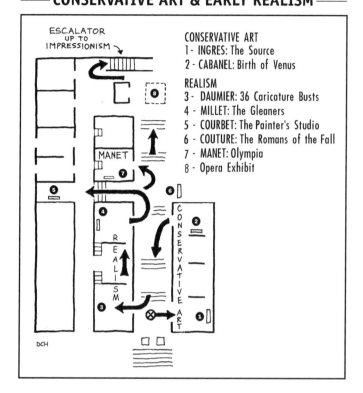

ESCALATOR
UP TO
IMPRESSIONISM

MANET

REALISM

CONSERVATIVE ART

DCH

CONSERVATIVE ART
1 - INGRES: The Source
2 - CABANEL: Birth of Venus

REALISM
3 - DAUMIER: 36 Caricature Busts
4 - MILLET: The Gleaners
5 - COURBET: The Painter's Studio
6 - COUTURE: The Romans of the Fall
7 - MANET: Olympia
8 - Opera Exhibit

gods, goddesses, nymphs, and winged babies, he painted simple rural scenes. He was strongly affected by the Revolution of 1848, with its affirmation of the working class. Here he captures the innate dignity of these stocky, tanned women who work quietly in a large field for their small reward.

This is "Realism" in two senses. It's painted "real"-istically, unlike the prettified pastels of Cabanel's *Birth of Venus*. And it's the "real" world—not the fantasy world of Greek myth, but the harsh life of the working poor.

• *Swoon briefly back out into the main gallery and hang a U-turn left, climbing the steps to a large alcove with two huge canvases. On the left . . .*

Courbet—*The Painter's Studio* (*L'Atelier du Peintre*)

In an age when "Realist painter" was equated with "bomb-throwing Socialist," it took great courage to buck the system. Rejected by the so-called experts, Courbet (coor-bay) held his own one-man exhibit. He built a shed in the middle of Paris, defiantly hung his art out, and basically "mooned" the shocked public.

Here we see Courbet himself in his studio, working diligently on a Realistic landscape, oblivious to the confusion around him. Looking on are ordinary citizens (not Greek heroes), a nude model (not a goddess but a woman), and a little boy with an adoring look on his face. Perhaps it's Courbet's inner child admiring the artist who sticks to his guns, whether it's popular or not.

• *Return to the main gallery. Back across the tracks, the huge canvas you see is...*

Couture—*The Romans of the Fall* (*Les Romains de la Décadence*)

We see a *fin de siècle* (end-of-century) society that's stuffed with too much luxury, too much classical beauty, too much pleasure; it's wasted, burned-out, and in decay. The old, backward-looking order was about to be slapped in the face.

• *Continue up the gallery, then left into Room 14 ("Manet, avant 1870"). Find the reclining nude.*

Manet—*Olympia*

"This brunette is thoroughly ugly. Her face is stupid, her skin cadaverous. All this clash of colors is stupefying." So wrote a critic when Edouard Manet's nude hung in the Salon. The public hated it, attacking Manet (man-nay) in print and literally attacking the canvas.

Think back on Cabanel's painting, *The Birth of Venus*—an idealized, pastel, Vaseline-on-the-lens beauty. Cabenel's nude was soft-core pornography, the kind you see selling lingerie and perfume. The public lapped it up (and Napoleon III purchased it).

Manet's nude doesn't gloss over anything. The pose is classic, used by Titian, Goya, and countless others. But the sharp outlines

and harsh, contrasting colors are
new and shocking. Her hand is a
clamp, and her stare is shockingly
defiant, with not a hint of the
seductive, hey-sailor look of most
nudes. This prostitute, ignoring
the flowers sent by her last customer, looks out to us as if to say,
"next." Manet replaced soft-core
porn with hard-core art.

Manet had an upper-class upbringing, some formal art
training, and he had been accepted by the Salon. He could have
cranked out pretty nudes and been a successful painter. Instead, he
surrounded himself with a group of young artists experimenting
with new techniques. With his reputation and strong personality,
he was their master, though he learned equally from them. Let the
Impressionist revolution begin.

• *Continue to the end of the gallery, where you'll walk on a glass floor
over a model of the city, ending up in front of a model of the Opera.*

Opera Exhibit

Expand to 100 times your size and hover over a scale model section of the city. There's the 19th-century Garnier Opéra House,
with its green roof in a diamond-shaped block in the center.

You'll also see a cross-section model of the Opera House.
You'd enter from the right end, buy your ticket in the foyer, then
move into the entrance hall with its grand staircase, where you could
see and be seen by *tout* Paris. At curtain time, you'd find your seat
in the golden auditorium, topped by a glorious painted ceiling. (The
current ceiling, done by Marc Chagall, is even more wonderful than
the model; for information on visiting the actual opera house, see
page 42). Notice that the stage is as big as the seating area, with
elaborate riggings to raise and lower scenery. Nearby, there are
models of set designs from some famous productions. These days,
Parisians enjoy their Verdi and Gounod at the modern opera house
at place Bastille.

• *Behind the Opéra model (go left around model), a covered escalator
leads to the often-crowded Impressionist rooms. To take a break and read
ahead, consider wandering to the quiet far left corner of the ground floor,
where you'll find a huge painting of a hot-air balloonist's-eye view of
pre–Eiffel Tower Paris (c. 1855).*

*Ride the escalator to the top floor. Take your first left for a com-
manding view of the Orsay. The second left takes you between a bookshop
and a giant "backwards" clock to the art.*

The Impressionist collection is scattered somewhat randomly through the next 10 or so rooms. Shadows dance and the displays mingle. You'll find nearly all of these paintings, but exactly where they're hung is a lot like their brushwork . . . delightfully sloppy. (If you don't see a described painting, move on. It's either hung farther down or on holiday.) Now, let there be light.

IMPRESSIONISM

The camera threatened to make artists obsolete. A painter's original function was to record reality faithfully, like a journalist. Now a machine could capture a better likeness faster than you could say Etch-a-Sketch.

But true art is more than just painting reality. It gives us reality from the artist's point of view, putting a personal stamp on the work. It records not only the scene—a camera can do that—but the artist's impressions of the scene. Impressions are often fleeting, so you have to work quickly.

The Impressionist painters rejected camera-like detail for a quick style more suited to capturing the passing moment. Feeling stifled by the rigid rules and stuffy atmosphere of the Academy, the Impressionists took as their motto, "out of the studio, into the open air." They grabbed their berets and scarves and took excursions to the country, setting up their easels on riverbanks and hillsides or sketching in cafés and dance halls. Gods, goddesses, nymphs, and fantasy scenes were out; common people and rural landscapes were in.

The quick style and simple subjects were ridiculed and called childish by the "experts." Rejected by the Salon, the Impressionists staged their own exhibition in 1874. They brashly took their name from an insult thrown at them by a critic who laughed at one of Monet's "Impression"s of a sunrise. During the next decade, they exhibited their own work independently. The public, opposed at first, was slowly drawn in by the simplicity, the color, and the vibrancy of Impressionist art.

Impressionism—Manet, Degas, Monet, Renoir

Light! Color! Vibrations! You don't hang an Impressionist canvas— you tether it. Impressionism features light colors, easygoing open-air scenes, spontaneity, broad brushstrokes, and the play of light.

The Impressionists made their canvases shimmer by a simple but revolutionary technique. If you mix, say, red, yellow, and blue together, you'll get brown, right? But Impressionists didn't bother to mix them. They'd slap a thick brushstroke of yellow down, then a stroke of green next to it, then red next to that. Up close, all you see are the three messy strokes, but as you back up . . . *voilà!* Brown! The colors blend in the eye at a distance. But while your

─── EARLY IMPRESSIONISM ───

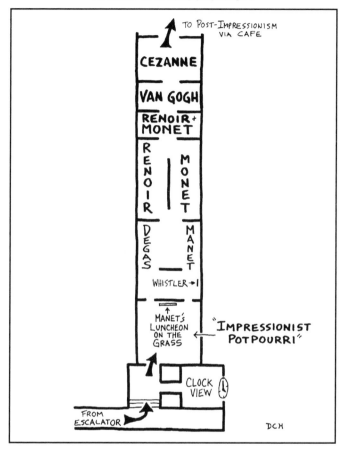

TO POST-IMPRESSIONISM
VIA CAFE

CEZANNE

VAN GOGH

RENOIR +
MONET

R
E
N
O
I
R

M
O
N
E
T

D
E
G
A
S

M
A
N
E
T

WHISTLER → |

↑
MANET'S
LUNCHEON
ON THE
GRASS

"IMPRESSIONIST
POTPOURRI"

CLOCK
VIEW

FROM
ESCALATOR

DCH

eye is saying "bland brown," your subconscious is shouting, "Red! Yellow! Blue! Yes!"

There are no lines in nature. Yet someone in the classical tradition (Ingres, for example) would draw an outline of his subject, then fill it in with color. But the Impressionists built a figure with dabs of paint... a snowman of color.

Manet—*Luncheon on the Grass* (*Le Déjeuner sur l'Herbe*)

Manet really got a rise out of people with this one. Once again the public judged the painting on moral terms rather than artistic ones. What are these scantily clad women doing with these fully clothed

men, they wondered? Or rather, what will they be doing after the last baguette is eaten?

A new revolutionary movement is budding: Impressionism. Notice the messy brushwork of the trees and leaves in the background, and the play of light on the pond in back and filtering through the trees onto the hazy woman stooping behind. And the strong contrasting colors (white skin, black clothes, green grass). And the fact that this is a true out-of-doors painting, not a studio production. The first shot had been fired.

Whistler—*Whistler's Mother* (*Portrait de la Mère de l'Auteur*)

Why so famous? I don't know either. It shouldn't be, of course, but it is. Perhaps because it's by an American, and we see in his mother some of the monumental solidity of our own ancestral moms made tough by pioneering the American wilderness.

Or perhaps because it was so starkly different in its day. In a roomful of golden goddesses, it'd stand out like a fish in a tree. The experts hated it and didn't understand it. (If music is the fear of silence, is art the fear of reality?) The subtitle is "Arrangement in Gray and Black," and the whole point is the subtle variations on dark shades softened by the rosy tint of her cheeks, but the critics kept waiting for it to come out in Colorization.

Degas—*The Dance Class* (*La Classe de Danse*)

Clearly, Degas loved dance and the theater. (Also catch his statue, *Tiny Dancer, 14 Years Old*, in the glass case.) The play of stage lights off his dancers, especially the halos of ballet skirts, is made to order for an Impressionist.

Edgar Degas (day-gah) was a rich kid from a family of bankers who got the best classical-style art training. Adoring Ingres' pure lines and cool colors, he painted in the Conservative style. His work was exhibited in the Salon. He gained success and a good reputation, and then... he met the Impressionists.

Degas blends classical lines with Impressionist color and spontaneity. His dancers have outlines, and he's got them in a classic 3-D setting—with the floor lines slanting to the upper right.

So why is Degas an Impressionist? First off, he's captured a candid, fleeting moment, a momentary "impression"—the dancers are tired and bored, at the tail end of a long rehearsal. Look at the girl on the left scratching her back restlessly, and the cuddly little bundle of dog in the foreground. Degas loved the unposed "snapshot" effect, catching his models off guard.

Finally, he's got that Impressionistic "fury" of the brush. In *The Dance Class*, look at the bright green bow on the girl with her back to us. Not only are the outlines sketchy, but see how he slopped green paint onto her dress and didn't even say, "*Excusez-moi.*"

Degas—*The Glass of Absinthe (Au Café, dit L'Absinthe)*

Degas hung out with low-life Impressionists discussing art, love, and life in the cheap cafés and bars in Montmartre (the original Bohemia-ville). He painted Impressionistic snapshots of everyday people. Here a weary lady of the evening meets morning with a last lonely coffin-nail drink in the glaring light of a four-in-the-morning café. The pale-green drink forming the center of the composition is that toxic substance, absinthe, that fueled many artists and burned out many more.

Look across the room at some later works by Manet. The old dog was learning new tricks from his former disciples.

• *The next rooms feature works by two Impressionist masters at their peak, Monet and Renoir. You're looking at the quintessence of Impressionism.*

Monet—*La Gare St. Lazare*

Claude Monet (mo-nay) is the father of Impressionism. He learned from Manet (*a* before *o*) but

quickly went beyond even Manet's shocking slabs of colors. Monet fully explored the possibilities of open-air painting and lighter, brighter colors.

He could even make this drab train station glow with reflected light. The sun diffuses through the skylight and mingles with the steam from the engine. The yellow buildings in the background merge with the blue smoke in the foreground to illuminate an otherwise colorless scene.

Stand a good six feet from the canvas and look at the tall building with the slanted Mansard roof behind the station. Looks fine? Now get close up. At six inches, it's a confusing pile of color blobs. And the smoke is truly "thick." Light on!

Monet—*The Cathedral of Rouen* (*La Cathédrale de Rouen*)

Monet went to Rouen, rented a room across from the cathedral, set up his easel...and waited. He wanted to catch "a series of differing impressions" of the cathedral facade at different times of day and year. He often had several canvases going at once. In all, he did 30 canvases, and each is unique. The time-lapse series shows the sun passing slowly across the sky, creating different-colored light and shadows. These five are labeled: in the morning, in gray weather, morning sun, full view, full sunlight.

As Monet zeroes in on the play of colors and light, the physical subject—the cathedral—is dissolving. It has become only a rack upon which to hang the light and color. Later artists would boldly throw away the rack, leaving purely abstract modern art in its place.

Monet—Paintings from Monet's Garden at Giverny

One of Monet's favorite places to paint was the garden of his home in Giverny, west of Paris (and worth a visit if you like Monet more than you hate crowds; see page 245).

You'll find several different views of it, along with the painter's self-portrait. The *Blue Water Lilies* is similar to the large and famous water lily paintings in the nearby L'Orangerie Museum (scheduled to re-open sometime in 2002, see page 184), across the river in the Tuileries Gardens.

Renoir—*Dance at the Moulin de la Galette* (*Bal du Moulin de la Galette*)

On Sunday afternoons, working-class folk would dress up and head for the fields on Butte Montmartre (near Sacré-Coeur church) to dance, drink, and eat little cakes (*galettes*) till dark.

Renoir (ren-wah) liked to go there to paint the common Parisians living and loving in the afternoon sun. The sunlight filtering through the trees creates a kaleidoscope of colors, like a 19th-century mirrored ball throwing darts of light on the dancers.

This dappled light is the "impression" that Renoir came away with. He captures it with quick blobs of yellow. Look at the sun-dappled straw hat (right of center) and the glasses (lower right). Smell the powder on the ladies' faces. The painting glows with bright colors. Even the shadows on the ground, which should be gray or black, are colored a warm blue. As if having a good time were required, even the shadows are caught up in the mood, dancing. Like a photographer who uses a slow shutter speed to show motion, Renoir paints a waltzing blur.

Renoir—*The City Dance/The Country Dance* (*La Danse à la Ville/La Danse à la Campagne*)

In contrast to Monet's haze of colors, Renoir clung to the more traditional technique of drawing a clear outline, then filling it in.

This two-panel "series" by Renoir shows us his exquisite draftsmanship, sense of beauty, and smoother brushwork. Like Degas, Renoir had classical training and exhibited at the Salon.

Renoir's work is lighthearted with light colors, almost pastels. He seems to be searching for an ideal, the pure beauty we saw on the ground floor. In later years he used more and more red tones, as if trying for even more warmth.

• *On the divider in the center of the room, you'll find...*

Pissarro and Others

We've neglected many of the founders of the Impressionist style. Browse around and discover your own favorites. Pissarro is one of mine. His grainy landscapes are more subtle and subdued than the flashy Monet and Renoir, but, as someone said, "He did for the earth what Monet did for the water."

You may find the painting *Young Girl in the Garden* (*Jeune*

Fille en Jardin) with a pastel style as pretty as Renoir's. It's by Mary Cassatt, an American who was attracted to the strong art magnet that was, and still is, Paris.
• *Take a break. Look at the Impressionist effect of the weather on the Paris skyline. Notice the skylight above you—these Impressionist rooms are appropriately lit by ever-changing natural light. Then carry on . . .*

POST-IMPRESSIONISM

Take a word, put "-ism" on the end, and you've become an intellectual. Commune-ism, sex-ism, cube-ism, computer-ism . . . Post-Impression-ism.

"Post-Impressionism" is an artificial and clumsy concept to describe those painters who used Impressionist techniques after Monet and Renoir. It might just as well be called something like "Premodernism," because it bridged Impressionism with the 20th century . . . or you could call it bridge-ism.
• *The Orsay's Post-Impressionist collection (we'll see van Gogh, Cézanne, Gauguin, Rousseau, Seurat, and Toulouse-Lautrec) flip-flops back and forth between here and the end of this gallery. Be prepared to skip around.*

Van Gogh

Impressionists have been accused of being "light"-weights. The colorful style lends itself to bright country scenes, gardens, sunlight on the water, and happy crowds of simple people. It took a remarkable genius to add profound emotion to the Impressionist style.

Vincent van Gogh (van-go, or van-HOCK to the Dutch and the snooty) was the son of a Dutch minister. He too felt a religious calling, and he spread the gospel among the poorest of the poor—peasants and miners. When he turned to painting, he channeled this same spiritual intensity into his work. Like Michelangelo, Beethoven, Rembrandt, Wayne Newton, and a select handful of others, he put so much of himself into his work that art and life became one. In this room you'll see both van Gogh's painting style and his life unfold.

Van Gogh—*Peasant* (*Paysanne près de l'Atre*)

As a young man, van Gogh left his steady clerking job to work with poor working people in overcast Belgium and Holland. He painted these hardworking, dignified folks in a crude, dark style reflecting the oppressiveness of their lives . . . and the loneliness of his own as he roamed northern Europe in search of a calling.

Van Gogh—*Self-Portrait, Paris* (*Portraite de l'Artiste*), 1887

Encouraged by his art-dealer brother, van Gogh moves to Paris

POST-IMPRESSIONISM

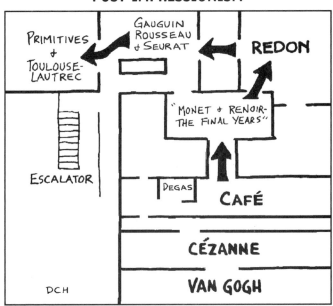

PRIMITIVES + TOULOUSE-LAUTREC

GAUGUIN ROUSSEAU + SEURAT

REDON

"MONET + RENOIR- THE FINAL YEARS"

ESCALATOR

DEGAS

CAFÉ

CÉZANNE

VAN GOGH

DCH

and, *voilà!* The color! He meets Monet and hobnobs with Gauguin and Toulouse-Lautrec. He rents a room in Montmartre, learning the Impressionist style. (See how he builds a bristling brown beard using thick strokes of reds and greens side by side.)

At first he paints like the others, but soon he develops his own style. By using thick, swirling brush strokes, he infuses life into even inanimate objects. Van Gogh's brush strokes curve and thrash around like a garden hose pumped with wine.

Van Gogh—*Midday (La Méridienne)*, 1890, based on a painting by Millet
The social life of Paris becomes too much for the solitary van Gogh. He moves to the south of France. At first, in the glow of the bright spring sunshine, he has a

period of incredible creativity and happiness, overwhelmed by the bright colors—an Impressionist's dream. Here again we see his love of the common people taking a glowing siesta in the noon sun.

Van Gogh—*Van Gogh's Room at Arles* (*La Chambre de Van Gogh à Arles*), 1889

But being alone in a strange country begins to wear on him. An ugly man, he finds it hard to get a date. The distorted perspective of this painting makes his tiny rented room look even more cramped. He invites his friend Gauguin to join him, but after two months together arguing passionately about art, nerves get raw. Van Gogh threatens Gauguin with a knife, driving him back to Paris. In crazed despair, van Gogh mutilates his own ear.

The people of Arles realize they have a madman on their hands and convince van Gogh to seek help. He enters a mental hospital.

Van Gogh—*The Church at Auvers-sur-Oise* (*L'Eglise d'Auvers-sur-Oise*), 1890

Van Gogh's paintings done in the peace of the mental hospital are more meditative—fewer bright landscapes, more closed-in scenes

with deeper and almost surreal colors.

There's also a strong sense of mystery. What's behind this church? The sky is cobalt blue and the church's windows are also blue, like we're looking right through the church to an infinite sky. There's something mysterious lurking on the other side. You can't see it, but you feel its presence like the cold air from an approaching Métro train still hidden in the tunnel. There's a road that leads from us to the church, then splits to go behind. A choice must be made. Which way? You can actually visit this church (see Auvers-Sur-Oise, page 246).

Van Gogh—*Self-Portrait, St. Remy*, 1889

Van Gogh wavered between happiness and madness. He despaired of ever being sane enough to continue painting.

This self-portrait shows a man engulfed in a confused but beautiful world. The background brush strokes swirl and rave, setting in motion the waves of the jacket. He's caught in the current, out of control. But in the midst of this rippling sea of mystery floats a still, detached island of a face with probing, questioning, wise eyes.

Do his troubled eyes know that only a few months on he will take a pistol, and put a bullet through his chest?

Cézanne

Cézanne's art brought Impressionism into the 20th century. There's less color here, less swirling brushwork, less passion. It's cleaner, chunkier, more intellectual. Cézanne (say-zahn) can be difficult to appreciate after the warmth of Renoir, and he won't give you the fireworks of van Gogh. But he's worth the effort.

Cézanne—*Self-Portrait* (*Portrait de l'Artiste*)

Cézanne was virtually unknown and unappreciated in his lifetime. He worked alone, lived alone, and died alone, ignored by all but a few revolutionary young artists who understood his efforts.

And Cézanne couldn't draw. His brush was a blunt instrument. With it, he'd bludgeon reality into submission, drag it across a canvas, and leave it there to dry. But Cézanne the mediocre painter was a great innovator. His works are not perfected, finished products but revolutionary works-in-progress—gutter balls with wonderful spin. His work spoke for itself—which is good because, as you can see here, he had no mouth.

Cézanne—*Landscape* (*Rochers près des Grottes au dessus de Château-Noir*)

Cézanne used chunks of color as blocks to build three-dimensional forms. The rocky brown cliffs here consist of cubes of green, tan, and blue that blend at a distance to create a solid 3-D structure. It only makes sense from a distance. Try this: Start at six inches and fade back. At some point the messy slabs become reality on the rocks.

Why is this revolutionary? Past artists created the illusion of 3-D with lines (like when we draw receding lines to turn a square into a cube). The Impressionists pioneered the technique of using blobs of color, not lines, to capture a subject. But most Impressionist art is flat and two-dimensional, a wall of color like Monet's *Cathedral of Rouen* series. Cézanne went 3-D with chunks.

These chunks are like little "cubes." No coincidence that his experiments in reducing forms to their geometric basics influenced the... cubists.

Cézanne—*The Card Players* (*Les Joueurs de Cartes*)

These aren't people. They're studies in color and pattern. The subject matter—two guys playing cards—is less important than the

pleasingly balanced pattern they make on the canvas, two sloping forms framing a cylinder (a bottle) in the center. Later, abstract artists would focus solely on the shapes and colors.

Again, notice how the figures are built with chunks of color. The jacket of the player to the right consists of tans, greens, and browns. As one art scholar put it: "Cézanne confused intermingled forms and colors, achieving an extraordinarily luminous density in which lyricism is controlled by a rigorously constructed rhythm." Just what I said—chunks of color.

Cézanne—*A Modern Olympia* (*Une Moderne Olympia*)

Is this Cézanne himself paying homage to Manet? And dreaming up a new, more radical style of painting? We've come a long way since Manet's *Olympia*, which seems tame to us now.

• *Exit to the café and consider a well-deserved break. From the café, continue ahead, walking under the large green beam, following signs saying, "suite de la visite."*

A hallway leads past WCs to a dark room in the right corner...

Redon

Now flip out the lights and step into his mysterious world. If the Orsay's a zoo, this is the nocturnal house. Prowl around. This is wild, wild stuff. It's intense—imagine Richard Nixon on mushrooms playing sax.

• *Coming out of the darkness, pass into the gallery lined with metal columns containing the primitive art of Rousseau and Gauguin. Start in the first alcove to the left.*

PRIMITIVISM

Henri Rousseau—*War* (*La Guerre ou La Chevauchée de la Discorde*)

Some artists, rejecting the harried, scientific, and rational world, remembered a time before "-isms," when works of art weren't scholarly "studies in form and color" but voodoo dolls full of mystery and magic power. They learned from the art of primitive tribes in Africa and the South Seas, trying to recreate a primal Garden of Eden of peace and wholeness.

In doing so, they created another "ism": Primitivism.

One such artist was Rousseau, a man who painted like a child. He was an amateur artist who palled around with all the great painters, but they never took his naive style of art seriously.

This looks like a child's drawing of a nightmare. The images are primitive—flat and simple, with unreal colors—but the effect is both beautiful and terrifying. War in the form of a woman with a sword flies on horseback across the battlefield, leaving destruction in her wake—broken bare trees, burning clouds in the background, and heaps of corpses picked at by the birds.

Gauguin—*The Beautiful Angel* (*La Belle Angele*)

A woman in peasant dress sits in a bubble, like the halos in a medieval religious painting. Next to it is a pagan idol. This isn't

a scene but an ordered collage of images with symbolic overtones. It's left to us to make the connection.

Paul Gauguin (go-gan) learned the bright clashing colors from the Impressionists, but diverged from this path about the time van Gogh waved a knife in his face.

Gauguin simplifies. His figures are two-dimensional, with thick dark outlines filled in with basic blocks of color. He turned his back on the entire Western tradition of realism begun in the Renaissance, which tried to recreate the 3-D world on a 2-D canvas. Instead he returns to an age where figures become symbols.

Gauguin—*Arearea* (*Pleasantries*) (*Joyeusetes*)

Gauguin got the travel bug early in childhood and grew up wanting to be a sailor. Instead, he became a stockbroker. In his spare time he painted and was introduced to the Impressionist circle. At the age of 35, he got fed up with it all, quit his job, abandoned his wife (see her stern portrait bust), and took refuge in his art. He traveled to the South Seas in search of the exotic, finally settling on Tahiti.

In Tahiti, Gauguin found his Garden of Eden. He simplified

his life to the routine of eating, sleeping, and painting. He simplified his painting still more to flat images with heavy black outlines filled in with bright, pure colors. He painted the native girls in their naked innocence (so different from Cabanel's seductive *Venus*). But this simple style had a deep undercurrent of symbolic meaning.

Arearea shows native women and a dog. In the "distance" (there's no attempt at traditional 3-D here), a procession goes by with a large pagan idol. What's the connection between the idol and the foreground figures who are apparently unaware of it? Gauguin makes us dig deep down into our medulla oblongatae to make a mystical connection between the beautiful women, the dog, and religion. In primitive societies, religion permeates life. Idols, dogs, and women are holy.

Seurat—*The Circus* (*Le Cirque*)

With pointillism, Impressionism is brought to its logical conclusion—little dabs of different colors placed side by side to blend in the viewer's eye. Using only red, yellow, blue, and green points of paint, Seurat (sur-rah) creates a mosaic of colors that shimmers at a distance, capturing the wonder of the dawn of electric lights.

Toulouse-Lautrec—*The Clownesse Cha-U-Kao*

Henri de Toulouse-Lautrec was the black sheep of a noble family. At age 15 he broke both legs, which left him a cripple. Shunned by

his family, a freak to society, he felt more at home in the underworld of other outcasts— prostitutes, drunks, thieves, dancers, and actors. He painted the nightlife lowlife in the bars, cafés, dance halls, and brothels he frequented. Toulose-Lautrec died young of alcoholism.

The Clownesse Cha-U-Kao is one of his fellow freaks, a fat lady clown who made her living being laughed at. She slumps wearily after a performance, indifferent to the applause, and adjusts her dress to prepare for the curtain call.

Toulouse-Lautrec was a true "Impression"-ist, catching his models in candid poses. He worked spontaneously, never correcting his mistakes, as you can see from the blotches on her dark skirt and the unintentional yellow sash hanging down. Can you see a bit of Degas here, in the subject matter, snapshot pose, and colors?

Toulouse-Lautrec—Jane Avril Dancing

Toulouse-Lautrec hung out at the Moulin Rouge dance hall in Montmartre. One of the most popular dancers was this slim, graceful, elegant, and melancholy woman who stood out above the rabble of the Moulin Rouge. Her legs keep dancing while her mind is far away. Toulouse-Lautrec the artistocrat might have identified with her noble face—sad and weary of the nightlife, but stuck in it.

• *You've seen the essential Orsay and are permitted to cut out (the exit is straight below you). But there's an "Other Orsay" I think you'll find entertaining.*

To reach the mezzanine ("niveau median"), cross to the other side of the gallery at this level and go down three flights. In front of you is the restaurant, behind you (at the foot of the escalator) are a grand ballroom and the mezzanine (which overlooks the main floor).

Peek into the restaurant Le Salon de Thé du Musée *(or enjoy*

the €9 salad bar or a cup of coffee). This was part of the original hotel that adjoined the station (built in 1900, abandoned after 1939, condemned, and restored to the elegance you see today). Then, find the palatial room of mirrors and chandeliers, marked "Salle des Fêtes" or "Arts et Decors de la IIIème République" (Room 52).

THE "OTHER" ORSAY—MEZZANINE

The beauty of the Orsay is that it combines all the art of the 1800s (1848–1914), both modern and classical, in one building. The classical art, so popular in its own day, has been maligned and was forgotten in the 20th century. It's time for a reassessment. Is it as gaudy and gawd-awful as we've been led to believe? From our end-of-century perspective, let's take a look at the opulent, *fin de siècle*, French high society and its luxurious art.

THE "OTHER" ORSAY

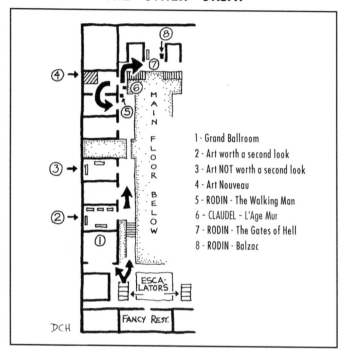

1 - Grand Ballroom
2 - Art worth a second look
3 - Art NOT worth a second look
4 - Art Nouveau
5 - RODIN - The Walking Man
6 - CLAUDEL - L'Age Mur
7 - RODIN - The Gates of Hell
8 - RODIN - Balzac

The Grand Ballroom
(*Arts et Decors de la IIIème République*)

This was one of France's most luxurious nightspots when the Orsay hotel was here. You can easily imagine gowned debutantes and white-gloved dandies waltzing the night away to the music of a chamber orchestra.

Notice:

1) The interior decorating: raspberry marble-ripple ice-cream columns, pastel ceiling painting, gold work, mirrors, and leafy strands of chandeliers.

2) The statue *Bacchante Couchée* sprawled in the middle of the room. Familiar pose? If not, you flunk this tour.

3) The statue *Aurore*, with her canopy of hair, hide-and-seek face, and silver-dollar nipples.

4) The large painting *The Birth of*

Venus (La Naissance de Venus) by William Bouguereau. Van Gogh once said: "If I painted like Bouguereau, I could hope to make money. The public will never change—they love only sweet things."

5) *La Nature*, with the only see-through veil of marble I've ever seen through.

So here's the question: Is this stuff beautiful or merely gaudy? Divine or decadent?

• *Return to the mezzanine overlooking the main gallery. Head toward the far end. Enter the first room on the left (#55).*

Art Worth a Second Look

We've seen some great art; now let's see some not-so-great art—at least, that's what modern critics tell us. This is realistic art with a subconscious kick, art from a neurotic society before Freud articulated its demons.

• *Working clockwise, you'll see . . .*

Cain

The world's first murderer, with the murder weapon still in his belt, is exiled with his family. Archaeologists had recently discovered a Neanderthal skull, so the artist shows them as a prehistoric hunter/gatherer tribe.

The Dream (*Le Rêve*)

Soldiers sleep, while visions of Gatling guns dance in their heads.

Payday (*La Paye des Moissonneurs*)

Peasants getting paid, painted by the man called "the grandson of Courbet and Millet." The subtitle of the work should be, "Is this all there is to life?"

The Excommunication of Robert Le Pieux

The bishops exit after performing the rite. The king and queen are stunned, the scepter dropped. The ritual candle has been snuffed out; it falls, fuming, echoing through the huge hall . . . . Again, is this art or only cheap theatrics?

• *Return to the mezzanine. Skip the next room, then go left into Room 59, labeled "Symbolisme."*

Art Not Worth a Second Look

The Orsay's director said: "Certainly we have bad paintings. But we have only the greatest bad paintings." And here they are.

Serenity
An idyll in the woods. Three nymphs with harps waft off to the right. These people are stoned on something.

The School of Plato (L'Ecole de Platon)
Subtitled "The Athens YMCA." A Christlike Plato surrounded by adoring, half-naked nubile youths gives new meaning to the term "Platonic relationship."

Will the pendulum shift so that one day art like *The School of Plato* becomes the new, radical avant-garde style?
• *Return to the mezzanine and continue to the far end. Enter the last room on the left (#65) and head for the far corner.*

ART NOUVEAU
The Industrial Age brought factories, row houses, machines, train stations, geometrical precision—and ugliness. At the turn of the century, some artists reacted against the unrelieved geometry of harsh, pragmatic, iron-and-steel Eiffel Tower art with a "new art"—Art Nouveau. Hmm. I think I had a driver's-ed teacher by that name.

Charpentier—Dining Room of Adrien Benard (Boiserie de la Salle à Mangé de la Propriété Benard)
Like nature, which also abhors a straight line, Art Nouveau artists used the curves of flowers and vines as their pattern. They were convinced that "practical" didn't have to mean "ugly" as well. They turned everyday household objects into art.

This wood-paneled dining room, with its organic shapes, is one of the finest examples of the Art Nouveau style (called *Jugendstil* in Germanic countries). Another is the curvy, wrought-iron work of some of Paris' early Métro entrances (some survive), built by the same man who commissioned this dining room for his home.
• *Browse through the Art Nouveau rooms to the left. You'll spill out back onto the mezzanine. Grab a seat in front of the Rodin statue of a man missing everything but his legs.*

Auguste Rodin

Rodin completes the tour—from classical sculpture to Impressionist painting to an artist who brought them both together. Rodin combined classical solidity with Impressionist surfaces to become the greatest sculptor since Michelangelo.

Rodin—*The Walking Man* (*L'Homme Qui Marche*)

This muscular, forcefully striding man could be a symbol of the Renaissance Man with his classical power. With no mouth or hands, he speaks with his body. But Rodin also learned a thing or two from the comparatively lightweight Impressionist painters. Get close and look at the statue's surface. This rough, "unfinished" look reflects light like the rough Impressionist brushwork, making the statue come alive, never quite at rest in the viewer's eye.

• *Near the far end of the mezzanine you'll see a small bronze couple* (L'Age Mur) *by Camille Claudel, a student of Rodin's.*

Claudel—*Maturity* (*L'Age Mur*)

Camille Claudel, Rodin's student and mistress, may have portrayed their doomed love affair here. A young girl desperately reaches out to an older man, who is led away reluctantly by an older woman. The center of the composition is the empty space left when their hands separate. In real life, Rodin refused to leave his wife, and Camille (see her head sticking up from a block of marble) ended up in an insane asylum.

Rodin—*The Gates of Hell* (*Porte de l'Enfer*)

Rodin worked for decades on these doors depicting Dante's Hell, and they contain some of his greatest hits, small statues that he later executed in full size. Find *The Thinker* squatting above the doorway, contemplating Man's fate. And in the lower left is the same kneeling man eating his children (*Ugolin*) you'll see in full size nearby. Rodin paid models to run, squat, leap, and spin around his studio however they wanted. When he saw an interesting pose, he'd yell, "freeze" (or "statue maker") and get out his sketch pad.

Rodin—*Balzac*

The great French novelist is given a heroic, monumental ugliness. Wrapped in a long cloak, he thrusts his head out at a defiant angle, showing the strong individualism and egoism of the 19th-century Romantic movement. Balzac is proud and snooty—but his body forms a question mark, and underneath the twisted features we can see a touch of personal pain and self-doubt. This is hardly camera-eye realism—Balzac wasn't that grotesque—but it captures a personality that strikes us even if we don't know the man.

From this perch, look over the main floor at all the classical statues between you and the big clock and realize how far we've come— not in years but in style changes. Many of the statues below—beautiful, smooth, balanced, and idealized—were done at the same time as Rodin's powerful, haunting works. Rodin is a good place to end the tour. With a stable base of 19th-century stone, he launched art into the 20th century.

POMPIDOU CENTER TOUR

paris

The Pompidou Center contains possibly Europe's best museum of 20th-century art. After the super-serious Louvre and Orsay, finish things off with this artistic kick in the pants. You won't find classical beauty here, no dreamy Madonnas-and-Children—just a stimulating, offbeat, and, if you like, instructive walk through nearly every art style of the wild and crazy last century.

Orientation

Cost: €5, covered by museum pass, 18 to 25 pay €3, under 18 and "job seekers" enter free. First Sun of the month is free. Buy tickets on ground floor. Other temporary exhibits require separate admission (or an all-day pass).

Hours: Wed–Mon 11:00–21:00, closed Tue and May 1.

Getting There: Métro: Rambuteau or Hôtel de Ville. The wild, color-coded exterior makes it about as hard to locate as the Eiffel Tower. To use the escalator to reach the museum (fourth floor), you need a ticket for the museum or a museum pass.

Information: Tel. 01 44 78 12 33, www.centrepompidou.fr. Parisians call the complex the "Centre Beaubourg" (sahn-truh boh-boor), but official publications call it the "Centre Pompidou."

Cloakroom: Ground floor.

Cuisine Art: You'll find a view restaurant on the sixth floor, a café on the mezzanine level, and a library cafeteria on second floor. This is a great café neighborhood. Across from the entrance/exit, on rue Rambuteau, is the mod and efficient Melodine self-service cafeteria.

Length of Our Tour: One hour.

Museum Tours: Audioguides cost €4.

Starring: Matisse, Picasso, Chagall, Dalí, Warhol, and contemporary art.

MODERN ART COLLECTION

The "Musée National d'Art Moderne: Collection Permanente" (what we'll see) is on the fourth floor, reached by the escalator to the left as you enter. But there's plenty more art scattered all over the building, some free, some requiring a separate ticket. Ask at the ground floor information booth or just wander.

The "permanent" collection . . . isn't. It changes so often that this chapter is intentionally general—to give you an overview.

• *Buy your ticket on the ground floor, then ride up the escalator (or run up the down escalator to get in the proper mood) to the fourth floor. When you see the view, your opinion of the Pompidou's exterior should improve a good 15 percent. Enter on the fourth floor and show your ticket. Past the ticket-checkers, hike the stairs to the fifth floor, which covers roughly 1900 to 1970. (You'll finish back here on the fourth floor, which brings us up to today.)*

The Exterior

That slight tremor you may feel comes from Italy, where Michelangelo has been spinning in his grave ever since 1977, when the Pompidou Center first revolted Paris. Still, it's an appropriate modern temple for the controversial art it houses.

The building is "exoskeletal" (like Notre-Dame or a crab), with its functional parts—the pipes, heating ducts, and escalator— on the outside, and the meaty art inside. It's the epitome of modern architecture where "form follows function."

MODERN ART FROM 1900 TO 1970 (FIFTH FLOOR)

A.D. 1900: A new century dawns. War is a thing of the past. Science will wipe out poverty and disease. Rational Man is poised at a new era of peace and prosperity . . .

Right. This cozy Victorian dream was soon shattered by two world wars and rapid technological change. Nietzsche murdered God. Darwin stripped off man's robe of culture and found a naked ape. Freud washed ashore on the beach of a vast new continent inside each of us. Einstein made every truth merely "relative." Even the fundamental building blocks of the universe, atoms, were behaving erratically.

The 20th century—accelerated by technology and fragmented by war—was exciting and chaotic, and the art reflects the turbulence of that century of change.

• *Twentieth century art resents being put in chronological order. I've described major modern art trends in a linear way, even though you'll find the rooms less orderly. Read and wander generally counterclockwise around this floor. If you don't see what you're looking for, it'll pop up later.*

POMPIDOU–FIFTH FLOOR

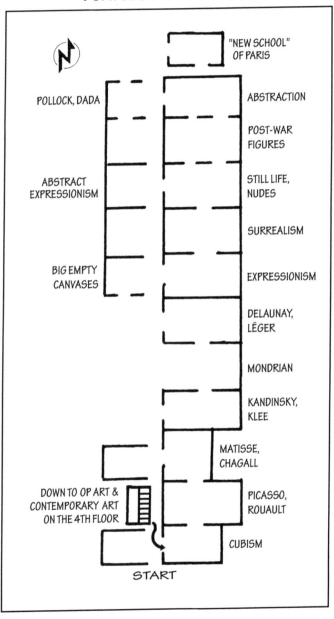

"NEW SCHOOL" OF PARIS

POLLOCK, DADA

ABSTRACTION

POST-WAR FIGURES

ABSTRACT EXPRESSIONISM

STILL LIFE, NUDES

SURREALISM

BIG EMPTY CANVASES

EXPRESSIONISM

DELAUNAY, LÉGER

MONDRIAN

KANDINSKY, KLEE

MATISSE, CHAGALL

DOWN TO OP ART & CONTEMPORARY ART ON THE 4TH FLOOR

PICASSO, ROUAULT

CUBISM

START

Cubism: Reality Shattered (1907–1912)

I throw a rock at a glass statue, shatter it, pick up the pieces, and glue them onto a canvas. I'm a Cubist.

Pablo Picasso (1881–1973) and Georges Braque (1882–1963)

Born in Spain, Picasso moved to Paris as a young man, settling into a studio (the Bateau-Lavoir) on Montmartre. He worked with next-door neighbor Georges Braque in poverty so dire they often didn't know where their next bottle of wine was coming from. They corrected each other's paintings (it's hard to tell whose is whose without the titles) and shared ideas, meals, and girlfriends while inventing a whole new way to look at the world.

They show the world through a kaleidoscope of brown and gray. The subjects are somewhat recognizable (with the help of the titles), but they're broken into geometric shards (let's call them "cubes," though there are many different shapes), then pieced back together.

Cubism gives us several different angles of the subject at once—say, a woman seen from the front and side angles simultaneously, resulting in two eyes on the same side of the nose. This involves showing three dimensions, plus Einstein's new fourth dimension, the Time it takes to walk around the subject to see other angles. Newfangled motion pictures could capture this moving, 4-D world, but how to do it on a 2-D canvas? The Cubist "solution" is a kind of Mercator projection, where the round world is sliced up like an orange peel and laid as flat as possible.

Notice how the "cubes" often overlap. A single cube might contain both an arm (in the foreground) and the window behind (in the background), both painted the same color. The foreground and background are woven together, so that the subject dissolves into a pattern.

Pablo Picasso (1881–1973): Synthetic Cubism (1912–1915) and Beyond

If the Cubists were as smart as Einstein, why couldn't they draw a picture to save their lives? Picasso was one modern artist who could draw exceptionally well (see his partly finished "Harlequin"). But he constantly explored and adapted his style to new trends, becoming the most famous painter of the century. Scattered throughout the museum are works from the many periods of Picasso's life.

Picasso soon began to use more colorful "cubes" (1912–1915). Eventually, he used curved shapes to build the subject, rather than the straight-line shards of early Cubism.

Picasso married and had children. Works from this period (the 1920s) are more realistic, with full-bodied (and big-nosed) women and children. He tries to capture the solidity, serenity, and volume of classical statues.

As his relationships with women deteriorated, he vented his sexual demons by twisting the female body into grotesque balloon-animal shapes (1925–1931).

All through his life, Picasso was exploring new materials. He made collages, tried his hand at making "statues" out of wood, wire, or whatever, and even made statues out of everyday household objects. These "multimedia" works, so revolutionary at the time, have become stock-in-trade today.

Marc Chagall (1887–1985)

Marc Chagall, at age 22, arrived in Paris with the wide-eyed wonder of a country boy. Lovers are weightless with bliss. Animals smile and wink at us. Musicians, poets, peasants, and dreamers ignore gravity, tumbling in slow-motion circles high above the rooftops. The colors are deep, dark, and earthy—a pool of mystery with figures bleeding through below the surface. (Chagall claimed his early poverty forced him to paint over used canvases, inspiring the overlapping images.)

Chagall's very personal style fuses many influences. He was raised in a small Russian village, which explains his "naive" outlook and fiddler-on-the-roof motifs. His simple figures are like Russian Orthodox icons. And his Jewish roots produce Old Testament themes. Stylistically, he's thoroughly modern—Cubist shards, bright Fauve colors, and Primitive simplification. This otherworldy style was a natural for religious works, and his murals and stained glass, with both Jewish and Christian motifs, decorate buildings around the world—including the ceiling of Paris' Garnier Opéra (Mo: Opéra).

Georges Rouault (1871–1958)

Young Georges Rouault was apprenticed to a stained-glass window maker. Enough said?

The paintings have the same thick, glowing colors, heavy black outlines, simple subjects, and (mostly) religious themes.

The style is modern, but the mood is medieval, solemn, and melancholy. Rouault captures the tragic spirit of those people—clowns, prostitutes, and sons of God—who have been made outcasts by society.

Henri Matisse (1869–1954)

Matisse's colorful "wallpaper" works are not realistic. A man is a few black lines and blocks of paint. The colors are unnaturally bright. There's no illusion of the distance and 3-D that were so important to Renaissance Italians. The "distant" landscape is as bright as things close up, and the slanted lines meant to suggest depth are crudely done.

Traditionally, the canvas was like a window that you looked "through" to see a slice of the real world stretching off into the distance. Now, a camera could do that better. With Matisse, you look "at" the canvas, like wallpaper. *Voilà!* What was a crudely drawn scene now becomes a sophisticated and decorative pattern of colors and shapes.

Though fully "modern," Matisse built on 19th-century art—the bright colors of van Gogh, the primitive figures of Gauguin, the colorful designs of Japanese prints, and the Impressionist patches of paint that only blend together at a distance.

Primitive Masks and Statues

Matisse was one of the Fauves ("wild beasts") who, inspired by African and Oceanic masks and voodoo dolls, tried to inject a bit of the jungle into bored French society. The result? Modern art that looked primitive: long, mask-like faces with almond eyes; bright, clashing colors; simple figures; and "flat," two-dimensional scenes.

Abstract Art

Abstract art simplifies. A man becomes a stick figure. A squiggle is a wave. A streak of red expresses anger. Arches make you want a cheeseburger. These are universal symbols that everyone from a caveman to a banker understands. Abstract artists capture the essence of reality in a few lines and colors, even things a camera can't—emotions, abstract concepts, musical rhythms, and spiritual states of mind. With abstract art, you don't look "through" the canvas to see the visual world, but "at" it to read the symbolism of lines, shapes, and colors.

Wassily Kandinsky (1866–1944)

The bright colors, bent lines, and lack of symmetry tell us that Kandinsky's world was passionate and intense.

Notice the titles like "Improvisation" and "Composition." Kandinsky was inspired by music, an art form that's also "abstract," though it still packs a punch. Like a jazz musician improvising a new pattern of notes from a set scale, Kandinsky plays with new patterns of related colors, looking for just the right combination. Using lines and color, Kandinsky translates the unseen reality into a new medium... like lightning crackling over the radio. Go, man, go.

Piet Mondrian (1872–1944)

Like blueprints for modernism, Mondrian's T-square style boils painting down to its basic building blocks (black lines, white canvas) and the three primary colors (red, yellow, and blue) arranged in orderly patterns.

(When you come right down to it, that's all painting ever has been. A schematic drawing of, say, the *Mona Lisa*, shows that it's less about a woman than about the triangles and rectangles she's composed of.)

Mondrian started out painting realistic landscapes of the orderly fields in his native Holland. Increasingly, he simplified them into horizontal and vertical patterns. For Mondrian, heavy into Eastern mysticism, "up vs. down" and "left vs. right" were the perfect metaphors for life's dualities: "good vs. evil," "body vs. spirit," "man vs. woman." The canvas is a bird's-eye view of Mondrian's personal landscape.

Constantin Brancusi (1876–1957)

Brancusi's curved, shiny statues reduce things to their essence. A bird is a single stylized wing, the one feature that sets it apart from other animals. He rounds off to the closest geometrical form, so a woman's head is a perfect oval on a cubic pedestal.

Humans love symmetry (maybe because our own bodies are roughly symmetrical), finding geometric shapes restful, even worthy of meditation. Brancusi follows the instinct for order that has driven art from earliest times, from circular Stonehenge to Egyptian pyramids to Greek columns to Roman arches to Renaissance symmetry to the American Indian medicine "wheel."

Paul Klee (1879–1940)

Paul Klee's small and playful canvases are deceptively simple, containing shapes so basic they could be read like universal symbols. Klee thought a wavy line, for example, would always suggest motion, and a stick figure would always mean a human (like the psychologist Carl Jung's universal dream symbols, part of our "collective unconscious").

Klee saw these universals in the art of children, who express themselves without censoring or cluttering things up with learning. His art has a childlike playfulness and simple figures, painted in an uninhibited frame of mind.

Klee also turned to nature. The same forces that cause the wave to draw a line of foam on the beach can cause a meditative artist to draw a squiggly line of paint on a canvas. The result is a universal shape. The true artist doesn't just paint Nature, he becomes Nature.

Design: Chairs by Rietveld and Alvar Aalto

Hey, if you can't handle modern art, sit on it! (Actually, don't.) The applied arts—chairs, tables, lamps, and vases—are as much a part of the art world as the fine ones. (Some say the first art object was the pot.) As machines became as talented as humans, artists embraced new technology and mass production to bring beauty to the masses.

Fernand Leger (1881–1955)

Fernand Leger's style has been called "Tubism"—breaking the world down into cylinder shapes rather than cubes. (He supposedly got his inspiration during World War I from the gleaming barrel of a cannon.) Leger captures the feel of the encroaching Age of Machines, with all the world looking like an internal combustion engine.

Robert and Sonia Delaunay

This husband-and-wife team's colorful, fragmented canvases (including a psychedelic Eiffel Tower) prove that the modern style does not have to be ugly or puzzling.

World War I: The Death of Values

Ankle-deep in mud, a soldier shivers in a trench, waiting to be ordered "over the top." He'll have to run through barbed wire, over fallen comrades, and into a hail of machine-gun fire, only to capture a few hundred yards of meaningless territory that will be lost the next day. This soldier was not thinking about art.

World War I left nine million dead. (During the war, France often lost more men in a single day than America lost in all of Vietnam.) The war also killed the optimism and faith in mankind that had guided Europe since the Renaissance. Now, rationality just meant scheming, technology meant machines of death, and morality meant giving your life for an empty cause.

Expressionism: Kirchner, Beckmann, Grosz, Soutine, Dix, and Kokoschka

Cynicism and decadence settled over postwar Europe. Artists "expressed" their disgust by showing a distorted reality that emphasized the ugly. Using the lurid colors and simplified figures of the Fauves, they slapped paint on in thick brushstrokes, depicting a hypo-critical, hard-edged, dog-eat-dog world that had lost its bearings. The people have a haunted look in their eyes, the fixed stare of corpses and of those who have to bury them.

Surrealism: Dalí, Ernst, and Magritte (1920–1940)

Greek statues with sunglasses, a man as a spinning top, shoes becoming feet, and black ants as musical notes—Surrealism. The world was moving fast, and Surrealists caught the jumble of images. The artist scatters seemingly unrelated things on the canvas, leaving us to trace the connections in a kind of connect-the-dots without numbers. If it comes together, the synergy of unrelated things can be pretty startling. But even if the juxtaposed images don't ultimately connect, the artist has made you think, rerouting your thoughts through new neural paths. As with Dada and so much other modern art, if you don't "get" it . . . you got it.

Complicating the modern world was Freud's discovery of the "unconscious" mind that thinks dirty thoughts while we sleep. Many a Surrealist canvas is an uncensored, stream-of-consciousness "land-scape" of these deep urges, revealed in the bizarre images of dreams.

In dreams, sometimes one object can be two things at once. "I dreamt that you walked in with a cat . . . no, wait, maybe you were the cat...no..." Surrealists paint opposites like these and let them speak for themselves.

Salvador Dalí (1904–1989)

Salvador Dalí could draw exceptionally well. He painted "unreal" scenes with photographic realism, making us believe they could really happen. Seeing famil-

iar objects in an unfamiliar setting—like a grand piano adorned with disembodied heads of Lenin—creates an air of mystery, the feeling that anything can happen. That's both exciting and unsettling. Dalí's images—crucifixes, political and religious figures, and naked bodies—pack an emotional punch. Take one mixed bag of reality, jumble in a blender, and serve on a canvas—Surrealism.

Abstract Surrealists: Miró, Calder, and Arp

Abstract artists described their subconscious urges using color and shapes alone—Rorschach inkblots in reverse.

The thin-line scrawl of Joan Miró's work is like the doodling of a three-year-old. You'll recognize crudely drawn birds, stars, animals, and strange cell-like creatures with whiskers ("Biological Cubism"). Miró was trying to express the most basic of human emotions using the most basic of techniques.

Alexander Calder's mobiles hang like Mirós in the sky, waiting for a gust of wind to bring them to life.

And talk about a primal image! Jean Arp builds human beings out of amoeba-like shapes.

Decorative Art: Bonnard, Balthus, and Later Picasso and Braque

Most 20th-century paintings are a mix of the real world ("representation") and the colorful patterns of "abstract" art. Artists purposely distort camera-eye reality to make the resulting canvas more decorative. So, Picasso flattens a woman into a pattern of colored shapes, Bonnard makes a man a shimmer of golden paint, and Balthus turns a boudoir scene into colorful wallpaper.

Patterns and Textures: Jean Dubuffet, Lucio Fontana, and Karel Appel

Increasingly, you'll have to focus your eyes to look "at" the canvases, not "through" them.

Enjoy the lines and colors, but also a new element: texture.

Some works have very thick paint piled on, where you can see the brush stroke clearly. Some have substances besides paint applied to the canvas, like Dubuffet's brown, earthy rectangles of real dirt and organic wastes. Fontana punctures the canvas so the fabric itself (and the hole) becomes the subject. Artists show their skill by mastering new materials. The canvas is a tray, serving up a delightful array of different substances with interesting colors, patterns, shapes, and textures.

Alberto Giacometti (1901–1966)

Giacometti's skinny statues have the emaciated, haunted, and faceless look of concentration camp survivors. Their simplicity is "Primitive," but these aren't stately, sturdy, Easter Island heads. Man is weak in the face of technology and the winds of history.

• *Now you're at the end of the floor. Circle across the main aisle and work your way back to where you started.*

Dada: Duchamp's Urinal (1917)

When people could grieve no longer, they turned to grief's giddy twin, laughter. The war made all old values a joke, including artistic ones. The Dada movement, choosing a purposely childish name, made art that was intentionally outrageous: a moustache on the *Mona Lisa*, a shovel hung on a wall, or a modern version of a Renaissance "fountain"—a urinal (by either Marcel Duchamp or I. P. Freeley, 1917). It was a dig at all the pompous prewar artistic theories based on the noble intellect of Rational Women and Men. While the experts ranted on, Dadaists sat in the back of the class and made cultural fart noises.

Hey, I love this stuff. My mind says it's sophomoric, but my heart belongs to Dada.

Abstract Expressionism: Pollock and Rothko

America emerged from World War II as the globe's superpower. With Europe in ruins, New York replaced Paris as the art capital. The trend was toward bigger canvases, abstract designs, and experimentation with new materials and techniques. It was called "Abstract Expressionism"—expressing emotions and ideas using color and form alone.

Jackson Pollock (1912–1956)

"Jack the Dripper" attacks convention with a can of paint, dripping and splashing a dense web onto the canvas. Picture Pollock in his studio, jiving to the hi-fi, bouncing off the walls, throwing paint in a moment of enlightenment. Of course, the artist loses some control this way—over the paint flying in mid-air and over himself in an ecstatic trance. Painting becomes a whole-body activity, a "dance" between the artist and his materials.

The act of creating is what's important, not the final product. The canvas is only a record of that moment of ecstasy.

Big, Empty Canvases: Newman and Rauschenberg

All those big, empty canvases with just a few lines or colors—what reality are they trying to show?

In the modern world, we find ourselves insignificant specks in a vast and indifferent universe. Every morning, each of us must confront that big, blank, Existentialist canvas and decide how we're going to make our mark on it. Like wow.

Another influence was the simplicity of Japanese landscape painting. A Zen master studies and meditates for years to achieve the state of mind where he can draw one pure line. These canvases, again, are only a record of that state of enlightenment. (What is the sound of one brush painting?)

On more familiar ground, postwar painters were following in the footsteps of artists such as Mondrian, Klee, and Kandinsky (whose work they must have considered "busy"). The geometrical forms here reflect the same search for order, but these artists painted to the 5/4 symmetry of "Take Five."

• *Descend to the fourth floor, which houses more current works.*

Pop Art: Andy Warhol (1930–1987)

America's postwar wealth made the consumer king. Pop art is created from the "pop"-ular objects of that throw-away society—a soup can, a car fender, mannequins, tacky plastic statues, movie icons, advertising posters. Take something out of Sears and hang it in a museum, and you have to think about it in a whole different way.

Is this art? Are these mass-produced objects beautiful? Or crap? If they're not art, why do we work so hard to acquire them? Pop art, like Dada, questions our society's values.

Andy Warhol (who coined "15 minutes of fame" and became a pop star) concentrated on another mass-produced phenomenon—celebrities. He took publicity photos of famous people and repeated them. The repetition—like the constant bombardment we get from repeated images on TV—cheapens even the most beautiful things.

THE CONTEMPORARY COLLECTION (FOURTH FLOOR)

The modern world is history. Picasso and his ilk are now gathering dust and boring art students everywhere. Enter the postmodern world as seen through the eyes of current artists.

You'll see very few traditional canvases or sculptures. Artists have traded paintbrushes for blowtorches, exploring new materials and new media. (Miró said he was out to "murder" painting.) Mixed media work is the norm, combining painting, sculpture, photography, welding, film/slides/video, and lighting and sound systems.

Here are some of the trends from the turn-of-20th-century odometer:

Op Art: "Op"-tical illusions play tricks with your eyes (like how a spiral starts to spin when you stare at it).

Found Art: Artists raid dumpsters, recycling junk into the building blocks for larger "assemblages."

Deconstruction: Modern artists critique (or "deconstruct") society by examining things so familiar we take them for granted. A familiar object loaded with meaning (a crucifix), removed from its usual circumstances (a church), and put it in a new setting (in a jar of urine, to cite one notorious art project), makes you see it in a different way.

Video and Film: Clips of inane, ordinary events, repeated ad nauseam.

Words: Plaques of inane slogans or ad copy, repeated ad nauseam.

The Occasional Sculpture: This is usually an abstract, unrecognizable form that emphasizes the material it's made from.

The Occasional Canvas: This comes as a familiar relief.

Natural Objects: A rock in an urban setting is inherently interesting.

New Realism: Hyper-realistic canvases try to recreate the "look" of a photo or video image.

Installations: An entire room is given to an artist to prepare. Like entering an art funhouse, you walk in without quite knowing what to expect (I'm always thinking, "Is this safe?"). Using the latest technology, the artist engages all your senses, controlling the lights, sounds, and sometimes even smells.

Contraptions: Weird, useless, Rube-Goldberg machines make fun of technology.

Interaction: Some exhibits require your participation, whether it's pushing a button to get the contraption going, just walking around the room, or touching something. In some cases, the viewer "does" art rather than just stares at it. If art is really meant to change, it has to move you, literally.

Performance Art: A kind of mixed media of live performance. Many artists that in another day would have painted canvases have turned to music, dance, theater, and performance art. This art form is often interactive, dropping the illusion of a performance and encouraging audience participation. When you finish with the Pompidou Center, go outside for some of the street theater.

Playful Art: Children love the art being produced today. If it doesn't put a smile on your face, well, then you must be a jaded grump like me, who's seen the same repetitious s#%t passed off as "daring" since Warhol stole it from Duchamp. I mean, it's *so* 20th century.

CARNAVALET MUSEUM TOUR

paris

At the Carnavalet Museum (Musée Carnavalet—Histoire de Paris), French history unfolds in a series of stills—like a Ken Burns documentary, except you have to walk. The Revolution is the highlight, but you get a good overview of everything, from Louis XIV to Napoleon to the belle époque.

Orientation

Cost: €5.50, 18 to 26 pay €3, under 18 free, covered by museum pass, free on Sun until 13:00.
Hours: Tue–Sun 10:00–17:40, closed Mon.
Getting There: It's in the heart of the Marais district at 23 rue de Sévigné (Mo: St. Paul), and on the Marais Walk (page 73).
Information: Get the free (necessary) map. Tel. 01 42 72 21 13.
Length of Our Tour: 90 minutes.
Starring: Francois I, Louis XIV, Louis XV, Louis XVI, Madame de Sévigné, the Bastille, Robespierre, the guillotine, Napoleon, Napoleon III, the Paris Commune, and la belle époque.

OVERVIEW

The museum, opened in 1880 and filling a Marais mansion built for a 16th-century aristocrat (and later expanded to fill an adjoining mansion), is frustrating for three reasons: there are no English descriptions, the rooms are numbered both out of order and out of historical sequence, and sections are closed at different times due to staffing shortages. Still, it's Paris' top history museum, nestled enjoyably in the charming Marais neighborhood near many recommended hotels and restaurants. To avoid running out of patience and steam, cover the pre-Revolution section in a random wander through the out-of-sequence rooms (ground floor and first floor in main building, with the help of the general commentary below).

Then become a serious student when you move into the adjoining mansion for the heart and soul of the museum: The 1789 to 1920 exhibits (which flow in easy and logical order).

MAIN BUILDING GROUND FLOOR AND FIRST FLOOR

Grab a velvety bench and read the following. Then wander whichever way room closures dictate through the ground floor (prehistory through the Reformation) and the first floor (17th and 18th centuries) of the main building. As you wander, you'll get a feel for the luxurious life of France's kings and nobles before the Revolution.

Ground Floor Rooms 1–4: Prehistory to 1500

Bone tools, broken columns, and stained leotards provide faint traces of Paris's first 2,000 years: The Celtic Parisii tribe fishing in the Seine (100 B.C.); Julius Caesar and the Romans (52 B.C.–A.D. 500); Clovis and his Germanic invaders (508); Charlemagne, who united the Franks (800); Hugh Capet, whose descendants ruled for 800 years (1000); and the English, who were finally driven out by Joan of Arc (1453), ending the Middle Ages and birthing modern France.

Ground Floor, Rooms 7–10: 1500s— Renaissance and Reformation

In Room 7, a **model of Ile de la Cité** (made by a monk around 1900) shows the medieval city before France became a world power—crowded, narrow-laned, and steeple-dotted, with houses piled even on top of bridges. There's Notre-Dame on the east end, and Sainte-Chapelle with its royal palace and gardens on the west. The only straight road in town was the old Roman road that splits the island north-south (and is still used today).

King François I (1494–1547, Room 7) brought Paris into the modern world. Handsome, athletic François—a writer of poems, leader of knights, and lover of women—embodied the optimism of the Italian Renaissance. "*Le grand roi François*" (it rhymes) centralized the government around his charismatic self and made a rebuilt Louvre his home. His absolute right to rule was affirmed every time he ordered something done—"For such is our pleasure!"

Renaissance open-mindedness brought religious debate, even leading to open warfare between Catholics and Protestants (called Huguenots in France). The Catholic **King Charles IX** and his mother, **Catherine de Medicis** (both depicted in room 8), plotted to assassinate several prominent Protestants, but it quickly snowballed into the slaughter of thousands of Parisian Huguenots on St. Bartholomew's Day, 1572. Paintings show events organized by the **Catholic League:** parades, Bible studies, and the occasional Protestant barbecue to keep the faithful in good spirits.

FIRST FLOOR

Rooms 13–20 (*Paris au XVII siècle*): 1600s—Louis XIII and XIV Modernize Paris

Many of the grand monuments that made Paris a world capital—the pont Neuf, the expanded Louvre, place Royale, and the Invalides dome—were begun or completed by **Louis XIII** (Room 14, rearing on his horse, with angels trumpeting his works) and his more glorious son, Louis XIV, the Sun King. They financed the arts (Le Brun, etc., in Room 15), shifting Europe's cultural axis from Italy to Paris.

Rooms 17 through 20, with their flowery walls, Greek-myth ceiling paintings, and powdered-wig portraits, give a tiny glimpse of the opulence of Louis XIV's greatest monument, the palace at Versailles. Versailles was the physical symbol of Louis' absolute power, ruling over the largest, most populous, and richest nation in Europe. Whenever the nobles got uppity, the larger-than-life Sun King wouldn't hesitate to put his foot down (Room 20).

Rooms 21–23 (*Madame de Sévigné et son temps*): Madame de Sévigné (1596–1696)

Esteemed hostess and letter writer Madame de Sévigné spent the last 20 years of her life living here at Hôtel Carnavalet. (See **portraits** of Madame, her daughter, and her son-in-law, M. de Grignan.) Widowed at age 25, Marie de Sévigné took her two young children to Paris and quickly charmed high society (including a young Louis XIV) with her beauty and wit. She hosted parties for writers (see **Molière**, acting the role of Caesar), thinkers, and political radicals. Her parties and romantic affairs were legendary. Still, in private, Marie stared out the windows of these rooms, missing her daughter—who had moved to the south of France. Madame wrote a letter to Mademoiselle almost every day for 20 years. Her subjects range from the everyday ("This morning, we had a good chicken soup and some good cabbages") to the poetic ("I have come here to say goodbye to the leaves. They are still on the trees, but, instead of green, they have taken on tones as varied as dawn, as varied as a magnificent, golden brocade") to playful gossip ("I am about to tell you the most astonishing thing…"). Most of all, the letters reveal her almost obsessive longing for her daughter ("Come visit me my darling, for as long as you're away, there is a dragon feasting on my heart"). Today, the vast store of letters is a gold mine of historical information, as well as a pioneering work that turned conversational speech and ordinary feelings into high art.

Rooms 24–48: Louis XV (ruled 1715–1774)

Louis XV (portrait in Room 25) ascended the throne of Europe's most powerful nation when his great-grandfather, the Sun King, died after reigning for 72 years. Only five years old at the time, he was forever a figurehead while the government was run by his mentors—a Regency during his childhood, his schoolteacher in youth, one of his many mistresses (Madame de Pompadour) in middle age, and bureaucrats at the end. Louis was intelligent and educated, and he personally embraced the budding democratic ideals of the Enlightenment, but he spent his time at Versailles, gaming and consorting with Europe's most cultured and beautiful people. Meanwhile, France's money was spent on costly wars with Austria and England (including the American "French and Indian War"). Louis, basking in the lap of luxury and the glow of the Enlightenment, looked to the horizon and uttered his prophetic phrase: "*Après moi— le deluge!*" ("After me—the flood!")

Rooms 49–64: Louis XVI (ruled 1774–1793), France's Last King

As you stroll through the first-floor rooms, you'll see luxurious wallpaper, tables, chairs, parquet floors, clocks, gaming tables, statues, paintings, and even a doghouse costing more than a peasant hut (Room 53). Look for subtle differences in decoration and furnishings:

Louis XIV Style: Baroque. In these gilded rooms, ceilings are decorated with curved ornamental frames (cartouches) holding paintings of Greek myths. The heavy tables and chairs have thick, curved legs, animal feet, and bronze-corner protectors.

Louis XV Style: Rococo. The rooms are decorated in pastel colors, with lighter decoration and exotic landscapes. The chairs are made of highly polished, rare woods, with delicate curved legs and padded seats and backs. Note the Chinese decor and objects (Ming vase).

Louis XVI Style: Neoclassical. Influenced by recently excavated Pompeii, the rooms are simpler—with classical motifs—and the furniture is straighter. The chairs' straight legs taper to a point.

Imagine these rooms during the *ancien régime* (the traditional chessboard society with king on top, pawns on bottom, and the bishops that walk diagonally), lit by chandeliers glimmering off mirrors, the sound of a string quartet, exotic foods from newly colonized lands, billiards in one room and high-stakes card games in another, a Molière comedy downstairs, dangerous talk by radicals like Voltaire and Rousseau in Room 48, and dangerous liaisons among social butterflies—male and female—dressed in high heels, make-up, wigs, and perfume.

• *From Room 45, walk down a long, blood-red corridor to another building, then upstairs to the second floor and* La Révolution française.

SECOND FLOOR

The Revolution: 1789–1799

No period of history is as charged with the full range of human emotions as the French Revolution. Bloodshed, martyrdom, daring speeches, lasting bonds of friendship, tolerance, murdering priests, emancipating women, feeding the starving, back-stabbing former friends—all done in the looming shadow of the guillotine. From the highest ideals to the pettiest jealousies, the bottled-up passions of ordinary men and women were suddenly uncorked, and what bubbled out wasn't always Dom Perignon. For the first time, common people with their everyday concerns were driving the engine of history....Or were they only foam bubbles swept along in the shifting tides of vast socioeconomic trends?

Room 101: The Estates General

It's 1789, France is bankrupt from wars and corruption, and the people want change. The large **allegorical painting by Dubois** shows King Louis XVI in the boat of France, navigating stormy seas. Lady Truth is trying to light the way, but the winged demon of tyranny keeps nagging at the king. Above shines the fleur-de-lis, whose petals are the three social groups that made France strong: clergy, king-and-people, and nobles.

In May, the king called these three groups together at Versailles to solve the financial crisis. But in a bold and unheard-of move, the Third Estate (the people), tired of being outvoted by the archaic system, split and formed their own National Assembly. Amid the chaos of speeches, debate, and deal-making, they raise their hands, bravely pledging to stick together until a new constitution is written (see *The Oath of the Jeu-de-Paume*, on wall opposite allegorical painting). **Louis XVI** (see his pink-faced portrait to the left), who seemed to vacillate between democratic change and royalist repression, ordered the Assembly to dissolve (they refused), sent 25,000 Swiss mercenary soldiers to Paris, and fired his most popular, liberal minister.

Room 102: The Bastille (July 14, 1789)

The Bastille (see the **model**) was a medieval fortress turned prison. With its eight towers and 30-meter-high (100-foot) walls, it dominated the Parisian skyline, a symbol of oppression. On the hot, muggy morning of July 14, Paris' citizens waited on edge for a

rumored attack by the king's Swiss guards. A crowd formed and marched on the Invalides armory (see series of **paintings**, left to right) and seized 30,000 rifles... but no gunpowder. Word spread it was stored across town at the Bastille. The mob grew bigger and angrier as it went. By noon, they stood at the foot of the walls of the Bastille, demanding gunpowder. The fort's governor stalled, but two citizens managed to scale the wall and cut the chains. The drawbridge crashed down, and the mob poured through. Terrified guards opened fire, killing dozens and wounding hundreds. At the battle's peak, French soldiers in red and blue appeared on the horizon... but whose side were they on? A loud cheer went up as they pointed their cannons at the Bastille, and soon the governor had no choice but to surrender. The mob trashed the Bastille, opened the dark dungeons, and brought seven prisoners into the light of day. They dragged the governor to City Hall (Hôtel de Ville) where he was literally torn apart by the hysterical crowd. His head was stuck on a stick and carried through the city. The Revolution had begun.

Today the events of July 14 are celebrated with equally colorful festivities every Bastille Day. The Bastille itself was soon dismantled stone by stone (nothing remains but the open space of place Bastille), but the memory became a rallying cry throughout the Revolution: *"Vive le quatorze Juillet!"* ("Long live July 14th!")

Room 103 (*La Fête de la Federation*): The Celebration (1789)

Imagine the jubilation! To finally be able to shout out loud things formerly whispered in fear.

French National Anthem: "La Marseillaise"

The genteel French have a gory past.

Allons enfants de la Patrie, (Let's go, children of
the fatherland,)

Le jour de gloire est arrivé. (The day of glory has arrived.)

Contre nous de la tyrannie (The blood-covered
flagpole of tyranny)

L'étendard sanglant est levé. (Is raised against us.)

Entendez-vous dans nos campagnes (Do you hear what's
happening in our countryside?)

Mugir les féroces soldats? (The ferocious soldiers are howling)

Qui viennent jusque dans nos bras (They're coming nearly
into our grasp)

Egorger nos fils et nos compagnes. (They're slitting the throats
of our sons and our women.)

Aux armes citoyens, (Grab your weapons, citizens,)

Formez vos bataillons, (Form your battalions,)

Marchons, marchons, (March on, march on,)

Qu'un sang impur (So that their impure blood)

Abreuve nos sillons. (Will fill our trenches.)

The large painting of **La Fête de la Federation** shows the joy and exuberance of the newly freed people, celebrating the first Bastille Day (July 14, 1790). Liberty! Equality! Fraternity! Members of every social class (even including, it appears, three women) hugged, kissed, and mingled on the Champ de Mars, where the Eiffel Tower stands today. An artificial mound was built for heroes of the Revolution to ascend while a choir sang. Women, dressed up to symbolize Truth, Freedom, Justice, and other capital-letter virtues, were worshiped in a new kind of secular religion. Public demonstrations like these must have infuriated the king, queen, bishops, and nobles, who were now quarantined in their palaces, fuming impotently.

The **Declaration of the Rights of Man and the Citizen** (see 2 different versions) made freedom the law. The preamble makes clear that "Le Peuple Francais" (the French people)—not the king—were the ultimate authority. "Men are born free and equal," it states, possessing "freedom of the individual, freedom of conscience, freedom of speech."

Room 104 (*de la Monarchie a la République*): Louis XVI Quietly Responds (1789–1792)

Louis XVI (1754–1793, see the bust)—studious, shy, aloof, and easily dominated—was stunned by the ferocious summer of 1789. The Bastille's violence spread to the countryside, where uppity peasants tenderized their masters with pitchforks. The Assembly was changing France with lightning speed, abolishing Church privileges, nationalizing nobles' land, and declaring the king irrelevant. Louis accepted his role as a rubber-stamp monarch, hoping the furor would pass, trying to appear idealistic and optimistic. But looming on the horizon was... *Le docteur Joseph-Ignace Guillotin* (1738–1814, see portrait).

The progressive Assembly abolished brutal medieval-style torture and executions. In their place, Dr. Guillotin proposed a kinder, gentler execution device that would make France a model of compassion. The guillotine—also known as "the national razor," or, simply, "The Machine"—could nearly instantly make someone "a head shorter at the top." (In 1977, it claimed its last victim; now capital punishment is abolished.)

Room 105 (*La famille royale*): Royalty Loses Its Head (1793)

Louis' wife, **Queen Marie-Antoinette** (several portraits), became the focus of the citizens' disgust. She spent extravagantly, plunging France into debt. More decisive than her husband, she steered him toward repressive measures to snuff out the Revolution. And worst of all, she was foreign-born, known simply as "The Austrian," and Austria was soon making war on the French, trying to preserve the monarchy. When Marie was informed that the Parisians had no bread to eat, a rumor spread that she sneered, "Let them eat cake!" ("Cake" was the term for the burnt crusts peeled off the oven and generally fed only to the cattle.)

Enraged and hungry, 6,000 Parisian women (backed by armed men) marched through the rain to Versailles to demand lower bread prices. On the night of October 5, 1789, a small band infiltrated the palace, burst into the Queen's room, killed her bodyguards, and chased her down the hall. The royal family was kidnapped and taken to Paris, where—though still monarchs—they were virtual prisoners in the Tuileries Palace (which once stood where, today, the Louvre meets the Tuileries Gardens).

Two years later, the royal family became actual prisoners (see the reconstructed and rather cushy **Prison du Temple** in Room 106) after trying to escape to Austria to begin a counter-revolution. One of their servants pretended to be a German baroness, while Louis dressed up as her servant (the irony must have been killing him). When a citizen recognized Louis from his portrait on a franc note, the family was captured, thrown into prison, and soon put on trial as traitors to France. The National Convention (the Assembly's successor) declared the monarchy abolished.

On January 21, 1793 (see **painting** in Room 105), King Louis XVI—excuse me, "Citizen Capet"—was led to the place de la Concorde, laid face down on a slab, and—shoop!—a thousand years of monarchy dating back before Charlemagne was decapitated.

A few months later, Marie-Antoinette was tearfully torn (see **painting**) from her eight-year-old son (Louis XVII) and moved to a prison in the Conciergerie. On October 16, 1793 (see **painting**), she too met her fate on place de la Concorde. Genteel to the end, she apologized to the executioner for stepping on his foot. The blade fell, the blood gushed, and her head was shown to the crowd on a stick—an exclamation point for the new rallying cry: *Vive la Nation*! (Louis XVII died in prison at age 10. Rumors spread that the boy-king had escaped, fueled by Elvis-type sightings and impersonators. But recent DNA evidence confirms that the *dauphin*—heir to the throne— did indeed die in prison in 1795.)

Room 108 (*La Convention–La Terreur*): The Reign of Terror (1793–1794)

Here are **portraits** of key players in the Revolutionary spectacle. Some were moderate reformers, some radical priest-killers. They all lived in fear that, with Europe ganging up on the Revolution, any backward step could tip the delicate balance of power back to the *ancien régime*. Enemies of the Revolution were everywhere— even in their own ranks.

By the summer of 1793, the left-of-center Jacobin party took control of France's fledgling democracy. Pug-faced but silver-tongued **Georges Danton** drove the Revolution with his personal charisma and bold speeches: "To conquer the enemies of the fatherland,  we need daring, more daring, daring now, always daring." He led the "Committee of Public Safety" to root out and execute those enemies, even guillotining moderates opposed to the Jacobins.

More radical still, **Jean-Paul Marat** (the "Friend of the People") dressed and burped like a man-of-the-street, but he wrote eloquently against all forms of authority. Wildly popular with the commoners, he was seen by others as a loose cannon. A beautiful 25-year-old noblewoman named **Charlotte Corday** decided it was her mission in life to save France by silencing him. On July 11, 1793, she entered his home under the pretext of giving him names of counter-revolutionaries. Marat, seated in a bathtub to nurse a skin condition, wrote the names down and said, "Good. I'll have them all guillotined." Corday stood up, whipped a knife out from under her dress, and stabbed him through the heart. Corday was guillotined, and Marat was hailed a martyr to the cause.

Marat's death was further "proof" that counter-revolutionaries were everywhere. For the next year (summer of 1793 to summer of 1794, see **paintings of guillotine scenes**), the Jacobin government arrested, briefly tried, then guillotined everyone suspected of being "enemies of the Revolution"—nobles, priests, and the rich, as well as many true Revolutionaries who simply belonged to the wrong political party. More than 2,500 Parisians were beheaded, 18,000 were executed by other means, and tens of thousands died in similar violence around the country. The violence begun at the **Bastille** in July 1789 would climax in July 1794.

Master of the Reign of Terror was **Maximilien Robespierre** (the portrait opposite Danton's), a 35-year-old lawyer who promoted the Revolution with a religious fervor. By July 1794, the guillotine was slicing 30 necks a day. In Paris' main squares, grim executions alternated with politically correct public spectacles honoring "Liberty," "Truth," and the heroes of France. As the death toll rose, so did public cynicism. Finally, Robespierre even sentenced to death his old friend Danton, when he spoke out against the bloodshed. As Danton knelt under the blade, he joked—"My turn." The people had had enough.

Room 109 (*Thermidor—Le Directoire*): Terror Ends (July 1794)

Engravings show Robespierre's meteoric fall from power. Food shortages, inflation, and Robespierre's own self-righteousness made him an easy target. On July 27, 1794, as Robespierre prepared to name the daily list of victims, his fellow committee members started yelling "Tyrant!" and shouted him down. Robespierre, stunned by the sudden fall from grace, tried to commit suicide by shooting himself in the mouth.

The next day, he walked the walk he'd ordered thousands to take. Hands tied behind his back, he was carried through the streets on a two-wheeled cart, while citizens jeered and spat on him. At the guillotine, the broken-down demagogue had no last words, thanks to his wounded jaw. When the executioner yanked off the bandage, Robespierre let out a horrible cry, the blade fell, and the Reign of Terror came to an end.

From 1795 to 1799, France caught its breath, ruled by the Directory, a government so intentionally weak and decentralized (2 houses of parliament and 5 executives, with no funding) that it could never create another Robespierre.

Room 110 (*La Guerre*): France vs. Europe

The blade that dropped on Louis XVI rattled royal teacups throughout Europe. Even as early as 1792, France had to defend its young democracy against Austria and Prussia. Surprisingly, France's new army—ordinary citizens from a universal draft, led by daring young citizen-officers, singing a stirring, bloodthirsty new song, "La Marseillaise"—quickly defeated the apathetic mercenaries they faced. France vowed to liberate all Europe from tyranny. Europe feared that, by "exporting Revolution," France would export democracy... plus senseless violence and chaos.

The 29-year-old General **Napoleon Bonaparte** (see the bust) rose quickly through the ranks, proving himself by fighting royalists in Italy, Egypt, and on the streets of Paris. In 1799, he returned to Paris a conquering hero. Backed by an adoring public, he dissolved the Directory, established order, and gave himself the Roman-style title of "first consul."

Room 111 (*Vandalisme et Conservation*): The Revolution vs. Religion

Three-fourths of France's churches were destroyed or vandalized during the Revolution, a backlash against the wealthy and politically repressive Catholic Church. In Notre-Dame, Christ was mothballed and a woman dressed as "Dame Reason" was worshiped on the altar.

Room 113: Souvenirs of Revolution

After Napoleon's dictatorship of 1799, "*Liberté, Egalité, Fraternité*" was just a slogan, remembered fondly on commemorative **plates and knickknacks**. The Revolution was over.

• *The visit continues downstairs—or down the elevator—on the ground floor.*

Room 115 (*Le Premier Empire*): Napoleon Conquers Europe (1799–1815)

Here's **Napoleon** (see portrait, also breastplate and death mask in glass case) at the peak of power, master of western Europe. Dressed in his general's uniform, he's checking the maps to see who's left to conquer. Behind him is a throne with his imperial seal. This Corsican-born commoner, educated in Paris' military schools, became a young Revolutionary and daring general, rising to prominence as a champion of democracy. Once in

power, he preached revolution but in fact became a dictator and crowned himself emperor (1804).

During the Empire, bishops such as **Talleyrand** and wealthy socialites such as **Juliette Recamier** could bring their fine clothes out of mothballs without fear of the guillotine. Paris was rebuilt (Room 117) with neoclassical monuments like the Arc de Triomphe to make it the "New Rome."

In 1812, Napoleon foolishly invaded Russia, starting a downward spiral that ended in defeat by allied Europe at the Battle of Waterloo in Belgium (1815). Napoleon was exiled, and died (1822) on the island of St. Helena, off the coast of Africa.

Room 118 (*La Restauration*): The Monarchy Restored (1815–1830)

After 25 years in exile, **Louis XVIII**—younger brother of headless Louis XVI—returned to Paris with the backing of Europe's royalty and reclaimed the crown as a constitutional monarch (see painted crowd scene of *3 mai 1814*).

The next king, retro-looking **Charles X**, in glorious coronation robes, revived the fashion and oppression of the *ancien régime*, plotting to dissolve the people's Assembly. But the French people were not about to turn the clock back.

Room 119 (*Juillet 1830*): Revolution of 1830

Parisians again blocked off the narrow streets with barricades to fight the king's soldiers. They **stormed the Louvre** (biggest painting) and the king's palace, and slaughtered the mercenary Swiss Guards. After "Three Glorious Days" of fighting, order was restored by Louis-Philippe (see **model**), an unassuming nobleman who appeared on the balcony of Hôtel de Ville and was cheered by royalists, the middle class, and peasants alike.

Room 120 (*La Monarchie de Juillet*): Constitutional Monarchy (1830–1848)

King Louis-Philippe (see black bust)—a former lieutenant turned banker, with a few drops of royal blood—was a true constitutional monarch, harmlessly presiding over an era of middle-class progress fueled by the industrial revolution. Still, liberal reforms came too slowly—new factories brought division between wealthy employers and poor workers, and only 200,000 out of 30 million French citizens (1:150) could vote.

Room 121 (*La Deuxième République*): Revolution of 1848

In February 1848—a time of Europe-wide depression and socialist strikes—Parisians took to the streets again (**battle scenes**), battling at Bastille, Palais-Royal, Panthéon, and Concorde, and toppling the king. Even prosperous accountants and shoe salesmen caught the spirit of revolution. After five decades of dictators (Napoleon), retread Bourbons (the Restoration), and self-proclaimed monarchs (Louis-Philippe), France was back in the hands of the people—the Second Republic.

Room 122 (*Le Romantisme*): Romanticism

Freedom of expression, the uniqueness of each person, the glories of the human spirit and the natural world—these values from the 1789 Revolution were continued by artists of the 1800s known as Romantics. Working clockwise, you'll see **caricature busts** of many famous Frenchmen and visitors to the center of European culture, Paris: Victor Hugo (author of *Les Misérables* and *Hunchback of Notre-Dame*), Johann Strauss, Sr. (inventor of the scandalous waltz craze), Paganini (touring violinist who played like a man possessed), Chopin (Polish pianist who charmed Parisian society), Adolphe Sax (-ophone), Giuseppe Verdi (composer of stirring operas—*Aida*, etc.), and Rossini (Lone Ranger theme). There are also **paintings** of Romantic painter Delacroix and of glamorous pianist Franz Liszt and his mistress Marie d'Agoult—the ultimate Romantic. She left her husband and children to follow the dynamic Liszt on a journey of self-discovery in Italy and Switzerland—"the years of pilgrimage."

• *Journey upstairs and to the left toward* "Paris: Du Second Empire à nos jours"—*From the Second Empire to Today.*

Room 128 (*Le Second Empire*): Napoleon III and the Second Empire (1852–1870)

Louis-Napoleon Bonaparte (in the big painting, with red pants

and sash, waxed moustache,
and goatee) was the nephew
of the famous Emperor
Napoleon I. He used his
famous name to be elected
president by a landslide in
1848, then combined
democracy with monarchy
to be voted "Emperor
Napoleon III." He sup-

pressed opposition but promoted liberal reforms and economic
and colonial expansion.

Here he hands an order to **Baron Georges Haussmann**
(mutton-chop sideburns) to modernize Paris. Haussmann cut
the wide, straight boulevards of today to move goods, open
up the crowded city . . . and prevent barricades for future revolutions. Parks, railroad stations, and the Garnier Opéra House
made Paris the model for world capitals. (Room 129 shows
building projects.)

The **boat-like cradle** (Room 128) is a copy of the famous
cradle of Napoleon II (1811–1832, known to history as the "King
of Rome"), the only son of Napoleon I, who died at 19 of tuberculosis before ever ruling anything.

Napoleon III pursued popular wars (the **model** in Room 129
celebrates Crimean War vets, 1855) and unpopular ones (backing
Austrian Emperor Maximilian in Mexico). In the summer of 1870,
he personally led a jubilant French Army to crush upstart Prussia—
"On to Berlin!" Uh-oh.

Room 130 (*Le siège de Paris*): The Franco-Prussian War (1870–1871)

Within weeks, the overconfident French were surrounded,
Napoleon III himself was captured, and he surrendered.
Paris was stunned. (See **painting of crowd** hearing the
news on the legislature steps.) The Germans quickly put a
stranglehold on Paris, and a long, especially cold winter
settled in.

Some would not give up. Without an emperor, they proclaimed yet another democratic republic (France's third in
a century) and sent minister Leon Gambetta in a newfangled
balloon (**painting**) over the Germans' heads to rally the countryside to come save Paris. The Parisians themselves held out
bravely (**painting** of Tuileries as army camp), but German
efficiency and modern technology simply overwhelmed
the French.

Room 131 (*La Commune*):
The Paris Commune (Spring 1871)

The Republic finally agreed to a humiliating surrender. Paris'
liberals—enraged at the capitulation after such a brave winter
and fearing a return of monarchy—rejected the surrender
and proclaimed their own government, the Paris Commune.
Portraits honor the proud idealists who barricaded themselves inside Paris' neighborhoods, refusing to bow to the
German emperor.

Then, in one "bloody week" in May (**battle scenes**),
French troops backing the Republic stormed through Paris,
leaving 15,000 dead, 5,000 jailed, and 8,000 deported. The
Commune was snuffed out, but the memory was treasured by
generations of liberals in popular **souvenirs**—a jar of bread
from the hungry winter, a carrier pigeon's feather, a box reading
"*Vive la Commune!*"

The church of Sacre-Coeur (**painting**) was built after the
war as a form of national penance.

Rooms 132–142 (*La Belle Epoque*):
The Beautiful Age (1871–1914)

The Third Republic restored peace to a prosperous middle-
class society. The **Eiffel Tower** (Room 132) marked the 1889
centennial of the Revolution, and the **Statue of Liberty** (Room
133) honored America's revolution.

Paris was a capital of world culture, a city of **Impressionist
painters** (Room 135); of the actress **Sarah Bernhardt** (Room
136), called the world's first international star ("a force of nature,
a fiery soul, a marvelous intelligence, a magnificent creature
of the highest order," raved one of the smitten); of **Georges
Bizet** (Room 136), composer of *Carmen*; of balls, carriages,
cafés, and parks (**paintings**, Rooms 137–140); and the city of
Art Nouveau.

Two delightful turn-of-the-century Parisian shops—spliced
into this old regime mansion—illustrate the curvy, decorative
Art Nouveau style: the *très chic* **Café de Paris** (Room 141)
and the **Boutique Fouquet** (Room 142). Imagine browsing
through jewelry in the spindly splendor of this Alfons Mucha–
created world of peacocks peering through stained glass and
nubile nymphs skinnying up lampposts.

Room 145: World War I (1914–1918)

Three costly wars with Germany—Franco-Prussian, World
War I, and World War II—drained France. Although **Marshall
Foch** (big painting) is hailed as the man who coordinated the

Allied armies to defeat Germany in World War I, France was hardly a winner. More than 1.5 million Frenchmen died, a generation was lost, and the country would be a pushover when Hitler invaded in 1940. France's long history as a global superpower was over.

Room 147 (*La vie litteraire XXe siècle*): Remembrance of Things Past

By producing such literary greats as the writer **Marcel Proust** (reconstructed bedroom) and the dreamy writer/filmmaker **Jean Cocteau**, France has remained a cultural superpower.

RODIN MUSEUM TOUR

paris

Auguste Rodin (1840–1917) was a modern Michelangelo, sculpting human figures on an epic scale, revealing through the body their deepest thoughts and feelings. Like many of Michelangelo's unfinished works, Rodin's statues rise from the raw stone around them, driven by the life force. With missing limbs and scarred skin, these are prefab classics, making ugliness noble. Rodin's people are always moving restlessly. Even the famous *Thinker* is moving. While he's plopped down solidly, his mind is a million miles away. The museum presents a full range of Rodin's work, housed in a historic mansion where he once lived and worked. The gardens are picnic perfect (BYO), but there's also a pleasant, if pricey, café.

Orientation

Cost: €4, €2.75 on Sun and for students, free for youth under 18 and for anyone on the first Sun of month; €0.75 for garden only; all covered by museum pass.

Hours: April–Sept Tue–Sun 09:30–17:45, garden closes at 18:45. Oct–March Tue–Sun 09:30–17:00, garden closes at 17:00. Closed Mon. Last entrance 30 minutes before closing.

Getting There: It's at 77 rue de Varennes, near Napoleon's Tomb (Mo: Varennes).

Information: Tel. 01 44 18 61 10, www.musee-rodin.fr.

Length of Our Tour: One hour.

Entrance Hall

Two bronze men stride forward, as bold as the often controversial Rodin. *The Walking Man* (*L'Homme Qui Marche*) plants his back foot forcefully as though he's about to step, while his front foot already has stepped. Rodin, who himself had one foot in the past, one in the future, captures two poses at once.

───── RODIN MUSEUM AND GARDENS ─────

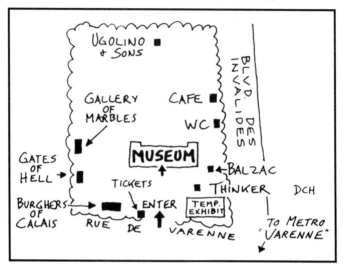

• *Pick up a museum plan with room numbers and walk left, through the shop, and to the far corner to start a circular tour of the ground floor.*

Room 1: Rodin's early works match the style of the time—pretty portrait busts and classical themes. Born of working-class roots, Rodin taught himself art by sketching statues at the Louvre and then sculpting copies.

The Man with the Broken Nose (*L'homme au nez casse*)—a deliberately ugly work—was 23-year-old Rodin's first break from the norm. He meticulously sculpted this deformed man (one of the few models the struggling sculptor could afford), but then the clay statue froze in his unheated studio, and the back of the head fell off. Rodin loved it! The Salon hated it. Rodin persevered.

See the painting of Rodin's future wife, Rose Beuret (*Portrait de Madame Rodin*), who suffered with him through obscurity and celebrity.

Room 2: To feed his new family, Rodin cranked out small works with his boss' name on them—portraits, ornamental vases, nymphs, and knickknacks to decorate buildings. Still, the series of mother-and-childs (Rose and baby Auguste?) allowed him to experiment on a small scale with the intertwined twosomes he'd do later.

His job gave him enough money to visit Italy, where he was inspired by Michelangelo's boldness, monumental scale, restless figures, and "unfinished" look. Rapidly approaching middle age, Rodin was ready to rock.

Room 3: He moved to Brussels, where his first major work, *The Bronze Age* (*L'âge d'airain*), brought controversy and the fame that surrounds it. This nude youth, perhaps inspired by Michelangelo's *Dying Slave* in the Louvre, awakens to a new world. It was so life-like that Rodin was accused of not sculpting it himself but simply casting it directly from a live body. The boy's left hand looks like he should be leaning on a spear, but it's just that missing element that makes the pose more tenuous and interesting.

The art establishment still snubbed Rodin the outsider, and no wonder. Look at his ultra-intense take on the symbol of France (*La Défense*)—this Marseillaise screams, "Off with their heads!" at the top of her lungs. Rodin was a slave to his muses, and some inspired monsters.

Room 4: Like the hand of a sculptor, *The Hand of God* (*La main de Dieu*) shapes Adam and Eve from the mud of the earth to which they will return. Rodin himself worked in "mud," using his hands to model clay figures, which were then reproduced in marble or bronze, usually by his assistants. Spin this masterpiece on its turntable. Rodin wants you to see it from every angle. He first worked from the front view, then checked the back and side profiles, then filled in the in-between.

Other works in this room show embracing couples who seem to emerge from the stone just long enough to love. Rodin left many works "unfinished," reminding us that all creating is a hard process of dragging a form out of chaos.

Room 5: The two hands that form the arch of *The Cathedral* (*La Cathèdrale*) are actually two right hands (a man's and a woman's?).

In *The Kiss*, a passionate woman twines around a solid man for their first, spontaneous kiss. In their bodies, we can almost read the thoughts, words, and movements that led up to this meeting of lips. *The Kiss* was the first Rodin work the public loved. Rodin despised it, think-ing it simple and sentimental.

Rodin worked with many materials—he chiseled marble (*The Kiss*), used clay (the smaller, red-brown *Kiss*—opposite the big kiss), cast bronze, worked plaster, painted, and sketched.

He often created different versions of the same subject in a different medium.

Room 6: This room displays works by Camille Claudel, mostly in the style of her master. The 44-year-old Rodin took 18-year-old Camille as his pupil, muse, colleague, and lover. We can follow the arc of their relationship:

Rodin was inspired by young Camille's beauty and spirit, and he often used her as a model. You'll see her head emerging from a block of marble.

As his student, "Mademoiselle C" learned from Rodin, doing portrait busts in his lumpy style. Her bronze bust of Rodin (by the door) shows the steely-eyed sculptor with strong front and side profiles, barely emerging from the materials he worked with.

Soon they were lovers. *The Waltz* (*La Valse*) captures the spinning exuberance the two must have felt as they embarked together on a new life. The couple twirls in a delicate balance.

But Rodin was devoted as well to his lifelong companion, Rose. *Maturity* (*L'Age Mur*) shows the breakup. A young girl on her knees begs the man not to leave her, as he's led away reluctantly by an older woman. The center of the composition is the hole left when their hands drift apart.

Rodin did leave Camille. Overwhelmed by grief and jealousy, she went crazy and had to be institutionalized until she died. *The Wave* (*La Vague*), carved in onyx in a very un-Rodin style, shows sensitive—perhaps fragile—women huddled under a wave about to engulf them.

Rooms 7 and 8: What did Rodin think of women? Here are many different images from which you can draw conclusions.

Eve buries her head in shame, hiding her nakedness. But she can't hide the consequences of that first sin—she's pregnant.

Rodin became famous, wealthy, and respected, and society ladies all wanted him to do their portraits. In Room 8, you'll also see his last mistress (*La Duchesse de Choiseul*), who lived with him here in this mansion.

Room 9: This dimly lit room is filled with Rodin's sketches. The first flash of inspiration for a huge statue might be a single line sketched on notepaper. Rodin wanted nude models in his studio at all times—walking, dancing, and squatting—in case they struck some new and interesting pose. Rodin thought of sculpture as simply "drawing in all dimensions."

• *Upstairs you'll find a glass display case that tries hard to explain how...*

Rodin made his bronze statues by pouring molten bronze into the narrow space between an original clay model and the mold around it. Once you had a mold, you could produce other copies, which is why there are famous Rodin bronzes all over the world.

As the display case clearly fails to make clear, the classic "lost wax" technique works like this:

1) The artist sculpts a clay model.

2) It is covered with materials that harden to make a shell that's hard on the outside, flexible inside. The shell is removed by cutting it into two halves that can be pieced back together—this is your mold.

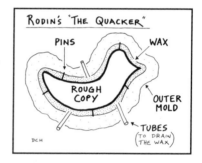

3) Cement is poured into the mold to make a durable, rough copy. The mold is removed.

4) The surface of the copy is sanded down slightly.

5) The mold is put back over it, using pins to keep a one-centimeter space between the mold and the rough copy. Hot wax is poured into the space, it cools, and the mold is removed. The artist touches up the wax "skin" of the rough copy into its final form.

6) The waxy piece of art is covered with materials that harden into a new mold. Ventilation tubes are added.

7) The whole contraption is coated with heat-resistant materials.

8) The wax is heated—it melts and drains away (gets "lost"), leaving a centimeter of open space between the rough copy and the mold. Molten bronze is poured in to fill the space. As the bronze cools, it takes the shape of the mold.

9) The mold and the tubing are removed, and the bronze halves are lifted off the rough copy. After the halves are soldered together, you have a hollow bronze statue ready to be polished and varnished.

Rooms 10 and 11: For decades, Rodin wrestled with a massive project—a doorway encrusted with characters from Dante's *Inferno*. These *Gates of Hell* were never completed (see unfinished piece in the garden), but his studies created some of Rodin's masterpieces—including *The Thinker*, who was to be the centerpiece.

Rodin's figures struggle to come into existence. Rodin was fascinated with the theory of evolution—not Darwin's version of the survival of the fittest, but the Frenchman Lamarck's. His figures survive not by the good fortune of random mutation (Darwin), but by their own striving (Lamarck). They are driven by the life force, a restless energy that animates and shapes dead matter (Lamarck and Bergson). Rodin must have felt that force even as a child, when he first squeezed soft clay and saw a worm emerge.

In Room 11, you'll see studies of the female body in all its aspects—open, closed, wrinkled.

Room 12: A virtual unknown until his mid-30s, Rodin slowly began receiving major commissions for public monuments. *The Burghers of Calais* depicts the actual event in 1347, when, in order to save their people, the city fathers surrendered the keys of the city—and their own lives—to the enemy. Rodin portrays them not in some glorious pose drenched in pomp and allegory, but as a simple example of men sacrificing their lives together. As they head to the gallows, with ropes already around their necks, each shows a distinct emotion: From courage to despair. Compare the small plaster model in the glass case with the final, life-size bronze group out the window in the garden (near the street behind the ticket booth).

Room 15: Rodin's feverish attempts to capture a portrait of the novelist Balzac ranged from a pot-bellied Bacchus to a headless nude cradling an erection. In a moment of inspiration, Rodin threw a plaster-soaked robe over the nude and watched it dry into what would become the final, definitive version.

Room 17: Legendary lovers kiss, embrace, and intertwine in yin-yang bliss.

Room 14: Rodin's portrait busts of celebrities and some paintings by (yawn, are we through yet?) van Gogh, Monet, and Renoir. Rodin enjoyed discussions with Monet and other artists and incorporated their ideas in his work. Rodin is often considered an Impressionist because he captured spontaneous "impressions" of figures and created rough surfaces that catch reflected light.

Room 13: By the end of his life, Rodin was more famous than his works. The museum's film clip shows Rodin making the marble chips fly. In fact, he rarely picked up a chisel, leaving that to assistants. Compare Rodin's small plaster "sketches" (in the glass case) with the final, large-scale marble versions executed by others.

THE GARDENS

Rodin lived and worked in this mansion, renting rooms alongside Matisse, the poet Rilke (Rodin's secretary), and the dancer Isadora Duncan. He loved placing his creations in the overgrown gardens. These are his greatest works, Rodin at his most expansive. The epic human figures are enhanced, not dwarfed, by nature.

• *Leaving the house, there are five more stops: Two on the left and three on the right. Beyond these stops is a big, breezy garden ornamented with statues, a cafeteria, and WC.*

The Thinker: Leaning slightly forward, tense and compact, every muscle working toward producing that one great thought, Man contemplates his fate. No constipation jokes, please.

This is not an intellectual, but a linebacker who's realizing there's more to life than frat parties. It's the first man evolving beyond his animal nature to think the first thought. It's anyone who's ever worked hard to reinvent himself or to make something new or better. Said Rodin: "It is a statue of myself."

There are 29 other authorized copies of this statue, arguably the most famous in the world.

• *To the left of* The Thinker *you'll find* . . .

Balzac: The iconoclastic novelist turns his nose up at the notion he should be honored with a statue. This final version also stands in the Musée d'Orsay and on a street median in Montparnasse. When the statue was unveiled, the crowd booed, a fitting tribute to both the defiant novelist and the bold man who sculpted him.

• *Along the street near the ticket booth are* . . .

The Burghers of Calais: The six city fathers trudge to their execution, and we can read in their faces and poses what their last thoughts are. They mill about, dazed, as each one deals with the decision he's made to sacrifice himself for his city.

• *Circling counterclockwise* . . .

The man carrying the key to the city tightens his lips in determination. The bearded man is weighed down with grief. Another buries his head in his hands. One turns, seeking reassurance from his friend, who turns away and gestures helplessly. The final key bearer (in back) raises his hand to his head.

Each is alone in his thoughts, but they're united by their mutual sacrifice, by the base they stand on, and by their weighty robes—gravity is already dragging them down to their graves.

Pity the poor souls, then salute King Edward III, who, at the last second, pardoned them.

• *Follow* The Thinker*'s gaze to the opposite side of the house. Standing before a tall white backdrop is a big dark door—the* Gates of Hell.

The Gates of Hell: These doors (never meant to actually open) were never finished for a museum that was never built. But the vision of Dante's trip into hell gave Rodin a chance to explore the dark side of human experience. "Abandon hope all ye who enter in," was hell's motto. The Three Shades at the top of the door point down—that's where we're going. Beneath The Shades, pondering the whole scene from above, is Dante as The Thinker. Below him, the figures emerge from the darkness just long enough to tell their sad tale of depravity. There's Paolo and Francesca (in the center of the right door), who were driven into an illicit love affair that brought them here. Ugolino (left door, just below center) crouches in prison over his kids. This poor soul was so driven by hunger that he ate the corpses of his own children. On all fours like an animal, he is the dark side of natural selection. Finally, find what some say is Rodin himself (at the very bottom, inside the right door jamb, where it just starts to jut out), crouching humbly.

You'll find some of these figures writ large in the garden. *The Thinker* is behind you, *The Shades* are 27 meters (90 feet) to the right, and *Ugolino* dines in the fountain at the far end.

It's appropriate that *The Gates*—Rodin's "cathedral"—remained unfinished. He was always a restless artist for whom the process of discovery was as important as the finished product.

• *To the right of the* Gates of Hell *is a glassed-in building, the*...

Gallery of Marbles: Unfinished, they show human features emerging from the rough stone. Imagine Rodin in his studio working to give them life.

Victor Hugo (at the far end of the Gallery), the great champion of Les Miz progress, leans back like Michelangelo's nude *Adam*, waiting for the spark of creation. He tenses his face and cups his ear, straining to hear the call from the blurry Muse above him. Once inspired, he can bring the idea to life (just as Rodin did) with the strength of his powerful arms. It's been said that all of Rodin's work shows the struggle of mind over matter, of brute creatures emerging from the mud and evolving into a species of thinkers.

MARMOTTAN
TOUR

paris

The Marmottan (or Musée Marmottan Monet) has the best collection of works by the master Impressionist, Claude Monet. In this mansion on the fringe of urban Paris, you can walk through Monet's life, from black-and-white sketches to colorful open-air paintings to the canvas that gave Impressionism its name. The museum's highlights are scenes of his garden at Giverny, including larger-than-life water lilies.

Orientation

Cost: €6, €4 for students under 25, free for children under 8. The Marmottan is not covered by the museum pass.
Hours: Tue–Sun 10:00–17:30 (last entrance 17:00), closed Mon, May 1, and Dec 25.
Getting There: It's in northwest Paris at 2 rue Louis Boilly (Mo: La Muette or RER-C: Boulainvilliers, then a 10-min walk, following signs; or bus #32, #63, #22, or #52).
Information: Tel. 01 44 96 50 33, www.marmottan.com.
Photography: Not allowed. Cameras must be checked.
Length of Our Tour: One hour.
Starring: Claude Monet, including *Impression: Sunrise* (shown above), Rouen Cathedral, Gare St. Lazare, Houses of Parliament, scenes from Giverny, water lilies.

OVERVIEW

The museum traces Monet's life chronologically, but in a way that's as rough and fragmented as a Monet canvas. Keep the big picture.

First Floor (upstairs): Works from the first half of Monet's life, plus paintings by Impressionist colleagues (Renoir, Pissarro, Morisot, and more).

Ground floor: Bookstore; old photos of Monet, his garden, and Giverny studio; an actual palette; and an eclectic collection of non-Monet objects.

Basement: Works from the last half of his life, mostly of his gardens at Giverny (including water lilies).

FIRST FLOOR: FROM LE HAVRE TO LONDON (1857–1900)

• *Start at the glass case at the top of the stairs.*

Portraits of Monet and his wife, Camille (by Renoir and others) and Memorabilia

Claude Monet (1840–1926) was the leading light of the Impressionist movement that revolutionized painting in the 1870s. Fiercely independent and dedicated to his craft, Monet gave courage to Renoir and others in the face of harsh criticism. The letters (in the glass case) from Monet asking for survival money from his friends show the price he paid for his bohemian principles.

Impression: Sunrise (1873)

Here's the painting—a simple, serene view of boats bobbing under an orange sun—that started the revolution. At the first public showing by Monet, Renoir, Degas, and others in Paris in 1874, critics howled at this work and ridiculed the title. "Wallpaper," one called it. The sloppy brushstrokes and ordinary subject looked like a study, not a finished work. The whole group and style got dubbed "Impression"-ist . . . a pretty accurate name.

The misty harbor scene obviously made an "impression" on Monet, who faithfully rendered the fleeting moment in quick strokes of paint. The waves are simple horizontal brushstrokes. The sun's reflection on the water is a few thick, bold strokes of orange tipped with white. They zigzag down the canvas, the way a reflection shifts on moving water.

• *Follow the arrow to the right, into "Debut d'exposition," passing through a big room of colorful canvases (which we'll return to later) into a smaller room in the corner.*

Growing up in Le Havre (1840–1860): Caricature Drawings (c. 1858)

Teenage Monet's first works—black-and-white, meticulously drawn, humorous sketches of small-town celebrities—are as different as can be from the colorful, messy oils that would make him famous. Still, they show his gift for quickly capturing an overall impression with a few simple strokes.

The son of a grocer, he defied his family, insisting he was

an artist, and sketched the world around him—beaches, boats, and small-town life. A fellow artist encouraged him to don a scarf, set up his easel outdoors, and paint the scene exactly as he saw it. (Well, duhh! But "open-air" painting was unorthodox for artists trained to study their subjects thoroughly in the perfect lighting of a controlled studio setting.)

The 1860s: Paris

At 19, Monet went to Paris but refused to enroll in the official art schools. He teamed up with Auguste Renoir and Alfred Sisley, leading them on open-air painting safaris to the countryside. Inspired by the realism of Edouard Manet, they painted everyday things—landscapes, seascapes, street scenes, ladies with parasols, family picnics—in bright, basic colors.

• *Return to the big room with colorful canvases (spanning 1870–1890). To follow Monet chronologically, you'll have to browse around this room and others on the first floor.*

The 1870s: Pure Impressionism

In 1870, Monet married his girlfriend, Camille, (the dark-haired woman in many of his paintings) and moved just outside Paris to the resort town of Argenteuil. Playing host to Renoir, Manet, and others, he perfected the Impressionist style—painting nature as a mosaic of short brushstrokes of different colors placed side by side, suggesting shimmering light.

First, he simplified. In *The Beach at Trouville* (1870), a lady's dress is simply a few thick strokes of paint. Gradually (*Stroll Near Argenteuil*, 1872), Monet broke things down into smaller dots of different colors. If you back up from a Monet canvas, the colors blend into one (for example, red plus green plus yellow equal a brown boat). Still, they never fully resolve, creating the effect of colorful, shimmering light. Monet limited his palette to a few bright colors—cobalt blue, white, yellow, two shades of red, and emerald green abound. But no black—even shadows are a combination of bright colors.

Monet's constant quest was to faithfully reproduce nature in colored blobs of paint. His eye was a camera lens set at a very slow shutter speed to admit maximum light. Then he "developed" the impression made on his retina with an oil-based, pigmented solution. Even as the heartbroken Monet watched Camille die of tuberculosis in 1879, he was (he admitted later) intrigued by the changing colors in her dying face.

The 1880s: Travels

In search of new light and new scenes, Monet traveled throughout France and Europe. As you look at canvases of fields, trees, seashores, churches, lakes, and farmhouses in all kinds of weather, picture Monet at work—hiking to a remote spot; carrying an easel, several canvases, brushes (large-size), a palette, tubes of paint (an invention that made open-air painting practical), food and drink, a folding chair, and an umbrella; and wearing his trademark hat, with a cigarette on his lip. He weathered the elements, occasionally putting himself in danger by clambering on cliffs to get the shot.

The key was to work fast before the weather changed and the light shifted, completely changing the colors. Monet worked "wet-in-wet," applying new paint before the first layer dried, mixing colors on the canvas, and piling them up into a thick paste.

The 1890s: Series

Monet often painted the same subject several times under different light (such as one of Paris' train stations, the *Gare St. Lazare*, 1870s). In the 1890s, he conceived of a series of paintings to be shown as a group, giving a time-lapse view of a single subject.

He rented a room overlooking the *Cathedral of Rouen* and worked on up to 14 different canvases at a time, shuffling the right one onto the easel as the sun moved across the sky. The cathedral is made of brown stone, but at sunset it becomes gold and pink with blue shadows, softened by thick smudges of paint. The true subject is not the cathedral, but the full spectrum of light that bounces off it.

These series—of the cathedral, of haystacks, poplars, and mornings on the Seine—were very popular. Monet, poverty-stricken until his mid-40s, was slowly becoming famous, first in America, then London, and finally in France.

The 1900s: London

Turning a hotel room into a studio, Monet—working on nearly a hundred different canvases simultaneously—painted the changing light on the River Thames. The *London Houses of Parliament*, reflected in the Thames, stretch and bend with the tide. *Charing Cross Bridge* is only a few smudgy lines enveloped in fog.

London's fog epitomized Monet's favorite subject—the atmosphere that distorts distant objects. That filtering haze gives even different-colored objects a similar tone, resulting in a more harmonious picture. When the light was just right and the atmosphere glowed, the moment of "instantaneity" had arrived, and Monet worked like a madman.

In truth, many of Monet's canvases were begun quickly in the open air, then painstakingly perfected later in the studio. He composed his scenes with great care—clear horizon lines give a strong horizontal, while diagonal lines (of trees or shorelines) create solid triangles. And he wasn't above airbrushing out details that might spoil the composition—such as Cleopatra's Needle near Charing Cross.

• *Find portraits of Monet's family in the small octagonal room.*

Monet's Two Families

Camille died in 1879, leaving Monet to raise 12-year-old Jean and babe-in-arms Michel. (Michel would grow up to inherit the family home and many of the paintings that ended up here.) But Monet was also involved with Alice Hoschede, who had recently been abandoned by her husband. Alice moved in with her six kids, took care of the dying Camille, and the two families made a Brady-Bunch merger. Baby Michel became bosom buddies with Alice's baby Jean-Pierre, and teenage Jean Monet and stepsister Blanche fell in love and later married.

In 1883, the brood settled into a farmhouse in Giverny (80 kilometers west of Paris). Monet would spend the next 40 years here, traveling less with each passing year. Financially stable and domestically blissful, he turned Giverny into a garden paradise—painting nature without the long commute.

• *Before leaving the first floor, check out the fine collection of paintings by Monet's Impressionist colleagues: Renoir, Gauguin, Pissarro, Morisot (if you like her, find her portrait by Manet), and others.*

BASEMENT: PAINTINGS OF GIVERNY (1883–1926)

These large, colorful canvases immerse you in Monet's garden at Giverny. He did his own landscaping: flower beds of lilies, iris, and clematis, arbors of climbing roses forming a tunnel-like "Grand Alley," and a Japanese garden with an arched footbridge, willows, bamboo, and a pond filled with water lilies.

In the last half of his life, Monet's world shrank—from the broad vistas of the world traveler to the tranquility of his home, family, and garden. But his artistic vision expanded as he painted smaller details on bigger canvases and helped invent modern abstract art.

• *Working roughly clockwise around the room . . .*

Path with Rose Trellises

The arched trellises form a natural tunnel effect that leads your eye down the path, "into" the canvas. But the canvas is fully saturated with color, with distant objects as bright as close ones. Monet's mosaic of brushstrokes forms a colorful design that's beautiful even if you just look "at" the canvas like wallpaper. He wanted his paintings to be realistic (3-dimensional), but with a pleasant (2-dimensional) pattern.

The Japanese Bridge (several versions)

In 1890, Monet started work on a Japanese garden, inspired by tranquil scenes from the Japanese prints he collected. He diverted a river to form a pond, planted willows and bamboo on the shores, filled the pond with water lilies, then crossed it with this wooden footbridge. As years passed (compare early and later canvases), the bridge became overgrown with wisteria. He painted it at different times of day and year, exploring different color schemes.

Monet uses the bridge as the symmetrical center of simple, pleasing designs. The water is drawn with horizontal brushstrokes that get shorter as you move up the canvas ("farther away"), creating the illusion of distance. The horizontal water contrasts with the vertical-stroke willows, while the bridge "bridges" the sides of the square canvas, lacing the scene together.

Monet—the greatest "vision"-ary, literally, of his generation—began to go blind. Cataracts distorted his perception of depth and color, and sent him into a tailspin of despair. The (angry?) red paintings date from this period.

Water Lilies (several versions)

As his vision slowly failed, he concentrated on painting close-ups of the surface of the pond and its water lilies (scientific name *Nympheas*), using red, white, yellow, lavender, and various combos. Some lilies are just a few broad strokes on a bare canvas (a study), while others are piles of paint formed with overlapping colors.

But the true subject is not the lilies, but the changing reflections on the surface of the pond—of the blue sky, white clouds, and green trees that line the shore. Pan slowly around the room and watch the pond turn from pre-dawn to bright sunlight to twilight. Monet, assisted by his favorite daughter, Blanche (a painter and a widow when Jean died young), worked on several canvases at once, moving with the sun from one to the next.

Early lily paintings (c. 1900) show the shoreline as a reference point. But increasingly, Monet cropped the scene ever closer until there was no shoreline, no horizon, no sense of what's up or down. Lilies float among clouds. Stepping back from the canvas, you see the lilies just hang there on the museum wall, suspended in space. The surface of the pond and the surface of the canvas are one. Modern, abstract art—a colored design on a flat surface—is just around the corner.

Big Weeping Willow

Get close—Monet did—and analyze the trunk. Rough "brown" bark is made of thick strokes (an inch wide and 4 inches long) of pink, purple, orange, and green. Impressionism lives. But to get these colors to resolve in your eye, you'd have to back up all the way to Giverny.

Later Water Lilies (1915–1926)

Like Beethoven going deaf, blind Monet wrote his final symphonies on a monumental scale. He planned a series of huge canvases (2 meters/6 feet tall) of water lilies to hang in special rooms at L'Orangerie (scheduled to re-open in 2002; see tour on page 184). He built a special studio with skylights and wheeled easels, and worked on them obsessively. A successful eye operation in 1923 gave him new energy. Here at the Marmottan are smaller-scale studies for that series.

Some lilies are patches of thick paint circled by a squiggly "caricature" of a lily pad. Monet simplifies in a way that Matisse and Picasso would envy. But getting close, you see that the lily is made of many brushstrokes, and also that each brushstroke is itself a mix of different colored paints.

Monet is thought of as a "light"-weight, but he deals with the fundamentals of life, especially in his later work: Green lilies floating among lavender clouds reflected in the blue water. Staring into Monet's pond, we see the intermingling of the four classical elements, earth (foliage), air (the sky), fire (sunlight), and water—the primordial soup where life begins.

When Monet died in 1926, he was famous. Starting with meticulous line drawings, he evolved to open-air realist to Impressionist color-analyst to serial painter to master of reflections. As the subjects of his work became fuzzier, the colors and patterns predominated. Monet builds a bridge between Impressionism and modern abstract art.

L'ORANGERIE
TOUR

paris

This Impressionist museum—lovely as a water lily—is due to reopen sometime in 2002 after renovation (for the latest, ask at a Paris TI or any Paris museum). When it opens, you can step out of the tree-lined, sun-dappled Impressionist painting that is the Tuileries Gardens, and into L'Orangerie (loh-rahn-zhay-ree), a little bijou of select works by Utrillo, Cézanne, Renoir, Matisse, and Picasso. On the ground floor, you'll find a line of eight rooms dedicated to these artists. Downstairs is the finale: Monet's water lilies. The museum's collection is small enough to enjoy in a short visit, but complete enough to see the bridge from Impressionism to the Moderns. And it's all beautiful.

Orientation
Cost: About €6 hours, covered by museum pass.
Hours: Approximately Wed–Mon 10:00–17:00, closed Tue.
Getting There: It's at the entry of the Tuileries Gardens near place de la Concorde, at the riverside (Mo: Concorde).
Information: Tel. 01 42 97 48 16.
Tour Length: One hour.

GROUND FLOOR
You'll encounter the work of these artists (possibly in a different order, following the renovation):

Maurice Utrillo (1883–1955)
This hard-drinking, streetwise bohemian artist is known for his postcard views of Montmartre—whitewashed buildings under perennially cloudy skies.

Cézanne (1839–1906)

These small canvases of simple subjects reinvented the way modern artists painted. In his landscapes, Cézanne the Impressionist creates "brown" rocks out of red, orange, and purple, and "green" trees out of green, lime, and purple. Cézanne the proto-Cubist builds the rocks and trees out of blocks of thick brushstrokes.

The fruits of his still-lifes are also "built" out of patches of color. There's no traditional shading to create the illusion of 3-D, but these fruits bulge out like cameos from the canvas. The fruits are clearly at eye level, yet they're also clearly placed on a table seen from above. Picasso was fascinated with Cézanne's strange new world that showed multiple perspectives at once.

Renoir (1841–1919)

Renoir loved to paint *les femmes*—women and girls, nude and innocent, all with rosy-red cheeks and a relaxed grace. We get a feel for the happy family life of middle-class Parisians during the belle époque—the beautiful age of the late 19th century. Renoir's warm, sunny colors (mostly red) are Impressionist, but he adds a classical touch with his clearer lines and, in the later nudes, the voluptuousness of classical statues and paintings.

Marie Laurencin (1883–1956)

Pink, blue, and gray pastels of women and animals.

Andre Derain (1880–1954)

Still-lifes, nudes, harlequins, portraits, landscapes—all of them in odd, angular poses. Contrast his sharp lines with the fuzziness of the earlier Impressionist style.

Matisse (1869–1954)

Languid women in angular rooms with arabesque wallpaper. Matisse, the original Fauve ("wild beast"), has tamed his colors a bit here. These paler tones evoke the sunny luxury of the Riviera. Traditional 3-D perspective is thrown out the occasional hotel window as the women and furnishings in the "foreground" blend with the wallpaper "background" to become part of the decor.

Picasso (1881–1973)

Pablo Picasso is a shopping-mall of 20th-century artistic styles. In this room alone, he passes through his "Blue" Period (sad and tragic), "Rose" Period (red-toned nudes with timeless, mask-like faces), and Cubism (flat planes of interwoven perspectives). He even seems a lover of women in the tradition of Renoir with his massive, sculptural nudes—warm blow-up dolls with substance. If all roads lead to Paris, all art styles flowed through Picasso.

Rousseau (1812–1867)

Henri Rousseau, a simple government official, never traveled outside France, but he created an exotic, dreamlike, completely unique world. A Parisian wedding is set amid tropical trees. Figures are placed in a 3-D world, but the lines of perspective recede so steeply into the distance that everyone is in danger of sliding down the canvas. The way he put familiar images in bizarre settings influenced the Surrealists. Enjoy France's biggest collection of Rousseaus.
•*Downstairs in two large rooms is L'Orangerie's highlight.*

CLAUDE MONET'S WATER LILIES

Hall I

These mammoth, curved, panels immerse you in Monet's garden. We're looking at the pond in his garden at Giverny—dotted with water lilies, surrounded by foliage—and at the reflections of the sky, clouds, and trees on the surface. The water lilies ("nympheas") range from plain green lily pads to flowers of red, white, yellow, lavender, and various combos.

The true subject is the play of light on the water. Monet (1840–1926) would work on several canvases at once, each one dedicated to the pond at a different time of day. He'd move with the sun from one to the next. Pan slowly around this hall. Watch the pond turn from pre-dawn to bright sunlight to twilight.

Get close to the yellow panel and see how Monet worked. Starting from the gray of blank canvas (lower right), he'd lay down big, thick brushstrokes of a single color, weaving them in a (mostly) horizontal and vertical pattern to create a dense mesh of foliage. Then, over this, he'd add more color for the dramatic highlights, until (in the center) he got a dense paste of piled-up paint. Up close it's a mess, but back up and the colors begin to resolve into a luminous scene of sunlight and trees on the water.

The panel (to right) on one of the long walls shows green lilies floating among lavender clouds reflected in blue water. Staring into Monet's pond, we see the intermingling of the four classical elements—earth (foliage), air (the sky), fire (sunlight) and water—the primordial soup from which all life springs.
• *Between the two halls, look for the bust of Monet with his Impressionist beard and old photos of the artist in his Giverny garden and studio.*

Hall II

Here the pond is framed by pillar-esque tree trunks and overhanging foliage. The compositions are a little more symmetrical and the color schemes more muted, with blue-and-lavender and green-brown.

But as you get close, you'll see that even a "brown" tree is a tangled Impressionist beard of purple, green, blue, and red. Each leaf is a long brushstroke and each lily pad a dozen smudges.

The darkest panel (at the end) is a mess of paint made symmetrical by the one rosy lily in the center. Get close to the lily, and you'll see that, yes, it's made of many brushstrokes, but also that each brushstroke is itself a mix of red, white, and pink paints.

Monet, who personally planned for these paintings to hang in this location, wanted the vibrant colors to keep firing your synapses. As the subjects become fuzzier, the colors and patterns alone are more important. Monet builds a bridge between Impressionism and modern abstract art.

NAPOLEON'S TOMB & LES INVALIDES TOUR

If you've ever considered being absolute dictator of a united Europe, come here first. Hitler did, before going out and making the same mistakes as his mentor. (Hint: Don't invade Russia.)

Napoleon's tomb can be seen where it rests beneath the golden dome of Les Invalides church. Around the church, in a one-time veterans' hospital built by Louis XIV, are various military museums. The best is the new WWII wing (see tour, below).

Orientation

Cost: €6, students and ages 12 to 17 pay €5, free for those under 12, covered by museum pass.

Hours: Daily April–Sept 09:00–17:45, Oct–March 10:00–16:45 (Napoleon's Tomb open June 15–Sept 15 until 18:45). Closed Jan 1, May 1, Nov 1, and Dec 25.

Getting There: The tomb is at Hôtel Les Invalides at 129 rue de Grenelle (near Rodin Museum, Mo: La Tour Maubourg, Varennes, or Invalides).

Information: Tel. 01 44 42 37 72, www.invalides.org.

Length of Our Tour: Women—two hours, men—three hours, Republican men—all day.

• *Start at Napoleon's tomb, underneath the golden dome. It's at the back end (farthest from the Seine) of this vast complex of churches and museums.*

NAPOLEON'S TOMB

Enter the church, gaze up at the dome, then lean over the railing and bow to the emperor lying inside the red porphyry, scrolled tomb. If the lid were opened, you'd find an oak coffin inside, which holds another ebony coffin, housing two lead ones, then mahogany, then tinplate . . . until finally you'd find Napoleon himself staring up, with his head closest to the door. When his body

was exhumed from the original grave and transported here, it was still perfectly preserved, even after 19 years in the ground.

Born of humble Italian heritage on the French-owned isle of Corsica, Napoleon Bonaparte (1769–1821) went to school at Paris' Ecole Militaire (Military School), then rose quickly through the ranks amid the chaos of the Revolution. The charismatic "Little Corporal" won fans by fighting for democracy at home and abroad. In 1799, he assumed power and, within five short years, conquered most of Europe. The great champion of the Revolution had become a dictator, declaring himself emperor of a new Rome.

Napoleon's red tomb on its green base stands 4.5 meters (15 feet) high in the center of a marble floor. It's exalted by the dome above (where dead Frenchmen cavort with saints and angels), forming a golden halo over Napoleon.

Napoleon is surrounded by family. After conquering Europe, he installed his big brother, Joseph, as king of Spain (turn around to see Joseph's tomb in the alcove to the left of the door); his little brother, Jerome, became king of Westphalia (to right of door); and his baby boy, Napoleon Junior (downstairs), sat in diapers on the throne of Rome.

In other alcoves, you'll find more dead war heroes (including World War I's Marshall Foch) and many painted saints, making this the French Valhalla in the Versailles of churches.

The Crypt

• *The stairs behind the altar (with the corkscrew columns) take you down to crypt level for a closer look at the tomb.*

Wandering clockwise, read the names of Napoleon's battles inlaid on the floor. Rivoli marks the battle where the rookie 26-year-old general took a ragtag band of "citizens" and thrashed the professional Austrian troops in Italy. He returned to Paris a celebrity. In Egypt (Pyramids), he fought Turks and tribesmen to a standstill, but the exotic expedition caught the public eye, and he returned home a legend.

Austerlitz made him Europe's top dog. At the head of the million-man Grand Army, he made a three-month blitz attack through Germany and Austria. As a general he was daring, relying on a mobile force of independent armies. His personal charisma on the battlefield was said to be worth 10,000 additional men.

Pause in the battles to gaze at the grand statue of Napoleon the emperor in the alcove at the head of the tomb—royal scepter and orb of Earth in his hands. By 1805, all of Europe was at his feet. He held an elaborate ceremony in Notre-Dame, where he proclaimed his wife, Josephine, as Empress, and himself—the 36-year-old son of humble immigrants—as Emperor. The laurel wreath, the robes, and the Roman eagles proclaim him the equal of the Caesars. The floor at the statue's feet marks the grave of his son, Napoleon II (Roi de Rome).

Around the crypt are relief panels showing Napoleon's constructive side. Dressed in toga and laurel leaves, he dispenses justice, charity, and pork-barrel projects to an awed populace.

• *In the first panel to the right of the statue . . .*

He establishes an Imperial University to educate naked boys throughout "*tout l'empire.*" The roll of great scholars links modern France with those of the past: Plutarch, Homer, Plato, and Aristotle.

Hail Napoleon. Then, at his peak, came his fatal mistake.

• *Continue around the tomb to the Battle of Moscow (Moscowa) . . .*

Napoleon invaded Russia with 600,000 men and returned to Paris with 100,000 frostbitten survivors. Two years later, the Russians marched into Paris, and Napoleon's days were numbered. After a brief exile on the isle of Elba, he skipped parole, sailed to France, bared his breast, and said, "Strike me down or follow me!" For 100 days they followed him, finally into Belgium, where the British finished him off at the Battle of Waterloo (conspicuously absent on the floor decor). Exiled again by a war tribunal, he spent his last days in a crude shack on the small South Atlantic island of St. Helena.

LES INVALIDES AND THE ARMY MUSEUM (*MUSÉE DE L'ARMÉE*)

Your tomb ticket also admits you to several military museums scattered around the complex (listed in free English map/guide in ticket hall). Most of it consists of dummies in uniforms and endless glass cases full of muskets, without historical context, but the wing on World War II is worthwhile.

Exiting the church with Napoleon's tomb, make a U-turn right and march past the ticket hall and café. Halfway down the long hallway, on the right, you'll see a bare stone slab beside weeping willows that originally marked Napoleon's grave on the island of St. Helena. There was no epitaph, since the French and British wrangled over what to call the hero/tyrant. The stones read simply, "Here lies . . ."

─── LES INVALIDES ───

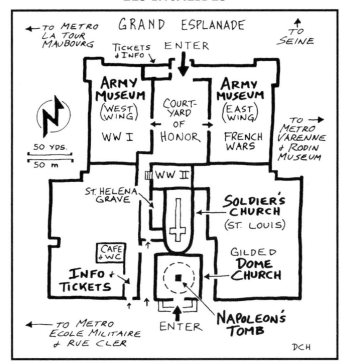

Continuing on, you'll spill out into the large Courtyard of Honor, where Napoleon honored his troops and de Gaulle once kissed Churchill. The Army Museum flanks both sides of the courtyard.

ARMY MUSEUM: EAST WING

This traces uniforms and weapons through French history, from Louis XIV to World War I. This is interesting for Napoleo-philes.

• *Enter under golden letters and go up to the second floor.*

As you circle this floor, you'll follow the history and art of French warfare from about 1700 to 1850: Pre-Revolution, Revolution, Napoleon, and Restoration.

The "First Republic: 1793–1804" section has early Napoleonic exhibits. In the Salle Boulogne are the emperor's hat and sword. The tent (behind screen) shows his bivouac equipment—a bed with mosquito netting, a director's chair, and a table that you can imagine his generals hunched over, making battle plans.

In the rooms covering "Napoleon and The Empire 1804–1814" (first room: Salle Austerlitz), you'll find the famous portrait by Ingres of Napoleon at his peak of power, stretching his right arm to supernatural lengths. Then comes Napoleon's beloved horse, Le Vizir, who weathered many a campaign and grew old with him in exile (stuffed in a glass case, third room: Salle Eylau).

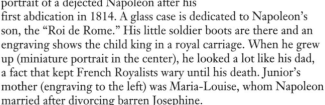

Later, in Salle Montmirail, there's a portrait of a dejected Napoleon after his first abdication in 1814. A glass case is dedicated to Napoleon's son, the "Roi de Rome." His little soldier boots are there and an engraving shows the child king in a royal carriage. When he grew up (miniature portrait in the center), he looked a lot like his dad, a fact that kept French Royalists wary until his death. Junior's mother (engraving to the left) was Maria-Louise, whom Napoleon married after divorcing barren Josephine.

Napoleon's big white dog (in a glass case after you turn the corner into the long blue Corridor de Tarascon) suffered the same fate as his horse. On the wall to the left of the dog hang proclamations of thanks and good-byes Napoleon sent to his soldiers and the French people, announcing the surrender at Waterloo. Directly behind the dog, a shining breastplate shows the effectiveness of British artillery in the Battle of Waterloo. In about the middle of the long blue room, you'll find Napoleon's death mask and a reconstruction of his final home on St. Helena. Picture a lonely man suffering from ulcers sitting here in his nightcap and slippers, playing chess, not war.

After the Salle Restauration (the mid-1800s, when France brought back the royalty), the last display before the exit is an American flag in a glass case, honoring General La Fayette of France, who helped George Washington take Yorktown. It has the only English-language description in the entire place.

ARMY MUSEUM: WEST WING

Across the courtyard is a twin museum in the West Wing. The ground floor covers military implements, from stone axes to Axis powers. Near the entry, two huge, interesting rooms of armor and medieval weaponry have good English descriptions.

Upstairs on the second floor, you'll find the World War I wing. Photos and films spice up the uniforms and guns.

The Musée des Plans Reliefs (top floor of West Wing) has 18th-century models of fortified cities (see flier at the door).

The Musée de l'Ordre de la Liberation (free, no English descriptions, located in another building back near Napoleon's gravestones) tells the story of the Resistance in World War II. The French refer to World War II as "The War of '39–40," but this proud collection makes it clear that the French were busy during the Nazi occupation.

ARMY MUSEUM: WORLD WAR II WING

World War II was the most destructive of earth's struggles. In this new exhibit, the war unfolds in photos, displays, and newsreels, with special emphasis on the French contribution. You may never have realized that it was Charles de Gaulle who won the war for us.

The wing is located in the southwest corner of the main courtyard; go upstairs, following signs to "General de Gaulle: Deuxième Guerre Mondiale, 39/45." The museum has two other names as well: "General de Gaulle, Seconde Guerre Mondiale" and "France Libre, France Combattante."

The free museum map is helpful for locating the displays we'll see.

Climb to the top floor and work back down, from Germany's quick domination (third floor) to the Allies turning the tide (second floor) to the final surrender (first floor).

There are fine English descriptions. Make time!

Third Floor: Axis Aggression

Room 1: Treaty of Versailles to 1939 (*Du Traité de Versailles à 1939*): In 1918, the "war to end all wars" ground to a halt, leaving 10 million dead, a defeated Germany, and a devastated (if victorious) France. For the next two decades, Adolf Hitler would feed off German resentment for the Treaty of Versailles, which had humiliated and ruined Germany.

Room 2: The Defeat of 1940 (*La Defaite de 1940*): On September 1, 1939, Hitler invaded Poland, starting World War II. France and Britain mobilized, but Germany did nothing for six months. Then, in the spring of 1940, came the Blitzkrieg ("lightning war"), and Germany's better-trained and better-equipped soldiers and tanks swept west through Belgium. France was immediately overwhelmed, and British troops barely escaped across the Channel from Dunkirk. Within a month, Nazis were goose-stepping down the Champs-Elysées, and Hitler was on his way to Napoleon's tomb.

Room 3: The Appeal of 18 June, 1940: Just like that, virtually all of Europe was dominated by fascists. During those darkest days, as France fell and Nazism spread across the Continent, one Frenchman—an obscure military man named Charles de Gaulle—refused to admit defeat. He escaped to London and made inspiring speeches over the radio, slowly convincing a small audience of French expatriates that victory was still possible.

Room 4: Charles de Gaulle
(1890–1970): This 20th-century John of Arc had an unshakable belief in his mission to save France. He was born into a literate, upper-class family, raised in military academies, and became a WWI hero and POW. After the war, he helped administer the occupied Rhineland. When World War II broke out, he was

only a minor officer (the title of "Brigadier General" was hastily acquired during the invasion). With limited political experience, he was virtually unknown to the French public. But he rallied France, became the focus of French patriotism, and later guided the country in the postwar years.

Room 6: The Vichy Government (*La France après l'Armistice, L'Empire colonial: un enjeu*): After the surrender, Germany ruled northern France (including Paris) but allowed the French to administer the south and the colonies (North Africa). This puppet government, centered in the city of Vichy, was right-wing and traditional, bowing to Hitler's demands as he looted France's raw materials and manpower for the war machine. (The movie *Casablanca*, set in Vichy-controlled Morocco, has French officials following Nazi orders while French citizens defiantly sing "The Marseillaise.")

Room 7: The Battle of Britain—June 1940–June 1941
(*La Bataille d'Angleterre, Du Refus de la Defaite a l'Esprit de Résistance*): Facing a "New Dark Age" in Europe, British Prime Minister Winston Churchill pledged, "We will fight on the beaches...We will fight in the hills. We will never surrender."

In June 1940, Germany mobilized to invade Britain across the Channel. From June to September, they paved the way, sending bombers—up to 1,500 planes a day—to destroy military and industrial sites. When Britain wouldn't budge, Hitler concentrated on London and civilian targets—this was "The Blitz" of the winter of 1940, which killed 30,000 and left London in ruins. But Britain hung on, armed with newfangled radar, speedy Spitfires, and an iron will.

They also had the Germans' secret "Enigma" code. The "Enigma" machine (in display case), with its set of revolving drums, allowed German commanders to scramble orders into a complex code to safely broadcast to their troops. The British captured a machine, broke the code (a project called "Ultra"), then monitored German airwaves. For the

rest of the war, they had advance knowledge of many top-secret plans. (Occasionally, Britain even let Germany's plans succeed—sacrificing their own people—to avoid suspicion.)

By spring of 1941, Hitler had given up any hope of invading the Isle of Britain. Churchill said of his people: "This was their finest hour."

Room 10: Germany Invades Russia—June 1941 (*L'Allemagne Envahit l'Union Sovietique*): Perhaps hoping to one-up Napoleon, Hitler sent his state-of-the-art tanks speeding toward Moscow (betraying his former ally, Josef Stalin). By winter, the advance had stalled at the gates of Moscow, bogged down by bad weather and Soviet stubbornness. The Third Reich had reached its peak. From

now on, Hitler would have to fight a two-front war. The French Renault tank (displayed) was downright puny compared to the big, fast, high-caliber German Panzers. This war was often a battle of factories, to see who could produce the latest technology fastest and in greatest number.

Room 12: The United States Enters the War (*Les Etats-Unis Entrent dans la Guerre*): "On December seventh, nineteen forty-one, a day that will live in infamy" (as F.D.R. put it), Japanese planes made a sneak attack on the U.S. base at Pearl Harbor, Hawaii, destroying the pride of the Pacific fleet in two hours. The United States quickly declared war on Japan and her ally, Germany. In two short years, America had gone from isolationist observer to supplier of Britain's arms to full-blown war ally against fascism. The United States now faced two wars—in Europe against Hitler, and against Japan's imperialist conquest of China, Southeast Asia, and the South Pacific.

America's first victory came in Hawaii when Japan tried a sneak attack on the U.S. base at Midway Island (June 3, 1942). This time—thanks to the Allies cracking the "Enigma" code—America had the U.S.S. *Enterprise* (see model) and two of her buddies lying in wait. In five minutes, three of Japan's carriers (with valuable planes) were fatally wounded, their major attack force was sunk, and Japan and the United States were dead even and settling in for a long war of attrition.

Though slow to start, America eventually had an army of 16 million strong, 80,000 planes, the latest technology, $250 million a day, unlimited raw materials, and a population fighting for freedom to a boogie-woogie beat.

• *Continue downstairs to the second floor.*

Second Floor: The Tide Turns

In 1942, the Continent was black with fascism and Japan was secure on a distant island. The Allies had to chip away on the fringes.

Room 13: Battle of the Atlantic (*La Bataille de l'Atlantique*): German U-boats (short for "Unterseeboot," see model) and battleships such as the *Bismarck* patrolled Europe's perimeter, keeping America from aiding Britain. (Until long-range transport planes were invented near war's end, virtually all military transport was by ship.) The Allies traveled in convoys with air cover, used sonar and radar, and dropped depth charges, but for years they endured the loss of up to 60 ships per month.

Room 14: El Alamein, Stalingrad, and Guadalcanal—The War Turns: Three crucial battles in autumn 1942 put the first chink in the fascist armor. Off the east coast of Australia, 10,000 marines took an airstrip on Guadalcanal, while 30,000 Japanese held the rest of the tiny, isolated island. For the next six months, the two armies were marooned together, duking it out in thick jungles and malaria-infested swamps while their countries struggled to reinforce or rescue them. By February 1943, America had won and gained a crucial launch pad for bombing raids.

A world away, German tanks under General Erwin Rommel rolled across the vast deserts of North Africa. In October 1942, a well-equipped, well-planned offensive by British General Bernard Montgomery attacked at El Alamein, Libya. "Monty" drove the "Desert Fox" east into Tunisia for the first real Allied victory against the Nazi Wehrmacht war machine.

Then came Stalingrad. In August 1942, Germany attacked the Soviet city, an industrial center and gateway to the Caucasus oil fields. By October, they'd battled their way into the city center and were fighting house-to-house, but their supplies were running low, the Soviets wouldn't give up, and winter was coming. The snow fell, their tanks had no fuel, and relief efforts failed. Hitler ordered them to fight on through the bitter cold. On the worst days, 50,000 men died. (America lost 58,000 in Vietnam.) Finally, on January 31, 1943, the Germans surrendered, against Hitler's orders. The six-month totals? Eight hundred thousand German and other Axis soldiers dead, 1.1 million Soviets dead. The Russian campaign put hard miles on the German war machine.

Also in 1942, the Allies began long-range bombing of German-held territory, including saturation bombing of civilians. It was global war and total war.

Room 16: The Allies Land in North Africa (*Le Débar-quement en Afrique du Nord, La Campagne de Tunisie*): Winston Churchill and U.S. President Franklin D. Roosevelt (see photo with de Gaulle), two of the century's most dynamic and strong-willed statesmen, decided to attack Hitler indi-

rectly by invading Vichy-controlled Morocco and Algeria. On November 8, 1942, 100,000 Americans and British—under the joint command of an unknown, low-key problem solver named General Dwight ("Ike") Eisenhower—landed on three separate beaches (including Casablanca). More than 120,000 Vichy French soldiers, ordered by their superiors to defend the fascist cause, confronted the Allies and ... gave up.

The Allies moved east, but bad weather, their own inexperi-ence, and the powerful Afrika Korps under Rommel stopped them in Tunisia. But with flamboyant General George S. ("Old Blood-and-Guts") Patton punching from the west and "Monty" pushing from the south, they captured the port town of Tunis (May 7, 1943). The Allies now had a base from which to retake Europe.

Room 17: The French Resistance (*L'Unification de la Résis-tance, La Lutte Clandestine*): Inside occupied France, other ordi-nary heroes fought the Nazis—the "underground," or Resistance. Bakers hid radios in loaves of bread to secretly contact London. Barmaids passed along tips from tipsy Nazis. Communists in black berets cut telephone lines. Farmers hid downed airmen in haystacks. Housewives spread news from the front with their gossip. Printers countered Nazi propaganda with pamphlets.

Jean Moulin (see photo), de Gaulle's assistant, secretly para-chuted into France and organized these scattered heroes into a unified effort. In May 1943, Moulin was elected chairman of the

National Council of the Resistance. A month later, he was arrested by the Gestapo (Nazi secret police), imprisoned, tortured, and sent to Germany, where he died in transit. Still, Free France now had a (secret) government again, rallied around de Gaulle and ready to take over when liberation came.

Room 18: The Red Army (*L'Armée Rouge Reprend l'Initiative*): Monty, Patton, and Ike were certainly heroes, but the war was won on the Eastern Front by Soviet grunts, who slowly bled Germany dry.

Room 21: The Allies Land in Italy (*Premiers Débarquements Allies en Europe*): On July 10, 1943, the assault on Hitler's European fortress began. More than 150,000 Americans and British sailed from Tunis, landing on the south shore of Sicily. (See maps showing the campaigns.) Speedy Patton and methodical Monty began a "horse race" to take the city of Messina (the United States won the friendly competition by a few hours). They met little resistance from 300,000 Italian soldiers, and were actually cheered as liberators by the Sicilian people. Their real enemies were the 50,000 German troops sent by Hitler to bolster his ally, Benito Mussolini. By September, the island was captured. On the mainland, Mussolini was arrested by his own people, and Italy surrendered to the Allies. Hitler quickly poured troops into Italy (and reinstalled Mussolini) to hold off the Allied onslaught.

In early September, the Allies launched a two-pronged landing onto the beaches of southern Italy. Finally, after four long years of war, free men set foot on the European continent.

Room 22: The Italian Campaign (*La Campagne d'Italie*): Lieutenant General Mark Clark, leading the slow, bloody push north to liberate Rome, must have been reminded of the French trenches he'd fought in during World War I. As in that bloody war, the fighting in Italy was a war of attrition, fought on the ground by foot soldiers, costing many lives to gain just a few miles.

In January 1944, the Germans dug in between Rome and Naples at Monte Cassino, a rocky hill topped by the monastery of St. Benedict. Thousands died as the Allies tried inching up the hillside. In frustration, the Allies air-bombed the historic monastery, killing hundreds of monks...but no Germans, who dug in deeper. Finally, after four months of vicious, sometimes hand-to-hand combat, the Allies—Americans, Brits, Free French, Poles, Italian partisans, Indians, etc.—stormed the monastery, and the Germans' back was broken.

Meanwhile, 50,000 Allies had landed on Anzio (a beach near

Rome), holding the narrow beachhead for months against massive German attacks. When reinforcements arrived, they broke out and joined the two-pronged assault on the capital. Rome fell without a single bomb threatening its historic treasures on June 4, 1944.

Room 23: D-Day—June 6, 1944, "Operation Overlord": Three million Allies and six million tons of materiel were massed in England in preparation for the biggest fleet-led invasion in history—across the Channel to France, then eastward to Berlin. The Germans, hunkered down in Northern France, knew an invasion was imminent, but the Allies kept it top secret. On the night of June 5, 150,000 soldiers boarded ships and planes, not knowing where they were headed until they were underway. Each one carried a note from General Eisenhower: "The tide has turned. The free men of the world are marching together to victory."

At 6:30 a.m. on June 6, 1944, Americans spilled out of troop transports into the cold waters off a beach in Normandy, codenamed Omaha. The weather was bad, seas were rough, and the prep bombing had failed. The soldiers, many seeing their first action, were dazed and confused. Nazi machine guns pinned them against the sea. Slowly, they crawled up the beach on their stomachs. A thousand died. They held on until the next wave of transports arrived.

All day long, Allied confusion did battle with German indecision—the Nazis never really counterattacked, thinking D-Day was just a ruse, not the main invasion. By day's end, the Allies had taken several beaches along the Normandy coast and began building artificial harbors, providing a tiny port-of-entry for the reconquest of Europe. The stage was set for a quick and easy end to the war. Right.
• *Go downstairs to . . .*

First Floor: The War Ends . . . Very Slowly (June 1944–Aug 1945)

Room 24: Battle of Normandy (*La Bataille de Normandie*): For a month, the Allies (mostly Americans) secured Normandy, taking bigger ports (Cherbourg and Caen) and amassing troops and supplies for the assault on Germany. In July they broke out and sped eastward across France, Patton's tanks covering up to 65 kilometers (40 miles) a day. They had "Jerry" on the run.

Room 25: Landing in Provence, August 1944 (*Le Debarque-ment de Provence*): On France's Mediterranean coast, American troops under General Alexander Patch landed near Cannes, took Marseilles, and headed north to meet up with Patton.

Room 26: "Les Maquis": French Resistance guerrilla fighters helped reconquer France from behind the lines. (Don't miss the folding motorcycle in its parachute case.) The liberation of Paris was started by a Resistance attack on a German garrison.

Room 27: Liberation of Paris: As the Allies marched on Paris, Hitler ordered his officers to torch the city—they sanely disobeyed and prepared to surrender. On August 26, General Charles de Gaulle walked ramrod-straight down the Champs-Elysées, followed by Free French troops and U.S. GIs passing out chocolate and Camels. Two million Parisians went ape.

Room 28: On to Berlin—Offensive from the West (*Vers Berlin—Offensives a l'Ouest*): The quick advance through France, Belgium, and Luxembourg bogged down at the German border in autumn of 1944. Patton outstripped supply lines, a parachute invasion of Holland (Battle of Arnhem) was disastrous, and bad weather grounded planes and slowed tanks.

On December 16, the Allies met a deadly surprise. An enormous, well-equipped, energetic German army appeared from nowhere, punched a "bulge" deep into Allied lines, and demanded surrender. General Anthony McAuliffe sent a one-word response—"Nuts!"—and the tide turned. The Battle of the Bulge was Germany's last great offensive.

The Germans retreated across the Rhine River, blowing up bridges behind them. The last bridge, at Remagen, was captured by the Allies just long enough to cross and establish themselves on German soil. Soon U.S. tanks were speeding down the autobahns and Patton could wire the good news back to Ike: "General, I have just pissed in the Rhine."

Soviet soldiers did the dirty work of taking fortified Berlin, launching a final offensive in January 1945, and surrounding the city in April. German citizens fled west to surrender to the more-benevolent Americans and Brits. Hitler, defiant to the end, hunkered in his underground bunker.

On April 28, 1945, Mussolini and his girlfriend were killed and hung by their heels in Milan. Two days later, Adolf Hitler and his new bride, Eva Braun, avoided similar humiliation by committing suicide (pistol in mouth) and having their bodies burned beyond recognition. Germany formally surrendered on May 8, 1945.

In Corridor to the left of Room 28: Concentration Camps
Lest anyone mourn Hitler or doubt this war's purpose, gaze on photos from Germany's concentration camps. Some camps held political enemies and prisoners of war (including 2 million French),

others were expressly built to exterminate peoples considered "genetically inferior" to the Aryan "master race"—namely, Jews, Gypsies, homosexuals, and the mentally ill.

Room 29: War Of The Pacific (*Pacifique—Les Grandes Offensives Americaines***):** Often treated as an afterthought, the final campaign against Japan was a massive American effort, costing many lives but saving millions from Japanese domination.

Japan was an island bunker surrounded by a vast ring of fortified Pacific islands. America's strategy was to take one island at a time, "island hopping" until close enough for B-29 Superfortress bombers to attack Japan itself. The war spread across thousands of miles. In a new form of warfare, ships carrying planes led the attack, preparing tiny islands for troops to land and build an airbase. While General Douglas MacArthur island-hopped south to retake the Philippines ("I have returned!"), others pushed north toward Japan.

In February 1945, marines landed on Iwo Jima, a city-size island-volcano close enough to Japan (1,300 kilometers/800 miles) to launch air raids. Twenty thousand Japanese had dug in on the volcano-top, picking off the advancing Americans. On February 23, several U.S. soldiers raised the Stars and Stripes on the mountain (that famous photo), inspiring their mates to victory at a cost of nearly 7,000 men.

Japan Surrenders (*Capitulation du Japon***):** On March 9, Tokyo was firebombed and 90,000 were killed. Japan was losing, but a land invasion would cost hundreds of thousands of lives. The Japanese had a reputation for choosing death over the shame of surrender—they even sent bomb-laden "kamikaze" planes on suicide missions.

America unleashed its secret weapon, an atomic bomb (originally suggested by German-turned-American Albert Einstein). On August 6, a B-29 dropped one (named "Little Boy") on the city of Hiroshima, instantly vaporizing 100,000 people and 6.5 square kilometers (4 square miles). Three days later, a second bomb fell on Nagasaki. The next day, Emperor Hirohito unofficially surrendered. The long war was over, and U.S. sailors returned home to kiss their girlfriends in public places.

War Totals (*Le Bilan de la Guerre***):** The death toll for World War II (Sept 1939–Aug 1945) totaled 80 million soldiers and civilians. The Soviet Union lost 26 million, China 13 million, France 580,000, and the United States 340,000.

World War II changed the world, with America emerging as

the dominant political, military, and economic superpower. Europe was split in two. The western half recovered, with American aid. The east remained under Soviet occupation. For 45 years, the United States and the Soviet Union would compete—without ever actually doing battle—in a "Cold War" of espionage, propaganda, and weapons production that stretched from Korea to Cuba, from Vietnam to the moon.

CLUNY MUSEUM TOUR

Musée National du Moyen Age

paris

The "National Museum of the Middle Ages" doesn't sound quite so boring as I approach middle age myself. Aside from the solemn religious art, there is some lively stuff here.

Paris emerged on the world stage in the "Middle" Ages, the time between ancient Rome and the Renaissance. Europe was awakening from a thousand-year slumber. Trade was booming, people actually owned chairs, and the Renaissance was moving in like a warm front from Italy.

Orientation

Cost and Hours: €6, €4 on Sun, covered by museum pass, Wed-Mon 09:15-17:45, closed Tue, tel. 01 53 73 78 00. Pick up the free and handy museum map guide.

Getting There: It's at 6 place Paul-Painlevé, near the corner of boulevards St. Michel and St. Germain (Mo: Cluny/La Sorbonne, St. Michel, or Odéon).

Baggage Check: Required and free.

Length of Our Tour: One hour.

THE TOUR BEGINS

Room 2: The first art you see is not some grim, gray crucifixion but a colorful tapestry depicting grape-stomping peasants during the Vendange (the annual autumn harvest/celebration). A peasant man treads grapes in a vat while his wife collects the juice. A wealthy man gives orders. Above that, a peasant with a pimple turns a new-fangled mechanical press. On the right,

——————— CLUNY–GROUND FLOOR ———————

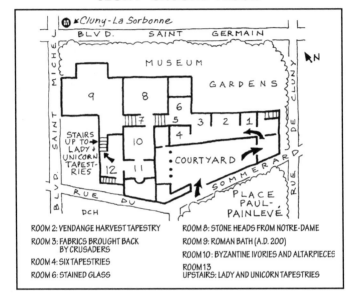

ROOM 2: VENDANGE HARVEST TAPESTRY

ROOM 3: FABRICS BROUGHT BACK BY CRUSADERS

ROOM 4: SIX TAPESTRIES

ROOM 6: STAINED GLASS

ROOM 8: STONE HEADS FROM NOTRE-DAME

ROOM 9: ROMAN BATH (A.D. 200)

ROOM 10: BYZANTINE IVORIES AND ALTARPIECES

ROOM 13 UPSTAIRS: LADY AND UNICORN TAPESTRIES

you'll see the joy of picking—pawns, knights, and queens all working side by side.

Having survived their Y1K crisis, these people realize the world won't end, and they turn their attention to the beauty of the world around them.

Room 3: Colorful woven fabrics were brought back to France by crusaders, who went off to conquer barbarian infidels but returned with tales of enlightened peoples on the fringes of Europe.

Room 4: Six tapestries in wool and silk show the rich enjoying the simple, secular pleasures of their estate. The humans mingle harmoniously with the trees, flowers, and animals of the glorious physical world.

Reading clockwise: 1) A lady with a puppy spins wool while her husband relaxes with the morning paper. 2) Out in the garden, the sexes mingle unchaperoned by the Church. A lady takes a breath mint while a troubadour puts the moves on her servant. 3) A lady embroiders a pillow. 4) The family picks fruit from their plentiful orchards. 5) A lord goes hunting with his falcon, dog, and servant. 6) A naked woman takes a chilly bath, enjoying fruits, jewels, and music—the good things of a material world becoming increasingly less sinful.

Room 6: Enter the Dark Ages, when life was harsh and violent, angels and demons made regular appearances, and the Church was your only refuge. This room offers a rare close-up look at stained glass, which gave the poor a glimpse of the glories of heaven and served as a visual aid for  teaching Bible lessons to the illiterate masses. These panels (many from the cathedral of light, Sainte-Chapelle) give us a window into the magical, supernatural, miraculous—and often violent— medieval mind.

Reading clockwise around the room, lowest level: 1) The angel Gabriel blasts his horn on Resurrection morning, rousting the grateful dead from their coffins. Notice that Gabriel's royal purple robe is made up of several different pieces of glass—purples, whites, blues— held together with lead. 2) King Herod seems—shocked? pleased?— to see the head of John the Baptist presented to him on a plate by Salome, his dancing stepdaughter. 3) A red-faced, horned, horny demon (with his equally lascivious wolf and henchman) carries off a frightened girl in red to do unspeakable acts. 4) Blond, pious Joseph is sold into slavery to camel merchants by his plotting brothers.

Next wall: 5) Samson is about to pull down the temple.... 6) Then, he has his eyes gouged out by Philistines. 7) Slaughter on the battlefield. Men with bloodstained hands and faces hack at each other with golden swords. 8) Aaron, disobeying God and Moses, worships a golden calf. 9) A king on a throne closes his eyes to all this wickedness.

Next wall (with some panels from the first Gothic church, St. Denis): 10) Two monks with prayer books gaze up as one of their brothers disappears into heaven. The Latin inscription, *"hec est via,"* means "This is the way." 11) Seated Jesus, in a royal purple robe, is consoled by two angels. 12) Theophilus ("Lover of God") has struck a Faustian deal with the devil and is now feeling buyer's remorse. 13) Sleeping St. Martin is visited by a heavenly vision. 14) Angels in Rock-and-Roll Heaven.

Last wall: Four apostles—John ("Ioanneus"), James, Peter ("Petrus," with key), and Paul.

Room 8: These 21 stone heads (sculpted 1220–1230) of the kings of Judah from the Bible once decorated the front of Notre-Dame. Then, in 1793, an angry and misinformed mob of revolutionaries mistook the kings of Judah for the kings of France and abused and decapitated the statues. (Today's heads on the Notre-Dame statues are reconstructions.) Someone gathered up the heads and buried them in his backyard near the present-day Opéra. There they slept for two centuries, unknown and noseless, until 1977, when some diggers accidentally unearthed them and brought them to an astounded world. Their stoic expressions accept what fate, time, and liberals have done to them.

The statue of Adam (on the left) is also from Notre-Dame. He's scrawny and flaccid by Renaissance standards. And it will be another 200 years before naked Adam can step out from behind that bush.

Room 9: This echoing cavern was a Roman frigidarium. Pretty cool. The museum is located on the site of a Roman bathhouse, a reminder of the Romans' centuries of occupation. After hot baths and exercise in adjoining rooms, ordinary Romans would take a cold dip in the sunken pool (in the alcove), then relax cheek to cheek with notables such as Emperor Julian the Apostate (see his statue), who lived right next door. The 12-meter (40-foot) ceiling is the largest Roman vault in France, and it took the French another 1,000 years to improve on that crisscross-arch technology. The sheer size of this room, constructed in A.D. 200 when Rome was at its peak, gives an idea of the epic scale the Romans built on, inspiring Europeans to greatness during the less civilized Middle Ages.

The four square columns (Pilier des Nautes) are the oldest man-made objects you'll see from Paris. These pillars once supported a 6-meter-high (20-foot) altar to the king of the gods in the Temple of Jupiter, where Notre-Dame now stands. The carving on one says it was built in the time of the Emperor Tiberius, A.D. 14 through 37 ("TIB. CAESARE"), and was paid for by the Parisian boatmen's union (see them holding their canoe-shaped boats).

Room 10: Rome lived on after the Fall. The finely carved Byzantine ivories (first glass case) show how pagan gods, emperors, and griffins became Christian saints, gargoyles, and icons. Constantinople—the eastern half of the empire that survived the Fall—preserved Roman tastes and imagery, like the willowy, bare-breasted, dreamy-eyed *Ariadne* (*Ariane*), with the sneaky satyr peek-
ing out. In painting, Byzantine gold-background icons inspired medieval altarpieces, like others in the room.

Rome also lived on in the Romanesque grandeur of Christian

churches like St. Germain-des-Près (the 12-column capitals). The central capital shows Christ in robes on a throne, ruling the world like a Roman emperor. These capitals were originally painted, much like the painted wooden statues across the room. Don't leave this room before eyeing the tusk of a narwhal (on the wall), which must have convinced superstitious folk to believe in unicorns.
• *Go upstairs to . . .*

"The Lady and the Unicorn" Tapestries

As Europeans emerged from the Dark Ages, they rediscovered the beauty of the world around them.

These six mysterious tapestries, designed by an unknown (but probably French) artist before 1500 and woven in Belgium out of wool and silk, are loaded with symbols, some serious, some playful. They have been interpreted many ways, but the series deals with each of the five senses.
• *Moving clockwise around the room . . .*

Taste: A blond lady takes candy from a servant's dish to feed it to her parakeet. A unicorn and a lion look on. At the lady's feet, a monkey also tastes something, while the little white dog behind her wishes he had some. This was the Age of Discovery, when Columbus and Vasco da Gama spiced up Europe's bland gruel with new fruits, herbs, and spices.

The lion (symbol of knighthood?) and unicorn (symbol of "bourgeois nobility," purity, or fertility?) wave flags with the coat of arms of the family that bought the tapestries—three silver crescent moons in a band of blue.

Hearing: Wearing a stunning dress, the lady plays sweet music on an organ, soothing the savage beasts around her. The pattern and folds of the tablecloth are lovely. Humans and their fellow creatures live in harmony in a blue, enchanted garden filled with flowers, set in a red background.

Sight: The unicorn cuddles up and looks at himself in the lady's mirror, pleased with what he sees. The lion turns away and snickers. As the Renaissance dawns, vanity is a less-than-deadly sin.

Admire the great artistic skill in some of the detail work, such as the necklace and the patterns in her dress. This tapestry had quality control in all its stages—drawing the scene, enlarging and transferring it to a cartoon, and weaving it. Still, the design itself is crude by Renaissance 3-D standards. The fox and rabbits, supposedly in the distance, simply float overhead, as big as the animals at the lady's feet.

Smell: The lady picks flowers and weaves them into a sweet-smelling wreath. On a bench behind, the monkey apes her. The flowers, trees, and animals are exotic and varied. Each detail is exquisite alone; but stepping back, they blend together into pleasing patterns.

Touch: This is the most basic and dangerous of the senses. The lady "strokes the unicorn's horn," if you know what I mean, and the lion gets the double-entendre. Unicorns, a species extinct since the Age of Reason, were so wild that only the purest virgins could entice and tame them. Medieval Europeans were exploring the wonders of love and the pleasures of sex. The Renaissance is coming.

Tapestry #6: The most talked-about tapestry gets its name from the words on our lady's tent: *A Mon Seul Désir* ("To My Sole Desire"). What *is* her only desire?

Is it jewelry, as she grabs a necklace from the jewel box? Or is she putting the necklace away, renouncing material things in order to follow her only desire?

Our lady has tried all things sensual and is now prepared to follow the one true impulse. Is it God? Or love? Her friends the unicorn and lion open the tent doors. Flickering flames cover the tent. Perhaps she's going in to meet the object of her desire. Or maybe she's stepping out. An old, dark age is ending and a new Renaissance world dawns.

THE REST OF THE MUSEUM

While the Unicorn tapestry is the Cluny's prize, there's much more: seventh-century Visigoth crowns (room 16), the chapel (room 20), and a medieval garden (outside and explained in the museum map guide).

VERSAILLES
TOUR

paris

If you've ever wondered why your American passport has French writing in it, you'll find the answer at Versailles (vehr-sigh). The powerful court of Louis XIV at Versailles set the standard of culture for all of Europe, right up to modern times. Versailles was every king's dream palace. Today, if you're planning to visit just one palace in all of Europe, make it Versailles. And if you have a car, or simply prefer a smaller town base for Paris, see my "Sleeping near Paris, in Versailles" recommendations on page 265.

Orientation

Cost: €7 (covered with museum pass); €5.50 after 15:30, on Sun, and for ages 18 to 25; under 18 free (the palace is also theoretically free for all teachers, professors, and architecture students). Admission is payable at entrances A, C, and D. Tours cost extra (see "Touring Versailles," below). The Grand and Petit Trianons cost €5 together, €3 after 15:30 (both covered with museum pass). Except for fountain-filled weekends (see "Fountain Spectacles," below), the gardens are free.

Hours: The **palace** is open May–Sept Tue–Sun 09:00–18:30, Oct–April Tue–Sun 09:00–17:30, closed Mon (last entry 30 minutes before closing). The **Grand and Petit Trianons** are open April–Oct Tue–Sun 12:00–18:00, Nov–March Tue–Sun 12:00–17:00, closed Mon. The **garden** is open from 07:00 to sunset (as late as 21:30).

In summer, Versailles is especially crowded around 10:00 and 13:00, and all day Tue and Sun. Remember, the crowds gave Marie-Antoinette a pain in the neck, too, so relax and let them eat cake. For fewer crowds, go early or late: Either arrive by 09:00 (when the palace opens, touring the palace first, then the gardens) or after 15:30 (you'll get a reduced entry ticket but you'll miss the

VERSAILLES

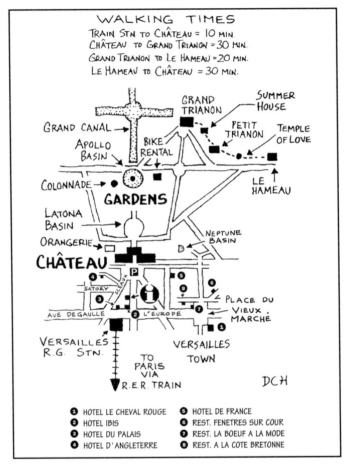

WALKING TIMES
TRAIN STN TO CHÂTEAU = 10 MIN.
CHÂTEAU TO GRAND TRIANON = 30 MIN.
GRAND TRIANON TO LE HAMEAU = 20 MIN.
LE HAMEAU TO CHÂTEAU = 30 MIN.

GRAND TRIANON
SUMMER HOUSE
GRAND CANAL
PETIT TRIANON
TEMPLE OF LOVE
APOLLO BASIN
BIKE RENTAL
COLONNADE
LE HAMEAU
GARDENS
LATONA BASIN
NEPTUNE BASIN
ORANGERIE
CHÂTEAU
SATORY
PLACE DU VIEUX MARCHÉ
AVE DE GAULLE
L'EUROPE
VERSAILLES R.G. STN.
VERSAILLES TOWN
TO PARIS VIA R.E.R. TRAIN
DCH

- ❶ HOTEL LE CHEVAL ROUGE
- ❷ HOTEL IBIS
- ❸ HOTEL DU PALAIS
- ❹ HOTEL D'ANGLETERRE
- ❺ HOTEL DE FRANCE
- ❻ REST. FENETRES SUR COUR
- ❼ REST. LA BOEUF A LA MODE
- ❽ REST. A LA COTE BRETONNE

last guided tours of the day, which generally depart at 15:00). If you arrive midday, see the gardens first and the palace later, at 15:00. The gardens and palace are great late. On my last visit, at 18:00 I was the only tourist in the Hall of Mirrors...even on a Tuesday.

Touring Versailles: Versailles' highlights are the State Apartments, the lavish King's Private Apartments, the Opera House, and the magnificent Hall of Mirrors. Most visitors are satisfied with a spin through the State Apartments (following my self-guided tour, below), the gardens, and the Trianons. Versailles

VERSAILLES' ENTRANCES

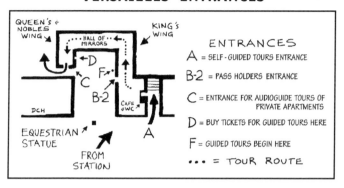

aficionados should spend the time (and money) for the King's Private Apartments, which can be visited only with an audioguide or live guide (neither tour covered by museum pass).

Self-guided tour—For the basic self-guided tour, join the line at entrance A if you need to pay admission. Those with a museum pass are allowed in through entrance B-2 without a wait. Enter the palace and take a one-way walk through the State Apartments (follow my tour, below) from the "King's Wing," through the Hall of Mirrors, and out via the "Queen's and Nobles' Wing."

Audioguide tours—Two informative but dry audioguide tours are available. One covers the State Apartments (€3.50, includes Hall of Mirrors and queen's bedchamber; start at entrance A or, if you have a museum pass, entrance B-2). The other includes more of the King's Private Apartments (Louis XIV) and a sampling of nobles' chambers (€4, entrance C). Both audioguide tours are sold until one hour before closing.

Guided tours—You may select a one-hour guided tour from a variety of themes, such as the daily life of a king or the lives of lesser-known nobles, such as the well-coiffed Madame Pompadour (€4, join first English tour available). Or consider the 90-minute tour (€6) of the King's Private Apartments (Louis XV, Louis XVI, and Marie-Antoinette) and the chapel. This tour, which is the only way visitors can see the Opera House, can be long; the occasional dull guide stretches it to eternity.

Make reservations for a live tour upon arrival, at entrance D, as tours can sell out by 13:00 (first tours generally begin at 10:00, last tours depart at 15:00 or 16:00). Guided tours begin at entrance F. The price of any tour is added to the €7 entry fee to Versailles (entry covered by museum pass, tours extra).

If you don't have a museum pass, and you think you might

want to take a guided tour after you've seen the palace on your own, remember to keep your ticket to prove you've already paid for admission.

Getting There: Take the **RER-C train** (€5 round-trip, 30 min one-way) to Versailles R.G. or "Rive Gauche" (not Versailles C.H., which is farther from the palace). Trains named "Vick" leave about five times an hour for the palace from these RER stops: Gare d'Austerlitz, St. Michel, Musée d'Orsay, Invalides, Pont de l'Alma, and Champ de Mars. Any train named Vick goes to Versailles; don't board other trains. Get off at the last stop (Versailles Rive Gauche), turn right out of the station, and turn left at the first boulevard. It's a 10-minute walk to the palace.

Your Eurailpass covers this inexpensive trip, but it uses up a valuable "flexi" day. If you really want to use your railpass, consider seeing Versailles on your way in or out of Paris. To get free passage, show your railpass at an SCNF ticket window—for example, at the Les Invalides or Musée d'Orsay RER stops—and get a *contremarque de passage.* Keep this ticket to exit the system.

When returning from Versailles, look through the windows past the turnstiles for the departure board. Any train leaving Versailles serves all downtown Paris RER line C stops (they're marked "all stations until d'Austerlitz").

Allow €35 each way for a **taxi** from Paris to Versailles.

To reach Versailles from Paris by **car**, get on the *périphérique* freeway that circles Paris and take the toll-free autoroute A-13 toward Rouen. Follow signs into Versailles, then look for "château" signs and park in the huge lot in front of the palace (pay lot). The drive takes about 30 minutes one-way.

Information: A helpful TI is just past Sofitel Hôtel on your walk from the station to the palace (May–Sept daily 09:00–19:00, Oct–April daily 09:00–18:00, tel. 01 39 24 88 88, www.chateauversailles .fr). You'll also find information booths inside the château (doors A, B-2, and C). The useful brochure, "Versailles Orientation Guide," explains your sightseeing options.

Fountain Spectacles: Classical music fills the king's backyard, and the garden's fountains are in full squirt, on Sat July–Sept and on Sun early April–early Oct (schedule for both days: 11:00–12:00, 15:30–17:00, and 17:20–17:30). On these "spray days," the gardens cost €5 (ages 18–25-€3.50, free if under 18, not covered by museum pass, ask for a map of fountains). Louis had his engineers literally reroute a river to fuel these fountains. Even by today's standards, they are impressive. Pick up the helpful brochure of the fountain show ("Les Grandes Eaux Musicales") at any information booth for a guide to the fountains. Also ask about the impressive *Les Fêtes de Nuit* nighttime spectacle (some Sat, July–mid-Sept).

Getting around the Gardens: It's a 30-minute hike from the palace, down the canal, past the two mini-palaces to the hamlet. You can rent bikes (€6/hr). The pokey tourist train runs between the canal and château (€5, 5/hr, 4 stops, you can hop on and off as you like; nearly worthless commentary).

Cuisine Art: The cafeteria and WCs are next to the general entrance, door A. There's a sandwich kiosk and a decent restaurant at the canal in the garden.

You'll find restaurants on the street to the right of the parking lot (as you face château), though the best places line the pleasant market square in the town center (turn right out of the train station, cross avenue de Paris, and continue about 5 blocks to place du Marché; see Eating chapter, page 277). A handy McDonald's is immediately across from the train station (WC without crowds).

Length of Our Tour: Allow two hours for the palace and two for the gardens. Including two hours to cover your round-trip transit time, it's a six-hour daytrip from Paris.

Starring: Louis XIV and the Old Regime.

KINGS AND QUEENS AND GUILLOTINES

• *Read this on the train ride out there. Relax, the palace is the last stop.*

Come the Revolution, when they line us up and make us stick out our hands, will you have enough calluses to keep them from shooting you? A grim thought, but Versailles raises questions like that. It's the symbol of the Old Regime, a time when society was divided into rulers and the ruled, when you were born to be rich or to be poor. To some it's the pinnacle of civilization, to others the sign of a civilization in decay. Either way, it remains one of Europe's most impressive sights.

Versailles was the residence of the king and seat of France's government for a hundred years. Louis XIV (reigned 1643–1715) moved out of the Louvre in Paris, the previous royal residence, and built an elaborate palace in the forests and swamps of Versailles, 19 kilometers (12 miles) west. The reasons for the move were partly personal—Louis loved the outdoors and disliked the sniping environs of stuffy Paris—and partly political.

Louis was creating the first modern, centralized state. At Versailles, he consolidated Paris' scattered ministries so he could personally control policy. More important, he invited to

Versailles all of France's nobles, so he could control them. Living a life of almost enforced idleness, the "domesticated" aristocracy couldn't interfere with the way Louis ran things. With 18 million people united under one king (England had only 5.5 million), a booming economy, and a powerful military, France was Europe's number-one power.

Versailles was also the cultural heartbeat of Europe. Every king wanted a palace like Versailles. Everyone learned French. French taste in clothes, hairstyles, table manners, theater, music, art, and kissing spread across the Continent. That cultural dominance has continued, to some extent, right up to this century.

Louis XIV

At the center of all this was Europe's greatest king. He was a true Renaissance man, a century after the Renaissance—athletic, good-looking, a musician, dancer, horseman, statesman, art-lover, lover. For all his grandeur, he was one of history's most polite and approachable kings, a good listener who could put even commoners at ease in his presence.

Louis called himself the Sun King because he gave life and warmth to all that he touched. He was also thought of as Apollo, the Greek god of the sun. Versailles became the personal temple of this god on earth, decorated with statues and symbols of Apollo, the sun, and Louis himself.

Louis was a hands-on king who personally ran affairs of state. All decisions were made by him. Nobles, who in other countries were the center of power, became virtual slaves dependent on Louis' generosity. For 70 years, he was the perfect embodiment of the absolute monarch. He summed it up best himself with his famous rhyme—"*L'état, c'est moi!*" ("The state, that's me!").

Another Louis or Two To Remember

Three kings lived in Versailles during its century of glory. Louis XIV built it and established French dominance. Louis XV, his great-grandson (Louis XIV reigned for 72 years), carried on the tradition and policies, but without the Sun King's flair. During Louis XV's reign, France's power abroad was weakening and there were rumblings of rebellion from within.

France's monarchy was crumbling, and the time was ripe for a strong leader to reestablish the old feudal order. They didn't get one. Instead, they got Louis XVI, a shy, meek bookworm, the kind of guy who lost sleep over Revolutionary graffiti . . . because it was misspelled. Louis XVI married a sweet girl from the Austrian royal family, Marie-Antoinette, and together they retreated into the idyllic gardens of Versailles while revolutionary fires smoldered.

THE TOUR BEGINS

This tour covers the ceremonial center of the palace (the State, or Grand Apartments) and the extensive grounds. It begins outside the palace at the equestrian statue of Louis XIV.

The central palace, the part we'll tour, forms a U around the courtyard in front of you. The right half (King's Wing) is separated from the left half (Queen's Wing) by the Hall of Mirrors ahead of you. Then two long wings shoot out to the right and left (north and south) of this U. In this tour, we'll walk counterclockwise through the U-shaped part on the middle floor.

The Original Château

The part of the palace directly behind the horse statue, at the far end of the courtyard, is the original château. Louis XIV's dad used to come out to the forests of Versailles to escape the worries of kingship. Here, he built this small hunting lodge. His son spent the happiest times of his boyhood at the lodge, hunting and riding. Louis XIV's three arched bedroom windows (beneath the clock) overlooked the courtyard. Naturally, it faced the rising sun. The palace and grounds are laid out on an East-West axis.

When he became king, Louis XIV spent more and more time here, away from the hubbub of Paris. He expanded the lodge, planted gardens, and entertained guests. The reputation spread about this "Enchanted Island," a kind of Disneyland for dukes and duchesses. As

visitors flocked here, Louis expanded around the original hunting château, attaching wings to create the present U-shape. Then, the long north and south wings were built. The total cost of the project has been estimated at half of France's entire GNP for one year.

Think how busy this courtyard must have been 300 years ago. There were as many as 5,000 nobles here at any one time, each with an entourage. They'd buzz from games to parties to amorous rendezvous in sedan-chair taxis. Servants ran about delivering secret messages and roast legs of lamb. Horse-drawn carriages arrived at the fancy gate with their finely dressed passengers, having driven up the broad boulevard that ran direct from Paris. (You can still see the horse stables lining the boulevard.) Incredible as it seems, both the grounds and most of the palace were public territory where even the lowliest peasant could come to gawk. Of course, this meant that there were,

then as now, hordes of tourists, pickpockets, and men selling
wind-up children's toys.
• *Enter at Entrance A (or at B-2 if you have a museum pass) and buy
your ticket. After showing your ticket, pass through the 21 rooms of the
history museum, with paintings on the background of Versailles and its
kings (or be directed immediately upstairs when these rooms are closed).*

Our tour starts upstairs, in the room that overlooks the lavish
Royal Chapel.

The State Apartments

Royal Chapel: In the vast pagan "temple" that is Versailles,
built to glorify one man, Louis XIV, this Royal Chapel is a paltry
tip of the hat to that "other" god, the Christian one. It's virtually
the first, last, and only hint of Christianity you'll see in the entire
complex. Versailles celebrates Man, not God, by raising Louis
to almost godlike status, the personification of all good human
qualities. In a way, Versailles is the last great flowering of
Renaissance humanism and revival of the classical world.

Louis attended Mass here every morning. While he sat on
the upper level, the lowly nobles below would turn their backs
to the altar and look up—worshiping Louis worshiping God.
Important religious ceremonies took place here, including the
marriage of young Louis XVI to Marie-Antoinette.
• *Take a seat in the next room, a large room with a fireplace and a
colorful painting on the ceiling.*

Hercules Drawing Room: Pleasure ruled. The main sup-
pers, balls, and receptions were held in this room. Picture
elegant partygoers in fine silks, wigs, rouge, and lipstick (and
that's just the men), dancing to the strains of Mozart played
by a string quartet.

On the wall opposite the fireplace is an appropriate painting
showing Christ in the middle of a Venetian party. The work by
Veronese, a gift from the Republic of Venice, was one of Louis'
favorites, so they decorated the room around it.

The ceiling painting of Hercules being crowned a god gives
the room its name. Hercules (with his club) rides up to heaven on
a chariot, where the king of the gods is ready to give him his
daughter in marriage. Louis XIV built the room for his own
daughter's wedding reception.
• *The following rooms are listed in order. The names of the rooms generally come from the paintings on the ceilings. From here on, it's a one-way
tour—getting lost is not allowed. Follow the crowds into the small green
room with a goddess in pink on the ceiling.*

The King's Wing

Cornucopia Room: If the party in the Hercules Room got too intense, you could always step in here for some refreshments. Silver trays were loaded up with liqueurs, coffee, juice, chocolates, and, on really special occasions, three-bean salad.

The ceiling painting shows the cornucopia of riches poured down on invited guests. Around the edges of the ceiling are painted versions of the king's actual dinnerware and treasures.

Louis himself might be here. He was a gracious host who enjoyed letting his hair down at night. If he took a liking to you, he might sneak you through those doors there (in the middle of the wall) and into his own private study, where he'd show off his collection of dishes, medals, jewels, or . . . the *Mona Lisa*, which hung on his wall.

Venus Room: Love ruled at Versailles. In this room, couples would cavort beneath a canopy of golden garlands (on the ceiling) sent down to Earth by the goddess of love to ensnare mortals in love. Notice how a painted garland goes "out" the bottom of the central painting, becomes a gilded wood garland held by a satyr, and then turns back to a painting again. Baroque artists loved to mix their media to fool the eye. Another illusion is in the paintings at both ends of the room, which extend this grand room into mythical courtyards.

Don't let the statue of a confident Louis as a Roman emperor fool you. He started out as a poor little rich kid with a chip on his shoulder. His father died before Louis was old enough to rule, and, during the regency period, the French Parliament treated little Louis and his mother like trash. They were virtual prisoners, humiliated in their home (the Louvre), surviving on bland meals, hand-me-down leotards, and pointed shoes. Once Louis attained power and wealth, there was one topic you never discussed in his presence—poverty. Maybe Versailles was his way of saying, "Living well is the best revenge."

Diana Room: This was the billiards room. Men played on a table that stood in the center of the room, while ladies sat surrounding them on Persian-carpet cushions.

The famous bust of Louis by Bernini (now in the center) shows a handsome, dashing, 27-year-old play-boy-king. His gaze is steady amid his windblown cloak and hair. Young Louis loved life. He hunted by day (notice Diana the Huntress on the ceiling) and partied by night.

Games were actually an important part of Louis' political strategy, known as "the domestication of the nobility." By distracting the nobles with the pleasures of courtly life, he was free to run the government his way. Billiards, dancing, and concerts were popular, but the biggest distraction was gambling, usually a card game similar to blackjack. Louis lent money to the losers, making them even more indebted to him. The good life was an addiction, and Louis kept the medicine cabinet well-stocked.

Mars Room: Decorated with a military flair, this was the room for Louis' Swiss bodyguards. On the ceiling, there's Mars, the Greek god of war, in a chariot pulled by wolves. The bronze cupids in the corners are escalating from love arrows to heavier artillery. Notice the fat walls that hid thin servants who were to be at their master's constant call—but out of sight when not needed. Don't miss the view of the sculpted gardens out the window.

Mercury Room: Louis' life was a work of art, and Versailles was the display case. Everything he did was a public event designed to show his subjects how it should be done. This room served as Louis' official bedroom, where the Sun King would ritually rise each morning to warm his subjects.

The tapestry on the wall shows how this ceremony might have looked. From a canopied bed, Louis would rise, dress, and take a seat for morning prayer. Meanwhile, the nobles (on the left) stand behind a balustrade, in awe of his piety, nobility, and clean socks. When Louis went to bed at night, the nobles would fight over who got to hold the candle while he slipped into his royal jammies. Bedtime, wake-up, and meals were all public rituals.

The two chests that furnish the room, with their curved legs, gilding, and heavy animal feet, are done in the "Louis the XIVth" style. Later furniture found in other rooms is lighter, straighter, and less ornamented. The clock dates from Louis' time. When the cocks crowed at the top of the hour and the temple doors opened, guess who popped out?

Apollo Room: This was the grand throne room. Louis held court from a 3-meter tall (10-foot) silver-canopied throne on a raised platform placed in the center of the room. (Notice the 4 metal bolts in the ceiling that once supported the canopy.)

Everything in here reminds us that Louis was not just any ruler, but the Sun King who lit the whole world with his presence.

The ceiling shows Apollo in his chariot, dragging the sun across the heavens every day. Notice the ceiling's beautifully gilded frame and Goldfinger maidens.

In the corners are the four corners of the world—all, of course, warmed by the sun. Counterclockwise from above the exit door are: 1) Europe, with a sword; 2) Asia, with a lion; 3) Africa, with an elephant; and 4) good old America, an Indian maiden with a crocodile.

The famous portrait by Rigaud over the fireplace gives a more human look at Louis. He's shown in a dancer's pose, displaying the legs that made him one of the all-time dancing fools of kingery. At night, they often held parties in this room, actually dancing around the throne.

Louis (who was 63 when this was painted) had more than 300 wigs like this one, and he changed them many times a day. This fashion first started when his hairline began to recede, then sprouted all over Europe, spreading even to the American colonies in the time of George Washington.

Louis may have been treated like a god, but he was not an overly arrogant man. His subjects adored him because he was a symbol of everything a man could be, the fullest expression of the Renaissance Man.

The War Room: Versailles was good propaganda. It showed the rest of the world how rich and powerful Louis was. One look at this eye-saturating view of the gardens sent visitors reeling.

But France's success also made other countries jealous and nervous. The semi-circles on the ceiling show Germany (with the double eagle), Holland (with its ships), and Spain (with a red flag and roaring lion) ganging up on Louis. Two guesses who won. Of course, these mere mortals were no match for the Sun King. The stucco relief on the wall shows Louis on horseback, triumphing over his fallen enemies.

But Louis' greatest triumph may be the next room, the one that everybody wrote home about.

The Hall of Mirrors: No one had ever seen anything like this hall when it was opened. Mirrors were still a great luxury at the time, and the number and size of these monsters were astounding. The hall is almost 75 meters long (250 feet). There are 17 arched mirrors matched by 17 windows with that breathtaking view of the gardens. Lining the hall are 24 gilded candelabras, eight busts of

Roman emperors, and eight
classical-style statues (7 of
them ancient). The ceiling
decoration chronicles Louis'
military accomplishments,
topped off by Louis himself
in the central panel (with
cupids playing cards at his
divine feet), doing what he
did best—triumphing.

This was where the grandest festivities were held for the most
important ambassadors and guests. The throne could be moved
from the Apollo Room and set up at the far end of the hall.
Imagine this place filled with guests dressed in silks and powdered
wigs, lit by the flames of thousands of candles. The mirrors are a
reflection of an age when beautiful people loved to look at themselves. It was no longer a sin to be proud of good looks or fine
clothes, or to enjoy the good things in life: laughing, dancing,
eating, drinking, flirting, and enjoying the view.

From the center of the hall, you can fully appreciate the epic
scale of Versailles. The huge palace (by architect Le Vau), the
fantasy interior (Le Brun), and the endless gardens (Le Notre)
made Versailles *le* best. In more recent times, the Hall of Mirrors
is where the Treaty of Versailles was signed, ending World War I
(and, some say, starting World War II).

• *Enter the small Peace Room and grab a bench.*

The Peace Room: "Louis
Quatorze was addicted to
wars..." but by the end of his
life, he was tired of fighting. In
this sequel to the War Room,
peace is granted to Germany,
Holland, and Spain as cupids
play with the discarded cannons,
armor, and swords.

The oval painting above the fireplace shows 19-year-old
Louis bestowing an olive branch on Europe. Beside him is his
wife, Marie-Thérèse, cradling their two-year-old twin daughters.
If being a father at 17 seems a bit young, remember that Louis
was married when he was four.

The Peace Room marks the beginning of the queen's half
of the palace. On Sundays, the queen held chamber-music concerts
here for family and friends.

• *Enter the first room of the Queen's Wing, with its canopied bed.*

The Queen's and Nobles' Wing

The Queen's Bedchamber: This was the queen's official bedroom. It was here that she rendezvoused with her husband. Two queens died here. This is where 19 princes were born. The chandelier is where two of them were conceived. Just kidding.

True, Louis was not the most faithful husband. There was no attempt to hide the fact that the Sun King warmed more than one bed, for he was above the rules of mere mortals. Adultery became acceptable—even fashionable—in court circles. The secret-looking doors on either side of the bed were for Louis' late-night liaisons—they lead straight to his rooms.

Some of Louis' mistresses became more famous and powerful than his rather quiet queen, but he was faithful to the show of marriage and had genuine affection for his wife. Their private apartments were connected, and Louis made a point of sleeping with the queen as often as possible, regardless of whose tiara he tickled earlier in the evening.

This room looks like it did in the days of the last queen, Marie-Antoinette. That's her bust over the fireplace, and the double eagle of her native Austria in the corners. The big chest to the left of the bed held her jewels.

The queen's canopied bed is a reconstruction. The bed, chair, and wall coverings switched with the seasons. This was the cheery summer pattern.

Drawing Room of the Nobles: The queen's circle of friends met here, seated on the stools. Discussions ranged from politics to gossip, food to literature, fashion to philosophy. The Versailles kings considered themselves enlightened monarchs who promoted the arts and new ideas. Folks like Voltaire—a political radical—and the playwright Molière participated in the Versailles court. Ironically, these discussions planted the seeds of liberal thought that would grow into the Revolution.

Queen's Antechamber: This is where the Royal Family dined publicly while servants and nobles fluttered around them, admiring their table manners and laughing at the king's jokes like courtly Paul Shaeffers. A typical dinner consisted of four different soups, two whole birds stuffed with truffles, plus mutton, ham slices, fruit, pastries, compotes, and preserves.

The central portrait is of luxury-loving, "Let-them-eat-cake" Marie-Antoinette, who became a symbol of decadence to the peasants. The portrait at the far end is a public-relations attempt to soften her image, showing her with three of her nine children.

Queen's Guard Room: On October 6, 1789, a mob of revolutionaries—appalled by their queen's taste in wallpaper—stormed the palace. They were fed up with the life of luxury led by the ruling class in the countryside while they were starving in the grimy streets of Paris.

The king and queen locked themselves in. Some of the revolutionaries got access to this upper floor. They burst into this room, where Marie-Antoinette had taken refuge, then killed three of her bodyguards and dragged her and her husband off. (Some claim that, as they carried her away, she sang "Louis, Louis, oh-oh . . . we gotta go now.")

The enraged peasants then proceeded to ransack the place, taking revenge for the years of poverty and oppression they'd suffered. Marie-Antoinette and Louis XVI were later taken to the place de la Concorde in Paris, where they knelt under the guillotine and were made a foot shorter at the top.

Did the king and queen deserve it? Were the revolutionaries destroying civilization or clearing the decks for a new and better one? Was Versailles progress or decadence?

Coronation Room: No sooner did they throw out a king than they got an emperor. The Revolution established democracy, but it was shaky in a country that wasn't used to it. In the midst of the confusion, the upstart general Napoleon Bonaparte took control and soon held dictatorial powers. This room captures the glory of the Napoleon years, when he conquered most of Europe. In the huge canvas on the left-hand wall, we see him crowning himself emperor of a new, revived "Roman" Empire. (This is a lesser-quality copy of a version hanging in the Louvre.)

Catch the portrait of a dashing, young, charismatic Napoleon by the window on the right. This shows him in 1796, when he was just a general in command of the Revolution's army in Italy. Compare this with the portrait next to it from 10 years later—looking less like a revolutionary and more like a Louis. Above the young Napoleon is a portrait of Josephine, his wife and France's empress. In David's *Distribution of Eagles* (opposite the *Coronation*), the victorious general (in imperial garb) passes out emblems of victory to his loyal troops. In *The Battle of Aboukir* (opposite the window), Napoleon looks rather bored as he slashes through a tangle of dark-skinned warriors. His horse, though, has a look of "What are we doing in this mob? Let's get out of here!" Let's.

• *Pass through a couple of rooms to the exit staircase on your left. The long Battle Gallery ahead of you shows 120 meters (400 feet) of scenes from famous French battles, arranged chronologically clockwise around the gallery. The exit staircase puts you outside on the left (south) side of the palace.*

The Gardens—Controlling Nature

Louis was a divine-right ruler. One way he proved it was by controlling nature like a god. These lavish grounds, so elaborately planned out, pruned, and decorated, showed everyone that Louis was in total command.

• *Exiting the palace into the gardens, veer to the left toward the concrete railing about 68 meters (225 feet) away. You'll pass by horse carriages for hire and through flowers and cookie-cutter patterns of shrubs and green cones. Stand at the railing overlooking the courtyard below and the Louis-made lake in the distance.*

The Orangerie: The warmth from the Sun King was so great that he could even grow orange trees in chilly France. Louis had a thousand of these to amaze his visitors. In winter they were kept in the greenhouses (beneath your feet) that surround the courtyard. On sunny days they were wheeled out in their silver planters and scattered around the grounds.

• *From the stone railing, turn about-face and walk back toward the palace, veering left toward the two large pools of water. Sit on the top stair and look away from the palace.*

View down the Royal Drive: This, to me, is the most impressive spot in all of Versailles. In one direction, the palace. Stretching out in the other, the endless grounds. Versailles was laid out along a 13-kilometer (8-mile) axis that included the grounds, the palace, and the town of Versailles itself, one of the first instances of urban planning since Roman times and a model for future capitals like Washington, D.C., and Brasilia.

Looking down the Royal Drive (also known as "The Green Carpet"), you see the round Apollo fountain way in the distance. Just beyond that is the Grand Canal. The groves on either side of the Royal Drive were planted with trees from all over, laid out in an elaborate grid and dotted with statues and fountains. Of the original 1,500 fountains, 300 remain.

Looking back at the palace, you can see the Hall of Mirrors—it's the middle story, with the arched windows.

• *Stroll down the steps to get a good look at the frogs and lizards that fill the round Latona Basin.*

The Latona Basin: The theme of Versailles is Apollo, the god of the sun, associated with Louis. This round fountain tells the story of the birth of Apollo and his sister, Diana. On top of the fountain are Apollo and Diana as little kids with their mother, Latona (they're facing toward the Apollo fountain). Latona, an unwed mother, was insulted by the local peasants. She called on the king of the gods, Zeus (the children's father), to avenge the insult. Zeus swooped down and turned all the peasants into the frogs and lizards that ring the fountain.

• *As you walk down past the basin toward the Royal Drive, you'll pass by "ancient" statues done by 17th-century French sculptors. The Colonnade is hidden in the woods on the left-hand side of the Royal Drive, about three-fourths of the way to the Apollo Basin.*

The Colonnade: Versailles had no prestigious ancient ruins, so the king built his own. This prefab Roman ruin is a 30-meter (100-foot) circle of 64 marble columns supporting arches. Beneath the arches are small birdbath fountains. Nobles would picnic in the shade to the tunes of a string quartet, pretending they were the enlightened citizens of the ancient world.

The Apollo Basin: The fountains of Versailles were its most famous attraction, a marvel of both art and engineering. This one was the centerpiece, showing the Sun God—Louis—in his sunny chariot, starting his journey across the sky. The horses are half-submerged, giving the impression, when the fountains play, of the sun rising out of the mists of dawn. Most of the fountains were only turned on when the king walked by, but this one played constantly for the benefit of those watching from the palace.

All the fountains are gravity-powered. They work on the same principle as when you block a hose with your finger to make it squirt. Underground streams feed into smaller pipes at the fountains that shoot the water high into the air.

Looking back at the palace from here, realize that the distance you just walked is only a fraction of this vast complex of buildings, gardens, and waterways. Be glad you don't have to mow the lawn.

The Grand Canal: Why visit Venice when you can just build your own? In an era before virtual reality, this was the next best thing to an actual trip. Couples in gondolas would pole along the waters accompanied by barges with orchestras playing *O Sole Mio*. The canal is actually cross-shaped, this being the long arm, 1.5 kilometers (1 mile) from end to end. Of course, this too is a man-made body of water with no function other than pleasing.

The Trianon Area—Retreat from Reality

Versailles began as an escape from the pressures of kingship. In a short time, the palace was as busy as Paris ever was. Louis needed an escape from his escape and built a smaller palace out in the tules. Later, his successors retreated still farther into the garden, building a fantasy world of simple pleasures from which to ignore the real world, which was crumbling all around them.

• *You can rent a bike or catch the TGV tram (5/hr, 4 stops, does not stop at Le Hameau), but the walk is half the fun. It's about a 30-minute walk from here to the end of the tour, plus another 30 minutes to walk back to the palace.*

Grand Trianon: This was the king's private residence away from the main palace. Louis usually spent a couple of nights a week here, but the two later Louises spent more and more time retreating.

The facade of this one-story building is a charming combination of pink, yellow, and white, a cheery contrast to the imposing Baroque facade of the main palace. Ahead you can see the gardens through the columns. The king's apartments were to the left of the columns.

The flower gardens were changed daily for the king's pleasure—for new color combinations and new "nasal cocktails."

Walk around the palace (to the right), if you'd like, for a view of the gardens and rear facade.

• *Facing the front, do an about-face. The Summer House is not down the driveway but about 180 meters (600 feet) away, along the smaller pathway at about 10 o'clock.*

The Summer House of the French Garden: This small white building with four rooms fanning out from the center was one more step away from the modern world. Here, the queen spent summer evenings with family and a few friends, listening to music or playing parlor games. All avenues of *la douceur de vivre*—"the sweetness of living"—were explored. To the left are the buildings of the Menagerie, where cows, goats, chickens, and ducks were bred.

• *Continue frolicking along the path until you run into . . .*

Petit Trianon: Louis XV developed an interest in botany. He wanted to spend more time near the French Gardens, but the Summer House just wasn't big enough. He built the Petit Trianon (the "small" Trianon),

a masterpiece of neoclassical architecture. This gray, cubical building has four distinct facades, each a perfect and harmonious combination of Greek-style columns, windows, and railings. Walk around it and find your favorite.

Louis XVI and his wife, Marie-Antoinette, made this their home base. Marie-Antoinette was a sweet girl from Vienna who never quite fit in with the fast, sophisticated crowd at Versailles. Here at the Petit Trianon, she could get away and re-create the simple home life she remembered from her childhood. On the lawn outside, she installed a merry-go-round.

• *Five minutes more will bring you to . . .*

The Temple of Love: A circle of 12 marble Corinthian columns supporting a dome decorates a path where lovers would stroll. Underneath, there's a statue of Cupid making a bow (to shoot arrows of love) out of the club of Hercules. It's a delightful monument to a society whose rich could afford that ultimate luxury, romantic love. When the Revolution came, I bet they wished they'd kept the club.

• *And finally you'll reach . . .*

Le Hameau—The Hamlet: Marie-Antoinette longed for the simple life of a peasant. Not the hard labor of real peasants—

who sweated and starved around her—but the fairy-tale world of simple country pleasures. She built this complex of 12 buildings as her own private village.

This was an actual working farm with a dairy, a water-wheel mill, and domestic

animals. The harvest was served at Marie's table. Marie didn't do much work herself, but she "supervised," dressed in a plain white muslin dress and a straw hat.

The Queen's House is the main building, actually two buildings connected by a wooden gallery. Like any typical peasant farmhouse, it had a billiard room, library, elegant dining hall, and two living rooms.

Nearby was the small theater. Here, Marie and her friends acted out plays far from the rude intrusions of the real world . . .

• *The real world and the main palace are a 30-minute walk to the southeast. Along the way, stop at the Neptune Basin near the palace, an impressive miniature lake with fountains, and indulge your own favorite fantasy.*

CHARTRES
TOUR

Many of the children who watched the old church burn to the ground on June 10, 1194, grew up to build Chartres cathedral and attend the dedication Mass in 1260. That's astonishing, considering that other Gothic cathedrals, such as Paris's Notre-Dame, took hundreds of years to build. Having been built so quickly, Chartres is arguably Europe's best example of pure Gothic, with a unity of architecture, statues, and stained glass that captures the spirit of the Age of Faith.

Chartres' pleasing, cobbled old center is overshadowed by its great cathedral. Discover the picnic-friendly park behind the cathedral and wander the quiet alleys and peaceful squares. The helpful TI has a map with a self-guided tour of Chartres. For accommodations, see the end of this chapter.

CHARTRES CATHEDRAL TOUR

Orientation

Cost and Hours: Free. Daily 07:00–19:00.

Getting There: Chartres is a one-hour train trip from Paris' Gare Montparnasse (about €11 one-way, 10/day, last train on Sat departs Chartres about 19:00; figure on a round-trip total of 3 hrs from Paris to cathedral doorstep and back). Upon arrival in Chartres, confirm your return schedule. Leaving the train station and heading uphill, you'll soon see the medieval church rise above the modern city of Chartres.

Bring: Binoculars, if you've got 'em.

Information: The TI (Mon–Sat 09:00–19:00, Sun 09:00–17:30, tel. 02 37 18 26 26) is located 100 meters (300 feet) in front of the church.

Cathedral Tours by Malcolm Miller: Fine one-hour tours Mon–Sat at 12:00 and 14:45 cost €6 and are led by either Malcolm Miller

─CHARTRES─

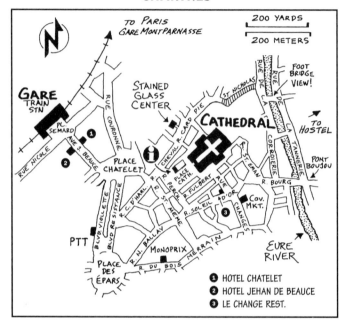

or his capable assistant. Tours begin at the gift shop inside the church. Private tours can be arranged (tel. 02 37 28 15 58, fax 02 37 28 33 03).

Length of Our Tour: One hour, but Chartres is an all-day excursion from Paris.

Accommodations and Restaurants: See end of chapter (page 238).

THE CHARTRES GENERATION—THE 1200s

• *Kill train time with this.*

From king to bishop to knight to pawn, French society was devoted to the Christian faith. It inspired knights to undertake the formidable Crusades, artists to re-create heaven in statues and stained glass, and architects to build skyscraping cathedrals filled with the mystic light of heaven. They aimed for a golden age, blending faith and reason, though misguided faith often outstripped reason, resulting in very un-Christian intolerance and violence.

Timeline

1194—The old cathedral burns down.

c. 1200—The University of Paris is founded, using human reason to analyze Christian faith. Borrowing from the pagan Greek philosopher Aristotle, scholars described the Christian universe as a series of concentric rings spinning around the Earth in geometrical perfection.

1202—The pope calls on all true Christians to rescue the Holy Land from Muslim "infidels" (including Genghis Khan) in the Fourth Crusade (1202–1204). This crusade ends disastrously in the sacking of Constantinople, a Christian city.

1206—Chartres' cornerstone is laid. The style is *opus francigenum* ("French-style work")—what the people in Gothic times called Gothic. Chartres is just one of several great cathedrals under construction in Europe.

1207—Francis of Assisi, a rebellious Italian youth, undergoes a conversion to a life of Christian poverty and love. His open spirit inspires many followers, including France's King Louis IX (a generation later).

1209—France's King Phillip Augustus, centered in Paris, invades southern France, massacring fellow Christians (the Cathars or Albigensians) as heretics.

1212—Thousands of boys and girls idealistically join the Children's Crusade (1212) to save the Holy Land. Most die in transit or are sold into slavery.

1220—The external structure of Chartres cathedral is nearly finished. Work begins on the statues and stained glass.

1226—Eleven-year-old Louis IX is crowned as *rex et sacerdos*, "King and Priest," beginning a 45-year Golden Age combining church and state. His mother, Blanche of Castile (granddaughter of Eleanor of Aquitaine), is his lifelong mentor.

1230—Most of Chartres' stained glass is completed.

1244—At age 30, Louis falls sick and sees a vision in a coma that changes his life. His personal trustworthiness helps unify the nation. He reforms the judicial system along Christian lines, helping the poor.

1245—The last Albigensian heretics are burned at Montsegur, in a crusade ordered by Louis and his mother, Blanche.

1248—Louis personally leads the Seventh Crusade by walking barefoot from Paris to the port of departure. During the fighting, he is captured and ransomed. He later returns home a changed man. Humbled, he adopts the poverty of the Franciscan brotherhood. His devotion earns him the title of Saint Louis.

1260—Chartres cathedral is dedicated. The church is the physical embodiment of the Age of Faith, with architecture as mathematically perfect as God's Creation, sculpture serving as sermons in stone, and stained glass lit by the light of God.

Mary's Church ("Notre-Dame" = "Our Lady" of Chartres)

The church is (at least) the fourth church on this spot dedicated to Mary, the mother of Jesus, who has been venerated here for some 1700 years. There's even speculation that the pagan Romans dedicated a temple to a mother-goddess. In earliest times, Mary was honored next to a natural spring with healing waters (not visible today). In the ninth century, the church acquired Mary's cloth birth tunic (which we'll see) as the focus of devotion. A crude wooden statue of Mary also attracted pilgrims (the statue was destroyed in 1793, but copies remain).

The Book of Chartres

Historian Malcolm Miller calls Chartres a picture book of statues, stained glass, and symbolic architecture, telling the entire Christian story—from Creation to Christ's birth (the north side of the church), from Christ and his followers up to the present (south entrance), to the end of time when Christ returns as judge (west entrance).

The Christian universe is a complex web of heaven and earth, angels and demons, and prophets and martyrs. Much of the medieval symbolism is obscure today. Expect to be overwhelmed by the thousands of things to see, but appreciate the perfect unity of this Gothic masterpiece.

THE TOUR BEGINS
1. The Main Entrance (West Facade), c. 1150:

The two mismatched steeples, three doors, rose window, and various statues are the only survivors of the intense, lead-melting fire that incinerated the rest of the church in 1194. The church of today was rebuilt behind this facade in a single generation (1194–1260).

Towers: The right (south) tower, with a stone steeple, is original Romanesque. The left (north) tower lost its wooden steeple in the 1194 fire. In the 1500s, it was topped by a steeple bigger than the tapered lower half was meant to hold.

The West Doors: Christ, the center of Christian history, sits above the **central door**, surrounded by symbolic animals.

The anorexic statues between the doors are pillars of the faith that foretold the coming of Christ. With solemn gestures and faces, they patiently endure the wait.

——— CHARTRES CATHEDRAL ———

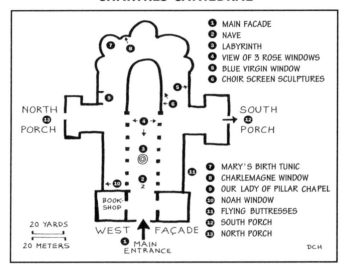

CHARTRES CATHEDRAL

- ❶ MAIN FACADE
- ❷ NAVE
- ❸ LABYRINTH
- ❹ VIEW OF 3 ROSE WINDOWS
- ❺ BLUE VIRGIN WINDOW
- ❻ CHOIR SCREEN SCULPTURES

NORTH ❸ PORCH

SOUTH ❷ PORCH

- ❼ MARY'S BIRTH TUNIC
- ❽ CHARLEMAGNE WINDOW
- ❾ OUR LADY OF PILLAR CHAPEL
- ❿ NOAH WINDOW
- ⓫ FLYING BUTTRESSES
- ⓬ SOUTH PORCH
- ⓭ NORTH PORCH

BOOK-SHOP

20 YARDS
20 METERS

WEST FAÇADE
❶ MAIN ENTRANCE

DCH

History's pivotal event is shown above the **right door**, where Mary (seated) produces baby Jesus from her loins. This Mary-and-baby sculpture is a 12th-century stone version of an older wooden statue (burned 1793). Centuries of pilgrims

have visited Chartres to see Mary's statue, gaze at her birth tunic (which we'll see), and ponder the mystery of how God in Heaven became Man on Earth, passing through immaculate Mary like sunlight through stained glass.

• *Enter the church and wait for your pupils to enlarge.*

2. Nave: The church has a long, tall central nave, flanked by raised side aisles for crowd flow, so pilgrims could circle the church without disturbing worshipers. The 12 pillars lining the nave support pointed crisscross arches on the ceiling, which lace together the heavy stone vaulting. The pillars are supported by flying buttresses on the outside of the church (which we'll see later). This skeleton structure was the miracle of Gothic, allowing tall buildings with ribbed walls and lots of stained-glass windows (like the big saints in the upper stories of the nave). The floor of the nave slopes in to the center, for easy drainage when hosing down dirty pilgrims who camped here.

3. The Labyrinth: The round maze inlaid in black stone on the floor of the nave is a spiritual journey. Pilgrims enter from the west rim by foot or on knees and wind inward, meditating. Three hundred meters (980 feet) later, they hope to meet God in the middle. (Current world record for reaching enlightenment is 3:42.)

• *Walk up the nave to where the transept crosses. As you face the altar, north is to the left.*

4. The Rose Windows—North, South, and West:

The three big, round "rose" (floral-shaped) windows over the entrances open like flowers to receive sunlight at different times of day. All three are predominantly blue and red, but each has different "petals," and each tells a different part of the Christian story in a kaleidoscope of fragmented images.

Having trouble making out the tiny, distant details? As we've all read, stained glass was a way to teach Bible stories to the illiterate medieval masses . . . who apparently owned state-of-the-art binoculars. Yes, the windows tell stories, but obviously, their main purpose was to light a dark church in a colorful and decorative way.

The **north rose window** charts history from the distant past up to the birth of Jesus. On the outer rim, murky, ancient (barely visible) prophets foretell Christ's coming. Then (circling inward), there's a ring of red squares with kings who are Christ's direct ancestors. Still closer, a circle of white doves and winged angels zero in on the central event of history—Mary, the heart of the flower, with her newborn baby, Jesus.

This window was donated by King Louis IX (who built Paris' Sainte-Chapelle) and his mom, Blanche of Castile. See their coats of arms just below the rose—Louis's yellow fleur-de-lis on a blue background and Blanche's yellow castles on a red background.

In the **south rose window**, the Old Testament prophecies are fulfilled. Christ sits in the center (dressed in blue, with a red background), setting in motion the radiating rings of angels, beasts, and apocalyptic elders who labor to bring history to its close. The five lancet windows below show Old Testament prophets lifting New Testament writers on their shoulders (in first window on left, see white-robed Luke riding piggyback on dark-robed Jeremiah), demonstrating how the ancients prepared the way for Christ. A dark Christ rings in history's final Day of Judgment at the center of the **west rose window**. Around him, winged angels blow their trumpets and the dead rise, are judged, and are sent to hell or raised to eternal bliss. The frilly edge of this glorious "rose" is flecked with tiny, clover-shaped dewdrops.

"Stained Glass Supreme"

- Melt one part sand with two parts wood ash to make glass.
- Mix in rusty metals to get different colors—iron makes red, cobalt makes blue, copper/green, manganese/purple, cadmium/yellow.
- Blow glass into a cylinder shape, cut lengthways, and lay flat.
- Cut into pieces with an iron tool, or by heating-and-cooling a select spot to make it crack.
- Fit pieces together to form a figure, using strips of lead to hold in place.
- Place masterpiece so high on a wall that no one can read it.

God = Light

You can try to examine the details, but a better way to experience the mystery of Chartres is to just sit and stare at these enormous panels, as they float in the dark of empty space like holograms or space stations or the Queen of Heaven's crown jewels. Ponder the medieval concept that God is light.

To the Chartres generation, the church was a metaphor for how God brings his creation to life, like the way light animates stained glass. They were heavy into mysticism, feeling a oneness with all creation in a moment of enlightenment. The Gospel of John (as well as a writer known to historians as the Pseudo-Dionysius) was their favorite. Here are select verses from John 1:1-12 (loosely translated):

"In the beginning was The Word.

He (Jesus) was the light of the human race.

The light shines in the darkness, and the darkness cannot resist it.

It was the real light coming into the world, the light that en-light-ens everyone.

He was in the world, but the world did not recognize Him. But to those who did, He gave the power to become the children of God."

5. The Blue Virgin Window: Mary, dressed in blue on a rich red background, cradles purple Jesus, while the dove of the Spirit descends on her. This is some of the oldest stained glass (1150), a survivor of the 1194 fire, which was reinserted into this new window frame around 1230. The Blue Virgin was one of the most popular stops for pilgrims—especially pregnant ones—of the cult of the Virgin-about-to-give-birth. Devotees prayed, carried stones to repair the church, or donated to the church coffers—Mary rewarded them with peace of mind, easy births, and occasional miracles.

Below Mary, see **Christ being tempted** by a red-faced, horned, smirking devil.

Hail, maiden, what's your sign? Pick up chicks at the **Zodiac Window** (second window to the left). The 12 signs are in the right half of the window; read from the bottom up—Pisces, Aries, Gemini (in the cloverleaf), Taurus, Cockroach, Leo, Virgo, etc.

6. The Choir Screen—Life of Mary: In the center of the church sits the stone **choir** (the enclosed area behind the altar where church officials sat), ringed with **41 statue-groups** illustrating Mary's life (by various sculptors, 1520–1714). Although the Bible says little about the mother of Jesus, legend and lore fleshed out her life.

Scene #1 (south side) shows an angel telling her dad that Mary's on the way. In #4, Anne gives birth to Mary. In #6, Mary marries Joseph. In #10, she gives birth to Jesus in a manger. In #12, the Three Kings arrive. Scenes #15, through #27, show her famous son's life. In #28, Jesus is crucified. In #34, the resurrected Jesus appears to his mother. In #38, Mary dies...in #39, she's raised by angels into heaven...and in #41, she's crowned Queen of Heaven by the Father, Son, and the Holy Ghost.

The **plain windows** surrounding the choir date from the 1770s, when the dark mystery of medieval stained glass was replaced by the open light of the French Enlightenment. The plain windows and the choir are some of the only "new" features. Most of the 1200s church has remained, despite style changes, Revolutionary vandals, and war bombs.

7. Mary's Birth Tunic: Sitting in a glass case with a gold frame held by angels, this is the torn, 2,000-year-old cloth **tunic** supposedly worn by Mary when she gave birth to Jesus. Since the ninth century, this has been the main object of adoration for the cult of the Virgin, and stories abound of its magical powers.

In A.D. 911, with the city surrounded by Vikings, the bishop hoisted the tunic like a battle flag and waved it at the invaders. It scared the bejesus out them with visions of extended labor, and the town was saved.

When the fire of 1194 incinerated the old church, the tunic was feared lost. Lo and behold, several days later they found it miraculously unharmed in the crypt (beneath today's choir). The people were so stoked, they worked like madmen to erect this grand cathedral to display it in.

8. Charlemagne Window: The window tells the story of how the tunic ended up here. **Charlemagne** (bottom left semi-circle), the great king of the Franks (A.D. 800), sits on his throne between two advisers and plans a great adventure—a crusade to the Holy City of Jerusalem. Next (the semicircle just above), he attacks the Muslim infidels occupying Jerusalem. Charlemagne (heart-shaped shield) stabs a Saracen (round shield) in the neck, driving the Muslims out of the city.

On the way home, Charlemagne stops in the great Christian city of Constantinople (in the diamond directly to the right), where he's welcomed at the gate by the emperor. The emperor rewards him (semicircle directly to the right) with three chests of holy relics...including Mary's tunic. Charlemagne returns home (the circle above the diamond) to his palace in Aix, kneels, and places the relics before the altar. Charlemagne's grandson, Charles the Bald, gave the tunic to Chartres in 876.

The fashion-conscious will notice the clothes are from the 1220s, when the window was made.

9. Chapel of Our Lady on the Pillar: A 16th-century **statue of Mary and baby**—draped in cloth, crowned and sceptered—sits on a column in a wonderful carved-wood alcove. This is today's pilgrimage center, built to keep visitors from clogging up the altar area. Modern pilgrims honor the Virgin by leaving flowers, lighting candles, and kissing the column.

10. The Noah Window: Read Chartres' windows from left to right and bottom to top.

Bottom-left is a man making a wheel. He's one of the donors of this window. His colleagues to the right are from the axe- and barrel-maker guilds.

Then comes the story of **Noah** (read from the bottom up): God tells Noah he'll destroy the earth (#1, bottom diamond). Noah hefts an axe to build an ark, while his son hauls wood (diamond #2). He loads horses (cloverleaf, above left), purple elephants (cloverleaf, above right), and other animals. The psychedelic ark sets sail (diamond #3). Waves cover the earth, drowning the wicked (two clover-leaves). The ark survives (diamond #4) and Noah releases a dove. Finally, up near the top (diamond #7), a rainbow arches overhead, God drapes himself over it, and Noah and his family give thanks.
• *Exit the church (through the main entrance or the door in the south transept) to view its south side.*

11. South Exterior—Flying Buttresses: Six flying but-tresses on the south side (the arches that stick out from the upper walls) push against six pillars lining the nave inside, helping to hold up the heavy stone ceiling and sloped, lead-over-wood roof. The ceiling and roof push down onto the pillars, of course, but also outward (north and south) because of the miracle of Gothic, the pointed arch. These flying buttresses push back, channeling the stress outward to the six vertical buttresses, then down to the ground. The result is a tall cathedral held up by slender pillars buttressed from the outside, allowing the walls to be opened up for stained glass.

The church is built from large blocks of limestone. Peasants trod in hamster-wheel contraptions to raise these blocks into place—a testament to their great faith.

12. South Porch: The three doorways of the south entrance show the world from Christ to the present, as Christianity triumphs over persecution.

Center Door—Christ and Apostles: Jesus stands between the double doors, holding a book and raising his arm in blessing. He's a simple, itinerant, bareheaded, barefoot rabbi, but underneath his feet he tramples symbols of evil, the dragon and lion (which is which?). Christ's face is among the most noble of all Gothic sculpture.

Christ is surrounded by his **apostles**, who spread the good news to a hostile world. **Peter** (to the left as you face Jesus), with curly hair and beard, holds the key to the kingdom of heaven and the slender cross on which he was crucified upside down. **Paul** (to the right of Jesus) fingers the sword of his martyrdom, contemplating the inevitable loss of his head and the hair upon it. In fact, all of the apostles were killed or persecuted, and their faces are humble, with sad eyes. But their message prevailed, and under their feet they crush the squirming emperors who once persecuted them.

The final triumph comes above the door in the **Last Judgment**. Christ sits in judgment, raising his hands, while Mary and John beg him to take it easy on poor humankind. Beneath Christ, the souls are judged—the righteous on our left, the wicked on the right, who are thrown into the fiery jaws of hell. Farther to the right (above the statues of Paul and the apostles), horny demons subject wicked women to an eternity of sexual harassment.

Left Door—Martyrs: Eight martyrs flank the left door. St. Lawrence (second from left) cradles the grill on which he was barbecued alive. His last brave words to the Romans actually were: "You can turn me over—I'm done on this side." St. George (far right) wears the knightly uniform of the 1200s, when Chartres was built and King Louis IX was crusading. Depicted beneath the martyrs are gruesome methods of torture (e.g., George stretched on the wheel), many of which were used in the 1200s against heretics, Muslims, Jews, and Albigensians (the Cathar sect of southern France).

Right Door—Confessors: Among these eight pillars of the faith, find Jerome (third from the right), holding the Bible he translated into everyday Latin; and Gregory (second from the right), the pope who organized church hierarchy and wrote Gregorian chants.

• *Reach the north side by circling around the back end of the church (great views) or cutting through the church.*

13. The North Porch: In the Book of Chartres, the north porch is chapter one, from the Creation up to the coming of Christ.

Center Door: Baby Mary (headless), in the arms of her mother Anne (the statue between the double doors), marks the culmination of the Old Testament world.

History begins in the tiny details in the concentric arches over the doorway. God creates Adam (at the peak of the outer arch) by cradling his head in his lap like a child.

Melchizedek (farthest to the left of Mary and Anne), with cap and cup, is the Biblical model of the *rex et sacerdos* (king-priest), the title bestowed on King Louis IX.

Abraham (second from left) holds his son by the throat and raises a knife to slit him for sacrifice. Just then, he hears something and turns his head up to see God's angel, who stops the bloodshed. The drama of this frozen moment anticipates Renaissance naturalism 200 years early.

John the Baptist (fourth to the right from Mary/Anne), the last Old Testament prophet who prepared the way for Jesus, holds a lamb, the symbol of Christ. John is skinny from his diet of locusts and honey. His body twists and flickers like a flame.

All these prophets, with their beards turning down the corners of their mouths, have the sad, wise look of having been around since the beginning of time, and having seen it all—from Creation to Christ to Apocalypse. They are some of the last work done on the church, completing the church's sermon in stone and glass.

Imagine all this painted and covered with gold leaf in preparation for the dedication ceremonies in 1260, when the Chartres generation could finally stand back and watch as their great-grandchildren, carrying candles, entered the cathedral.

The Rest of the Church

Malcolm Miller's tours and books: This fascinating English scholar illuminates a new detail of the church with each tour (see "Orientation," above). His tours are worthwhile even if you've taken this self-guided tour. For a detailed look at Chartres' windows, sculpture, and history, pick up Malcolm Miller's two guidebooks (sold at the church bookstore).

The crypt: The foundations (below the present church) can be visited only as part of a guided tour in French. You'll see remnants of the earlier churches, a modern copy of the old wooden Mary-and-baby statue, and hints of the old well and Roman wall (30-min tours start in La Crypte bookstore, located outside church near south porch).

Climb the north tower: Three hundred steps lead to a great view (€4, students-€2.50, children free, Mon–Sat 09:00–18:00 in summer, Sun 13:00–18:00, entrance inside church near bookstore).

Sleeping and Eating in Chartres
(€1.10 = about $1, country code: 33, zip code: 28000)

Chartres, which makes a good getaway from Paris, can also serve as a convenient first or last night for those flying to/from Orly airport. These two hotels face each other, 200 meters (650 feet) straight out of the train station, 300 meters below the cathedral: **Hôtel Jehan de Beauce**** is basic, but clean and quiet, with some tiny bathrooms (S-€24, D-€27, Ds-€31, Db-€37–47, Tb-€38, CC, 19 avenue Jehan de Beauce, tel. 02 37 21 01 41, fax 02 37 21 59 10). **Hôtel Chatelet***** is comfortable, from its welcoming lobby to its spotless, spacious, well-furnished rooms (Sb-€56–72, Db-€66, extra person-€9, streetside rooms are cheaper, CC, 6 avenue Jehan de Beauce, tel. 02 37 21 78 00, fax 02 37 36 23 01, e-mail: hchatel@club-internet.fr).

Eating in Chartres: Le Pichet, a short hop from the TI, is a reasonable, friendly, and homey place (19 rue du Cheval Blanc, tel. 02 37 21 08 35). **Le Change** serves fine food at good prices (€11/€21 *menus*, closed Sun, 45 rue des Changes, tel. 02 37 21 99 36). Le **Bistrot de la Cathédrale** is good for salads and basic bistro fare (on south side of cathedral at 1 Cloître Notre-Dame, tel. 02 37 36 59 60).

MORE DAYTRIPS FROM PARIS

Grand Châteaux near Paris • Impressionist Excursions: Giverny and Auvers-sur-Oise • Disneyland Paris

paris

GRAND CHÂTEAUX NEAR PARIS

The region around Paris (the Ile de France) is dotted with sumptuous palaces. Paris' booming upper class made this the heartland of European château–building in the 16th and 17th centuries. Most of these châteaux were lavish hunting lodges—getaways from the big city. The only things they defended were noble and royal egos.

Consider four very different châteaux:

▲▲▲**Versailles**—for its history, grandeur, and accessibility (closed Mon)

▲▲▲**Vaux-le-Vicomte**—for sheer beauty and intimacy (open daily)

▲▲**Fontainebleau**—for its history, fine interior, and pleasant city (closed Tue)

▲**Chantilly**—for its beautiful setting and fine collection of paintings (closed Tue except in summer)

If you only have time for one château, choose between Vaux-le-Vicomte and Versailles (see tour on page 209). Except for Versailles, these châteaux are quiet on weekdays. Versailles, Fontainebleau, and Chantilly are covered by the Paris museum pass.

Vaux-le-Vicomte

While Versailles is most travelers' first choice for its sheer historic weight, Vaux-le-Vicomte (voh-luh-vee-komt) offers a more intimate interior and a far better sense of 17th-century château life. Sitting in a huge forest, with magnificent gardens and no urban sprawl in sight, Vaux-le-Vicomte gave me just a twinge of palace envy.

Vaux-le-Vicomte was the architectural inspiration of Versailles and set the standard for European châteaux to come. The proud

——DAYTRIPS FROM PARIS——

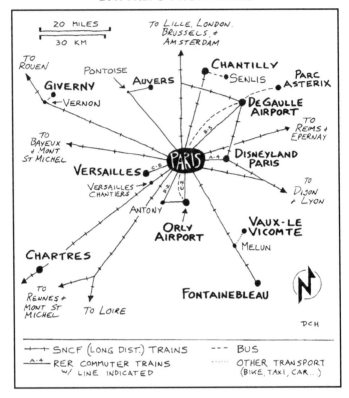

owner, Nicolas Fouquet (Louis XIV's finance minister), threw a
château-warming party. Louis was so jealous that he arrested his host,
took his architect (Le Vau), artist (Le Brun), and landscaper
(Le Notre), and proceeded with the construction of the bigger and
costlier (but not necessarily more splendid) palace of Versailles.
Monsieur Fouquet is thought to be Alexandre Dumas' man in
The Man in the Iron Mask, which was filmed here.

Vaux-le-Vicomte is more expensive to get to (because of
cab fare) but a joy to tour. While the gift shop's souvenir booklet
has helpful information, your ticket includes an English audioguide
tour and most rooms have English explanations. Outside the
gift shop is a reasonable café (open 11:30–18:00 and, during candlelit visits, until midnight). Start your tour with the fine horse-
carriages exhibit (*équipages*) in the old stables. Wax figures and
an evocative soundtrack get you in the proper mood. Next, stroll

like a wide-eyed peasant across the stone bridge (any fish down there?) and up the front steps into the château. Turn around to admire the symmetry and elegance of the stables; horses lived well here.

As you wander through Fouquet's dream home, you'll understand Louis' jealousy. Versailles was a rather simple hunting lodge when this was built. The furniture in Vaux-le-Vicomte is not original—Louis confiscated it for Versailles. You'll see cozy bedrooms upstairs and grand living rooms downstairs (billiards room, library, card room, and dining room; feel free to fast-forward the 90-min audioguide tour). The kitchen and wine cellar are in the basement. Climb the cupola for a great view.

Survey the garden from the back steps of the palace. This was the landscaper Le Notre's first claim to fame. This garden was the cutting edge of sculpted French gardens. He integrated ponds, shrubbery, and trees in a style that would be copied in palaces all over Europe. Take the 30-minute walk (one-way) to the Hercules viewpoint atop the grassy hill way in the distance. Rentable golf carts (Club Cars, €12/45 min, €122 deposit) make the trip easier. Picnics are not allowed.

Cost and Hours: €10 for gardens, château, and carriage museum (includes audioguide tour), not covered by museum pass; €5 for gardens and carriage museum only. Open March–Oct daily 10:00–18:00, closed off-season, tel. 01 64 14 41 90. The impressive fountains run 15:00–18:00 the second and last Sat of each month (April–Oct).

Candlelit Visits: Two thousand candles and piped-in classical music illuminate the palace on Sat and holiday nights (open 20:00–24:00) May–October (except July 14—call to ask about any upcoming holidays). These *visites aux chandelles* are worth the €12 entry, but remember, it doesn't get really dark until 22:00 in late May, June, and early July, and the last train to Paris leaves Melun at about 22:00.

Getting to Vaux-le-Vicomte: To reach Vaux-le-Vicomte by a train-and-taxi combination, you can take the RER train to Melun from Paris' Gare du Nord or Chatelet stations. Faster SNCF Banlieue trains leave from Paris' Gare de Lyon to Melun (€7 one-way, hrly, 35 min). From Melun's station, taxis make the 10-minute drive to Vaux-le-Vicomte (€13 weekdays, €16 eves and Sun, taxi phone number posted above taxi stand). Ask a staff person at the château to call a cab for your return or schedule a pick-up time with your driver. In either direction, split the fare with other travelers. There's a bus from the station on weekends and holidays only (departs from Melun station at 10:55 and returns from Vaux-le-Vicomte at 12:27 or 17:40). Melun's **TI** is at 17 rue Paul Doumier (Tue–Sat 10:00–12:00, 14:00–18:00, closed Sun–Mon, tel. 01 64 37 11 31).

By car from Paris, take the A-6 autoroute toward Lyon, then follow signs to Melun. In Melun, follow signs to Meaux (N-36), then Vaux-le-Vicomte.

Adding Fontainebleau: Vaux-le-Vicomte and Fontainebleau can be combined into a full, though manageable, daytrip by car or train from Paris (except on Tue, when Fontainebleau is closed). Fontainebleau is 12 minutes by train from Melun.

Sleeping near Vaux-le-Vicomte: The modern and ugly but handy **Ibis Hôtel** is between Melun and the château, just off N-105 (Db–€47, CC, less on weekends, tel. 01 60 68 42 45, fax 01 64 09 62 00). The bypassed town of Melun has more appealing hotels in its handsome old center; pick up a hotel list from the TI (see above). Also consider sleeping in nearby Fontainebleau (see below).

Château of Fontainebleau

Fontainebleau's history rivals Versailles'. Many French kings have called this glamorous hunting lodge home. Napoleon welcomed the pope here during his coronation celebration, and it was here that he abdicated his rule when exiled to Elba in 1814. General Patton set up headquarters at this château on his way to Berlin.

While Vaux-le-Vicomte and Versailles are French-designed, Fontainebleau was built a century earlier by an Italian. The palace you see today was largely financed by Renaissance King Francois I. Inspired by his travels through Renaissance Italy, he hired Italian artists to build his palace.

Orient with a quick visit to the château information room, with its huge model of the château (first door on your right in the grand courtyard). The palace entry is next-door. Your ticket provides access to the Chinese rooms and the main rooms of the château. Napoleon

buffs will enjoy the little museum of Napoleonic history, which requires an additional ticket and a guided tour in French (€2.75, mornings only). The €3 guidebooks give excellent room-by-room descriptions, though basic English explanations are posted throughout.

Start downstairs with the small but impressive Chinese collection of the Empress of Napoleon III, then climb to the main rooms of the palace. Highlights include the stunning Renaissance hall of Francois I, the opulent dance hall with piped-in music (*salle de bal*), Napoleon's throne room, and Diana's Gallery (library). The gardens, designed a century later by the landscaper Le Notre, are worth a stroll. Rent a rowboat for the *étang des carpes* (carp pond), or walk its path for a good view of the château complex.

Cost and Hours: €5.50, covered by museum pass, Wed–Mon 09:30–18:00, closed Tue, last entry 45 minutes before closing.

Getting to Fontainebleau: Catch a train from Paris' Gare de Lyon in the direction of Montereau (about €8.50 one-way, 40 min) to the Fontainebleau-Avon station, where a bus goes to the château (Cars Verts, about €1.50, 4/hr; schedules posted in English). Taxis to the château cost about €6; to nearby Vaux-le-Vicomte costs about €34.

Town of Fontainebleau: Turn right out of the château courtyard and keep right to reach the town center, where cafés and restaurants abound. The helpful **TI** is two blocks up from the château behind Hôtel Londres and has hiking maps, bike rental, and hotel listings (Mon–Sat 10:00–18:30, Sun 10:00–16:00, tel. 01 60 74 99 99).

Sleeping and Eating in Fontainebleau: The **Hôtel Londres***** offers a helpful staff and very pleasant rooms, many with point-blank views of the château (Db-€104–137, family rooms-€122–152, CC, 1 place du General de Gaulle, tel. 01 64 22 20 21, fax 01 60 72 39 16, www.hotellondres.com). Turn right out of the château entrance and keep right for about five blocks to reach these hotels: **Hôtel Legris et Parc***** is a quiet, dreamy getaway with a pleasant garden, pool, and an elegant restaurant (Db-€78–90, suites-€130, CC, 36 rue Paul Seramy, tel. 01 64 22 24 24, fax 01 64 22 22 05, www.chateauxhotels.com/legrisparc). **Hôtel a la Carpe d'Or**** is one block away, above the Bakardi bar (Db-€53, CC, 7 rue d'Aven, tel. 01 64 22 28 64, fax 01 64 22 39 95). To eat well, try one of these central places: **Croquembouche** (*menus* from €20, closed Wed, 43 rue de France, tel. 01 64 22 01 57) or **Chez Arrighi** (*menus* from €15, closed Mon, 53 rue de France, 01 64 22 29 43).

Château of Chantilly

Chantilly (shahn-tee-yee), 35 minutes north of Paris, floats serenely on a reflecting pond amid grand gardens. Unfortunately, the château interior is disappointing. Its best rooms can be seen only on a boring French-language guided tour, and the fine works of art in the picture galleries are poorly displayed. Still, Chantilly can be a pleasant experience if approached in the right way. Allow most of a day for Chantilly.

This extravagant hunting palace was destroyed during the Revolution. Today's château was largely rebuilt during the 19th century. It's divided into two parts: The painting gallery, with paintings by Raphael, Titian, Poussin, Delacroix, and others; and the private apartments, which require a French-language tour. The highlight of the otherwise dull apartments is the first stop, the prince's library, lined with more than 13,000 books and beautiful copies of pages from *Les Très Riches Heures du Duc du Berry*, a much-admired 15th-century illuminated manuscript.

The gardens immediately behind the château are formal and austere. With your back to the château, follow the signs to the right to *le Hameau*. This little hamlet, with a delightful garden café, was the prototype for the more famous *Hameau* at Versailles. Just beyond is a small kiosk offering a tethered balloon ride (€7, great view) and boat trips along the canals (€5.50, tel. 03 44 57 35 35).

Cost and Hours: €6, €3 for gardens only, covered by museum pass, March–Oct Wed–Mon 10:00–18:00, Nov–Feb Wed–Mon 10:30–12:45, 14:00–17:00, closed Tue except in July–Aug; tel. 03 44 62 62 62.

Live Horse Stables (Les Ecuries Vivant): The Prince de Conde believed he'd be reincarnated as a horse, so he built this opulent horse château for his next go-round. You'd have to have similar beliefs to pay the €8 entry for this horse museum (although it's impressive and thorough). The museum features 40 live horses in their stables, and a daily demonstration, generally at 15:30, more often during summer weekends (April–Oct Wed–Mon 10:30–17:30, also open Tue in summer; Nov–March Wed–Fri 14:00–17:30, Sat–Sun 10:30–17:30, tel. 03 44 57 13 13).

Getting to Chantilly: Leave from Paris' Gare du Nord for Chantilly-Gouvieux. While the RER serves Chantilly, service is faster on the main lines at Grandes Lignes level. Ask at the information desk opposite track 18 for the next departure (about €7 one-way, nearly hrly, 35 min). Upon arrival in Chantilly, confirm return times (fewer trips on weekends). The **TI** is a block in front of the station. To get to the château, it's a €6 taxi ride, a free ride on a rare city bus (ask at station), or a 30-minute walk (follow signs, stay on path, turn right before BP gas station, cross grass field, "château" in distance is stables, real château is beyond that).

IMPRESSIONIST EXCURSIONS:
GIVERNY AND AUVERS-SUR-OISE

Giverny

From 1883 to 1926, Monet spent 43 of his most creative years at Giverny (zhee-vayr nee), the Camp David of Impressionism. Monet's gardens and home are, unfortunately, split by a busy road and very popular with tourists. Buy your ticket, walk through the gardens, and take the underpass into the artist's famous lily-pad land. The path leads over the Japanese Bridge, under weeping willows, and past countless scenes that leave artists aching for an easel. For Monet fans, it's strangely nostalgic. Back on the other side, continue your visit with a wander through his more robust and structured garden and his mildly interesting home. The jammed gift shop at the exit is the actual sky-lit studio where Monet painted his water-lily masterpieces. While lines may be long and tour groups may trample the flowers, true fans still find magic in those lily pads. Minimize crowds by arriving before 10:00 (get in line) or after 16:00 (€5.50, €4 for gardens only, April–Oct Tue–Sun 10:00–18:00, closed Mon and Nov–March, tel. 02 32 51 94 65).

Getting to Giverny: Take the Rouen-bound train from Paris' Gare St. Lazare station to Vernon (about €21 round-trip, long gaps in service, know schedule before you go). From the Vernon train station to Monet's garden (4 km/2.5 miles one-way), try the Vernon-Giverny bus (4/day, scheduled to meet most trains). Make sure the driver knows you plan to return by bus and on which trip, otherwise he may not make the last Giverny pickup. If you miss the last bus, find others to share a taxi (about €11 for up to 3, €12 for 4, tel. 07 76 08 50 78). You can also rent a bike at the bar opposite the train station (€12, tel. 02 32 21 16 01, crummy ride on a busy road). The ticket office at Monet's home in Giverny has bus schedules and can call a taxi if you don't see one waiting by the bus stop (tel. 02 32 51 70 17 or 06 07 34 36 68). Bus stops are in the parking lot across from the entry to Monet's home and just beyond the American Impressionist Art Museum. Big tour companies do a Giverny daytrip from Paris for around €65. Ask at your hotel.

The **American Impressionist Art Museum** (turn left when leaving Monet's place and walk 90 meters/300 feet) is devoted to American artists who followed Claude to Giverny. Giverny had a great influence on American artists of Monet's day. This bright, modern gallery is well-explained in English, has a good little Mary Cassatt section, and gives Americans a rare chance to see French people appreciating our artists (same price and hours as Monet's home).

Sleeping and Eating in Giverny: The adorable **Hôtel La**

Musardiere**, two blocks to the right out of Monet's home, makes an ideal Paris escape or stopover on your way farther into Normandy (Db-€46–69, Tb-€63–73, CC, 132 rue Claude Monet, 27620 Giverny, tel. 02 32 21 03 18, fax 02 32 21 60 00). You'll find a café and sandwich stand near the entry to Monet's home, but the garden café at the overlooked American Impressionist Museum is better—peaceful and surrounded by gardens Monet would appreciate (€9 salads, picnics possible at the far end).

Auvers-sur-Oise

There's no better place to appreciate life during the Impressionist era than here on the banks of the Oise river, about a 45-minute drive (or 1-hr train ride) northwest of Paris. Auvers-sur-Oise (oh-vay-soor-wahz) is most famous as the village where Vincent Van Gogh committed suicide, though many other artists enjoyed this peaceful rural retreat, including Daubigny, Corot, Pissarro, and Cézanne. Today, this little town offers a handful of interesting sights, posted walking trails leading to scenes painted by the artists, and a tranquil break from the big city. Most sights are closed Mondays and Tuesdays; a few are open only after lunch.

Stop by the **TI,** which has good information on all village sights and a €0.50 map of Auvers showing the walking routes, with famous art scenes posted. The TI (daily 09:00–12:00, 14:00–18:00, tel. 01 30 35 10 06) is housed with Musée Daubigny in Manoir des Colombières (below).

The most worthwhile sight in Auvers is **Château d'Auvers,** where the entire château has been brilliantly transformed into a re-creation of life during the Impressionist years. Elaborate multi-media displays use headphones, video screens, and lasers to guide you along the Impressionist route that led from Montmartre to the sea, giving you a keen appreciation of life's daily struggles and pleasures during this time (€10, April–Sept Tue–Sun 10:30–18:00, summer Mon 14:00–18:00; Oct–March Tue–Sun 10:30–16:30, closed Mon; tel. 01 34 48 48 48). The **Musée Daubigny** houses a small but pleasing collection of works from artists who came to work with Monsieur Daubigny, an ardent defender of the Impressionists (€3, Wed–Sun 14:00–18:00, closed Mon–Tue, next to TI in Manoir des Colombières). You can visit **Daubigny's studio** and appreciate its serene setting and the murals inside (€4, Wed–Sun 14:00–18:30, closed Mon–Tue).

Van Gogh fans seek out the **Auberge Ravoux** to see the room where Vincent tragically shot himself (€5, daily 10:00–18:00; food connoisseurs skip the room and have a tasty lunch in the *auberge's* perfectly preserved restaurant). To complete a van Gogh pilgrimage, visit the **Church at Auvers** (see painting at Orsay), above the train station. Vincent and his brother Theo are buried at the cemetery up rue Bernard from the church. Beginning in 2002, visitors can visit the home of Vincent's physician, Dr. Gachet (get details at TI).

The little café **Museum of Absinthe** is fun for aficionados (€5, includes a mini-guided tour, open June–Sept Wed–Sun 11:00–18:00, closed Mon–Tue, Oct–May Sat–Sun only 11:00–18:00).

Sleeping and Eating in Auvers (zip code: 95430): Auvers is a handy first or last stop for drivers using Charles de Gaulle airport. If you want to begin or end your trip with style, sleep luxuriously at the small, friendly, and polished **Hostellerie du Nord*****, with modern, spacious rooms and a seriously good restaurant requiring reservations (Db-€93–124, suites-€185, CC, *menus* from €43, a block from train station at 6 rue du Général de Gaulle, tel. 01 30 36 70 74, fax 01 30 36 72 75, www.hostelleriedunord.fr). **Ecuries d'Auvers** is a nine-room *chambre d'hôte* on the river side of the main road below the TI (Sb, Db, or Tb-€37, no CC, 5 bis rue de la Bourgogne, tel. 01 30 36 81 44, fax 01 30 36 87 43). The place to eat in Auvers is **Auberge Ravoux**, unchanged since 1876, where painters would meet over a good meal (closed Sun eve and all day on Mon, below TI on place de la Mairie, tel. 01 30 36 60 60).

Getting to Auvers: Take the Banlieue **train** from Paris' Gare du Nord to Pontoise (2/hr, 40 min, departs from tracks 30–36), then transfer to Auvers-sur-Oise (2/hr, 10 min, allow 1 hr for entire trip one-way). Turn left on the main road leaving Auvers' station to reach the TI.

By **car**, Auvers is about 45 minutes northwest of Paris, off autoroute A-15 (exit #7, then follow direction: Beauvais).

DISNEYLAND PARIS

Europe's Disneyland is a remake of California's, with most of the same rides and smiles. The main difference is that Mickey Mouse speaks French (and you can buy wine with your lunch). My kids went ducky. It's easy to get to and worth a day if Paris is handier than Florida or California. Crowds are a problem (tel. 01 64 74 30 00 for the latest). If possible, avoid Saturday, Sunday, Wednesday, school holidays, and July and August. After dinner, crowds are gone. Food is fun, but prepare for Paris prices (or smuggle in a picnic). The free FASTPASS system is a worthwhile timesaver (get FASTPASS card at entry, good for 5 most popular rides, at ride insert card in machine to get a window of time to enter—often within about 45 min). You'll also save time by buying your tickets ahead (at airport TIs, over 100 Métro stations, or along the Champs-Elysées at the TI, Disney Store, or Virgin Megastore). Disney brochures are in every Paris hotel. For Disneyland information and reservations, contact: tel. 01 60 30 60 30, fax 01 60 30 60 65, www.disneylandparis.com.

Cost and Hours: From March 31 through Nov 4, adults pay €37 for one day (€70 for 2 days, €97 for 3 days) and kids aged 3 to 11 pay €28.50 for one day (€54 for 2 days, €75 for 3 days). On summer evenings (17:00–23:00), everyone (age 3 and up) pays €18. Kids under 3 are always free. Regular prices are about 25 percent less off-season. Open daily April–June 09:00–20:00, July–Aug daily 09:00–23:00, Sept–March Mon–Fri 10:00–20:00, Sat–Sun 09:00–20:00.

Sleeping at Disneyland: Most are better off sleeping in reality (Paris), though with direct buses and freeways to both airports, Disneyland makes a convenient first or last night stop. Seven different Disney-owned hotels offer accommodations at or near the park in all price ranges, from the cheapest, **Davy Crockett** (requires a car), to the most expensive, **Disneyland Hotel** (at the park entry). The prices you'll be quoted include entry to the park; ask about package deals including park entry and transportation. To reserve any Disneyland hotel, call 01 60 30 60 30, fax 01 60 30 60 65, or check www.disneylandparis.com.

Hôtel Sante Fe** is the best value, with shuttle service to the park every 12 minutes (Db-€214 includes breakfast and 2-day park pass, CC). The **Disneyland Hotel****** costs more, but it's right at the park (Db-€427 for the same deal, CC).

Transportation Connections—Disneyland Paris

By train: TGV trains connect Disneyland directly with: **Charles de Gaulle airport** (10 min), the **Loire Valley** (1.5 hrs, Tours-St. Pierre des Corps station, 15 min from Amboise), **Avignon** (3 hrs, TGV station), **Lyon** (2 hrs, Part Dieu station), and **Nice** (6 hrs, main station).

By RER: From downtown Paris, take RER line A-4 to Marne-la-Vallee (from Etoile, Auber, Chatelet, and Gare de Lyon stations, about €7 each way, hrly, drops you off right in the park). The last train back to Paris leaves shortly after midnight.

By bus: Both airports have direct shuttle buses (€13, daily from 08:30–19:45, every 45 min).

By car: Disneyland is east of Paris by about 40 minutes on the A-4 autoroute (direction Nancy/Metz, exit #14). Parking is €7 per day at the park.

SLEEPING
IN PARIS

paris

I've focused on three safe, handy, and colorful neighborhoods: rue Cler, Marais, and Contrescarpe. For each, I list good hotels, helpful hints, and restaurants (see chapter on Eating, page 267). Before reserving, read the descriptions of the three neighborhoods closely. Each offers different pros and cons, and your neighborhood is as important as your hotel for the success of your trip.

Reserve ahead for Paris, the sooner the better. Conventions clog Paris in September (worst), October, May, and June (very tough). In August, when Paris is quiet, some hotels offer lower rates to fill their rooms (if you're planning to visit Paris in the summer, the extra expense of an air-conditioned room can be money well spent). Most hotels accept telephone reservations, require prepayment with a credit-card number, and prefer a faxed follow-up to be sure everything is in order. For more information, see "Making Reservations" on page 12.

French hotels are rated by stars (indicated in this book by an *). One star is simple, two has most of the comforts, and three is generally a two-star with a mini-bar and fancier lobby. Four stars offers more luxury than you have time to appreciate.

Old, characteristic, budget Parisian hotels have always been cramped. Retrofitted with elevators, toilets, and private showers (as most are today), they are even more cramped. Even three-star hotel rooms are small and often not worth the extra expense in Paris. Some hotels include the hotel tax (*taxe du séjour*, about €0.60–€1 per person per day), though most will add this to your bill. Two- and three-star hotels are required to have an English-speaking staff. Nearly all hotels listed will have someone who speaks English.

Recommended hotels have an elevator unless otherwise noted. Quad rooms usually have two double beds. Because rooms with double beds and showers are cheaper than rooms with twin beds and baths, room prices vary within each hotel.

You can save as much as €15 by finding the increasingly rare room without a private shower, though some hotels charge for down-the-hall showers. Singles (except for the rare closet-type rooms that fit only 1 twin bed) are simply doubles used by one person. They rent for only a little less than a double. Continental breakfasts average €6, buffet breakfasts (baked goods, cereal, yogurt, and fruit) cost €7.75 to €9.25. Café or picnic breakfasts are cheaper, but hotels usually give unlimited coffee.

Get advice from your hotel for safe parking (consider long-term parking at Orly Airport and taxi in). Meters are free in August. Garages are plentiful (€14–23/day, with special rates through some hotels). Self-serve Laundromats are common; ask your hotelier for the nearest one (*Où est un laverie automatique?*; ooh ay uh lah-vay-ree auto-mah-teek).

If you have any trouble finding a room using my listings, try www.parishotel.com and www.hotelboulevard.com. You can select from various neighborhood areas (e.g., Eiffel Tower area), give the dates of your visit and preferred price range, and presto—they'll list options with rates. You'll find the hotels listed in this book to be better located and more objectively reviewed, though as a last resort these services are handy.

Sleep Code

S = Single, **D** = Double/Twin, **T** = Triple, **Q** = Quad, **b** = bathroom, **s** = shower only, **CC** = Credit Cards accepted, **no CC** = Credit Cards not accepted, * = French hotel rating system (0–4 stars).
Exchange rate: 1 euro (€) = about 90 cents and €1.10 = $1.
Country code: 33.

Rue Cler Orientation

Rue Cler, a village-like pedestrian street, is safe, tidy, and makes me feel like I must have been a poodle in a previous life. How such coziness lodged itself between the high-powered government district and the wealthy Eiffel Tower and Invalides areas, I'll never know. This is a neighborhood of wide, tree-lined boulevards, stately apartment buildings, and lots of Americans. The American Church, American library, American University, and many of my readers call this area home.

Become a local at a rue Cler café for breakfast or join the afternoon crowd for *une bière pression* (a draft beer). On rue Cler, you can eat and browse your way through a street full of tart shops, delis, cheeseries, and colorful outdoor produce stalls. For an after-dinner cruise on the Seine, it's just a short walk to the river and the Bâteaux-Mouches (see page 30).

Your neighborhood **TI** is at the Eiffel Tower (May–Sept daily 11:00–18:42, no kidding, tel. 01 45 51 22 15). The Métro station (Ecole Militaire) and a **post office** are at the end of rue Cler on avenue de la Motte Piquet, and there's a handy **SNCF office** at 78 rue St. Dominique (Mon–Fri 09:00–19:00, Sat 10:00–12:20, 14:00–18:00). The Banque Populaire (across from Hôtel Leveque) changes money. Rue St. Dominique is the area's boutique-browsing street. The Epicerie de la Tour **grocery** is open until midnight (197 rue de Grenelle).

The **American Church and College** is the community center for Americans living in Paris and should be one of your first stops if you're planning to stay a while (reception open Mon–Sat 09:00–22:30, Sun 09:00–19:30, 65 quai d'Orsay, tel. 01 40 62 05 00). Pick up copies of the *Paris Voice* for a monthly review of Paris entertainment, and *France-U.S.A. Contacts* for information on housing and employment through the community of 30,000 Americans living in Paris. The interdenominational service at 11:00 on Sunday, the coffee hour after church, and the free Sunday concerts (18:00, not every week, Sept–May only) are a great way to make some friends and get a taste of émigré life in Paris.

Afternoon *boules* (lawn bowling) on the esplanade des Invalides is a relaxing spectator sport. Look for the dirt area to the upper right as you face the Invalides.

You should try at least one of these helpful **bus routes:** Line #69 runs along rue St. Dominique and serves Les Invalides, Orsay, Louvre, Marais, and Père-Lachaise cemetery. Line #92 runs along avenue Bosquet and serves the Arc de Triomphe and Champs-Elysées in one direction and the Montparnasse Tower in the other. Line #87 runs on avenue de la Bourdonnais and serves St. Sulpice, Luxembourg Gardens, and the Sevres-Babylone shopping area. Line #28 runs on boulevard La Tour Maubourg and serves the St. Lazare station.

Sleeping in the Rue Cler Neighborhood
(7th arrondissement, Mo: Ecole Militaire, zip code: 75007)

Rue Cler is the glue that holds this pleasant neighborhood together. From here you can walk to the Eiffel Tower, Napoleon's Tomb, the Seine, and the Orsay and Rodin Museums.

Many of my readers stay in this neighborhood. If you want to disappear into Paris, you'll do it better at the hotels away from the rue Cler, or in the other neighborhoods I list. And if nightlife matters, sleep elsewhere. The first seven hotels listed below are within Camembert-smelling distance of rue Cler; the others are within a 5- to 10-minute stroll. Warning: The first two hotels are popular with my readers.

Hôtel Leveque** is ideally located, with a helpful staff and a singing maid. It's a big place with well-designed rooms that have all the comforts (S-€53, Db-€84–91, Tb-€114, breakfast-€7, first breakfast free for readers of this book, CC, air-con planned for 2002, 29 rue Cler, tel. 01 47 05 49 15, fax 01 45 50 49 36, www.hotel-leveque.com, e-mail: info@hotelleveque.com).

Hôtel du Champ de Mars**, with charming, pastel rooms and helpful English-speaking owners Françoise and Stephane and right-hand man Slim, is a cozier rue Cler option. The hotel has a Provence-style, small-town feel from top to bottom. Rooms are small, but comfortable and a good value. Single rooms can work as tiny doubles (Sb-€66, Db-€72–76, Tb-€92, CC, 30 meters off rue Cler at 7 rue de Champ de Mars, tel. 01 45 51 52 30, fax 01 45 51 64 36, www.hotel-du-champ-de-mars.com, e-mail: stg @club-internet.fr).

Hôtel Cadran*** charges too much for its fine location and cozy lobby. Rooms are tight and narrow but air-conditioned (Sb-€148, Db-€165, CC, 10 rue de Champs de Mars, tel. 01 40 62 67 00, fax 01 40 62 67 13, www.cadran.com).

Hôtel Relais Bosquet*** is modern, spacious, and a bit upscale, with snazzy, air-conditioned rooms and big beds (Sb-€123–148, standard Db-€140, spacious Db-€163, extra bed-€31, parking-€14, CC, 19 rue de Champ de Mars, tel. 01 47 05 25 45, fax 01 45 55 08 24, www.relaisbosquet.com).

Hôtel Beaugency***, on a quieter street just off rue Cler, has small but comfortable rooms, a lobby you can stretch out in, and friendly Nadine in charge (Sb-€104, Db-€111, Tb-€127, CC, buffet breakfast, 21 rue Duvivier, tel. 01 47 05 01 63, fax 01 45 51 04 96, www.hotel-beaugency.com).

Hôtel la Motte Piquet**, at the end of rue Cler, is reasonable, spotless, and cozy (Ss-€54, Sb-€60–69, Db-€69–79, CC, most rooms face a busy street, 30 avenue de la Motte Piquet, tel. 01 47 05 09 57, fax 01 47 05 74 36).

Sleeping near rue Cler: The following listings are a 5- to 10-minute walk west of rue Cler and are listed in order of proximity.

Hôtel Prince**, just across avenue Bosquet from the Ecole Militaire Métro stop, has fair-value rooms, many overlooking a busy street (Db-€74–97, CC, 66 avenue Bosquet, tel. 01 47 05 40 90, fax 01 47 53 06 62).

Hôtel le Tourville**** is the most classy and expensive

RUE CLER HOTELS

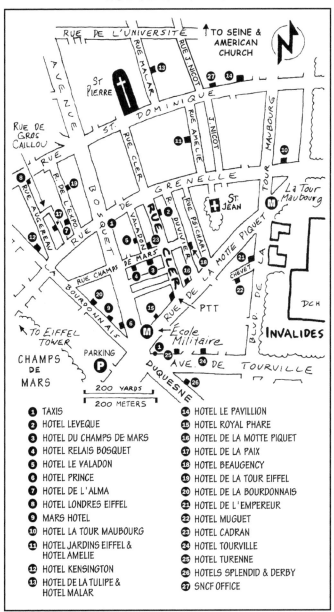

1. TAXIS
2. HOTEL LEVEQUE
3. HOTEL DU CHAMPS DE MARS
4. HOTEL RELAIS BOSQUET
5. HOTEL LE VALADON
6. HOTEL PRINCE
7. HOTEL DE L'ALMA
8. HOTEL LONDRES EIFFEL
9. MARS HOTEL
10. HOTEL LA TOUR MAUBOURG
11. HOTEL JARDINS EIFFEL & HOTEL AMELIE
12. HOTEL KENSINGTON
13. HOTEL DE LA TULIPE & HOTEL MALAR
14. HOTEL LE PAVILLION
15. HOTEL ROYAL PHARE
16. HOTEL DE LA MOTTE PIQUET
17. HOTEL DE LA PAIX
18. HOTEL BEAUGENCY
19. HOTEL DE LA TOUR EIFFEL
20. HOTEL DE LA BOURDONNAIS
21. HOTEL DE L'EMPEREUR
22. HOTEL MUGUET
23. HOTEL CADRAN
24. HOTEL TOURVILLE
25. HOTEL TURENNE
26. HOTELS SPLENDID & DERBY
27. SNCF OFFICE

of my rue Cler listings. This four-star gem is surprisingly intimate and friendly, from its welcoming lobby to its air-conditioned, pastel rooms, and vaulted breakfast area (small standard Db-€138, superior Db-€170, Db with private terrace-€215, extra bed-€15.50, CC, 16 avenue de Tourville, Mo: Ecole Militaire, tel. 01 47 05 62 62, fax 01 47 05 43 90, e-mail: hotel@tourville.com).

Hôtel de Turenne**, with comfortable, air-conditioned rooms, is a great value when it's hot, and has five truly single rooms (Sb-€61, Db-€71–81, Tb-€96, extra bed-€9.50, CC, 20 avenue de Tourville, tel. 01 47 05 99 92, fax 01 45 56 06 04, e-mail: hotel.turenne.paris7@wanadoo.fr).

Hôtel Londres Eiffel*** is my closest listing to the Eiffel Tower and Champs de Mars park. It offers small but thoughtfully-appointed rooms, cozy public spaces, and an Internet station. Helpful Esther and Cedric take good care of their guests (Sb-€90–102, Db-€103–112, Tb-€135, CC, use handy bus #69 or the RER Alma stop, 1 rue Augerau, tel. 01 45 51 63 02, fax 01 47 05 28 96, www.londres-eiffel.com).

Mars Hôtel**, with an ambitious, engaging new owner, is a solid mid-range value with mostly spacious rooms and a beam-me-up-Jacques, coffin-sized elevator. The front rooms are noisier but have a view of the Eiffel Tower (small Db-€70, large Db-€85, extra bed-€18.50, CC, 117 avenue de la Bourdonnais, tel. 01 47 05 42 30, fax 01 47 05 45 91).

Hôtel de la Bourdonnais***, best known for its renowned restaurant, is a perfectly Parisian place. It mixes Old World elegance with professional service, generally spacious rooms, and pleasant public spaces (Sb-€110, Db-€130, Tb-€140, Qb-€150, Qb suite-€200, CC, 111 avenue de la Bourdonnais, tel. 01 47 05 45 42, fax 01 45 55 75 54, www.hotellabourdonnais.fr).

Hôtel Kensington** feels less personal but is a fair value, with tiny and warmly decorated rooms (Sb-€53, Db-€67–82, CC, 79 avenue de la Bourdonnais, tel. 01 47 05 74 00, fax 01 47 05 25 81, www.hotel-kensington.com).

Hôtel de la Paix is bare-bones basic and cheap (S-€29, Ds-€51, Db-€54, Tb-€74, no CC, no elevator, no frills, 19 rue du Gros-Caillou, tel. 01 45 51 86 17, fax 01 45 55 93 28).

Hôtel de la Tulipe** is a unique place two blocks from rue Cler toward the river, with artistically decorated rooms (each one different) above a wood-beamed lounge and a peaceful, leafy courtyard (Db-€105–110, Tb-€140, CC, no elevator, cable TV, 33 rue Malar, tel. 01 45 51 67 21, fax 01 47 53 96 37, www.hoteldelatulipe.com).

Sleeping near Métro stop La Tour Maubourg: The next

four listings are within two blocks of the intersection of avenue de la Motte Piquet and Les Invalides.

Hôtel le Pavillon** is a quiet place with unrealized potential, set back from the street. A small courtyard greets clients and its pastel rooms are adequate, but the bathrooms need work (Sb-€72, Db-€80, CC, family suites-€105, 54 rue St. Dominique, tel. 01 45 51 42 87, fax 01 45 51 32 79, e-mail: patrickpavillon@aol.com).

Hôtel Les Jardins Eiffel*** is a bit pricey, but merits its three stars with professional service, a spacious lobby, outdoor patio, and comfortable, air-conditioned rooms—some with private balconies. Ask for a room *avec petit balcon* (Sb-€92–128, Db-€100–€152, extra bed-€21, parking-€17/day, CC, 8 rue Amelie, tel. 01 47 05 46 21, fax 01 45 55 28 08, e-mail: eiffel@unimedia.fr).

What the roomy **Hôtel de l'Empereur**** lacks in personality, it makes up for in value. Its pleasant rooms offer all the comforts except air-conditioning. Streetside rooms have views but some noise; fifth floor rooms have small balconies and better views (Sb-€68–72, Db-€73–82, Tb-€103, Qb-€118, CC, 2 rue Chevert, tel. 01 45 55 88 02, fax 01 45 51 88 54, www.hotelempereur.com).

Reserve early for the **Hôtel Muguet**,** a peaceful and clean hotel where you get three-star comfort for the price of two. The hotel offers sharp, air-conditioned rooms, a small garden courtyard, and several good family rooms (Sb-€85, Db-€94–102, Tb-€130, CC, 11 rue Chevert, tel. 01 47 05 05 93, fax 01 45 50 25 37, www.hotelmuguet.com).

Lesser values: Given this fine area, these are acceptable last choices. **Hôtel Malar*** (Db-€78–86, CC, 29 rue Malar, tel. 01 45 51 38 46, fax 01 45 55 20 19, www.hotelmalar.com); **Hôtel de la Tour Eiffel**** (Sb-€61, Db-€76, Tb-€79, CC, 17 rue de l'Exposition, tel. 01 47 05 14 75, fax 01 47 53 99 46, Muriel speaks English); **Hôtel Royal Phare**** (Db-€61–74, CC, facing Ecole Militaire Métro stop, 40 avenue de la Motte Piquet, tel. 01 47 05 57 30, fax 01 45 51 64 41); **Hôtel Amelie**** (Db-€87, CC, 5 rue Amelie, tel. 01 45 51 74 75, fax 01 45 56 93 55); **Hôtel de l'Alma***** (Db-€114, CC, 32 rue de l'Exposition, tel. 01 47 05 45 70, fax 01 45 51 84 47, e-mail: almahotel@minitel.net); **Derby Eiffel Hôtel***** (Db-€116–139, CC, air con, 5 avenue Duquesne, tel. 01 47 05 12 05, fax 01 47 05 43 43, e-mail: info@derbyeiffelhotel.com); **Hôtel Splendid***** (Db-€122–145, CC, most rooms have Eiffel Tower views, 29 avenue Tourville, tel. 01 45 51 24 77, fax 01 44 18 94 60, e-mail: splendid@club-internet.fr); and the basic, overpriced **Hôtel La Serre*** (Db-€84, CC, has good location on rue Cler but generates readers' complaints for its rude staff and bizarre hotel practices—you can't see room in advance or get a refund, 24 rue Cler, across from Hôtel Leveque, Mo: Ecole Militaire, tel. 01 47 05 52 33, fax 01 40 62 95 66).

These are last resorts. The following two hotels are decent and well-located, but are poorly and erratically run by the same rude owner. **Hôtel La Tour Maubourg***, with spacious Old World rooms, overlooks a lawn within sight of Napoleon's tomb (Sb-€107, Db-€122–137, CC, includes breakfast, immediately at La Tour Maubourg Métro stop, 150 rue de Grenelle, tel. 01 47 05 16 16, fax 01 47 05 16 14). **Hôtel Valadon****, one block west of rue Cler, is small, quiet, and sleekly furnished. Avoid the musty, windowless basement room (Sb-€61, Db-€78–86, CC, 16 rue Valadon, tel. 01 47 53 89 85, fax 01 44 18 90 56).

Marais Orientation

Those interested in a more Soho-Greenwich Village locale should make the Marais their Parisian home. The Marais is a more happening area than rue Cler, with great access to many museums: Picasso, Carnavalet, Jewish History, and Pompidou Center. It's narrow, medieval Paris at its finest, where elegant stone mansions sit alongside trendy bars, antique shops, and slick boutiques. Only 15 years ago, it was a forgotten Parisian backwater, but now the Marais is one of Paris' most popular residential, tourist, and shopping areas.

The nearest **TIs** are in the Louvre (Wed–Mon 10:00–19:00, closed Tue) and Gare de Lyon (daily 08:00–20:00, tel. 01 43 43 33 24, answered by live English-speaker). The **Banque de France** changes money, with good rates and long lines (Mon–Fri 09:00–11:45, 13:30–15:30, closed Sat–Sun, at corner of rue St. Antoine and place de la Bastille). Most banks and other services are on the main drag, rue de Rivoli/St. Antoine. You'll find one **taxi stand** on the north side of rue St. Antoine, where it meets rue Castex, and another on the south side of St. Antoine, in front of the St. Paul church.

The Bastille opera house, Promenade Plantée Park, place des Vosges (Paris' oldest square), the Jewish Quarter (rue des Rosiers), and nightlife-happening rue de Lappe are all nearby. Be sure to stroll into place des Vosges after dark. The massive budget **department store** is BHV, next to Hôtel de Ville. Marais **post offices** are on rue Castex and on the corner of rues Pavée and Francs Bourgeois.

Helpful **bus routes:** Line #69 on rue St. Antoine takes you to the Louvre, Orsay, Rodin, and Napoleon's Tomb and ends at the Eiffel Tower. Line #86 runs down boulevard Henri IV, crossing Ile St. Louis and serving the Latin Quarter along boulevard St. Germain. Line #96 runs on rues Turenne and François Miron and serves the Louvre and boulevard St. Germain (near Luxembourg Gardens). Line #65 serves the train stations Austerlitz, Est, and Nord from place de la Bastille.

Sleeping in the Marais Neighborhood
(4th arrondissement, Mo: St. Paul or Bastille, zip code: 75004)

The Marais runs from the Pompidou Center to the Bastille (a 15-min walk), with most hotels located a few blocks north of the main East-West drag, rue de Rivoli/St. Antoine (it's the same street, just changes names). It's about 15 minutes on foot from any hotel in this area to Notre-Dame, Ile St. Louis, and the Latin Quarter. Strolling home (day or night) from Notre-Dame along the Ile St. Louis is marvelous.

The St. Paul Métro stop puts you right in the heart of the Marais, while the Hôtel de Ville stop serves its Western end, and the Bastille stop serves its eastern limit.

Hôtel Castex** is a clean, well-run, and cheery place—a great value with comfortable rooms, many stairs, and a good location on a relatively quiet street. Reserve by phone and leave your credit-card number (Sb-€47, Db-€55–58, Tb-€74, CC, no elevator, just off place de la Bastille and rue St. Antoine, 5 rue Castex, Mo: Bastille, tel. 01 42 72 31 52, fax 01 42 72 57 91, e-mail: info @castexhotel.com). The owners have another decent-value hotel two Métro stops away, in a less appealing location that often has rooms when others don't: **Hôtel de la République**** (Sb-€53, Db-€61, CC, cable TV, 31 rue Albert Thomas, 75010 Paris, Mo: République, tel. 01 42 39 19 03, fax 01 42 39 22 66, www.republiquehotel.com).

Grand Hôtel Jeanne d'Arc**, a warm, welcoming place with thoughtfully appointed rooms, is ideally located for connoisseurs of the Marais. Rooms on the street can be noisy until the bars close. Sixth-floor rooms have a view, and corner rooms are wonderfully bright in the City of Lights. Reserve this place way ahead (small Db-€70, standard Db-€94, Tb-€109, good Qb-€125, CC, 3 rue Jarente, Mo: St. Paul, tel. 01 48 87 62 11, fax 01 48 87 37 31).

Hôtel Bastille Speria***, a short block off the Bastille, feels family-run while offering business-type service. The 45 plain but cheery rooms have air-conditioning and thin walls. It's English-language friendly, from the *Herald Tribune*s in the lobby to the history of the Bastille posted in the elevator (Sb-€90–98, Db-€100–125, Tb-€143, CC, 1 rue de la Bastille, Mo: Bastille, tel. 01 42 72 04 01, fax 01 42 72 56 38, e-mail: speria@micronet.fr).

Hôtel Lyon-Mulhouse**, with half of its rooms on a busy street just off place de la Bastille, is a good value. Rooms are large and pleasant (Sb-€55–75, Db-€65–85, Tb-€75–95, Qb-€102, CC, 8 boulevard Beaumarchais, tel. 01 47 00 91 50, fax 01 47 00 06 31, e-mail: hotelyonmulhouse@wanadoo.fr).

Hôtel de la Place des Vosges** is well-located on a quiet

MARAIS HOTELS

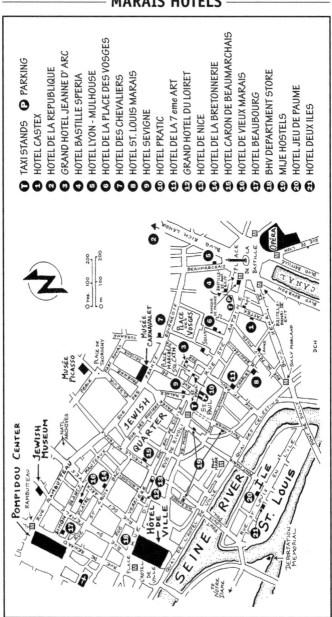

- ① TAXI STANDS ℗ PARKING
- ① HOTEL CASTEX
- ② HOTEL DE LA REPUBLIQUE
- ③ GRAND HOTEL JEANNE D' ARC
- ④ HOTEL BASTILLE SPERIA
- ⑤ HOTEL LYON - MULHOUSE
- ⑥ HOTEL DE LA PLACE DES VOSGES
- ⑦ HOTEL DES CHEVALIERS
- ⑧ HOTEL ST. LOUIS MARAIS
- ⑨ HOTEL SEVIGNE
- ⑩ HOTEL PRATIC
- ⑪ HOTEL DE LA 7 eme ART
- ⑫ GRAND HOTEL DU LOIRET
- ⑬ HOTEL DE NICE
- ⑭ HOTEL DE LA BRETONNERIE
- ⑮ HOTEL CARON DE BEAUMARCHAIS
- ⑯ HOTEL DE VIEUX MARAIS
- ⑰ HOTEL BEAUBOURG
- ⑱ BHV DEPARTMENT STORE
- ⑲ MIJE HOSTELS
- ⑳ HOTEL JEU DE PAUME
- ㉑ HOTEL DEUX ILES

street just off place des Vosges. The owners plan to renovate all rooms in 2002—the following prices are estimates (Sb-€84–99, Db-€107–122, CC, elevator begins one floor up, 12 rue de Biraque, Mo: St. Paul, tel. 01 42 72 60 46, fax 01 42 72 02 64, e-mail: hotel.place.des.vosges@gofornet.com).

Hôtel des Chevaliers*, a little boutique hotel one block northwest of place des Vosges, offers small, pleasant rooms with modern comforts. Rooms off the street are quiet (Db-€114–130, CC, skip overpriced breakfast, 30 rue de Turenne, Mo: St. Paul, tel. 01 42 72 73 47, fax 01 42 72 54 10).

Hôtel Sévigné** is less personal but central, offering sufficient rooms at fair prices with the cheapest breakfast in Paris—€3.50 (Sb-€56, Db-€60–63, Tb-€69, CC, 2 rue Malher, Mo: St. Paul, tel. 01 42 72 76 17, fax 01 42 78 68 26, www.le-sevigne.com).

Hôtel Pratic* has a terrific location on a fun, people-friendly square and charges accordingly. Its stairs are many and its overpriced rooms are modern, but nothing special (Db-€90, CC, no elevator, 9 rue d'Ormesson, Mo: St. Paul, tel. 01 48 87 80 47, fax 01 48 87 40 04, e-mail: practic.hotel@wanadoo.fr).

Hôtel St. Louis Marais**, well-situated between the river and rue St. Antoine, has a fine lobby and cozy, if pricey, rooms (small Db-€108, standard Db-€125, CC, no elevator, 1 rue Charles V, tel. 01 48 87 87 04, fax 01 48 87 33 26, www.saintlouismarais.com).

Hôtel de 7ème Art**, two blocks south of rue St. Antoine, is a relaxed, Hollywood-nostalgia place, run by young, friendly, hip Marais types, with a full service café/bar and Charlie Chaplin murals. Most rooms are adequate, but the few large double rooms at €107 are plenty nice (Sb or Db-€82–93, large Db-€107–125, extra bed-€21, CC, 20 rue St. Paul, Mo: St. Paul, tel. 01 44 54 85 00, fax 01 42 77 69 10, e-mail: hotel7art@wanadoo.fr).

MIJE Youth Hostels: The Maison Internationale de la Jeunesse des Etudiants (MIJE) runs three classy, old residences clustered a few blocks south of rue St. Antoine. Each offers simple, clean, single-sex, one- to four-bed rooms for families and travelers under the age of 30 (exceptions are made for families). Prices are per person; you can pay more to have your own room or be roomed with as many as three others (Sb-€37, Db-€27, Tb-€24, Qb-€22, no CC, includes breakfast but not towels, which you can get from a machine; required membership card-€2.50 extra/person; rooms locked 12:00–15:00 and at 01:00). **MIJE Fourcy** (cheap dinners, 6 rue de Fourcy, just south of rue Rivoli), **MIJE Fauconnier** (11 rue Fauconnier), and the best, **MIJE Maubisson** (12 rue des Barres), share the same contact information (tel. 01 42 74 23 45, fax 01 40 27 81 64,

www.mije.com) and Métro stop (St. Paul). Reservations
are accepted.

Sleeping near the Pompidou Center: The remaining
hotels are farther West and closer to the Pompidou Center
than to place Bastille.

Hôtel de Nice**, on the Marais' busy main drag, is a cozy
"Marie Antoinette does tie-dye" place. Its narrow halls are littered
with paintings, and rooms are filled with lots of thoughtful touches.
Twin rooms, which cost the same as doubles, are larger but on
the street side—with effective double-paned windows (23 rooms,
Sb-€58, Db-€92, Tb-€110, CC, 42 bis rue de Rivoli, Mo: Hôtel
de Ville, tel. 01 42 78 55 29, fax 01 42 78 36 07).

Hôtel de la Bretonnerie***, three blocks North and East of
Hôtel de Ville, is a fine Marais splurge. It has elegant decor and
tastefully-decorated rooms with an antique, open-beam warmth
(standard Db-€105, Db with character-€136, the standard Db has
enough character for me, family-friendly suites-€175, CC, closed
Aug, between rue du Vielle du Temple and rue des Archives at
22 rue Sainte Croix de la Bretonnerie, Mo: Hôtel de Ville, tel.
01 48 87 77 63, fax 01 42 77 26 78, www.bretonnerie.com).

At the inexpensive, laid-back **Grand Hôtel du Loiret****,
you get what you pay for (S-€37, Sb-€47–60, D-€42, Db-€56–
73, Tb-€70–82, CC, just north of rue de Rivoli, 8 rue des Garçons
Mauvais, Mo: Hôtel de Ville, tel. 01 48 87 77 00, fax 01 48 04
96 56, e-mail: hotelloiret@aol.com).

Hôtel Caron de Beaumarchais***, its lobby cluttered with
bits from an elegant 18th-century Marais house, rents rooms that
antique collectors would appreciate (Db-€135–150, CC, air-con,
12 rue Vielle du Temple, Mo: Hôtel de Ville, tel. 01 42 72 34 12,
fax 01 42 72 34 63, www.carondebeaumarchais.com).

Hôtel de Vieux Marais**, tucked away on a quiet street
two blocks east of the Pompidou Center, offers bright and fairly
spacious rooms with air-conditioning, simple decor, and we-try-
harder owners. Say hello to Leeloo, the hotel hound (Sb-€95–105,
Db-€105–120, extra bed-€23, CC, just off rue des Archives at
8 rue du Platre, Mo: Rambuteau/Hôtel de Ville, tel. 01 42 78
47 22, fax 01 42 78 34 32).

Hôtel Beaubourg*** is a good three-star value within spitting
distance of the Pompidou Center. The rooms are wood-beam
comfy, and public spaces are warm and pleasant (Db-€104–113,
some with balconies-€122, includes breakfast, CC, 11 rue Simon
Lefranc, Mo: Rambuteau, tel. 01 42 74 34 24, fax 01 42 78 68 11,
e-mail: htlbeaubourg@hotellerie.net).

Sleeping near the Marais on Ile St. Louis: The peaceful,
residential character of this island, its central location, and great

ice cream have drawn Americans for decades, allowing hotels to charge top euro for their generally standard, though comfortable, rooms. There are no budget values here, but the island's coziness and proximity to the Marais, Notre-Dame, and the Latin Quarter compensate for high room rates. These hotels are on the island's main drag, the rue St. Louis en l'Ile, where I list several restaurants (see chapter on Eating, page 277).

Hôtel Jeu de Paume**** is the most expensive hotel I list in Paris. When you enter its magnificent lobby—with high ceilings and half-timbered walls—you'll understand why. It has fine public spaces and charming rooms, most of which face a central garden (Db-€210–255, Db suite-€415–445, CC, 54 rue St. Louis en l'Ile, tel. 01 43 26 14 18, fax 01 40 46 02 76, www.jeudepaumehotel.com).

Hôtel Des Deux Iles*** is the best value on the island, with an appealing lobby and well-appointed rooms (Sb-€122, Db-€140, CC, air-con, must cancel 1 week in advance or pay fees, 59 rue St. Louis en l'Ile, tel. 01 43 26 13 35, fax 01 43 29 60 25, www.hotel-ile-saintlouis.com). Its sister hotel, **Hôtel de Lutece*****, is next door (#65), with the same rates but smaller rooms (CC, tel. 01 43 26 13 35, fax 01 43 29 60 25).

Contrescarpe Orientation

This lively, colorful neighborhood is like Montmartre with fewer tourists. It's just south of the Latin Quarter, encompassing the area between Luxembourg Gardens and rue Monge.

The nearest **TI** is at the Louvre Museum. The **post office** (PTT) is between rue Mouffetard and rue Monge at 10 rue de l'Epée du Bois. Place Monge hosts a colorful **outdoor market** on Wednesday, Friday, and Sunday until 13:00. The **street market** at the bottom of rue Mouffetard bustles daily except Monday (Tue–Sat 08:00–12:00, 15:30–19:00, Sun 08:00–12:00, 5 blocks south of place Contrescarpe). Lively cafés at place Contrescarpe hop with action from the afternoon into the wee hours. **Bus #47** runs along rue Monge north to Notre-Dame, the Pompidou Center, and Gare du Nord.

The flowery Jardin des Plantes park is just east, and the sublime Luxembourg Gardens are just west. Both are ideal for afternoon walks, picnics, naps, and kids. The doorway at 49 rue Monge leads to a hidden **Roman arena** (Arènes de Lutèce). Today, *boules* players occupy the stage while couples cuddle on the seats. Admire the Panthéon from the outside (it's not worth paying to enter), and peek inside the exquisitely beautiful St. Etienne-du-Mont church.

Sleeping in the Contrescarpe Neighborhood
(5th arrondissement, Mo: place Monge,
zip code: 75005)
Hotels here are a 20-minute walk from Notre-Dame, Ile de la
Cité, and Ile St. Louis, and a 5- to 10-minute walk from the
Luxembourg Gardens and the grand boulevards St. Germain and
St. Michel. Fewer tourists sleep in Contrescarpe, and I find the
hotel values generally better than in most other neighborhoods.
Most hotels listed are on or very near rue Mouffetard, the spine of
this area, running from the perfectly Parisian place Contrescarpe
south to rue Bazelles. Two thousand years ago, rue Mouffetard
was the principal Roman road south to Italy. Today, this small,
meandering street has a split personality. The lower part thrives
in the daytime as a pedestrian market street. The upper part sleeps
during the day but comes alive after dark, teeming with bars,
restaurants, and nightlife. These hotels are listed in order of proximity to the Seine and Notre-Dame.

Hôtel Central* defines unpretentiousness, with a charming
location, a steep, slippery, castle-like stairway, so-so beds, and
simple rooms (all with showers, though toilets are down the hall).
It's a fine budget value (Ss-€27–29, Ds-€37–41, no CC, no elevator, 6 rue Descartes, Mo: Cardinal Lemoine, tel. 01 46 33 57 93).

Hôtel des Grandes Ecoles*** is simply idyllic. A short
alley leads to three buildings that protect a flowering garden courtyard, preserving a sense of tranquility that is rare in a city this
size. Rooms are spacious and comfortable with large beds. This
romantic place is deservedly popular, so call well in advance (Db-
€90–114, extra bed-€15, parking-€20, CC, 75 rue de Cardinal
Lemoine, Mo: Cardinal Lemoine, tel. 01 43 26 79 23, fax 01 43
25 28 15, www.hotel-grandes-ecoles.com, mellow Marie speaks
some English).

Sleeping between the Panthéon and Luxembourg Gardens:
The following five hotels are a five-minute walk from place Contrescarpe. For these listings, the RER stop Luxembourg (with
direct connections to the airports) is closer than the nearest
Métro stop, Maubert Mutualité. The first two face the Panthéon's
right transept.

Hôtel du Panthéon*** offers a seductively comfy lobby
and rooms decorated in "country-French." Rooms are well-
designed, with air-conditioning and every comfort. Fifth-floor
rooms have balconies, but sixth-floor rooms have the best views
(Db-€190–220, CC, tel. 01 43 54 32 95, fax 01 43 26 64 65,
www.hoteldupantheon.com).

Hôtel des Grandes Hommes*** has spacious, wood-
beamed rooms, which are scheduled for renovation in 2002

—CONTRESCARPE HOTELS AND RESTAURANTS—

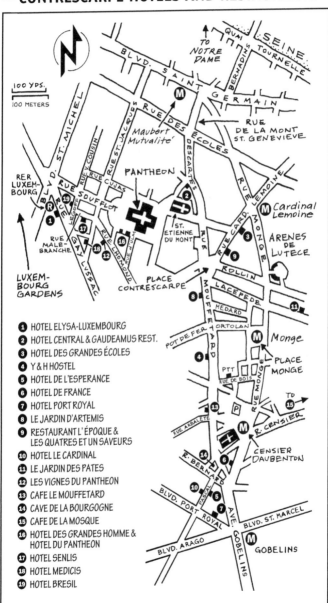

1. HOTEL ELYSA-LUXEMBOURG
2. HOTEL CENTRAL & GAUDEAMUS REST.
3. HOTEL DES GRANDES ÉCOLES
4. Y & H HOSTEL
5. HOTEL DE L'ESPERANCE
6. HOTEL DE FRANCE
7. HOTEL PORT ROYAL
8. LE JARDIN D'ARTEMIS
9. RESTAURANT L'ÉPOQUE &
   LES QUATRES ET UN SAVEURS
10. HOTEL LE CARDINAL
11. LE JARDIN DES PATES
12. LES VIGNES DU PANTHEON
13. CAFE LE MOUFFETARD
14. CAVE DE LA BOURGOGNE
15. CAFE DE LA MOSQUE
16. HOTEL DES GRANDES HOMME &
    HOTEL DU PANTHEON
17. HOTEL SENLIS
18. HOTEL MEDICIS
19. HOTEL BRESIL

(Db-€190–230, prices are estimates, CC, 17 place du Panthéon, tel. 01 46 34 19 60, fax 01 43 26 67 32, e-mail: reservation@hoteldesgrandeshommes.com).

Hôtel Senlis** hides quietly two blocks from Luxembourg Gardens with modest rooms, all with beamed ceilings and TVs (Sb-€65, Db-€70–85, Tb-€95, Qb-€107, CC, 7 rue Malebranche, tel. 01 43 29 93 10, fax 01 43 29 00 24, e-mail: hoteldesenlis@wanadoo.fr).

Hôtel Brésil** lies one block from Luxembourg Gardens and offers less character, and some smoky rooms, at reasonable rates (Sb-€62, Db-€62–85, CC, 10 rue le Goff, tel. 01 43 54 76 11, fax 01 46 33 45 78, e-mail: hoteldubresil@wanadoo.fr).

Hôtel Medicis is as cheap, stripped-down, and basic as it gets, with a soiled linoleum charm, a helpful owner, and a great location (S-€15, D-€30, 214 rue St. Jacques, tel. 01 43 54 14 66, Denis speaks English).

Hôtel Elysa-Luxembourg*** sits on a busy street at Luxembourg Gardens and charges top euro for its plush, air-conditioned rooms (Sb-€107, Db-€134, CC, 6 rue Gay Lussac, tel. 01 43 25 31 74, fax 01 46 34 56 27, www.elysa_luxembourg.fr).

Sleeping at the bottom of rue Mouffetard: Of my recommended accommodations in the Contrescarpe neighborhood, these are farthest from the Seine and other tourists, and lie in an appealing work-a-day area. They may have rooms when others don't.

Y&H Hostel offers a great location, easygoing, English-speaking management, Internet access, kitchen facilities, and basic but acceptable hostel conditions (beds in 4-bed rooms-€18, beds in double rooms-€21, sheets-€2.50, no CC, rooms closed 11:00–16:00 but reception stays open, 02:00 curfew, reservations require deposit, 80 rue Mouffetard, Mo: Cardinal Lemoine, tel. 01 47 07 47 07, fax 01 47 07 22 24, e-mail: smile@youngandhappy.fr).

Hôtel de l'Esperance** is nearly three stars for the price of two. It's quiet, pink, fluffy, and comfortable, with thoughtfully-appointed rooms complete with canopy beds, hair dryers, and a flamboyant owner (Sb-€70, Db-€72–86, small Tb-€101, CC, 15 rue Pascal, Mo: Censier-Daubenton, tel. 01 47 07 10 99, fax 01 43 37 56 19).

Hôtel le Cardinal*** is a new, well-designed hotel with pleasing décor, air-conditioning, and modern comforts (Sb-€93, standard Db-€115, large Db-€185, Tb-€205, CC, 20 rue Pascal, tel. 01 47 07 41 92, fax 01 47 07 43 80, e-mail: hotelcardinal@aol.com).

Hôtel de France**, set on a busy street, has fine, modern rooms and hardworking, helpful owners (Jean and Christine). The best and quietest rooms are *sur le cour* (on the courtyard), though streetside rooms are fine (Sb-€62, Db-€74–78, CC, requires 1 night non-refundable deposit, 108 rue Monge,

Mo: Censier-Daubenton, tel. 01 47 07 19 04, fax 01 43 36 62 34, e-mail: hotel.de.fce@wanadoo.fr).

Don't let **Hôtel Port Royal***'s lone star fool you—this place is polished bottom to top and has been well-run by the same family for 66 years. Its clean and comfy rooms come at fair prices. Ask for a room off the street (S-€35–46, Db-€63–73, no CC, climb stairs from rue Pascal to busy boulevard de Port Royal, 8 boulevard de Port Royal, Mo: Gobelins, tel. 01 43 31 70 06, fax 01 43 31 33 67).

Sleeping near Paris, in Versailles

For a laid-back alternative to Paris within easy reach of the big city by RER train (5/hr, 30 min), Versailles, with easy, safe parking and reasonably-priced hotels, can be a good overnight stop (see map on page 210). Park in the château's main lot while looking for a hotel, or leave your car there overnight (free from 19:30–08:00). Get a map of Versailles at your hotel or at the TI. For restaurant recommendations, see page 277.

Hôtel Le Cheval Rouge**, built in 1676 as Louis XIV's stables, now houses tourists. It's a block behind place du Marché in a quaint corner of town on a large, quiet courtyard with free, safe parking and sufficiently comfortable rooms (Ds-€49, Db-€58–72, Tb-€86, Qb-€90, CC, 18 rue Andre Chenier, tel. 01 39 50 03 03, fax 01 39 50 61 27).

Ibis Versailles** offers fair value and modern comfort, but no air-conditioning (Db-€71, cheaper weekend rates can't be reserved ahead, CC, across from RER station, 4 avenue du General de Gaulle, tel. 01 39 53 03 30, fax 01 39 50 06 31).

Hôtel du Palais, facing the RER station, has clean, sharp rooms—the cheapest I list in this area. Ask for a quiet room off the street (Ds-€43, Db-€49, extra person-€11, CC, miles of stairs, 6 place Lyautey, tel. 01 39 50 39 29, fax 01 39 50 80 41).

Hôtel d'Angleterre**, away from the frenzy, is a tranquil old place with comfortable and spacious rooms. Park nearby in the palace lot (Db-€56–72, extra bed-€15, CC, just below palace to the right as you exit, 2 rue de Fontenay, tel. 01 39 51 43 50, fax 01 39 51 45 63).

Hôtel de France***, in an 18th-century townhouse, offers four-star value, with air-conditioned, appropriately royal rooms, a pleasant courtyard, comfy public spaces, a bar, and a restaurant (Db-€125–130, Tb-€168, CC, just off parking lot across from château, 5 rue Colbert, tel. 01 30 83 92 23, fax 01 30 83 92 24, www.hotelfrance-versailles.com).

For Longer Stays

Staying a week or longer? Consider the advantages that come with renting a furnished apartment. Complete with a small, equipped kitchen and living room, this option is great for families. Among the many English-speaking organizations ready to help, the following have proven most reliable. Their Web sites are generally excellent and essential to understanding your options.

Paris Appartements Services rents studios and one-bedroom apartments in the Opéra, Louvre, and Marais neighborhoods (2 rue d'Argout, 75002 Paris, tel. 01 40 28 01 28, fax 01 40 28 92 01, www.paris-appartements-services.fr).

Apalachee Bay is British-owned and offers an extensive range of carefully selected, furnished apartments (21 rue de Madrid, 75008 Paris, tel. 01 42 94 13 13, fax 01 42 94 83 01, www.apalachee.com).

Locaflat offers accommodations ranging from studios to five-room apartments (tel. 01 43 06 78 79, fax 01 40 56 99 69, www.locaflat.com).

EATING
IN PARIS

Paris is France's wine and cuisine melting pot. While it lacks a style of its own (only French onion soup is truly Parisian), it draws from the best of France. Paris could hold a gourmet's Olympics and import nothing.

Picnic or go to bakeries for quick take-out lunches, or stop at a café for a lunch salad or *plat du jour*, but linger longer over dinner. You can eat well, restaurant style, for €15 to €25. Your hotel can usually recommend nearby restaurants in the €15 range. Remember, cafés are happy to serve a *plat du jour* (garnished plate of the day, about €11) or a chef-like salad (€9) day or night, while restaurants expect you to enjoy a full dinner. Famous places are often overpriced, overcrowded, and overrated. Find a quiet neighborhood and wander, or follow a local recommendation. Restaurants open for dinner around 19:00, and small local favorites get crowded after 21:00. Most of the restaurants listed below accept credit cards.

To save piles of euros, review the budget eating tips in this book's introduction and consider dinner picnics (great take-out dishes available at *charcuteries*). My recommendations are centered around the same three great neighborhoods listed in the Sleeping chapter; you can come home exhausted after a busy day of sightseeing and have a good selection of restaurants right around the corner. And evening is a fine time to explore any of these delightful neighborhoods, even if you're sleeping elsewhere.

Restaurants

The Parisian eating scene is kept at a rolling boil. Entire books (and lives) are dedicated to the subject. If you are traveling outside of Paris, save your splurges for the countryside, where you'll enjoy regional cooking for less money. I've listed places that conveniently fit a busy sightseeing schedule and places near recommended hotels. If you'd like to visit a district specifically to eat, consider the many romantic restaurants that line the cozy Ile St. Louis' main street and the colorful, touristy-but-fun string of eateries along rue Mouffetard behind the Panthéon (in the Contrescarpe neighborhood). Beware: Many restaurants close Sunday and Monday. Most restaurants offer several fixed-price *menus*, often between €15 and €25. In most cases, the few extra euros you pay for not choosing the least expensive option is money well spent, as it opens up a variety of better choices. You decide.

Cafeterias and Picnics

Many Parisian department stores have huge supermarkets hiding in the basement and top-floor cafeterias offering not really cheap but low-risk, low-stress, what-you-see-is-what-you-get meals.

For lunch and dinner picnics, you'll find handy little groceries (*épiceries*) and delis (*charcuteries*) all over town, but rarely near famous sights. Good picnic fixings include roasted chicken, drinkable yogurt, fresh bakery goods, melons, and exotic pâtés and cheeses. Great take-out deli-type foods like gourmet salads and quiches abound. *Boulangeries* make good, cheap mini-quiches and sandwiches. While wine is taboo in public places in the United States, it's *pas de problème* in France.

Romantic Picnic Spots: My favorite dinner-picnic places are the pedestrian bridge (Pont des Arts) across from the Louvre, with unmatched views and plentiful benches; the Champ de Mars park under the Eiffel Tower; and the western tip of Ile St. Louis, overlooking Ile de la Cité. Bring your own dinner feast and watch the riverboats or the Eiffel Tower light up the city for you. The Palais Royal (across the street from the Louvre) is a good spot for a peaceful, royal picnic, as is the little triangular Henry IV Park on the west tip of Ile de la Cité. For lunch picnics with great people-watching, try the Pompidou Center (by the *Homage to Stravinsky* fountain), the elegant place des Vosges (closes at dusk), the gardens at the Rodin Museum, and the Luxembourg Gardens.

Eating in the Rue Cler Neighborhood

The rue Cler neighborhood isn't famous for its restaurants. That's why I enjoy eating here. Several small, family-run places serve great dinner *menus* for €15 and *plats du jour* for €9 to €12. My first two recommendations are easygoing cafés, ideal if what you want is a light dinner (good dinner salads) or more substantial but simple meals.

Café du Marché, with the best seats, coffee, and prices on rue Cler, serves hearty salads and good €9 *plats du jour* for lunch or dinner to a trendy, smoky, mainly French crowd (at the corner of rue Cler and rue Champ de Mars); arrive before 19:30 or wait at the bar. A chalkboard listing the plates of the day—each a meal—will momentarily be hung in front of you. You'll find the same dishes and prices with better (but smoky) indoor seating at their other restaurant, **Le Comptoir du Septième**, at the École Militaire Métro stop (39 avenue de la Motte Piquet, tel. 01 45 55 90 20).

Café le Bosquet is a vintage Parisian brasserie. Come here for a bowl of French onion soup, a salad, or a three-course set *menu* for €16 (many choices, closed Sun, 46 avenue Bosquet, tel. 01 45 51 38 13).

Leo le Lion, a warm, charming souvenir of old Paris, is popular with locals. Expect to spend €23 per person for fine à la carte choices (closed Sun, 23 rue Duvivier, tel. 01 45 51 41 77).

Vegetarians will appreciate the Mediterranean cuisine at **7ème Sud** (closed Sun, at corner of rue de Grenelle and rue Duvivier). A few blocks toward the river, **l'Ami de Jean** is a lively place to sample Basque cuisine (closed Sun, 27 rue Malar, tel. 01 47 05 86 89). Almost next door, **L'Affriole** is an intimate place and well-deserving of its rave reviews. Item selections change daily and the wine list is extensive, with some good bargains (€29 *menu*, closed Sun, 17 rue Malar, tel. 01 44 18 31 33).

The next three places are closer to La Tour Maubourg Métro stop. **La Bressanne** is a country-warm place with a good €21 *menu* (16 avenue de la Motte Piquet, tel. 01 47 05 98 37). The tiny **Au Petit Tonneau** is a purely Parisian experience, where owner-chef Madame Boyer prepares everything herself (allow €30/person with wine, open daily, 20 rue Surcouf, tel. 01 47 05 09 01). **Thoumieux**, the neighborhood's classy, traditional Parisian brasserie, is deservedly popular. It's big and dressy with formal but good-natured waiters. Skip the *menu* and order à la carte (allow €30/person with wine, 79 rue St. Dominique, tel. 01 47 05 49 75).

I like browsing the handful of fine places that line rue de l'Exposition one block west of avenue Bosquet between rue St. Dominique and rue de Grenelle. Each of these places is a hard-working, mom-and-pop organization with plenty of charm and a distinct ambience. Eat early with tourists or late with locals. **Restaurant La Serre**, at #29, has a fun atmosphere but an unpredictable staff (*plats* €8–11, daily from 19:00, often a wait after 21:00, good onion soup and duck specialties, tel. 01 45 55 20 96, Marie-Alice and Philippe speak English). **Le P'tit Troquet**, across the street at #28, is delightfully Parisian, popular with locals, and gracefully run by Dominique—allow €24 per person for dinner (closed Sun–Mon, tel. 01 47 05 80 39). **La Casa di Sergio**,

RUE CLER RESTAURANTS

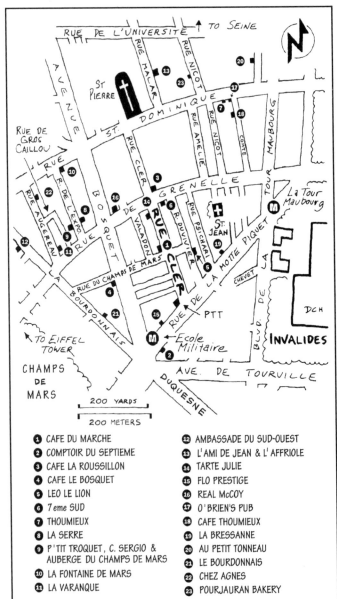

1. CAFE DU MARCHE
2. COMPTOIR DU SEPTIEME
3. CAFE LA ROUSSILLON
4. CAFE LE BOSQUET
5. LEO LE LION
6. 7eme SUD
7. THOUMIEUX
8. LA SERRE
9. P'TIT TROQUET, C. SERGIO & AUBERGE DU CHAMPS DE MARS
10. LA FONTAINE DE MARS
11. LA VARANQUE
12. AMBASSADE DU SUD-OUEST
13. L'AMI DE JEAN & L'AFFRIOLE
14. TARTE JULIE
15. FLO PRESTIGE
16. REAL McCOY
17. O'BRIEN'S PUB
18. CAFE THOUMIEUX
19. LA BRESSANNE
20. AU PETIT TONNEAU
21. LE BOURDONNAIS
22. CHEZ AGNES
23. POURJAURAN BAKERY

at #20, is where I go in Paris for gourmet Italian cuisine served family-style by Sicilian Sergio. Sergio says he's waited his entire life to open a restaurant like this. While not cheap, the food is remarkable. Sit down and let Sergio do the rest (€26–34 *menus*, closed Wed, tel. 01 45 51 37 71). The softly lit tables and red velvet chairs of **Auberge du Champ de Mars**, at #18, draw a romantic crowd (€15 *menu*, expensive wines, closed Sun). For top à la carte-only cuisine, locals reserve early for the charmingly situated **La Fontaine de Mars.** Skip it if you don't get a table downstairs (allow €38/person with wine, where rue de l'Exposition and rue St. Dominique meet, tel. 01 47 05 46 44).

These four places are closer to the Champs de Mars park. Just off rue de Grenelle, the friendly and unpretentious **La Varanque** is a good budget bet, with €9 *plats* and a €12 *menu* (27 rue Augereau, tel. 01 47 05 51 22). **Chez Agnes** is tiny, a good value, and run by engaging Agnes (closed Mon, next to recommended Hôtel Londres Eiffel at 1 rue Augereau, tel. 01 45 51 06 04). **Ambassade du Sud-Ouest**, a wine and food boutique/restaurant, specializes in southwestern French cuisine, such as cassoulet (46 avenue de la Bourdonnais, tel. 01 45 55 59 59). For a truly special occasion, the **Le Bourdonnais** has one Michelin star and a warm, intimate feel. Micheline Croat, your hostess, will take good care of you (€64 *menu*, 113 avenue de la Bourdonnais, tel. 01 47 05 47 96).

Picnicking: The rue Cler is a moveable feast that gives "fast food" a good name. The entire street is clogged with connoisseurs of good eating. Only the health-food store goes unnoticed. A festival of food, the street is lined with people whose lives seem to be devoted to their specialty: polished produce, rotisserie chicken, crêpes, or cheese.

For a magical picnic dinner at the Eiffel Tower, assemble it in no fewer than five shops on rue Cler and lounge on the best grass in Paris (the police don't mind after dusk), with the dogs, Frisbees, a floodlit tower, and a cool breeze in the Parc du Champ de Mars.

The **crêpe stand** next to Café du Marché does a wonderful top-end dinner crêpe for €4. Asian delis (generically called *Traiteur Asie*) provide tasty, low-stress, low-price, take-out treats (two with tables on the rue Cler—one across from Hôtel Leveque, and the other near the rue du Champs de Mars). For a variety of savory quiches or a tasty pear-and-chocolate tart, try **Tarte Julie's** (take-out or stools, 28 rue Cler). The elegant **Flo Prestige** *charcuterie* (at the Ecole Militaire Métro stop) is open until 23:00 and offers mouthwatering meals to go. **Real McCoy** is a little shop selling American food and sandwiches (194 rue de Grenelle). A good, small, late-night grocery is at 197 rue de Grenelle.

The bakery (*boulangerie*) on the corner of rue Cler and rue de Grenelle is the place for sandwiches, *pain au chocolat*, or almond croissants. And the **Pourjauran** bakery, offering great baguettes, hasn't changed in 70 years (20 rue Jean Nicot). The bakery at 112 rue St. Dominique is worth the detour, with classic decor and tables to enjoy your *café au lait* and croissant.

Cafés and Bars: If you want to linger over coffee or a drink at a sidewalk café, try **Café du Marché** (see above), **Petite Brasserie PTT** (local workers eat here, opposite 53 rue Cler), or **Café le Bosquet** (46 avenue Bosquet, tel. 01 45 51 38 13). **Le Sancerre** wine bar/café is wood-beam warm and ideal for a light lunch or dinner, or just a glass of wine after a long day of sightseeing. The owner's cheeks are the same color as his wine (open until 21:30, great omelets, 22 avenue Rapp, tel. 01 45 51 75 91). **Maison Altmayer** is a hole-in-the-wall place good for a quiet drink (09:00–19:30, next to Hôtel Eiffel Rive Gauche, 6 rue du Gros Caillou). Cafés like this originated (and this one still functions) as a place where locals enjoyed a drink while their heating wood, coal, or gas was prepared for delivery.

Nightlife: This sleepy neighborhood is not the place for night owls, but there are a few notable exceptions. **Café du Marché** and its brother, **Le Comptoir du Septième** (both listed above), hop with a Franco-American crowd until about midnight, as does the flashier **Café La Roussillon** (at corner of rue de Grenelle and rue Cler). **O'Brien's Pub** is a relaxed, Parisian rendition of an Irish pub (77 St. Dominique). **Café Thoumieux** (younger brother of the brasserie listed above) has big-screen sports and a trendy young crowd (4 rue de la Comete, Mo: Latour Maubourg).

Eating in the Marais Neighborhood

The sidewalks of the Marais are filled with locals and tourists in search of a good meal from, unfortunately, an abundance of average eateries. I've worked hard to find the best in this area, where too often you must choose between the quality of the atmosphere or cuisine. The Ile St. Louis is a short walk away (see below), offering those sleeping in the Marais a pleasant alternative for restaurants.

For starters, stroll the rue Vieille du Temple (near rue des Rosiers), home to several lively cafés providing traditional fare (some even serve Sunday brunch), and a handful of good restaurants worth the detour. **Au Petit Fer à Cheval,** named for its horseshoe-shaped bar, is an authentic gem with mirrored walls and tiled floors. To avoid crowds, come for lunch, an early dinner, or a nightcap. The restaurant in back serves daily specials to diners seated on old wooden Métro seats (daily until 02:00, 30 rue Vieille du Temple, tel. 01 42 72 47 47). **Le Colimacon,** at #44, is a romantic little place offering two-course (€14) or three-course (€20) *menus* of traditional cuisine, including *magret de canard aux fruits de saison*—duck breast with a sauce of seasonal fruit (daily except Tue eve, reservations required, tel. 01 48 87 12 01).

You'll find several places that rely more on the quality of their charming location than their cuisine at place du Marché Ste. Catherine, a tiny square just off rue St. Antoine between the St. Paul Métro stop and place des Vosges. Try the outdoor tables at the side-by-side **Le Marché** or **Au Bistrot de la Place** (allow €23/person, 2 place du Marché Ste. Catherine). For reliably good cuisine with a Basque emphasis, find **L'Auberge de Jarente** (€18 *menu*, closed Sun–Mon, just off the square at 7 rue Jarente, tel. 01 42 77 49 35).

Dinners under the candlelit arches of the place des Vosges are *très* romantic. The mod and pastel **Nectarine** at #16 is a teahouse serving good salads, quiches, and reasonable *plats du jour* both day and night (tel. 01 42 77 23 78). **Ma Bourgogne** is bigger, darker, and more traditional (allow €38/person with wine, open daily, dinner reservations smart, no CC, at northwest corner, tel. 01 42 78 44 64). Just off the place des Vosges, **L'Impasse** (or **Chez Robert**) is a cozy neighborhood bistro located on a quiet alley next to a Laundromat. Clean your clothes while you dine from a classic bourgeois *menu* with a variety of €6 first courses, €13.50 second courses, and €6 desserts (closed Sun, 4 impasse Guéménée, tel. 01 42 72 08 45). A few blocks west you'll find **Camille**, a traditional corner brasserie with white-aproned waiters serving €9 salads and very French *plats du jour* for €15 (daily, 24 rue des Francs-Bourgeois at corner of rue Elzevir, tel. 01 42 72 29 50).

The following places sit near the intersection of rues Castex and St. Antoine. For a break from French cooking, find a table at the tiny, tasty **Trattoria Delizie Italiane** (closed Sun–Mon, 6 rue Castex, tel. 01 44 54 00 33). Across the street at #13, the tight little **Café de la Poste** offers good €9 *plats du jour* (closed Sun). On the other side of rue St. Antoine, **Gaspard de la Nuit** is cozy and a worthwhile step up, with a good €24 *menu* (a block off rue St. Antoine at 6 rue des Tournelles, tel. 01 42 77 90 53). Farther up at 38 rue des Tournelles, **Baracane-Bistro de l'Oulette** offers specialties from southwestern France and a descriptive and reasonable wine list. The €37 *menu* is a good value with an *apéritif*, three fine courses, a half bottle of wine per person, and coffee (closed Sun, tel. 01 42 71 43 33). If the weather's good, grab a table on the terrace at **Chez Janou**, a Provençal bistro, then make your selection from a tempting à la carte menu (2 rue Roger-Verlomme, at the corner of rue des Tournelles and rue Roger-Verlomme, tel. 01 42 72 28 41).

MARAIS RESTAURANTS

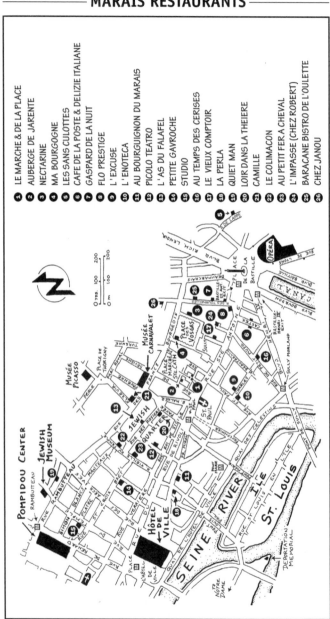

1. LE MARCHE & DE LA PLACE
2. AUBERGE DE JARENTE
3. NECTARINE
4. MA BOURGOGNE
5. LES SANS CULOTTES
6. CAFE DE LA POSTE & DELIZIE ITALIANE
7. GASPARD DE LA NUIT
8. FLO PRESTIGE
9. L'EXCUSE
10. L'ENOTECA
11. AU BOURGUIGNON DU MARAIS
12. PICOLO TEATRO
13. L'AS DU FALAFEL
14. PETITE GAVROCHE
15. STUDIO
16. AU TEMPS DES CERISES
17. LE VIEUX COMPTOIR
18. LA PERLA
19. QUIET MAN
20. LOIR DANS LA THEIERE
21. CAMILLE
22. LE COLIMACON
23. AU PETIT FER A CHEVAL
24. L'IMPASSE (CHEZ ROBERT)
25. BARACANE BISTRO DE L'OULETTE
26. CHEZ JANOU

For a real treat, cross place de la Bastille and roam the lively rue de Lappe to the popular, zinc-bar classic **Bistrot les Sans Culottes** (€20 *menu*, 27 rue de Lappe, tel. 01 48 05 42 92).

Vegetarians will appreciate the excellent cuisine at the popular **Picolo Teatro** (closed Mon, near rue des Rosiers, 6 rue des Ecouffes, tel. 01 42 72 17 79) or the **L'As du Falafel**, which serves the best falafel on rue des Rosiers (#34). **Le Loir Dans La Theiere,** an artsy café, is another local favorite with mismatched chairs and good vegetarian options (daily from 10:00, last order at 19:00, 3 rue des Rosiers, tel. 01 42 72 90 61). On the other side of rue de Rivoli, wine-lovers shouldn't miss the superb Burgundy wines and exquisite, though limited, selection at **Au Bourguignon du Marais** (closed Sat–Sun, call by 19:00 to reserve, 52 rue Francois Miron, tel. 01 48 87 15 40).

For a fast, cheap change of pace, eat at (or take out from) the Chinese-Japanese **Delice House**. Two can split 200 grams of chicken curry (or whatever, €5) and rice (€3). There's lots of seating, with pitchers of tap water at the ground-floor tables and a roomier upstairs (open until 21:00, 81 rue St. Antoine). For dirt-cheap French cooking, try the charmingly basic **Petite Gavroche** (15 rue Sainte Croix de la Bretonnerie).

Closer to the Pompidou Center, the **Studio** is wonderfully located on a 17th-century courtyard below a dance school. The tasty salads, €12 *plats du jour*, and Tex-Mex food are good day or night (41 rue de Temple, tel. 01 42 74 10 38).

Near Hôtel du 7ème Art, splurge at the romantic and dressy **L'Excuse** (€30 *menu*, closed Sun, reserve ahead, 14 rue Charles V, tel. 01 42 77 98 97). Across the street, **L'Enoteca** (wine bar) has lively and reasonable Italian cuisine in a relaxed, open setting (closed Sun, at rue St. Paul and Charles V, tel. 01 42 78 91 44).

Picnicking: Picnic at the peaceful place des Vosges (closes at dusk). Hobos stretch their euros at the supermarket in the basement of the **Monoprix** department store (near place des Vosges on rue St. Antoine), and connoisseurs prefer the gourmet take-out places all along rue St. Antoine, such as **Flo Prestige** (open until 23:00, on the tiny square where rue Tournelle and rue St. Antoine meet). A couple of small grocery shops are open until 23:00 on rue St. Antoine (near intersection with rue Castex). An **open-air market**, held Sunday morning, is just off place de la Bastille on boulevard Richard Lenoir.

For a cheap breakfast, try the tiny *boulangerie/pâtisserie* where the hotels buy their croissants (coffee machine-€0.50, baby quiches-€1.50, *pain au chocolat*-€0.75, 1 block off place de la Bastille, corner of rue St. Antoine and rue de Lesdiguieres).

Cafés and Bars: In heart of the Marais, a *très* local wine bar,

Au Temps des Cerises, is a relaxed and amiably run, if smoky, place (open until 20:00, around the corner from Hôtel Castex, rue du Petit Musc and rue de Cerisaie). **Le Vieux Comptoir** is tiny, lively, and just hip enough (just off place des Vosges at 8 rue Biraque). **La Perla** is trendy and full of Parisian yuppies in search of the perfect margarita (26 rue Francois Miron). **The Quiet Man** is a traditional Irish pub with happy hour from 16:00 to 20:00 (5 rue des Haudriettes).

Nightlife: The trendiest cafés and bars are clustered on rues Vielle du Temple, Archives, and Ste. Croix de la Bretonnerie (open generally until 02:00), and are popular with gay men.

Eating in the Contrescarpe Neighborhood

There are a few diamonds for fine dining in this otherwise rough area. Most come here for the lively and cheap eateries that line rues Mouffetard and du Pot-de-Fer. Study the many *menus*, compare crowds, then dive in and have fun (see map on page 263).

Le Jardin d'Artemis is one of the better values on rue Mouffetard, at #34 (€13.50 and €21 *menus*), though **Restaurant l'Epoque** is the best place I found for fine cuisine at moderate prices (basic €13.50 *menu*, €19 *menu* is worth it, a block off place Contrescarpe at 81 rue Cardinal Lemoine, tel. 01 46 34 15 84). Across the street, **Les Quatres et Une Saveurs** is a hard-core, gourmet vegetarian place and worth a detour (closed Mon, 72 rue Cardinal Lemoine, tel. 01 43 26 88 80). **Le Jardin des Pates** is popular with less strict vegetarians, serving pastas and salads at fair prices (near Jardins des Plantes, 4 rue Lacepede, tel. 01 43 31 50 71).

The next two places are near the Panthéon. **Gaudeamus,** with a low-profile café on one side and a cozy bistro on the other, has friendly owners and cheap *menus* (daily, just below the Panthéon, 47 rue Montagne Ste. Genevieve, tel. 01 40 46 93 40). **Les Vignes du Panthéon** has Old World appeal and is popular with locals (allow €23 for à la carte, closed Sat–Sun, 4 rue des Fossés, tel. 01 43 54 80 81).

Cafés: The cafés on place Contrescarpe are popular until late. Both indoors and outdoors provide good people-watching. **Café Le Mouffetard** is in the thick of the street-market hustle and bustle (at corner of rue Mouffetard and rue de l'Arbalete). The outdoor tables at **Cave de la Bourgogne** are picture-perfect (at the bottom of rue Mouffetard on rue Bazelles). At **Café de la Mosque,** you'll feel like you've been beamed to Morocco. In this purely Arab café, order a mint tea, pour in the sugar, and enjoy the authentic interior and peaceful outdoor terrace (behind mosque, 2 rue Daubenton).

Eating on Ile St. Louis

The Ile St. Louis is popular with Americans for good reason: It's a romantic and peaceful place to window-shop for plenty of promising dinner possibilities. Cruise the island's main street for a variety of good options, from cozy *crêperies* to romantic restaurants. After dinner, sample Paris' best sorbet and ice cream at any place advertising "les glaces Berthillon" (the original Berthillon shop is at 31 rue St. Louis en l'Ile). Then stroll across to the Ile de la Cité to see an illuminated Notre-Dame.

All listings below line the rue St. Louis en l'Ile and begin at the end of the island closest to Notre-Dame. **Café Med**, at #77, serves inexpensive salads, crêpes, and lighter *menus* in a cheery setting (open daily). Nearby at #72, **Coin Sud** offers much of the same with warmer ambience; **La Castafiore**, at #51–53, serves fine Italian in a black-and-white-tile atmosphere (€28 *menu*). Farther down are three small and generally reliable places: **Le Tastevin** at #46 wins the ambience award (good €25 *menus*, tel. 01 43 54 17 31). Next door, **Au Gourmet de l'Isle** is a fun, good bet with a €25 *menu* (closed Mon–Tue). **Auberge de la Reine Blanche** is worth a visit for its consistently good cuisine and pleasant owners (open daily).

For a crazy, touristy, cellar atmosphere and hearty, fun food, feast at **La Taverne du Sergeant Recruiter**. The "Sergeant Recruiter" used to get young Parisians drunk and stuffed here, then sign them into the army. It's all-you-can-eat, including wine and service, for €31 (daily from 19:00, #41, tel. 01 43 54 75 42). There's a near-food-fight clone next door at **Nos Ancêtres Les Gaulois** ("Our Ancestors the Gauls," daily from 19:00, tel. 01 46 33 66 07).

Eating in Versailles

In the pleasant town center, around place du Marché Notre-Dame, you'll find a variety of reasonable restaurants, cafés, and a few cobbled lanes (market days Sun, Tue, and Fri until 13:00; see map on page 210). The square is a 15-minute walk from the château (veer left when you leave château). These places are on or near the square—place du Marché Notre-Dame—and all are good for lunch or dinner. **La Boeuf à la Mode** offers fine, traditional cuisine right on the square (€23 *menu*, 4 rue au Pain, tel. 01 39 50 31 99). **Fenêtres sur Cour** is the romantic's choice; it feels like you're dining in an Impressionist painting (closed Mon all year and Tue–Wed eves in summer, just below the square in "antique village," on place de la Geole, tel. 01 39 51 97 77). **A la Cote Bretonne** is the place to go for crêpes in a cozy setting (a few steps off the square on the traffic-free rue des Deux Ponts, #12).

Rue Satory is another pedestrian-friendly street with restaurants (10-min walk, go right out of the château).

LES GRANDS CAFÉS DE PARIS

Please see "Café Culture" (page 15) in this book's Introduction for tips on Parisian cafés.

History of Cafés in Paris

The first café in the Western world was in Paris—established in 1686 at Le Procope (still a restaurant today, see below). The French had just discovered coffee, and their robust economy was growing a population of pleasure-seekers and thinkers looking for places to be seen, to exchange ideas, and to plot revolutions both political and philosophical. And with the advent of theaters like La Comédie Française, the necessary artsy, coffee-sipping crowds were birthed. By 1700, more than 300 cafés had opened their doors; at the time of the Revolution (1789), there were over 1,800 cafés in Paris. Revolutionaries from Marat to Napoleon to Dalí enjoyed the spirit of free thinking that the cafés engendered.

Café society took off in the early 1900s. Life was changing rapidly, with the Industrial Revolution and wars on a global scale. Many retreated to Parisian cafés to try to make sense out of the confusion. Vladimir Lenin, Leon Trotsky, Igor Stravinsky, Ernest Hemingway, Scott Fitzgerald, James Joyce, Albert Einstein, Jean-Paul Sartre, Gene Openshaw, and Albert Camus were among the devoted café society. Some virtually lived at their favorite café, keeping their business calendars, entertaining friends, and having every meal. Parisian apartments were small, walls were thin (still often the case), and heating (particularly during war times) was minimal, making the warmth of cafés all the harder to leave.

There are more than 12,000 cafés in Paris today, though their numbers are shrinking. They're still used for business meetings, encounter sessions, political discussions, and romantic interludes. Most Parisians are loyal to their favorites and know their waiter's children's names. And with the recently approved 35-hour workweek, most will have even more time to linger longer over their *café crème*.

Here's a short list of grand Parisian cafés, worth the detour only if you're not in a hurry and don't mind paying outrageous prices for a shot of espresso. Think of these cafés as museums. Try to understand why they matter just as much today as they did yesterday.

GRAND CAFÉS BY NEIGHBORHOOD

St. Germain

Where the boulevard St. Germain meets rue Bonaparte (Mo: St. Germain-des-Près), you'll find two famous cafés. **Les Deux Magots** offers great outdoor seating and a warm interior. Once a favorite of Ernest Hemingway (in *The Sun Also Rises*, Jake met

Brett here) and of Jean-Paul Sartre (he and Simone de Beauvoir met here), the café is today filled with international tourists. **Le Café de Flore**, right next door, feels more local, hip, and literary—wear your black turtleneck. Picasso was a regular here while painting *Guernica*. The smoky interior is popular with Europeans.

For great outdoor seating and the same great view for less, skip these places and set up for coffee or a light lunch at **Café Bonaparte** (fine salads big enough for 2, from Les Deux Magots 1 block down rue Bonaparte toward river). You're farther from the large boulevards and exhaust fumes here, but still in the thick of this pleasant café-sitting area.

The first and most famous **Café Le Procope** lies an enchanting five-minute stroll away. From the Café Bonaparte, walk down the rue de l'Abbaye (consider a 20-step detour onto place Furstembourg en route), then continue onto rue de Bourbon le Château, veer left on the picturesque rue de Buci (many fine cafés here), and turn right just after crossing rue de l'Ancienne Comédie. Go up the passageway at 59–61 to find Le Procope (13 rue de l'Ancienne Comédie). Here Voltaire would consume dozens of coffees each day as he worked. Other famous patrons included Rousseau, Balzac, Zola, and Maupassant.

Boulevard Montparnasse

An eclectic assortment of historic cafés gathers along the busy boulevard Montparnasse at the intersection with boulevard Raspail (Mo: Vavin). Combine these historic cafés with the Luxembourg Gardens that lie just a few blocks away down rue Vavin (next to Café le Select).

La Coupole, built in the 1920s, was decorated by aspiring artists (Leger, Brancusi, and Chagall, among others) in return for free meals. This cavernous place feels like a classy train station, with grand chandeliers, velvet booths, brass decor, and waiters by the dozen. Today an unappealing glass building towers above. Bring your friends and make noise. The food is fine, but not the reason you came. In fact, I prefer coffee and drinks rather than dinner here (102 boulevard Montparnasse, tel. 01 43 26 70 50).

Le Dome sits right at the intersection of Raspail and Montparnasse and forms a dramatic contrast to the party atmosphere of La Coupole. Smaller, more elegant, and refined in every way, this place makes me want to dress up and look better than I do. Have a drink at the tables just inside, facing the sidewalk. While La Coupole is not known for its cuisine, Le Dome is. Come here for a splurge dinner (figure €38/person, tel. 01 43 35 25 81).

Le Select was popular with the more rebellious types—Leon Trotsky, Jean Cocteau, and Pablo Picasso loved it. It feels more conformist today, with good salads (€9–11), outdoor seating, and pleasant tables just inside the door (99 boulevard Montparnasse, across from La Coupole).

Champs-Elysées

Le Fouquet's, which opened in 1899, served as James Joyce's dining room. Today it's known as the film stars' place to go. Those golden plaques at the entry are from winners of France's version of our Oscar awards, the Césars. While the intimidating interior is impressive, the outdoor setting is Champs-Elysées great—and you can buy the most expensive shot of espresso I found in Paris (€4.50). Fouquet's was recently saved from foreign purchase and eventual destruction when the government declared it a historic monument (99 Avenue du Champs-Elysées, Mo: George V).

Near the Louvre

Within a short walk of the Louvre, you'll find melt-in-your-chair cafés (Mo: Palais Royal/Musée du Louvre). The staunchly Parisian **Café Le Nemours,** serving great light lunches, is tucked into the corner of Palais Royal adjacent to Comédie Française (leaving the Louvre, cross rue Rivoli and veer left). Brass-and-art-deco elegant, with outdoor tables under an arcade two minutes from the pyramid, this place makes a great post-Louvre retreat (2 place Colette).

On Place de la Concorde

Hotel de Crillon's four-star elegance can be yours for an afternoon. Considered the most exclusive hotel in Paris (and the last of the great hotels to be French-owned), this is the place to experience château life. Wear the best clothes you packed, arrive after 15:00, let the bellhop spin the door, and settle into the royal blue chairs in the *salon du thé* (€8.50 for a pot of tea or double *café au lait*, €28.50 for high tea). You'll be serenaded by a harpist and surrounded by famous people you won't recognize.

paris

PARIS WITH
CHILDREN

Paris is surprisingly kid-friendly. After enjoying so many parks, squares, and such a variety of kid-friendly sights, your children may want to return to Paris before you do. Consider these tips.

Before You Go:
- Get your kids in the spirit (rent or read Madeleine stories, *The Hunchback of Notre-Dame*, or *The Man in the Iron Mask*).
- Hotel selection is critical. Stay in a kid-friendly area near a park. The rue Cler neighborhood is ideal. If you're staying a week or more, rent an apartment (see "For Longer Stays," page 265).
- Bring plenty of kids' books; they're hard to find and expensive in Paris.

In Paris:
- Don't overdo it. Tackle one key sight each day (Louvre, Orsay, Versailles) and mix with a healthy dose of fun activities. The double-decker bus tours (see page 29) are a great way to start your visit.
- Follow this book's crowd-beating tips to a tee. Kids despise long lines more than you do.
- Eat dinner early (19:30 at restaurants, earlier at cafés). Skip famous places. Try relaxed cafés (or fast-food restaurants) where kids can move around without bothering others. Picnics work well.
- The best, cheapest toy selection is in the large department stores, such as Bon Marché (see Shopping chapter, page 285).
- French marionette shows, called *guignols*, are fun for everyone. They take place in several locations in Paris, mostly in big parks. See *Pariscope* or *L'Officiel des Spectacles* (sold at newsstands), under

"Marionettes," for times and places. The plots, while in French, are easy to follow. Arrive 20 minutes early for good seats.
• Involve your children in the trip. Let them help choose daily activities, lead you through the Métro, and so on.

TOP TEN KIDS' SPOTS IN PARIS

1. Luxembourg Gardens: This is my favorite place to mix kid business with pleasure. This perfectly Parisian park has it all: an extensive big-toys play area with imaginative slides, swings, and jungle gyms (kids-€2.70, adults-€1.80, good for all day, open daily, many parents watch from chairs outside the play area); pedal go-carts; a fun merry-go-round; toy sailboats in the main pond (€2.70/hr, daily in summer, otherwise Wed and Sat–Sun); and big open areas perfect for kicking a ball. Near the main building is a toddler wading pool and sandpit (free). Adults and kids enjoy the terrific puppet shows (*guignols*) held in the afternoons (Mo: St. Sulpice, Odéon, or Notre-Dame-des-Champs, tel. 01 43 26 46 47).

2. Jardin des Plantes: These pleasant, colorful gardens are short on grass, but have a small zoo, a plant maze, and several kid-friendly natural-science museums (closed Tue). Kids love the dinosaur exhibit at the Galerie d'Anatomie Comparée et de Paléontologie (no English explanations, but no real need, kids-€3.10, adults-€4.60, Wed–Mon 10:00–17:00, closed Tue, includes Musée de Mineralogie). From the park entrance on place Valhubert, the museums line the left side of the park (Mo: Gare d'Austerlitz or Jussieu).

3. Eiffel Tower and Champ de Mars Park: (see also "Trocadero," below): A ride up the tower is a hit day or night. See the video on the first floor. The vast Champ de Mars park stretches out from the tower's base; near the southwestern corner of the park (about halfway between the tower and the military school) are grassy play areas (bring your own ball, play after dusk), big toys, pony rides, and picnic-perfect benches (Mo: Ecole Militaire). For more information on the tower, see page 36.

4. Trocadero: All ages enjoy the view from Trocadero across the river to the Eiffel Tower, especially after dark (Mo: Trocadero). In-line skaters and skateboarders make the area below the Trocadero a teenage scene, particularly during afternoons and evenings. Two kid-friendly museums flank the Trocadero square in the Palais de Chaillot: the Naval Museum (*Musée de la Marine*) and the extensive Museum of Man (*Musée de l'Homme*). Neither offers much information in English, but both are pretty self-explanatory. An impressive collection of ship models, submarines, torpedoes, and naval you-name-it—including a small boat made for Napoleon—are docked at the Naval Museum (kids-€4, adults-€7, covered by museum pass, Wed–Mon 10:00–17:50, closed Tue, on the left side of the Trocadero square with your back to the Eiffel Tower). On the other side of the square, the sprawling Museum of Man is an anthropologist's dream, as cultures from Thailand to Lapland are creatively displayed on several floors with tools, costumes, and musical instruments (under 27-€3.10, adults-€4.60, not covered by museum pass, Wed–Mon 09:45–17:15, closed Tue).

5. Notre-Dame, Towers, and Crypt: Paris' famous Gothic cathedral doesn't have to be dry and dull. Replay Quasimodo's stunt and climb the tower. Kids love being on such a lofty perch with an in-your-face look at a gargoyle. The crypt on the square in front of Notre-Dame is quick and interesting. Kids can push buttons to highlight remains of Roman Paris and leave with a better understanding of how different civilizations build on top of each other. The small but beautiful park along the river and behind Notre-Dame has sandboxes, picnic benches, and space to run (Mo: Cité). ✪ See Historic Paris Walk, page 47.

6. Seine River Boat Rides: A variety of boats offer one-hour Seine cruises on huge glass-domed boats, with departures until 23:00. Or hop on a Bâteau-Bus, a river bus connecting six stops along the river: Eiffel Tower, Orsay/place de la Concorde, Louvre, Notre-Dame, Hôtel de Ville, and St. Germain-des-Près. Use the Bâteau-Bus by day, and take a twilight cruise on a Bateau-Mouche. See "Boat Tours," page 29.

7. Arc de Triomphe and Champs-Elysées: Watch the crazy traffic rush around the Arc de Triomphe for endless entertainment, then stroll the Champs-Elysées, with its car dealerships (particularly Renault's car-concept exhibit), Virgin Megastore (music), Disney Store, and the river of humanity that flows along its broad sidewalks. Take your teenager to see a movie on the Champs-Elysées ("v.o." next to the show time means original-version language). ✪ See Champs-Elysées Walk, page 66.

8. Versailles: This massive complex of palaces, gardens, fountains, and forest can be a good family getaway if well-planned. Do the gardens first and the interior late, when crowds subside. Then you can do cartwheels in an empty Hall of Mirrors. Rent a bike for the gardens or a rowboat for the canal. The Hameau has barnyard animals nearby. Be careful of weekend crowds when the fountains are flowing. ✪ See Versailles Tour, page 209.

9. Pompidou Center: The Pompidou Center appeals more
to teens, with its crazy outdoor entertainers, throngs of young people, happening cafés, and fun fountains next door. Inside, the temporary exhibits on the main floor are visually impressive. The *Star Wars* escalator to the top is fun for all ages, but you need to have a museum pass or a ticket for the museum (Modern Art) to escalate (Mo: Rambuteau). ✪ See Pompidou Center Tour, page 139.

10. The Cité des Sciences in the Parc de la Vilette:
This is like a city of its own, filled with hands-on science museums (closed Mon). It's well-organized, with something for all ages, and provides helpful information in English for most exhibits. Walk up from the Métro Porte de la Vilette into the huge metal building and stop at the information desk to explore your options. Pick up the essential brochure ("The Keys to the Cité") explaining the exhibits, which include separate discovery/play areas for kids ages 3 to 5 and 5 to 11, and a Technocité for those ages 12 and up (each €3.80); the most important Explora museum (€8.40, helpful English audioguide-€3.80); an aquarium (€5.30); the Geode (a giant spherical movie screen, €7); and a planetarium (€5.30). Whew, you could go broke if you don't focus—the Explora museum and the Geode are the most famous. Most of these areas have allotted times when you can enter, generally limited to 90 minutes per area (Tue–Sat 10:00–18:00, Sun until 19:00, closed Mon, tel. 01 40 05 12 12).

SHOPPING
IN PARIS

paris

Shopping can provide a good break between Paris' many heavy-weight museums and monuments. And if approached carefully, shopping can be a culturally enlightening experience. Here you'll find information on shopping for souvenirs, clothing, food, and bargains.

Most travelers are interested in finding a few souvenirs and maybe an article of clothing. Here's a simplified approach that works for most:

1) If you just need souvenirs, hit a souvenir shop.

2) For more elaborate purchasing plans, the city's large department stores offer relatively painless one-stop shopping in elegant surroundings.

3) Neighborhood boutiques offer the greatest reward at the highest risk. While clerks and prices can be intimidating, the selection is more original and the experience totally Parisian.

Tips

Before you enter a Parisian store, remember:

- In small stores, always say *bonjour, Madame/Mademoiselle/Monsieur* when entering and *au revoir, Madame/Mademoiselle/Monsieur* when leaving.
- The customer is not always right. In fact, figure the clerk is doing you a favor by waiting on you.
- Except for in department stores, it's not normal for the customer to handle clothing. Ask first if you can look at an item.
- Forget returns (and don't count on exchanges).
- Saturdays are busiest.
- Observe French shoppers. Then imitate.

Souvenir Shops

Avoid souvenir carts in front of famous monuments. Prices and

Key Phrases

Just looking. - *Je regards.* (zhuh ruh-gar)
How much is it? - *Combien?* (kohm-bee-en)
Too big/small/expensive. - *Trop grand/petit/cher.* (troh grahn/puh-tee/sher)
May I try it on? - *Je peut l'essayer?* (zhuh puh luh-say-yay)
Can I see more? - *Puis-je en voir d'autres?* (pweezh en vwahr doh-truh)
I'll think about it. - *Je vais y penser.* (zhuh vay ee pahn-say)
I'd like this. - *Je voudrais ça.* (zhuh voo-dray sah)

selection are better in shops. Look under the arcades of rue de Rivoli (across from Tuileries Gardens), around the Pompidou Center, on the streets of Montmartre, and in department stores (see below). The riverfront stalls near Notre-Dame sell a variety of used books, magazines, and tourist paraphernalia in the most romantic setting.

Department Stores (*Les Grandes Surfaces*)

Like cafés, department stores were invented here (surprisingly, not in America). While the stores seem overwhelming at first, they generally work like ours, and those listed here are accustomed to foreign shoppers. These stores are not only beautiful monuments to more elegant times, but also a great lesson on how others live. Most have spectacular perfume sections, a good selection of souvenirs and toys at fair prices, great view terraces, reasonably priced restaurants, and helpful information desks (near the front door, pick up the handy store floor-plan). Stores are generally open Monday through Saturday from 10:00 to 19:00. Choose from these four great Parisian department stores:

Galeries Lafayette and Printemps

You'll find both Galeries Lafayette and Printemps (pran-tom) department stores in many Parisian neighborhoods. The most convenient and busiest are side by side behind the old Opéra. Both stores sprawl over three buildings and consume entire city blocks. The selection is huge. Don't miss the belle époque dome at Galeries Lafayette. Fashion shows open to the public are held at both stores all year on Tuesdays at 11:00 and from April to October on Fridays at 14:30 (call 01 48 74 02 30 to reserve; Mo: Chaussee d'Antin, Havre-Caumartin, or Opéra). Continue your shopping by walking from this area to the place Vendôme (see "Boutiques," below).

Samaritaine
Samaritaine (sah-mah-ree-ten) is Paris' most central department store (on the Seine at Pont Neuf, Mo: Pont Neuf, see Historic Paris Walk, page 47). Old World elegant yet not high-priced, this is a handy place to take care of shopping business and enjoy one of the best views of Paris. Review the history of the store in dioramas at the top of the elevator. Then climb to the panorama terrace on the 11th floor.

Bon Marché
Combine this fine department store with a great neighborhood shopping experience (Mo: Sevres-Babylone). Bon Marché, quieter and more relaxed than the others, is surrounded by pleasant shopping streets (see "Boutiques," below). Graze through the gourmet grocery store in the basement (ideal for food souvenirs like mustards, teas, and chocolates).

Boutiques
I enjoy window-shopping on city streets, pausing at cafés, and observing the rhythm of neighborhood life. While the shops are more intimate, sales clerks are more formal—mind your manners. Here are four very different areas to sample:

Sevres-Babylone to St. Sulpice
Start at the elegant Bon Marché department store, described above (Mo: Sevres-Babylone), then shop the smart boutiques that line the streets between Bon Marché and St. Sulpice Church. The rue de Sevres (turns into rue du Four) is the spine of this upscale area. Explore rues du Dragon, Cherche Midi, Bonaparte, and Vieux Colombier. End your shopping stroll in the Luxembourg Gardens or at a grand café on the boulevard St. Germain (see "Les Grands Cafés de Paris," on page 278).

Le Marais
For more eclectic, avant-garde stores, peruse the shops between the Pompidou Center and place des Vosges. Stick to the West-to-East axis formed by rue Ste. Croix de la Bretonnerie, rue des Rosiers, rue Franc Bourgeois, and rue St. Antoine. (These streets are part of the Marais Walk on page 73.) Rue Franc Bourgeois throbs with trendy boutiques between place des Vosges and the Carnavalet Museum. On Sunday afternoons, this area is jammed with shoppers and café crowds.

Place Vendôme
The ritzy streets connecting Galeries Lafayette with place de la

Concorde are a miracle mile of jewelry stores, four-star hotels, perfumeries, and exclusive clothing boutiques.

From place de l'Opéra (Mo: Opéra), walk down rue de la Paix to place Vendôme. The *très* elegant place Vendôme is home to the Ritz Hôtel (Hemingway liberated the bar in World War II) and equally exclusive boutiques. The square was created by Louis XIV in the 17th century as a setting for a statue of himself. One hundred and fifty years later, Louis was replaced by a statue of Napoleon.

Continue on rue Castiglione, window-shopping the arcades, to rue de Rivoli. Turn right on Rivoli, passing Paris' largest English bookstore, W. H. Smith, at #248, to reach place de la Concorde.

Bercy Village

For a very different shopping experience, take Métro 14 to the futuristic station, Cours St. Emilion. Exit and follow signs to Paris' latest urban renewal project, Bercy Village.

In this renovated warehouse district, you'll find less frenetic shopping and more relaxed cafés and bistros. A small yet fine selection of stores cluster in an open courtyard, offering everything from pets to perfume. Animal-lovers must check out the chic *Animalis* boutique. Continue through Bercy Village to place des Vins de France (the wine square of France), with several wine shops, some offering tastings.

Flea Markets

Paris plays host to several sprawling flea markets (*marché aux puces*; mar-shay-oh-poose; literally translated since *puce* is French for flea). These oversized garage sales were started in the Middle Ages, when middle-men would sell old, flea-infested clothes and discarded possessions of the wealthy at bargain prices to eager peasants. Buyers were allowed to rummage through piles of virtual aristocratic garbage.

No event better brings together the melting-pot population of Paris than these almost carnival-like markets. Some find them claustrophobic, crowded, monster versions of those back home, though others find their French diamonds-in-the-rough and return happy. All of Paris' flea markets take place over weekends, and a few are open Mondays (which are by far quieter). Come early (most open at 07:30) for the best deals and fewest crowds. You can bargain a bit, and you'll generally do better by paying with cash. Note: Wear your moneybelt; pickpockets enjoy these wall-to-wall shopper events.

The **Puces St.-Ouen** (poose-sah-wahn) is the biggest and oldest of them all, with well over 2,000 vendors selling everything under the sun, from furniture to faucets (Sat-Mon 07:30-19:30, Mo: Clingacourt). **Puces de Vanves** is comparatively tiny and civilized (Sat-Sun 07:30-19:00, Mo: Porte de Vanves). The mega-**Puces de Montreuil** is the least organized and most traditional of them all, with chatty sellers and competitive buyers (Sat-Mon 07:30-19:00, Mo: Porte de Montreuil).

Street Markets

Several traffic-free street markets (like on the rue Cler) overflow with flowers, produce, fish vendors, and butchers, illustrating how most Parisians shopped until the invention of supermarkets and department stores. Browse these markets for picnics, or find a corner café from which to appreciate the scene.

Here is a list of Paris' most appealing street markets (open daily except Sun afternoons and Mon, also closed for lunch between 13:00-15:00): **Rue Cler** is a refined street market serving an upscale neighborhood near the Eiffel Tower (Mo: Ecole Militaire, for details see Rue Cler Walk, page 79). **Rue Montorgueil** is less touristy but central to many sights, and famous as the last vestige of the once massive Les Halles market (just north of St. Eustache Church, Mo: Etienne Marcel). **Rue Mouffetard** is touristy but fun. Combine a visit to this market with the Luxembourg Gardens (start at place Contrescarpe and work your way down, Mo: Cardinal Lemoine or Censier-Daubenton; for more, see Luxembourg Gardens, page 40, and "Contrescarpe Orientation," page 261). **Rue Daguerre**, near the Catacombs, is the least touristy of the four (off avenue du General Leclerc, Mo: Denfert-Rochereau, for Catacombs description, see page 41).

Offering cheaper prices and more selection, weekly markets take over selected boulevards and squares throughout Paris (08:00-13:00). Expect a lively combination of flea and street market atmosphere and items. **Marché Bastille** is huge, with a vast selection of products (Thu and Sun, Mo: Bastille); consider combining this with a stroll through Promenade Plantée park (page 45) and the Marais Walk route (page 73). **Marché Place Monge** is comparatively minuscule, specializing in high-quality foods (Wed, Fri, and Sun, near rue Mouffetard, Mo: Monge). **Marché Boulevard de Grenelle**, a few blocks southwest of the Champs de Mars park, is packed with produce and non-perishable goods (between Mo: Duplex and Mo: La Motte Picquet-Grenelle). **Marché Belleville** is big and feels very local (Tue and Fri, Mo: Belleville).

paris

PARIS AT NIGHT

Paris is brilliant after dark. Save energy from your day's sightseeing and get out at night. Whether it's a concert at Sainte-Chapelle, a boat ride on the Seine, an elevator up the Arc de Triomphe, or a late-night café, experience the City of Lights lit. *Pariscope* magazine (€0.50 at any newsstand, in French) offers a complete weekly listing of music, cinema, theater, opera, and other special events—I decipher this useful periodical for you below. The *Paris Voice* newspaper, in English, has a monthly review of Paris entertainment (available at any English-language bookstore, French-American establishments, or the American Church, www.parisvoice.com).

A Tour of *Pariscope*

The weekly *Pariscope* (€0.50) or *L'Officiel des Spectacles* (€0.30) are both cheap and essential if you want to know what's happening. Pick one up at a newsstand and page through it. For a head start, *Pariscope* has a Web site: www.pariscope.fr (in French).

Each begins with culture news. Skip the bulky "Théâtres" and "Dîners/Spectacles" sections and anything listed as "des environs" (outside of Paris). "Musique" or "Concerts Classiques" follow, listing each day's events (program, location, time, and price). Venues with phone numbers and addresses are listed in an "Adresses des Salles de Concerts" sidebar. Touristic venues (such as Sainte-Chapelle and Eglise de la Madeleine) are often featured in display ads. "Opéras, Musique Traditionelle, Ballet/Danse," and "Jazz/Rock" listings follow.

Half of these magazines are devoted to cinema—a Parisian forte. After the "Films Nouveaux" section trumpets new releases, the "Films en Exclusivité" pages list all the films playing in town. While a code marks films as "Historique, Karate, Erotisme," and so on, the key mark for tourists is "v.o.," which means *version originale* (American films have their English soundtracks). Films are listed alphabetically, with theaters and their *arrondissements* at the end of each entry. Then films are listed by neighborhood ("Salles Paris") and by genre. First-runs are shown at cinemas on the Champs-Elysées and on place de l'Odéon; art films and older films are best found in the Latin Quarter. To find a showing near your hotel, simply match the *arrondissement*. (But don't hesitate to hop on the Métro for the film you want.) "Salles Périphérie" are out in the suburbs.

Pariscope has a small English "Time Out" section listing the week's events. The "Musées" sections ("Monuments," "Jardins," "Autres Curiosités," "Promenades," "Activites Sportives," "Piscines") give the latest hours of the sights, gardens, curiosities, boat tours, sports, swimming pools, and so on ("tlj" stands for daily—*tous les jours*). "Clubs de Loisirs" are various athletic and social clubs. "Pour les Jeunes" is for young people (kids' films, animations/cartoons, marionettes, circuses, and amusement parks such as Asterix and Disney). "Conferences" are mostly lectures. For cancan mischief, look under "Paris la Nuit," "Cabarets," or the busty "Spectacles Erotiques."

Finally, you'll find a TV listing. Paris has four countrywide stations: TF1, France 2, France 3, and the new Arte station (a German/French cultural channel). M6 is filled with American series. Canal Plus (channel 4) is a cable channel that airs an American news show at seven in the morning and an American sports event on Sunday evening.

Music

Jazz Clubs: With a lively mix of American, French, and international musicians, Paris has been an internationally acclaimed jazz capital since World War II. You'll pay from €6 to €24 to enter a jazz club (1 drink may be included; if not, expect to pay €5–9 per drink; beer is cheapest). See *Pariscope* magazine under "Musique" for listings, or better, the American Church's *Paris Voice* paper for a good monthly review, or drop by the clubs to check out their calendars posted on the front door. Music starts after 21:00 in most clubs. Some offer dinner concerts from about 20:30 on. Here are several good bets:

Caveau de la Huchette, a characteristic old jazz club, fills an ancient Latin Quarter cellar with live jazz and frenzied dancing every night (€9 weekday, €12 weekend admission, €5 drinks, Tue–Sun 21:30–02:30 or later, closed Mon, 5 rue de la Huchette, Mo: St. Michel, recorded info tel. 01 43 26 65 05).

For a hotbed of late-night activity and jazz, go to the two-block-long rue des Lombards, at boulevard Sebastopol, midway between the river and Pompidou Center (Mo: Chatelet). **Au Duc des Lombards**, right at the corner, is one of the most popular and respected jazz clubs in Paris, with concerts generally at 21:00 (42 rue des Lombards, tel. 01 42 33 22 88). **Le Sunset** and **le Sunside** sit side by side a block west, offering more traditional jazz—Dixieland and big band—and fewer crowds, with concerts generally at 21:00 (60 rue des Lombards, Sunset tel. 01 40 26 46 60, Sunside tel. 01 40 26 21 25).

At the more down-to-earth and mellow **Le Cave du Franc Pinot**, you can enjoy a glass of chardonnay at the main-floor wine bar, then drop downstairs for a cool jazz scene (good dinner-and-jazz values as well, located on Ile St. Louis where Pont Marie meets the island, 1 quai de Bourbon, Mo: Pont Marie, tel. 01 46 33 60 64).

Classical Concerts: For classical music on any night, consult *Pariscope* magazine; the "Musique" section under "Concerts Classiques" lists concerts (free and fee). Look for posters at the churches. Churches that regularly host concerts include St. Sulpice, St. Germain-des-Prés, Basilique de Madeleine, St. Eustache, St. Julien-le-Pauvre, and Sainte-Chapelle. It's worth the €15 to €23 entry for the pleasure of hearing Mozart surrounded by the stained glass of the tiny Sainte-Chapelle. Look also for daytime concerts in parks, such as the Luxembourg Gardens. Even the Galeries Lafayette department store offers concerts. Many concerts are free (*entrée libre*), such as the Sunday atelier concert sponsored by the American Church (18:00, not every week, Sept–May, 65 quai d'Orsay, Mo: Invalides, RER: Pont de l'Alma, tel. 01 40 62 05 00).

Opera: Paris is home to two well-respected opera venues. The Opéra de la Bastille is the massive modern opera house that dominates place de la Bastille. Come here for state-of-the-art special effects and modern interpretations of classic ballets and operas (Mo: Bastille, tel. 01 43 43 96 96). The Opéra Garnier, Paris' first opera house, hosts opera and ballet performances. Come here for less expensive tickets and grand belle époque decor (Mo: Opéra, tel. 01 44 73 13 99). For tickets, call 01 44 73 13 00, go to the opera ticket offices (open 11:00–18:00), or, best, reserve on the Web at www.ticketavenue.com (for both operas).

Bus Tours
Paris Illumination Tours, run by Paris Vision, connect all the great illuminated sights of Paris with a 100-minute bus tour in 12 languages. Double-decker buses have huge windows, but customers continuing to the overrated Moulin Rouge get the most desirable front seats.

You'll stampede on with a United Nations of tourists, get an audioguide, and listen to a tape-recorded spiel (interesting but occasionally hard to hear). Uninspired as it is, this provides an entertaining first-night overview of the city at its floodlit and scenic best (bring your city map to stay oriented as you go). Left-side seats are marginally better. Visibility is fine in the rain. You're entirely on the bus except for one five-minute cigarette break at the Eiffel Tower viewpoint (adult-€23, kids under 11 ride free, departures at 20:30 nightly all year, also 21:30 April–Oct only, departs from Paris Vision office at 214 rue de Rivoli, across the street from Mo: Tuileries).

The same company will take you on the same route for twice the price by minivan—pick-up is at your hotel, the driver is a qualified guide, and there's a maximum of seven clients (adult-€46, kids ages 4–11-€23).

These trips are sold through your hotel (brochures in lobby) or at Paris Vision (214 rue de Rivoli, tel. for bus and minivans 01 42 60 30 01, fax 01 42 86 95 36, www.parisvision.com).

Seine River Cruises

The Bâteaux-Mouches offers one-hour cruises on huge glass-domed boats with departures along the Seine, including the Eiffel Tower (every 20 to 30 min 10:00–22:30; see "Organized Tours of Paris," on page 29).

Walks

Go for a walk to best appreciate the City of Lights. Break for ice cream, pause at a café, and enjoy the sidewalk entertainers as you join the post-dinner Parisian parade. Consider these walks:

Champs-Elysées and the Arc de Triomphe— ✪ See Champs-Elysées Walk, page 66. This is brilliant after dark. Start at the Arc de Triomphe, then stroll down the lively Champs-Elysées. A right turn on avenue George V leads to the Bâteaux-Mouches river cruises. A movie on the Champs-Elysées is a fun experience (weekly listings in *Pariscope* under "Cinema").

Trocadero and Eiffel Tower—These monuments glimmer at night. Take the Métro to the Trocadero stop and join the party on place de la Trocadero for a magnificent view of the glowing Eiffel Tower. It's a festival of gawkers, drummers, street acrobats, and entertainers. Pass the fountains and cross the river to the base of the tower, worth the effort even if you don't go up. See "Eiffel Tower," page 36.

From the Eiffel Tower, you can stroll through the Parc du Champ de Mars past Frisbees, soccer balls, and romantic couples and take the Métro home (Ecole Militaire stop, across avenue de la Motte Piquet from the far southeast corner of the park). Or, to head home sooner, there's a handy RER stop (Champ de Mars-Tour Eiffel) two blocks west (downriver) of the Eiffel Tower.

Ile St. Louis and Notre-Dame— ✪ See Historic Paris Walk, page 47. Take this beautiful evening stroll after having dinner on Ile St. Louis (see page 277 of Eating chapter).

To get to Ile St. Louis, take the Métro to the Pont Marie stop (line 7), then cross Pont Marie to Ile St. Louis. Turn right up rue St. Louis-en-Ile, stopping for dinner—or a Berthillon ice cream at #31. At the end of Ile St. Louis, cross Pont St. Louis to Ile de la Cité with a great view of Notre-Dame. Cross to the left bank on quai de l'Archeveché and drop down to the river to the right for the best floodlit views. End your walk on place du Parvis in front of Notre-Dame or continue across the river to the Latin Quarter.

TRANSPORTATION
CONNECTIONS

This chapter covers Paris' two airports, six train stations, and main bus station. When leaving Paris, arrive at your departure point early to allow time for waiting in lines (3 hrs for an overseas flight, or 1 hr before a flight within Europe, a train trip—including Eurostar—or a bus ride).

CHARLES DE GAULLE AIRPORT

Paris' primary airport has three main terminals: T-1, T-2, and T-9. Air France uses T-2, charters dominate T-9, and U.S. carriers use T-1. Terminals are connected every few minutes by a free *navette* (bus), and the RER (Paris subway) stops at T-1 and T-2 terminals. The TGV (*train à grande vitesse*; tay-zhay-vay) station is at T-2. There is no bag storage at the airport.

Those flying to or from the United States will probably use T-1, and the information that follows is for that terminal. The ADP (quasi–tourist office) is ground zero for tourist information, with museum passes and free maps and brochures (daily 07:00–22:00, follow signs to *Meeting Point* area). A *Relay* store sells *Kertel* phone cards. A bank (with lousy rates) is near gate 16. An American Express cash machine and an ATM are near gate 32. Car-rental offices are on the arrival level from gates 10 to 22; the SNCF (train) office is at gate 22. For flight information, call 01 48 62 22 80.

Those departing from this terminal will find restaurants, a PTT (post office), a pharmacy, boutiques, and a handy grocery store one floor below the ticketing desks at level 2.

Transportation between Charles de Gaulle Airport and Paris: Three efficient public-transportation routes, taxis, and airport shuttle vans link the airport's T-1 and T-2 terminals with central Paris. At T-1 (where most flights land), **RER trains** run every 15 minutes to central Paris. From gate 36, take the elevator down to level (*niveau*) 2, walk outside, cross the street, and catch the green bus to *Roissypole*. Transfer to RER trains there (€8, stops at Gare du Nord, Chatelet, St. Michel, and Luxembourg Gardens). When coming from Paris to the airport, T-1 is the first RER stop at Charles de Gaulle; T-2 is the second stop.

The **Roissy Bus** runs every 15 minutes between gate 30 and Paris' Opéra Garnier (€8, 40 min, buy ticket inside terminal at gate 30; the Opéra stop is on rue Scribe at the American Express office). The **Air France Bus** leaves every 15 minutes from gate 34 and serves the Arc de Triomphe and Porte Maillot in about 40 minutes for €10, and the Montparnasse Tower in 60 minutes for €11; from any of these stops, you can reach your hotel by taxi. (The RER Roissy Rail, Roissy Bus, and Air France bus described above serve the T-2 terminal as efficiently and economically as T-1; for most people, the RER Roissy Rail works best.)

A **taxi** ride with luggage costs about €38; a taxi stand is at gate 20 in T-1. The **Disneyland Express bus** departs from gate 32. The **TGV station** is at T-2 (from gate 36, take elevator down to *niveau* 2, walk outside, cross the street, and catch the red bus to T-2).

For a stress-free trip between either of Paris' airports and downtown, consider an **airport shuttle minivan**, ideal for single travelers or families of four or more. Reserve from home and they'll meet you at the airport (€23 for 1 person, €27 for 2, €41 for 3, €55 for 4, plan on a 30-min wait if you ask them to pick you up at the airport). Choose between **Airport Connection** (tel. 01 44 18 36 02, fax 01 45 55 85 19, www.airport-connection.com) and **Paris Airport Services** (tel. 01 49 62 78 78, fax 01 49 62 78 79, www.magic.fr/pas, e-mail: pas@magic.fr).

Sleeping at or near Charles de Gaulle Airport: Hôtel Ibis**, outside the RER Roissy Rail station for T-1 (the first RER stop coming from Paris), offers standard and predictable accommodations (Db-€85, CC, near *navette* bus stop, free shuttle bus to either terminal takes 2 min, tel. 01 49 19 19 19, fax 01 49 19 19 21, e-mail: h1404@accor-hotels.com). **Novotel***** is similar (Db-€133–145, CC, tel. 01 49 19 27 27, fax 01 49 19 27 99). A 15-minute drive from the airport is another Ibis hotel in the village of Roissy, with shuttle service.

Drivers wanting to avoid rush-hour traffic may consider sleeping north of Paris in either **Auvers-sur-Oise** (30 min west of airport, see "More Daytrips from Paris," page 239), or in the medieval town of Senlis (15 min north of airport) at **Hostellerie de la Porte Bellon** (Db-€65, CC, in the center at 51 rue Bellon, near rue de la République, tel. 03 44 53 03 05, fax 03 44 53 29 94).

ORLY AIRPORT

This airport feels small. Orly has two terminals: Sud and Ouest. International flights arrive at Sud. After exiting Terminal Sud's baggage claim (near gate H), you'll see signs directing you to city transportation, car rental, and so on. Turn left to enter the main terminal area, and you'll find exchange offices with bad rates, an ATM machine, the ADP (a quasi–tourist office that offers free city maps and basic sightseeing information, open until 23:00), and an SNCF French rail desk (closes at 18:00, sells train tickets and even Eurailpasses, next to the ADP). Downstairs are a sandwich bar, WCs, a bank (same bad rates), a newsstand (buy *télécarte* phone card), and a post office (great rates for cash or American Express traveler's checks). Car-rental offices are located in the parking lot in front of the terminal. For flight info on any airline serving Orly, call 01 49 75 15 15.

Transportation between Paris and Orly Airport: There are three efficient public-transportation routes, taxis, and a couple of airport shuttle services linking Orly Sud and central Paris. The gate locations listed below apply to Orly Sud, but the same transportation services are available from both terminals. The **Air France bus** (outside gate G) runs to Paris' Invalides Métro stop (€8, 4/hr, 30 min) and is best for those staying in or near the rue Cler neighborhood (from Invalides terminal, take the Métro 2 stops to Ecole Militaire to reach recommended hotels). The **Jetbus #285** (outside gate F, €5, 4/hr) is the quickest way to the Paris subway and the best way to the recommended hotels in the Marais and Contrescarpe neighborhoods (take Jetbus to Villejuif Métro stop, buy a *carnet* of 10 Métro tickets, then take the Métro to the Sully Morland stop for the Marais area, or the Censier-Daubenton or place Monge stops for the Contrescarpe area). If going to the airport, make sure your train serves Villejuif, as the route splits at the end of the line.

The **Orlybus** (outside gate H, €5.50, 4/hr) takes you to the Denfert-Rochereau RER-B line and the Métro, offering subway access to central Paris. The **Orlyval trains** are overpriced (€9) and require a transfer at the Antony stop to reach RER line B (serving Luxembourg, Chatelet, St. Michel, and Gare du Nord stations in central Paris). **Taxis** are to the far right as you leave the terminal, at gate M. Allow €26 for a taxi into central Paris.

Airport shuttle minivans are ideal for single travelers or families of four or more (see "Charles de Gaulle Airport," above, for the companies to contact; from Orly, figure about €18 for 1 person, €12/person for 2, less for larger groups and kids).

Sleeping near Orly Airport: Hôtel Ibis** is reasonable and close by (Db-€61, CC, tel. 01 56 70 50 60, fax 01 56 70 50 70). **Hôtel Mercure***** provides more comfort for a price (Db-€114, tel. 01 46 87 23 37, fax 01 46 87 71 92). Both have free shuttles to the terminal.

PARIS' TRAIN STATIONS

Paris is Europe's rail hub, with six major train stations, each serving different regions: Gare de l'Est (Eastbound trains), Gare du Nord (northern France and Europe), Gare St. Lazare (northwestern France), Gare d'Austerlitz (southwest France and Europe), Gare de Lyon (southeastern France and Italy), and Gare Montparnasse (northwestern France and TGV service to France's southwest). Any train station can give you schedule information, make reservations, and sell tickets for any destination. Buying tickets is handier from an SNCF neighborhood office (e.g., Louvre, Invalides, Orsay, Versailles, airports) or at your neighborhood travel agency—worth their small fee (SNCF signs in their window indicate they sell train tickets). For schedule information, call 08 36 35 35 35 (€0.50/min, English sometimes available).

All six train stations are connected by Métro, bus, and taxi. All have banks or change offices, information desks, telephones, cafés, lockers (*consigne automatique*), newsstands, and clever pickpockets. Each station offers two types of rail service: long distance to other cities, called *Grandes Lignes* (major lines); and suburban service to outlying areas, called *Banlieue* or RER. Both *Banlieue* and RER serve outlying areas and the airports; the only difference is that *Banlieue* lines are operated by SNCF (France's train system) and RER lines are operated by RATP (Paris' Métro and bus system). Paris train stations can be intimidating, but if you slow down, take a deep breath, and ask for help, you'll find them manageable and efficient. Bring a pad of paper for clear communication at ticket/info windows. All stations have helpful *accueil* (information) booths; the bigger stations have roving helpers, usually in red vests.

Station Overview

Here's an overview of Paris' major train stations. Métro, RER, buses (BUS), and taxis are well-signposted at every station. When arriving by Métro, follow signs for *Grandes Lignes*-SNCF to find the main tracks.

Gare du Nord: This station serves cities in northern France and international destinations to the North of Paris (including Amsterdam, Copenhagen, and the Eurostar to London, see "The Eurostar Train to London," below) as well as two of the daytrips described in this book (Auvers-sur-Oise and Chantilly). Arrive early to allow time to navigate this huge station. From the Métro, follow *Grandes Lignes* signs and keep going up and up until you reach the tracks at street level. Main lines (*Grandes Lignes*) depart from tracks 1–29, suburban (*Banlieue*) lines from tracks 30–36, and RER trains depart from tracks 37–44 (tracks 40–44 are 1 floor below). Train

PARIS' TRAIN STATIONS

PARIS TRAIN STATIONS & DESTINATIONS

❶ ST-LAZARE - TO NORMANDY (GIVERNY)

❷ NORD - TO LONDON & BRUSSELS VIA EUROSTAR
     TO NORTH EUROPE, THALYS TRAINS & AUVERS

❸ L'EST - TO EASTERN FRANCE, SOUTHERN GERMANY
     SWITZERLAND & AUSTRIA

❹ LYON - TO SOUTHEAST FRANCE & ITALY
     ALSO FONTAINEBLEAU & MELUN
     (FOR VAUX LE VICOMTE)

❺ AUSTERLITZ - TO SOUTHWEST FRANCE, LOIRE & SPAIN

❻ MONTPARNASSE - TO NORMANDY, BRITTANY, CHARTRES,
     TGV TRAINS TO LOIRE &
     SOUTHWEST FRANCE

information booths are opposite tracks 8 and 18, and information staff circulate around the station to help you (all rail staff are required to speak English). Information booths for the Thalys (high-speed trains to Brussels and elsewhere) are opposite track 8. All non-Eurostar ticket sales are opposite tracks 3 through 8. Passengers departing on the **Eurostar** (London via Chunnel) can buy tickets and must check in on the second level, opposite track 6. (Note: Britain's time zone is 1 hour earlier than the Continent's; times listed on

TRAIN ROUTES

Eurostar tickets are local times.) A peaceful waiting area is provided on the upper level overlooking the tracks (great station view). Storage lockers, baggage check, taxis, and rental cars are at the far end, just opposite track 3 and down the steps.

Key destinations served by Gare du Nord Grandes Lignes: Brussels (21/day, 1.5 hrs, see "To Brussels and Amsterdam," below), **Bruges** (18/day, 2 hrs, change in Brussels, 1 direct), **Amsterdam** (10/day, 4 hrs; see "To Brussels and Amsterdam," below), **Copenhagen** (1/day, 16 hrs, 2 night trains), **Koblenz** (6/day, 5 hrs, change in Köln), **London** via Eurostar Chunnel (17/day, 3 hrs, tel. 08 36 35 35 39, www.raileurope.com, www.eurostar.co.uk; for details, see "The Eurostar Train to London," below). **By Banlieue/RER lines to: Chantilly-Gouvieux** (hrly, fewer on weekends, 35 min), **Charles de Gaulle airport** (2/hr, 30 min, runs 05:30–23:00, track 4).

Key Train Phrases

accueil (ah-koy) = information assistance
niveau (nee-voh) = level
billets (bee-yay) = tickets
départs (day-par) = departures
arrivées (ah-ree-vay) = arrivals
aller simple (ah-lay sam-pluh) = one-way
aller-retour (ah-lay ruh-toor) = round-trip
voyageurs munis de billets = travelers with tickets
Grandes Lignes (grahnd leen) = major domestic
    and international lines
RER (air-ay-air) = suburban lines
Banlieue (bahn-lee-yuh) = suburban lines
quai (kay) = platform
voie (vwah) = track
retard (ruh-tar) = delay
salle d'attente (sahl dah-tahnt) = waiting room
consigne automatique (kohn-seen auto-mah-teek) =
    storage lockers
première classe (pruhm-yair klahs) = first class
deuxième classe (duhz-yehm klahs) = second class

Gare Montparnasse: This big and modern station covers three floors, serves Lower Normandy and Brittany, and offers TGV service to the Loire Valley and southwestern France, and suburban service to Chartres. At street level, you'll find a bank, Banlieue trains (serving Chartres; you can also reach the Banlieue trains from the second level), and ticket windows in the center, just past the escalators. Lockers (*consigne automatique*) are on the mezzanine level between levels 1 and 2. Most services are provided on the second level, where the Grandes Lignes arrive and depart (ticket windows to the far left with your back to glass exterior). Banlieue trains depart from tracks 10 through 19. The main rail information office is opposite track 15. Taxis are to the far left as you leave the tracks.

    Key destinations served by Gare Montparnasse: Chartres (20/day, 1 hr, Banlieue lines), **Pontorson-Mont St. Michel** (5/day, 4.5 hrs, via Rennes, then take bus; or take train to Pontorson via Caen, then bus from Pontorson), **Dinan** (7/day, 4 hrs, change in Rennes and Dol), **Bordeaux** (14/day, 3.5 hrs), **Sarlat** (5/day, 6 hrs, change in Bordeaux, Libourne, or Souillac), **Toulouse** (11/day, 5 hrs, most require change, usually in Bordeaux), **Albi** (7/day, 6–7.5 hrs, change in Toulouse, also night train), **Carcassonne** (8/day,

6.5 hrs, most require changes in Toulouse and Bordeaux, direct trains take 10 hrs), **Tours** (14/day, 1 hr).

Gare de Lyon: This huge and bewildering station offers TGV and regular service to southeastern France, Italy, and other international destinations. *Banlieue* trains serve Melun (near Vaux-le-Vicomte) and Fontainebleau. All trains arrive and depart from one level but are divided into two areas (tracks A-N and 5-23). They are connected by the long platform along tracks A and 5, and by the hallway adjacent to track A and opposite track 9. This hallway has all the services, ticket windows, ticket information, banks, and shops. *Banlieue* ticket windows are just inside the hall adjacent to track A (*Billets Ile de France*). *Grandes Lignes* and *Banlieue* lines share the same tracks. A Paris TI and the main train information office are opposite track L. From the RER or Métro, follow signs for "Grandes Lignes Arrivées" and take the escalator up to reach the platforms. Train information booths (*accueil*) are opposite tracks G and 13. Taxis wait in front of the station.

   Key destinations served by Gare de Lyon: Melun (hrly, 30 min), **Fontainebleau** (nearly hrly, 45 min), **Beaune** (12/day, 2.5 hrs, most require change in Dijon), **Dijon** (15/day, 1.5 hrs), **Chamonix** (9/day, 9 hrs, change in Lyon and St. Gervais, direct night train), **Annecy** (8/day, 4–7 hrs), **Lyon** (16/day, 2.5 hrs), **Avignon** (9/day in 2.5 hrs, 6/day in 4 hrs with change), **Arles** (14/day, 5 hrs, most with change in Marseille, Avignon, or Nîmes), **Nice** (14/day, 5.5–7 hrs, many with change in Marseille), **Venice** (3/day, 3/night, 11–15 hrs, most require changes), **Rome** (2/day, 5/night, 15–18 hrs, most require changes), **Bern** (9/day, 5–11 hrs, most require changes, night train).

Gare de l'Est: This station serves eastern France and European points to the East of Paris. Much smaller than the Gare du Nord, this single-floor station (with underground Métro) is a snap. Train information booths are at tracks 1 and 26; ticket windows and the main exit to buses and Paris are opposite track 8; luggage storage is opposite track 12.

   Key destinations served by Gare de l'Est: Colmar (12/day, 5.5 hrs, change in Strasbourg, Dijon, or Mulhouse), **Strasbourg** (14/day, 4.5 hrs, many require changes), **Reims** (12/day, 1.5 hrs), **Verdun** (5/day, 3 hrs, change in Metz or Chalon), **Munich** (5/day, 9 hrs, some require changes, night train), **Vienna** (7/day, 13–18 hrs, most require changes, night train), **Zurich** (10/day, 7 hrs, most require changes, night train), **Prague** (2/day, 14 hrs, night train).

Gare St. Lazare: This relatively small station serves Upper

Normandy, including Rouen and Giverny. All trains arrive and depart one floor above street level. Follow signs to *Grandes Lignes* from the Métro to reach the tracks. You'll pass a mini-mall. Ticket windows and a Thomas Cook exchange are in the first hall on the second floor. The tracks are through the small hallways (lined with storage lockers). Grandes Lignes (main lines) depart from tracks 17 through 27; Banlieue suburban trains depart from 1 through 16. The train information office (*accueil*) is opposite track 15; the reservation office is opposite track 16. Baggage consignment and the post office are along track 27, and WCs are opposite track 19.

Key destinations served by Gare St. Lazare: Giverny (train to Vernon, 5/day, 45 min; then bus or taxi 10 min to Giverny), **Rouen** (15/day, 75 min), **Honfleur** (6/day, 3 hrs, via Lisieux, then bus), **Bayeux** (9/day, 2.5 hrs, some with change in Caen), **Caen** (12/day, 2 hrs).

Gare d'Austerlitz: This small station provides non-TGV service to the Loire Valley, southwestern France, and Spain. All tracks are at street level. The information booth is opposite track 17, and a Thomas Cook exchange and all ticket sales are in the hall opposite track 10. Baggage consignment and car rental are near Porte 27 (along the side, opposite track 21).

Key destinations served by Gare d'Austerlitz: Amboise (8/day in 2 hrs, 12/day in 1.5 hrs with change in St. Pierre des Corps), **Cahors** (7/day, 5–7 hrs, most with changes), **Barcelona** (1/day, 9 hrs, change in Montpellier, night trains), **Madrid** (2 night trains only, 13–16 hrs), **Lisbon** (1/day, 24 hrs).

The Eurostar Train to London

The fastest and most convenient way to London is by rail. Eurostar is the speedy passenger train that zips you from downtown Paris to London (17/day, 3 hrs) faster and easier than flying. The train goes 190 mph in France but a doddering 80 mph in England. (When the English segment gets up to speed, the journey time will shrink to 2 hours.) The actual tunnel crossing is a 20-minute, black, silent, 100-mile-per-hour nonevent. Your ears won't even pop. Eurostar trains also run direct to London from Charles de Gaulle Airport or even Disneyland Paris.

Channel fares are reasonable but complicated. For the latest, call 800/EUROSTAR in the United States. These are prices from 2001: The "Leisure Ticket" is affordable ($219 first class, $139 second class, 50 percent refundable up to 3 days before departure). "Full Fare" first class costs $279 and includes a meal (a dinner departure nets you more grub than breakfast); "full fare" second class costs $199 (fully refundable even after departure date). Discounts are available to railpass holders ($155/first class, $75/second class, railpass must include France or Britain); seniors over 60 ($189/first class only), youths under 26 ($79/second class); and children under 12 (about half the fare of your ticket).

Cheaper seats can sell out. Book from home if you're ready to commit to a date and time. Compare fares sold by U.S. rail agents (www.raileurope.com) and French agents (www.eurostarplanet.com, French only). If you're ready to commit to a date, time, and U.S. prices, you can book by calling 800/EUROSTAR, visiting www.raileurope.com, or having your travel agent do it all for you (prices do not include FedEx ticket delivery).

You can buy your Eurostar ticket in Europe at any major train station. Eurostar tickets are sold in Paris at all of the train stations, neighborhood SNCF offices, and most travel agencies. Or order by phone (tel. 08 36 35 35 39). Those with a railpass pay about €85 (second class) one-way, any day. Without a railpass, a same-day round-trip on a Saturday or Sunday costs €154. Various deals are available. For instance, if you stay over on a Saturday night, you'll pay €115 for a second-class round-trip (7-day advance purchase necessary). Round-trip tickets over a Saturday are often cheaper than the basic one-way fare ...you know the trick. Note that first-class and business-class fares are substantially higher.

To Brussels and Amsterdam

The pricey Thalys train has the monopoly on this route. The cheapest way to connect Paris with Brussels and Amsterdam is by bus (see "Buses," below). Without a railpass, you'll pay about $100 second-class for the Paris-Amsterdam train (compared to $33 by Eurolines bus) or about $70 second-class for the Paris-Brussels train (compared to $24 by Eurolines bus). Even with a railpass, you need to pay for reservations ($14/second class, $30/first class). Book at least a day ahead as seats are limited. Or hop on the bus, Gus.

BUSES

The main bus station is Gare Routière du Paris-Gallieni (28 avenue du General de Gaulle, in suburb of Bagnolet, Mo: Gallieni, tel. 01 49 72 51 51). Buses provide cheaper—if less comfortable and more time-consuming—transportation to major European cities (Eurolines' buses depart from here, tel. 08 36 69 52 52, www.eurolines.com).

APPENDIX

French (and Parisian) History

Celts and Romans (52 B.C.–A.D. 500)
Julius Caesar conquered the Parisii, turning Paris from a tribal fishing village into a European city. The mix of Latin (southern) and Celtic (northern) cultures, with Paris right in the middle, defined the French character.

Paris Sites: Cluny Museum (Roman baths), Louvre (Roman antiquities), and Archaeological Crypt near Notre-Dame.

Dark Ages (500–1000)
Roman Paris fell to German pirates ("Franks" = France) and later to the Vikings ("Norsemen" = Normans). During this turbulent time, Paris was just another island state ("Ile de France") in the midst of many warring kingdoms. The lone bright spot was the reign of Charlemagne (A.D. 800), who briefly united the Franks, giving a glimpse of the modern nation-state of France.

Paris Sites: Cluny Museum artifacts and statue of Charlemagne near Notre-Dame.

Border Wars with England (1066–1500)
In 1066, the Norman king, William ("the Conqueror"), invaded and conquered England. This united England, Normandy, and much of what is today western France, sparking centuries of border wars and French-speaking kings of England. In 1328, a Norman-English king declared war on the king of France, leading to more than 100 years of Franco-Anglo battles (called the Hundred Years' War). Rallied by the teenage visionary Joan of Arc, the French finally united north and south, driving the English across the Channel in 1453. Modern France was born, with Paris as its capital.

Paris Sites: Notre-Dame, Sainte-Chapelle, Cluny Museum tapestries, Carnavalet Museum, Sorbonne, and the Latin Quarter.

Renaissance and Religious Wars (1500s)
A strong centralized France emerged, with French kings setting Europe's standard. François I made Paris a cultural capital, inviting Leonardo and *Mona Lisa* to visit. Catholics and Protestants fought openly, and 2,000 Parisians were slaughtered in the St. Bartholomew's Day Massacre.

Paris Sites: Louvre (palace and Renaissance art), pont Neuf, place des Vosges, and Fontainebleau.

Louis XIV, the Absolute Monarch (1600s)
Louis XIV centralized the power, neutered the nobility, and moved the capital to Versailles, which also became the center of European culture. France's wealth sparked "Enlightened" ideas. With these came the seeds of democracy.

Paris Sites: Versailles, Vaux-le-Vicomte, Les Invalides, paintings by Poussin and Lorraine.

Decadence and Revolution (1700s)
A financial crunch from wars and royal excess drove the French people to revolt. On July 14, 1789, they stormed the Bastille. Later they kidnapped and beheaded the king and queen. Thousands lost their heads—guillotined if suspected of hindering progress. A charismatic commoner rose amid the chaos, promising stability—Napoleon Bonaparte. Along with Napoleon, this was the age of Louis XV, Louis XVI, Marie-Antoinette, Voltaire, Rousseau, and Robespierre.

Paris Sites: Versailles, place de la Concorde, place de la Bastille, Conciergerie, and paintings by Watteau, Boucher, Fragonard, and David.

Elected Emperors and Constitutional Kings (1800s)
Napoleon conquered Europe, crowned himself emperor, invaded Russia, and ended up defeated on the battlefields of Waterloo. The monarchy was restored, but a series of popular uprisings (1830, 1848, and 1870) forced rulers to toe the democratic line. Napoleon's nephew, Napoleon III, presided over a wealthy, middle-class nation with a colonial empire in slow decline. France's political clout was fading, even as Paris remained the world's cultural center during the belle époque, or beautiful age.

Paris Sites: Arc de Triomphe, Haussman's wide boulevards, Eiffel Tower, Les Invalides and Napoleon's Tomb, pont Alexandre, Grand and Petit Palais, Montmartre, Opéra Garnier, paintings

by Ingres and Delacroix at the Louvre, and Impressionist and
Post-Impressionist paintings (Manet, Monet, Renoir, Degas,
Toulouse-Lautrec, Cézanne, and so on) at the Orsay, Marmottan,
and L'Orangerie (scheduled to re-open in 2002).

War and Depression (1900–1950)
France began the turn of the century as top dog, but the two
World Wars with Germany (and the earlier Franco-Prussian
War of 1870) wasted the country. France lost millions of men in
World War I, sank into a depression, and was easily overrun by
Hitler in World War II. Paris, now dirt cheap, attracted foreign
writers and artists.

This was the age of Picasso, Ravel, Debussy, Satie, Stravinsky,
Nijinsky, Hemingway, Fitzgerald, Stein, Pound, Sartre, Edith
Piaf, and Maurice Chevalier.

Paris Sites: Picasso Museum, Deportation Memorial,
Pompidou Center.

Postwar France (1950–Present)
Wartime hero Charles de Gaulle reestablished a democratic
Republic. France's colonial empire dissolved after bitter wars in
Algeria and Vietnam. Immigrants from former colonies flooded
Paris. The turbulent '60s, progressive '70s, socialist-turned-
conservative '80s, and the middle-of-the-road '90s bring us to
the *début de siècle*, or the beginning of the century.

Paris Sites: Montparnasse Tower, La Défense, Louvre's
pyramid, and Pompidou Center.

Contemporary Politics in France
The key political issues in France today are high unemployment
(about 9 percent), a steadily increasing percentage of ethnic
minorities, and the need to compete in a global marketplace.
The challenge is to address these issues while maintaining the
social benefits the French expect from their government. As a
result, national policies seem to conflict with each other (e.g.,
France supports the lean economic policies of the European
Union but has recently reduced the French workweek to 35 hours).

The unification of Europe has been powered by France and
Germany. The 15-member European Union, which is well on its
way to becoming a "United States of Europe," is dissolving borders
and freeing up trade. It has established an all-European currency
called the euro.

French national politics are fascinating. While only two
parties dominate American politics, France has five major parties.
From left to right, these include the reformed Communists (PCF—

Parti Communiste Française), the moderate Socialists (PS—Parti
Socialiste), the aristocratically conservative UDF (Union pour la
Démocratie Française), the center-right RPR (Rassemblement pour
la République), and the racist Front National. In general, the UDF
and RPR split the conservative middle ground and the Socialists
dominate the liberal middle ground. But in France, unlike in the
United States, informal coalitions are generally necessary for any
party to "rule." At the fringes, you'll read about the racist Front
National party, led by Jean-Marie Le Pen and Bruno Megret (who
seem more interested in fighting with each other than working
together). Le Pen's "France for the French" platform calls for the
expulsion of ethnic minorities and broader police powers. As unemployment rose in the '90s, so did the popularity of this far-right party
(getting as much as 15 percent in national elections, Le Pen was able
to force center-right parties farther in his direction). But now that
unemployment is dropping, the extreme right cause appears to be
floundering. On the far left, the reformed Communists, still recover-
ing from the fall of the Soviet Union, have had to work more flexibly
with the less radical Socialists and the environmental (Green) parties.

While the French president is elected by popular vote every
five years, he is more of a figurehead than his American counterpart.
The more powerful prime minister is elected by the parliament
(Assemblée Nationale) every five years. With five major parties, a
single majority is rare—it takes a coalition to elect a prime minister.
Currently, the left is working together better than the right. The
Socialist, Green, and Communist parties run the country today.
France has a liberal prime minister (socialist Lionel Jospin) and a
conservative president (Jacques Chirac). This "cohabitation," as it's
called in French, is similar to an American president having to deal
with a Congress controlled by an opposing party. These two party
leaders will square off against each other in national elections in
the spring of 2002; the race will likely be very close.

Let's Talk Telephones

Here are general instructions for making phone calls. (For information specific to France, see page 10). International access
codes and country codes are listed below.

Making Calls within a European Country: About half of
all European countries use area codes (like we do); the other half
uses a direct-dial system without area codes.

To make calls within a country that uses a direct-dial system
(Belgium, Denmark, France, Italy, Portugal, Norway, Spain, and
Switzerland), you dial the same number whether you're calling
across the country or across the street.

In countries that use area codes (such as Austria, Britain,

Czech Republic, Finland, Germany, Ireland, Netherlands, and
Sweden), you dial the local number when calling within a city, and
you add the area code if calling long-distance within the country.

   Making International Calls: You always start with the international access code (011 if you're calling from America or Canada,
or 00 from virtually anywhere in Europe), then dial the country
code of the country you're calling (see chart below).

   What you dial next depends on the phone system of the country you're calling. If the country uses area codes, drop the initial
zero of the area code, then dial the rest of the number.

   Countries that use direct-dial systems (no area codes) vary in
how they're accessed internationally by phone. For instance, if
you're making an international call to Denmark, Italy, Norway,
Portugal, or Spain, simply dial the international access code, country code, and phone number. But if you're calling Belgium, France,
or Switzerland, drop the initial zero of the phone number.

International Access Codes
When dialing direct, first dial the international access code. For
the United States and Canada, it's 011. Virtually all European
countries use "00" as their international access code; the only
exceptions are Finland (990) and Lithuania (810).

Country Codes
After you've dialed the international access code, then dial the
code of the country you're calling.

Austria—43	Greece—30
Belgium—32	Ireland—353
Britain—44	Italy—39
Canada—1	Morocco—212
Czech Repub.—420	Netherlands—31
Denmark—45	Norway—47
Estonia—372	Portugal—351
Finland—358	Spain—34
France—33	Sweden—46
Germany—49	Switzerland—41
Gibraltar—350	United States—1

Calling-Card Operators
AT&T	**MCI**	**Sprint**
0800-990-011	0800-990-019	0800-990-087

Handy Phone Numbers
Directory assistance for Paris and France (some English
   spoken): 12

Lost property (Bureau des Objets Trouvés): Open Tue and
   Thu 8:30-20:00, 36 rue des Morillons, Mo: Convention,
   tel. 01 55 76 20 20
American Church: 65 quai d'Orsay, tel. 01 40 62 05 00
Office of American Services (lost passports, etc): tel. 01 43 12 22 22
Sunday Banks: 115 and 154 avenue des Champs-Elysées

Emergency/Medical Needs
Police: 17
Emergency medical assistance: 15
American Hospital: 63 boulevard Victor Hugo, in suburb of
   Neuilly, Mo: Porte Maillot, then bus #82, tel. 01 46 41 25 25
English-speaking pharmacy: tel. 01 45 62 02 41 (24 hrs,
   Mo: Georges V)
Chiropractic Centers: tel. 01 43 54 26 25 or 01 43 87 81 62
SOS Doctors: tel. 01 47 07 77 77 or 01 48 28 40 04
SOS Help (English-speaking hotline): Open daily 15:00-23:00,
   tel. 01 47 23 80 80

Consulates/Embassies
U.S. Consulate: 2 rue St. Florentin, tel. 01 43 12 22 22.
U.S. Embassy: 2 avenue Gabriel, tel. 01 43 12 22 22, Mo:
   Concorde for both consulate and embassy.
Canadian Consulate and Embassy: 35 avenue Montaigne,
   Mo: Franklin-Roosevelt, tel. 01 44 43 29 00.

Tourist and Transportation Information
Paris Tourist Information: tel. 01 43 43 33 24 (live person,
   English spoken), 08 36 68 31 12 (long menu), or 01 49 52 53 10
Ile de France Tourist Information: (Paris area, for example,
   Fontainebleau, Vaux-le-Vicomte, Chantilly): tel. 01 42 60 28 62
Train (SNCF) Information: tel. 08 36 35 35 35 (some
   English usually spoken)
Bus and Métro (RATP) Information: tel. 08 36 68 77 14
   (French only)

Travel Companies
The American Express Travel Company (11 rue Scribe, Mo: Opéra,
tel. 01 47 77 77 07) is a popular hangout for American travelers,
but you'll find cheaper flights at Voyageurs en Amerique du Nord
(55 rue Sainte Anne, Mo: Pyramides, tel. 01 42 86 17 30).

Airports
Charles de Gaulle: tel. 01 48 62 22 80
Orly: tel. 01 49 75 15 15

Airlines

(Note: Any number beginning with 08 is a fee call.)

Aer Lingus: tel. 01 55 38 38 55
Air Canada: tel. 08 25 88 08 81
Air France: tel. 08 20 82 08 20
Alitalia: tel. 08 02 31 53 15
American Airlines: tel. 08 01 87 28 72
British Airways: tel. 08 25 82 54 00
BMI British Midlands: tel. 01 41 91 87 04
Continental: tel. 01 42 99 09 09
Delta: tel. 08 00 35 40 80
Iberia: tel. 08 02 07 50 75
KLM: tel. 08 10 55 65 56
Lufthansa: tel. 08 02 02 00 30
Northwest: tel. 01 44 56 18 18
Olympic: tel. 01 44 94 58 58
Sabena: tel. 08 20 83 08 30
SAS: tel. 08 01 25 25 25
Swissair: tel. 08 02 30 04 00
TWA: tel. 08 01 89 28 92
United: tel. 08 01 72 72 72
US Air: tel. 08 01 63 22 22

Classes

French-Language Classes

• American University of Paris (tel. 01 40 62 07 20, fax 01 47 05 34 32, www.aup.fr)
• France Ecole Langue (tel. 01 45 00 40 15, fax 01 45 00 53 41, www.france-langue.fr)

Cooking Schools

These have demonstration courses:
• Le Cordon Bleu (tel. 01 53 68 22 50, fax 01 48 56 03 96)
• Ritz Escoffier Ecole de Gastronomie Française (tel. 01 43 16 30 50)

Wine Classes

• Maison de la Vigne (tel. 01 47 20 20 76)

Numbers and Stumblers

• Europeans write a few of their numbers differently than we do. 1 = 1 , 4 = 4 , 7 = 7 . Learn the difference or miss your train.
• In Europe, dates appear as day/month/year, so Christmas is 25/12/02.

- Commas are decimal points and decimals commas. A dollar and a half is 1,50, and there are 5.280 feet in a mile.
- When pointing, use your whole hand, palm down.
- When counting with fingers, start with your thumb. If you hold up your first finger to request one item, you'll probably get two.
- What Americans call the second floor of a building is the first floor in Europe.
- Europeans keep the left "lane" open for passing on escalators and moving sidewalks. Keep to the right.

Metric Conversion (approximate)

1 inch = 25 millimeters	32 degrees F = 0 degrees C
1 foot = 0.3 meter	82 degrees F = about 28 degrees C
1 yard = 0.9 meter	1 ounce = 28 grams
1 mile = 1.6 kilometers	1 kilogram = 2.2 pounds
1 centimeter = 0.4 inch	1 quart = 0.95 liter
1 meter = 39.4 inches	1 square yard = 0.8 square meter
1 kilometer = .62 mile	1 acre = 0.4 hectare

Paris' Climate

First line, average daily low; second line, average daily high; third line, days of no rain.

J	F	M	A	M	J	J	A	S	O	N	D
34°	34°	39°	43°	49°	55°	58°	58°	53°	46°	40°	36°
43°	45°	54°	60°	68°	73°	76°	75°	70°	60°	50°	44°
14	14	19	17	19	18	19	18	17	18	15	15

Basic French Survival Phrases

Hello (good day).	**Bonjour.**	bohn-zhoor
Do you speak English?	**Parlez-vous anglais?**	par-lay-voo ahn-glay
Yes. / No.	**Oui. / Non.**	wee / nohn
I'm sorry.	**Désolé.**	day-zoh-lay
Please.	**S'il vous plaît.**	see voo play
Thank you.	**Merci.**	mehr-see
Goodbye.	**Au revoir.**	oh vwahr
Where is...?	**Où est...?**	oo ay
...a hotel	**...un hôtel**	uhn oh-tehl
...a youth hostel	**...une auberge**	ewn oh-behrzh
	de jeunesse	duh zhuh-nehs
...a restaurant	**...un restaurant**	uhn rehs-toh-rahn
...a grocery store	**...une épicerie**	ewn ay-pee-suh-ree
...the train station	**...la gare**	lah gar
...the tourist info office	**...l'office du tourisme**	loh-fees dew too-reez-muh
Where are the toilets?	**Où sont les toilettes?**	oo sohn lay twah-leht
men / women	**hommes / dames**	ohm / dahm
How much is it?	**Combien?**	kohn-bee-an
Cheaper.	**Moins cher.**	mwan shehr
Included?	**Inclus?**	an-klew
Do you have...?	**Avez-vous...?**	ah-vay-voo
I would like...	**Je voudrais...**	zhuh voo-dray
...a ticket.	**...un billet.**	uhn bee-yay
...a room.	**...une chambre.**	ewn shahn-bruh
...the bill.	**...l'addition.**	lah-dee-see-ohn
one	**un**	uhn
two	**deux**	duh
three	**trois**	twah
four	**quatre**	kah-truh
five	**cinq**	sank
six	**six**	sees
seven	**sept**	seht
eight	**huit**	weet
nine	**neuf**	nuhf
ten	**dix**	dees
At what time?	**À quelle heure?**	ah kehl ur
Just a moment.	**Un moment.**	uhn moh-mahn
Now.	**Maintenant.**	man-tuh-nahn
today / tomorrow	**aujourd'hui / demain**	oh-zhoor-dwee / duh-man

For more user-friendly French phrases, check out *Rick Steves'
French Phrase Book and Dictionary* or *Rick Steves' French, Italian &
German Phrase Book and Dictionary*.

Faxing Your Hotel Reservation

Use this handy form for your fax (or find it online at
www.ricksteves.com/reservation). Photocopy and fax away.

One-Page Fax

To: _____ @ _____
                    hotel   *fax*

From: _____ @ _____
                    name   *fax*

Today's date: ____ / ____ / ____
                    day   month   year

Dear Hotel _____ ,

Please make this reservation for me:

Name: _____

Total # of people: _____   # of rooms: _____   # of nights: _____

Arriving: ____ / ____ / ____   My time of arrival (24-hr clock): _____
              day   month   year   (I will telephone if I will be late)

Departing: ____ / ____ / ____
                day   month   year

Room(s): Single___ Double___ Twin___ Triple___ Quad___

With: Toilet___ Shower___ Bath___ Sink only___

Special needs: View___ Quiet___ Cheap___ Ground Floor___

Credit card: Visa___ MasterCard___ American Express___

Card #: _____

Expiration date: _____

Name on card: _____

You may charge me for the first night as a deposit. Please fax, e-mail, or
mail me confirmation of my reservation, along with the type of room
reserved, the price, and whether the price includes breakfast. Please also
inform me of your cancellation policy. Thank you.

_____
Signature

_____
Name

_____
Address

_____
City   *State*   *Zip Code*   *Country*

_____
E-mail Address

Road Scholar Feedback for PARIS 2002

We're all in the same travelers' school of hard knocks. Your feedback helps us improve this guidebook for future travelers. Please fill this out (or use the online version at www.ricksteves.com/feedback), attach more info or any tips/favorite discoveries if you like, and send it to us. As thanks for your help, we'll send you our quarterly travel newsletter free for one year. Thanks! **Rick**

Of the recommended accommodations/restaurants used, which was:

Best _____

    Why? _____

Worst _____

    Why? _____

Of the sights/experiences/destinations recommended by this book, which was:

Most overrated _____

    Why? _____

Most underrated _____

    Why? _____

Best ways to improve this book:

_____

_____

I'd like a free newsletter subscription:

_____ Yes   _____ No   _____ Already on list

_____
Name

_____
Address

_____
City, State, Zip

_____
E-mail Address

    Please send to: ETBD, Box 2009, Edmonds, WA 98020

INDEX

FREE-SPIRITED TOURS FROM

Rick Steves

Great Guides

Big Buses

Small Groups

No Grumps

**Best of Europe ■ Village Europe ■ Eastern Europe ■ Turkey ■ Italy ■ Britain
Spain/Portugal ■ Ireland ■ Heart of France ■ South of France ■ Village France
Scandinavia ■ Germany/Austria/Switzerland ■ London ■ Paris ■ Rome**

Looking for a one, two, or three-week tour that's run in the Rick Steves style? Check out Rick Steves' educational, experiential tours of Europe.

Rick's tours include much more in the "sticker price" than mainstream tours. Here's what you'll get with a Europe or regional Rick Steves tour...

■ **Group size:** Your tour group will be no larger than 26.

■ **Guides:** You'll have two guides traveling and dining with you on your fully guided Rick Steves tour.

■ **Bus:** You'll travel in a full-size 48-to-52-seat bus, with plenty of empty seats for you to spread out and read, snooze, enjoy the passing scenery, get away from your spouse, or whatever.

■ **Sightseeing:** Your tour price includes all group sightseeing. There are no hidden extra charges.

■ **Hotels:** You'll stay in Rick's favorite small, characteristic, locally-run hotels in the center of each city, within walking distance of the sights you came to see.

■ **Price and insurance:** Your tour price is guaranteed for 2002. Single travelers do *not* pay an extra supplement (we have them room with other singles). ETBD includes prorated tour cancellation/interruption protection coverage at no extra cost.

■ **Tips and kickbacks:** All guide and driver tips are included in your tour price. Because your driver and guides are paid salaries by ETBD, they can focus on giving you the best European travel experience possible.

Interested? Call (425) 771-8303 or visit www.ricksteves.com for a free copy of Rick Steves' 2002 Tours booklet!

Rick Steves' Europe Through the Back Door

130 Fourth Avenue North, PO Box 2009, Edmonds, WA 98020 USA
Phone: (425) 771-8303 ■ Fax: (425) 771-0833 ■ www.ricksteves.com

FREE TRAVEL GOODIES FROM

Rick Steves

EUROPEAN TRAVEL NEWSLETTER

My *Europe Through the Back Door* travel company will help you travel better *because* you're on a budget—not in spite of it. To see how, ask for my 64-page *travel newsletter* packed full of savvy travel tips, readers' discoveries, and your best bets for railpasses, guidebooks, videos, travel accessories and free-spirited tours.

2002 GUIDE TO EUROPEAN RAILPASSES

With hundreds of railpasses to choose from in 2002, finding the right pass for your trip has never been more confusing. To cut through the complexity, ask for my 64-page *2002 Guide to European Railpasses.* Once you've narrowed down your choices, we give you unbeatable prices, including important extras with every Eurailpass, *free:* my 90-minute *Travel Skills Special* video or DVD; your choice of one of my 16 country guidebooks and phrasebooks; and answers to your "top five" travel questions.

RICK STEVES' 2002 TOURS

We offer 18 different one, two, and three-week tours (180 departures in 2002) for those who want to experience Europe in Rick Steves' Back Door style, but without the transportation and hotel hassles. If a tour with a small group, modest family-run hotels, lots of exercise, great guides, and no tips or hidden charges sounds like your idea of fun, ask for my 48-page 2002 Tours booklet.

YEAR-ROUND GUIDEBOOK UPDATES

Even though the information in my guidebooks is the freshest around, things do change in Europe between book printings. I've set aside a special section at my website (www.ricksteves.com/update) listing *up-to-the-minute changes* for every Rick Steves guidebook.

Call, fax, or visit www.ricksteves.com to get your...

- ☑ **FREE EUROPEAN TRAVEL NEWSLETTER**
- ☑ **FREE 2002 GUIDE TO EUROPEAN RAILPASSES**
- ☑ **FREE RICK STEVES' 2002 TOURS BOOKLET**

Rick Steves' Europe Through the Back Door

130 Fourth Avenue North, PO Box 2009, Edmonds, WA 98020 USA
Phone: (425) 771-8303 ■ Fax: (425) 771-0833 ■ www.ricksteves.com

**AVALON
TRAVEL**
p u b l i s h i n g

How far will our travel guides take you? As far as you want.

Discover a rhumba-fueled nightspot in Old Havana, explore
prehistoric tombs in Ireland, hike beneath California's centuries-
old redwoods, or embark on a classic road trip along Route 66.
Our guidebooks deliver solidly researched, trip-tested
information—minus any generic froth—to help globetrotters
or weekend warriors create an adventure uniquely their own.

And we're not just about the printed page. Public television view-
ers are tuning in to Rick Steves' new travel series,
Rick Steves' Europe. On the Web, readers can cruise the
virtual black top with *Road Trip USA* author Jamie Jensen
and learn travel industry secrets from Edward Hasbrouck
of The *Practical Nomad*.

In print. On TV. On the Internet.

We supply the information. The rest is up to you.

Avalon Travel Publishing

Something for everyone

www.travelmatters.com

Avalon Travel Publishing guides are available at
your favorite book or travel store.

MOON HANDBOOKS

provide comprehensive coverage of a region's arts, history, land, people, and social issues in addition to detailed practical listings for accommodations, food, outdoor recreation, and entertainment. Moon Handbooks allow complete immersion in a region's culture—ideal for travelers who want to combine sightseeing with insight for an extraordinary travel experience in destinations throughout North America, Hawaii, Latin America, the Caribbean, Asia, and the Pacific.

WWW.MOON.COM

Rick Steves shows you where to travel and how to travel—all while getting the most value for your dollar. His Back Door travel philosophy is about making friends, having fun, and avoiding tourist rip-offs.

Rick has been traveling to Europe for more than 25 years and is the author of 22 guidebooks, which have sold more than a million copies. He also hosts the award-winning public television series *Rick Steves' Europe.*

WWW.RICKSTEVES.COM

ROAD TRIP USA

Getting there is half the fun, and Road Trip USA guides are your ticket to driving adventure. Taking you off the interstates and onto less-traveled, two-lane highways, each guide is filled with fascinating trivia, historical information, photographs, facts about regional writers, and details on where to sleep and eat—all contributing to your exploration of the American road.

"[Books] so full of the pleasures of the American road, you can smell the upholstery."
                                          ~BBC radio

WWW.ROADTRIPUSA.COM

FOGHORN OUTDOORS guides are for campers, hikers, boaters, anglers, bikers, and golfers of all levels of daring and skill. Each guide focuses on a specific U.S. region and contains site descriptions and ratings, driving directions, facilities and fees information, and easy-to-read maps that leave only the task of deciding where to go.

"Foghorn Outdoors has established an ecological conservation standard unmatched by any other publisher." **~Sierra Club**

WWW.FOGHORN.COM

TRAVEL SMART guidebooks are accessible, route-based driving guides focusing on regions throughout the United States and Canada. Special interest tours provide the most practical routes for family fun, outdoor activities, or regional history for a trip of anywhere from two to 22 days. Travel Smarts take the guesswork out of planning a trip by recommending only the most interesting places to eat, stay, and visit.

"One of the few travel series that rates sightseeing attractions. That's a handy feature. It helps to have some guidance so that every minute counts." **~San Diego Union-Tribune**

CiTY·SMaRT™ guides are written by local authors with hometown perspectives who have personally selected the best places to eat, shop, sightsee, and simply hang out. The honest, lively, and opinionated advice is perfect for business travelers looking to relax with the locals or for longtime residents looking for something new to do Saturday night.

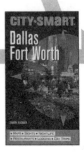